an other

Black Outdoors Innovations in the Poetics of Study

A SERIES EDITED BY J. KAMERON CARTER AND SARAH JANE CERVENAK

an other

a black feminist
consideration of
animal life

Sharon Patricia Holland

DUKE UNIVERSITY PRESS / DURHAM AND LONDON / 2023

© 2023 DUKE UNIVERSITY PRESS
Printed and bound by CPI Group (UK) Ltd,
Croydon, CR0 4YY
Project Editor: Brian Ostrander
Designed by Matthew Tauch
Typeset in Garamond Premier Pro, Futura Std,
and Sang Bleu Kingdom by Westchester Publishing Services

Library of Congress Cataloging-in-Publication Data
Names: Holland, Sharon Patricia, author.
Title: An other : a black feminist consideration of animal life / Sharon Patricia
Holland.
Other titles: Black feminist consideration of animal life | Black outdoors.
Description: Durham : Duke University Press, 2023. | Series: Black outdoors:
innovations in the poetics of study | Includes bibliographical references and
index.
Identifiers: LCCN 2022056722 (print)
LCCN 2022056723 (ebook)
ISBN 9781478025078 (paperback)
ISBN 9781478020097 (hardcover)
ISBN 9781478027065 (ebook)
Subjects: LCSH: MOVE (Organization) | Human-animal relationships. |
Human-animal relationships—Pennsylvania—Philadelphia—History—
20th century. | African Americans—Pennsylvania—Philadelphia. | Feminist
theory. | BISAC: SOCIAL SCIENCE / Black Studies (Global)
Classification: LCC QL85 .H655 2023 (print) | LCC QL85 (ebook) |
DDC 590—dc23/eng/20230407
LC record available at https://lccn.loc.gov/2022056722
LC ebook record available at https://lccn.loc.gov/2022056723

Cover art: Painting by Judith Raphael. Courtesy of the artist and
Tony Phillips.

for amani & zadie
because they asked me to

an-oth-er
(determiner and noun)

1   Middle English. *an other* until the sixteenth century.
2   Used to refer to an additional person or thing of the same type as one already mentioned or known about; one more; a further.
3   Used to refer to a different person or thing from one already mentioned or known about.
4   A hum:animal world.
5   An insurgence.
6   Something out of vision.
7   Your mama.
8   Your daddy too.
9   A kind of living.

Me, I have two rituals. I chant, and then, before I mount the horse, I breathe him in. I know it sounds a little Horse-Whisperer-ish, but when I breathe in a horse, it's as if we are kindred souls. We are one.

SYLVIA HARRIS, *Long Shot* (2011)

The distinction between the human and the non-human no longer marks the outer limits of the social world, as against that of nature, but rather maps a domain within it whose boundary is both permeable and easily crossed.

TIM INGOLD, *The Perception of the Environment* (2000)

For the heart to truly share another's being, it must be an embodied heart, prepared to encounter directly the embodied heart of another. I have met the "other" in this way, not once or a few times, but over and over during years spent in the company of "persons" like you and me, who happen to be nonhuman.

BARBARA SMUTS, reflecting in Coetzee's *The Lives of Animals* (1999)

The difference between poetry and rhetoric
is being ready to kill
yourself
instead of your children.

AUDRE LORDE, "Power" (1978)

contents

how to read this book

The animal looks at us, and we are naked
before it. Thinking perhaps begins there.
JACQUES DERRIDA, *The Animal That
Therefore I Am* (2008)

Lone black filly. Finished . . .
JOY PRIEST, "Elegy for Kentucky,"
Horsepower (2020)

What happens when Black people *do* things with animals? To write
this book, I returned to the birthplace of my maternal line, spent
over a decade working with horses, and sometimes failed miserably
at becoming with, being with, and loving with them. In short, I did
a lot of field work for this project.

This book is therefore riddled with what the animal said, at the
same time as it collapses the meaning-making of the term *animal*
altogether. This is a feminist text, as it follows a line of argument
that concerns itself with females, and all of their hot mess.

Andrea Long Chu sets our teeth on edge in *Females* by coming
after a few sacred points about gender (a politics of sex): "Everyone is female. . . . The entire incarcerated population is female. All
rape survivors are females. All rapists are females. Females master-
minded the Atlantic slave trade. All the dead are female. All the
dying too. . . . I am female. And you, dear reader, you are female,
even—especially—if you are not a woman. Welcome. Sorry."[1] In
thinking with Valerie Solanas's work, from her play *Up Your Ass* to
the oft-referred to but little quoted *SCUM Manifesto*, Chu writes
that Solanas was "brushing off a decade of feminist organizing like
a fat, drunk tick" (9). There goes Heidegger's tick again, but at least
in this world, the tick is satiated, feels release.

For Chu, not only are we females, but we are especially so if we are not women, a nod to Judith Butler and also perhaps TERF wars in feminist encampments. I want to take note here especially that in this catalogue of possibilities for female, being *female* means you can send up the whole history of a people's embodied living as enslaved peoples in and as the master's mind, which reveals itself just so (female). Certainly not the "female" that Hortense J. Spillers refers to in "Mama's Baby, Papa's Maybe," as Chu has no time for a biology that engenders. If we take this word—*engenders*—at its root, then the repudiation here is of the *male* parts, and their situatedness at the top of orders of being, doing, and becoming. I bring Chu's text into this brief praxis for reading because it posits several categories of being we think we know: blackness, hum/animal distinction, and, yes, females. This book in many ways works against *knowing* as a rule of thumb.

In the beginning, I was writing a book called *Vocabularies of Vulnerability*—I wanted to cite all of the ways in which blackness, and perhaps Black life, could be taken in this world(ing) that we find ourselves in. Then I "fell"—a rider's euphemism for being bucked off of or politely deposited on the ground by a horse—and shattered my left collarbone. In that moment, I discovered things about my body that I didn't know, I considered my own vulnerability to *an* other, and, perhaps most importantly for this work, I moved past my indebtedness to ontological modes of being and understanding and began to see things through the prism of ethical relation, always already a dog's eye.

My inquiry therefore is about relation, rather than difference, or its resolution. The book's organizing structure is *peripatetic*—I sniff the ground, following the scent of ordinary objects and the theoretical scaffolding they might/must build, then I move on, get bored, find another patch of awful/offal to enjoy. Animal life is, after all, mostly unreasonable and hard to manage. I move at a curiosity, but not always an argument, culled from the thin edge of a knife; I allow some of my finer points to fall away, I get comfortable with my failure to master.

The Black feminist thought that *tracks* best here is from that dirty south, the one we live every day. The one bell hooks refers to that engenders "dissident thinking and living."[2] hooks contends that to even speak of this place, to claim it, is "an act of counterhegemonic resistance" (5). If you don't know this place, if you don't do your working and living and dying in its arms, this book is not for you. I'm sorry too . . .

I use several terms throughout this book to make my most salient points. When I use the term *hum/animal,* I refer to the philosophical distinction between human being and nonhuman animal being. My use of the term *hum:animal* is to have us reflect upon how the animal opens to the human and the human opens to the animal; this configuration sees *relation.*[3] When I say "animal life," I am intentionally blurring the distinction, hum/animal, encouraging us to rethink what we mean by "animal life," and incline our heads elsewhere.

Along the way there are some impolite questions and outrageous assertions. Some nudity and nakedness. Several moments of ill humor and misbehaving. And among them, yes, love.

primer : what the animal said

Hast thou given the horse strength?
Hast thou clothed his neck with thunder?
JOB 39:19

A mess is an accident.
IAN BOGOST, *Alien Phenomenology* (2012)

accident

How dare I write to you about accident before love. The autocorrect for oxycodone is oxymoron. I will have to tell friends that my trouble is not a literary one. The ground comes up quickly below me and I am not stunned, but indignant. Fuckityfuckfuck am I really going down? Where is he? How far to my right? Will my outstretched leg catch his panicked hindquarter? This could end very badly, I think, but before I hit the ground I take a calculated risk, triangulate the vectors and decide to twist my body toward the horse. Avoiding the face plant and head injury, I choose my left shoulder—am lucky to choose.

Blackhawkdown

Blackhawkdown

I spring up and in the corner of my eye I see the foamy backend of Petey, all sixteen hands moving away from me at a long-stride canter with a few bucks thrown in for good measure or for scorn—I cannot say because he is not mine and at this point never will be. Nonetheless, I notice the sheen of his coat and mourn for our fleeting partnership.

What happened?

An oxymoron

Updown

Slowlyfaster

Unseatedrider

I get up so fast that my trainer cheers—I turn to her after seeing Petey galloping down the far fence line and I raise my right arm for the thumbs-up. When I go to lift my left arm, something between brain and shoulder breaks down. I point to the general region of my collarbone and shake my head, her voice begins to come from far away; I am broken; getting high on my personal stash of endogenous morphine.

Help. To Morristown regional hospital for the verdict: I am indeed broken—a wing that cannot be fixed without incident . . . my x-ray is a vision of small bones shattered like glass. I need to see a specialist. I hear the soundtrack to *The Bionic Woman* playing in my head; I will finally get to meet Lindsay Wagner. I smile.

The Demerol begins to make me drool; I tell my trainer that I love her . . . *really* and the nurse too and the little boy by the front desk who stares at me in wide-eyed panic, clutching his mother for dear life against the woman with the shredded shirt and paper bag of hydrocodone and the mud stains down the left side of her riding pants.

I will have surgery in five days; in the interim, I teach my summer class in a sling, cook dinner for a friend reminding myself not to move my left wing that little half-inch to the right. I forego all attempts to read as I have the attention span of a twelve-year-old. I am pleased that my masturbating hand is still good.

My left eye now possesses a horse's vision. I see my enemies from two separate flanks and rapid movement makes me rear. Recipe for repair of a shattered wing: do I want a long pin or screws and a plate? The latter. Do I have people who can be with me before, during, and after surgery? Absolutely. Am I allergic to any medications? What? Do I intend to ride again? Yes! Am I insane? Probably. My surgeon comes in and with military precision he marks the spot where the incision will go, noting the fall of my undershirt. He wants to make his mark but not leave it.

My sister flies down from Boston with my nieces in tow. The Face-book post from the oldest reads: "My crazy auntie got bucked from a horse and we have to go take care of her." None of us are actually related by blood—we are blood-strangers. Twenty-four hours after surgery, they walk into my bedroom with the quiet hum of the ice machine circulating, pumping what is now lukewarm water to the wrap under my arm and around my bandaged incision.

"Use of this device cuts down by 50% both pain and swelling after surgery"

I am a mess of sheets and blankets in the apathy of anesthesia ringed by a halo of oxycodone. They are worried. How many did you take . . . no, really? Shite, I am a purist and unused to narcotics. The youngest climbs onto the bed, dragging along her father's iPad. She knows what to do and the rest follow until we become a collection of Mac products fanned out among the bed linens along with the limbs of the dogs, enjoying our togetherness in a haze of cyberlove.

During my months-long rehab, I read the online results from my rib x-rays and find that they do not describe anyone I know.

Impression:

> *1. The cardiac silhouette is unremarkable for the patient's age.*
> *2. No acute abnormalities in the lungs.*
> *3. Mild scoliosis.*[1]

love

My oxycodone dreams are vivid and reek of horseflesh. I no longer recognize my silhouette. Something has happened to me of my own accord; I am now metal, severed nerve, and organic matter.

A year later, I circle, urge Annie on, kicking just before the jump cycle to get her up and over. We leave the ground together. This might be what love is. Sherah with Joy.

1 vocabularies : possibility

Give me your fingers.
Under this hair shirt steams the vocabulary
of flesh, crosshatched into meaning.
VIEVEE FRANCIS, "Smoke under the Bale," *Horse in the Dark* (2012)

From now on it seems impossible to remain in the inner certitude of him who perceives: seen from without perception glides over the things and does not touch them. At most one will say, if one wishes to admit the perception's own perspective upon itself, that each of us has a private world: these private worlds are "worlds" only for their titulars; they are not the world.
MAURICE MERLEAU-PONTY, *The Visible and the Invisible* (1964)

Time is a horse you never have to whip.
C. E. MORGAN, *The Sport of Kings* (2016)

worlding

If Heidegger were to have his way (instead of *us* having our way with him—which I plan to do momentarily), human being would set itself apart from the being of nonhuman animals in such splendid fashion that we could simultaneously break from the uncomfortably hierarchized biological relationship we have with animals (at least in the philosophical tradition) while also maintaining a kind of uber-mastery over the world in which we face the truth, unconcealed. That such a move to mastery is predicated (always already?) upon the acceptance of an unspoken but nonetheless a priori lie makes for an uncomfortable kind of dominance. In many ways, human being is constantly unsettled by the conditions of its own existence—without such anxiety, we would have no need for philosophical inquiry or the psychotherapist's comfy couch and box of tissues.

The world is not just a receptacle for life; it is the situation in which the truth (what Heidegger will eventually call "the open") of relation unfolds.[1] In terms of human being, there is no better evidence for our participation in such an environment called "world" than the fact that we can have a perspective on it that simultaneously sees it as *a* world and *the* world. If truth is a kind of disclosure or unconcealment, then in the light of the open, human being is able to see not only its own existence but also that of others (the Being of human being and the being of others). This is a powerful situation indeed, one replete with the kind of tricky mastery that produces teleology from the tautological.

an other is an extended engagement with the discourses surrounding the hum:animal question.[2] It seeks not to immerse itself in these conversations so much as to think through their various critical and, yes, *practical* investments. In particular, the work endeavors to create an intersection between this work on the Being of beings (something that for the most part only a human can do, right?) and the kind of work that the category of blackness does to both disrupt the neat alignment of hum/animal as well as absent itself from the open where beings often collide and collude.[3] In this work, I want to have the freedom to explore species alongside Being, not as an alternative to it but as a question that arises when the work of being cannot help but recall a centering of the human and its juxtapositions.[4] Blackness often stands as that middle-ground*ing* in the neat negotiation of hum:animal. At the same time, Black critical inquiry up until now has sensed the uncomfortability of its alignment with the animal, and so it tended to move away from emphasizing animal life, and toward some kind of meaningful negotiation with the human as its constant interlocutor.[5]

This project therefore represents a fervent desire to interrogate the intellectual roots of the "problem" posed above; roots that could take us anywhere really, since there is no stated beginning for the intersection that is hum:animal:blackness. As a result, this work is a bit rough around the edges as I want to eschew disciplinary structures and freely associate—a phrase that figures if not incorporates my practice. But I want to assure you that this gritty texture is intentional, as I attempt to explore the crevasse between what we know as "blackness" (something at once immaterial and with its own ontology) and what we understand as "the distinction" or hum/animal divide. The purpose of this work is to add to a discourse about vulnerable subjects and our thought about such vulnerability. I hope to mind the gap, treating the utterances of our persistent ignorance of the interstitial nature of all *being* in the trope of the constant refrain of the underground operator. We mind the gap every day by recognizing it long enough to step over it on our way to someplace—to work, to leisure, to hospital, and to death. Concerned neither with animality or humanity, per se, I want to locate my critique by minding the gap/relation between and among hum:animal and how Black b/Being both understates and overstates its commitment to the category.

In order to answer the burning question here, this work moves through genres and critical terrains and therefore has no "home"; instead it is anchored in the relentlessness of lack, at the edge of what we cannot know. To traverse the crevasse, to get us in the mood for suture here, I leave this brief in the hands of the following observation: A climber once saved his own life by doing the most counterintuitive thing. With one badly broken leg, he descended into the crevasse rather than attempt to climb out of it. He came out of the unfathomable darkness into bright sunlight.[6] This is a true story.

....

The story that begins this project creates the condition for intersection between *accident* and *love*, playing with the potentiality that "the open"— both Heidegger's and Agamben's—attempts to track. It is a true story, more or less. The body in question is my own, and I am, at least culturally and certainly phenotypically, Black. One could argue that animal love is held away from blackness by accident, by the citation of instances where animal love fails to cohere, where animal love is either overlooked or replaced by a descent into the realm of undervalued flesh. The role blackness has to play in regard to the animal iterates a constant failure of relation—signals crossed, relationship forestalled. Often, this exercise in relation among hum:animal:blackness focuses on vocabularies of vulnerability that riddle epistemological approaches to our attempts to engage, at least (w)holistically, this threesome.

There are a myriad or more ways to die in this world, and each step over a threshold is a reminder of just how many. From the nightly news to the conference circuit, there is a market—in the flesh, in *discourse*—for vulnerability. Vulnerability is ubiquitous. And it is better still if one can be made vulnerable to something or someone. To be (made) vulnerable is to be descended upon by the state, by one's neighbors (remember Derrida's warning about that thing called "hospitality"), or even by the dis-ease of despair. In the wake of Sanford (Florida), Ferguson (Missouri), Staten Island (New York), North Charleston (South Carolina), Atlanta (Georgia), Minneapolis (Minnesota), and perhaps little-known Bladen County (North Carolina) . . .

the work of vulnerability opens up people of color and, for the purposes of my observations here, Black people to *a particular* and *constant* scene of racialized violence.[7] Our vulnerability is a narrative told often and always and most importantly it is chosen *for* us.

In many ways, the vocabularies used to describe our present state are relentless. I rehearse a few of them here: crisis, nakedness, terror, nakedness, precarity, love, perishment, family, management, sovereignty, and diversity. I hope you have noted the inclusion of some of the more benign vocabularies for our global condition, and in one instance, their repetition. I observe here that these words might do as much to unmake us as do the regimes of power they attempt to illuminate. Vocabularies of vulnerability and their attendant narratives tell three signal and oft-repeated stories about the lived experience of people of color and Indigenous peoples: one is of the Indigenous person's archaic-ness, fading into that good night of yesteryear; another is of the person of color's perpetual foreign-ness, opening a worlding presence to a constant unbelonging; and the third is the Black body's never-ending descent into an *animal* and simultaneous potentiality for destruction *like* an animal. It is a strange temporality, the getting there and being there *already*. It is important to note here that I am referring to the stories often told about these communities, rather than to the tales such human beings would tell about themselves, or to the ways in which each and every one of the narrative assignments above bleed into one another, as managed life becomes swiftly interchangeable. It does not matter whose body, so long as it is *some*body.

To say that hum:animal:blackness represents blackness's return to animality would not be accurate without qualification here. What I am driving at is that we *need* and *mean* an animality so tied to transgression and excess that the cuteness or cuddliness or the potentiality of the animal to return the human to its humanity is something foreclosed by this necessary ordering. When we compare hum:animal:blackness, we exclude the playfulness of the cub or colt and go straight for the one, full grown in its predation and potential to harm. Puppies are for kids. Really.

Thankfully, critics have begun the pushback on biopower's catastrophic reach, pulling us all away from the spectacular—known to Lauren Berlant as the "event"—and back into the quotidian, the ordinary—a space always already thoroughly interrogated by critical race theory since 1973.[8] Having overindulged in the catastrophic we are now to return to our belief in the efficacy of the everyday. Temporality shifts whenever the possibilities of critical theory are exhausted, or to put it more bluntly, "definitions belong to the definers, not the defined."⁹ More recently, Alexander Weheliye's assessment of Black feminism's and, by extension, Black studies' reach into genres of the human finds biopower, bare life, and state of exception lacking. He writes: "The concepts of bare life and biopolitics . . . are in dire need of recalibration if we want to understand the workings of and abolish our extremely uneven global power structures."¹⁰

In a chapter on property and law, Weheliye observes, "Taking in other instantiations of mere life such as colonialism, racial slavery, or indigenous genocide opens up a sociopolitical sphere in which different modalities of life and death, power and oppression, pain and pleasure, inclusion and exclusion form a continuum that embody the hidden and not-so-veiled matrices of contemporary sovereignty."¹¹ The signal and important contribution here—and I cannot help but think of Charles Mills's work on white supremacy and contract theory in *The Racial Contract*—is that once the theoretical territory is reimagined with the practices of chattel slavery, colonialism, and Indigenous dispossession clearly in our scope, it is therefore possible to imagine a worlding that is other than the order of things so neatly packaged to us as modernity's foothold on the neck of human being. Weheliye's groundbreaking work, especially his focus on "pain and pleasure," returns the potentiality of worlding to thresholds of blackness, though my work here would steer clear of binaries and move into the uncomfortable space of ambivalence—*at every animal turn.* In forgetting these thick-on-the-ground histories of potential conquest, containment, and power, critics render the taking of Black life unto itself as a natural impossibility. I want to argue that this emphasis on *human* being can be shattered, was shattered, by African-descended practices and imaginaries at the boundary of hum/animal. I want to open Weheliye's "different modalities" and perhaps the polarizing vocabularies of "pain and pleasure," "inclusion and exclusion" even further, by considering a relationship among hum:animal:blackness that does not carry the stigma of dichotomous difference or solipsistic sameness. This project departs from other posthuman work in that it insists on relation rather than difference to mark its central inquiry. It moves outside of the problem of human relation to nonhuman animal beings and the affective life/vulnerable life Black subjects (literally and figuratively) make with them. There are narratives that place Black being, blackness, in direct relation to the animal in modes of consideration, relation, and mutual observation that do not always already follow a prescription for violent trespass, possible descent, or what I would call negative mimetic relation.

In Berlant's assessment of the crisis of crisis (and its failed management),

the rhetoric of crisis effects a slippage or transfer of the notion of the urgency of a situation to the level of the temporalities of the lives of those who are deemed the locus of the crisis. Yet since catastrophe means change, crisis rhetoric belies the constitutive point—that slow death, or the structurally motivated attrition of persons notably because of their membership in certain populations, is neither a state of exception nor the opposite, mere banality, but a domain of revelation where an upsetting scene of living that has been muffled in ordinary consciousness is revealed to be interwoven with ordinary life after all, like ants revealed scurrying under a thoughtlessly lifted rock.[12]

Mobilizing "slow death" as a "domain of revelation," Berlant brings us to the ant—a species whose biomass is equal to that of all the humans on the earth, and a species capable of rendering its own members into biopolitical machines (slaves) for the purposes of the colony. I am not sure if Berlant's analogy is intentional, but the "muffled" and "upsetting scene of living" of ants reveals itself as the socio-life, the political life of a species not unlike human being.[13] In both instances, Berlant and Weheliye move against the notion of precarity as *surprise* in culture, recognizing that such "structurally motivated attrition" is a constant state. I will have a closer look at this phenomenon in chapter 3, "diversity : a scarcity."

Leaving alone those ants for a moment. . . . As Charles Mills observes in *The Racial Contract*, "Thus, in effect, on matters related to race, the Racial Contract prescribes for its signatories an inverted epistemology, an epistemology of ignorance, a particular pattern of localized and global cognitive dysfunctions (which are psychologically and socially functional), producing the ironic outcome that whites will in general be unable to understand the world they themselves have made."[14] Given Mills's assessment, the revelation of political life—bare life—"revealed . . . under a thoughtlessly lifted rock" produces human discovery as sustained ignorance—a reduced capacity to imagine the possibility of other worlds, other circumlocutions, and *an* other who cocreates them. Moreover, this site now becomes the locus of an "upsetting scene of living," projected onto the colony, revealed to be hidden in plain sight and, yes, *ordinary*. It is not that the living is "upsetting" in and of itself, it is that its revelation means something in the negative to the human lifting said rock. It is this emotional life that then is conferred to the ant; it might be living its best life, but such life makes the rock lifter feel some type of way, and that feeling produces the crime for which there must be a penalty. The quotidian nature of this "scene of living" recalls the work of critical race theory decades earlier, where scholars attempted to incline our heads to think differently about how racism works and moves in the world, to think away from spectacularity and "event" toward something much more basic and pernicious. This work subtends Berlant's assessment, though it goes unremarked upon. Like Kathleen Stewart's randomized purposefulness in *Ordinary Affects*, Berlant "tries to provoke attention to the forces that come into view as habit or shock, resonance or impact."[15] In this way, Berlant's project seems much like Elizabeth Povinelli's work in *Economies of Abandonment* where she explores structures of capital that produce constant and somewhat relentless practices of endurance from marginalized peoples. I get to that work in chapter 4, "love : livestock."

What would a world, perhaps *the* world, look like if we paid attention not to human being but to animal life in its living, a perpetual present laced through perhaps with a Steinian logic; one that serves as the scaffolding for Melanctha's story but nevertheless still misunderstands *her*? Gertrude Stein sees Melanctha as shaped by a present she inhabits, rather than understands Melanctha as a capacity builder in her own right.[16] How have modes of Black genius in particular created hum:animal worlds within and without these structured vulnerabilities? I lay work in this book alongside Black feminist inquiry in the work of Katherine McKittrick, Danielle Purifoy, and Tiffany L. King, all of whom have cited Black "livingness" as an antidote to antiblackness and have dedicated themselves to an exploration of these attempts to refashion a world.[17] Rather than focus on blackness and Black living as a particular counterpoint to annihilation, or as an analysis of space and place, I come at this same query about living and life with a dog's vision—a relentless focus on *animal life* in order to discover where it might lead. What if the scene of living or that thing that looks like "endurance" were not so "upsetting" and the rock were to be lifted with care, in the presence of great *thoughtfulness* under a watchful eye, as *kin*? Or what if the rock stays in place, hum:animal?

My larger theoretical project attempts to join this conversation from the vantage point of animal life and blackness's consideration of "it"—a vantage point that can be written in the language of affect at times, history at others, but is, for the most part, speculative. What this project seeks to do is arrive at the threshold—a clearing, a space for meeting, *an* other worlding. For scholars and critics of biopower and bare life, the threshold is always spectacular, an event (contra Berlant) that moves endangered bodies toward a kind of vulnerability that almost seems like natural selection. The subject never chooses it—that is, it is always random but scripted nonetheless. In short, the kinds of violence that Black bodies endure produce a conundrum for basic notions of the human and, as I argue above, temporality itself.

First and foremost, I want to contemplate the possibility of a threshold without such naturalized selection, a threshold where the event upon connection is not only chosen by (Black) humanity but one in which animal being is taken into account, thus opening the possibility for ethical *and* affective relation. I want to be clear about the language of choice here. As a child of existentialism in my college years, I have affinity for the language of bad faith and free choice, essence and existence. When I say "choice," I am not suggesting, for example, in my discussion below of lynching that Black subjects choose lynching. That would be absurd. To the contrary, I focus instead on the logical consequences of choosing *against* the law (of the father:master:state) and perhaps *for* ethical connection, one that challenges the efficacy of the self's own will to live and the antiblack world that opens up to us as father, master, state. This is a moment that opens up the space for other types of potentialities to emerge; for discussions of slavery's *ethical* life, rather than its biopolitical consequence.

Gilles Deleuze and Félix Guattari have defined threshold and self with the following question: "The self is only a threshold, a door, a becoming between two multiplicities. . . . And at each threshold or door, a new pact?"[18] I take this particular definitional query as instructive because I admire how their definition of the self is in fact an opening unto itself; the possibilities for other emerging narratives—even contradictory ones—are kept alive *within* the human capacity to world *even* before one opens the self to the world-view of another. Put more pointedly, they offer "no one, not even God, can say in advance whether two borderlines will string together or form a fiber, whether a given multiplicity will or will not cross over into another given multiplicity, or even if given heterogeneous elements will enter symbiosis, will form a consistent, or cofunctioning, multiplicity susceptible to transformation."[19] While I chuckle at the chutzpah of knowing what God or anyone can say, one can see how the new materialism's tension with the motive will of humans as a singular "political" force falls on the heels of Deleuze and Guattari's expansion of what's possible for cofunctioning multiplicities. By proliferating the possibilities of contact and (human?) endeavor itself, thus troubling the grounding of progress at the heart of humanity's (constant) overcoming, Deleuze and Guattari produce the work of *being human* as ancillary to work *an* other already engages in that is un(der)acknowledged.

They open the political's narrow and temporal frame of reference, quite possibly (re)turning our gaze in other ethical directions, toward other practices. And feminists love themselves a good, hearty *praxis*.

Scholars and feminists from Donna Haraway to Sara Ahmed, from Jasbir Puar to Jane Bennett, and from Katherine McKittrick to Alexander Weheliye track Deleuze and Guattari's use of theories of *assemblage* to tell the story of how various temporalities and sometimes beings all collapse into a multivalent capacity to *create* political life. The benefit of much of the work of the assemblage is that elements of its construction are often unknown, hard to track, and this inability to measure reminds me of Elizabeth Freeman's and José Esteban Muñoz's work on the temporal—the ephemerality of queer life.[20] That I am tracking what cannot or does not leave a trace makes the timelessness of the assemblage's collective force a queer space for theorizing. While I hold open this queer space, I also let it go—constantly—recognizing that it is also a center that cannot hold. I am forever reaching for that which cannot be held by me; that which ought not be mine alone.

In her pithy and shattering manifesto *Vibrant Matter*, which attempts to plot what constitutes *political* action, political scientist Jane Bennett puts forth "a theory of action and responsibility that crosses the human-nonhuman divide."[21] Contributing to work begun by anthropologist Kathleen Stewart in *Ordinary Affects*, Bennett offers "to affirm a vitality distributed along a continuum of ontological types and to identify the human-nonhuman assemblage as a locus of agency" (37). Taking the category of the "human" out of the biopolitical moment in which it is entirely enmeshed is both to resituate the human and its agential capacities *and* to remake our approach to politics; an approach still grounded in "ontological types." Remembering that the proof is in the pudding, or that politics is in the proof, *pace* Derrida, Bennett urges us toward a less human-centered politics that can overcome "[a] moralized politics of good and evil, of singular agents who must be made to pay for their sins . . . [that] becomes unethical to the degree that it legitimates vengeance and elevates violence to the tool of first resort" (38). This might answer a question like: What to do with George Zimmerman's "punishment" in light of our collective goal of prison abolition and reparative justice? How do our politics align with our ethics? Not very well, most of the time. But this is because Bennett's argument rests squarely in the work of the mainstream; were she to venture into the arena of abolitionist organizing—*an* other type of *political* work—she would find necessary company in the efforts of activists and scholars like Mariame Kaba, who observes that "being intentionally in relation to one another, a part of a collective, helps to not only imagine new worlds, but also to imagine ourselves differently."[22] Abolitionist and organizer Kaba reminds us that abolitionist work "is a *political* framework."[23]

Bennett's question about the "elevation of violence" is a serious one and must be considered. What are our options for social justice and how might we achieve them in a culture of violence that shapes what our response can be? That Bennett's query is a Black feminist one, there is no doubt, whether she credits this thought or not. I am reminded here again of that nagging difference sited in Audre Lorde's poem "Power"—"the difference between poetry and rhetoric / is being ready to kill / yourself . . ." What could she possibly mean by that? Why is the word "yourself" set apart, emphasizing the selfish-ness of the human and its isolation? For years, I read the poem's first lines as an absurdity, a poetic sleight of hand, not a possible truth at all, but a pretty line, nonetheless. I was dead wrong, and as I wrote the first complete draft of this book in retreat with poet, colleague, and friend Meta Jones, she reminded me of Lorde's line and I was shocked into *understanding*. In thinking through decades of Black feminist thought and its uncomfortable questions, these lines of Lorde's poem—which centers after all on *power*, another feminist num-num—I began to see a simple and awful truth of our collective history. Black feminists and novelists have opened up uncomfortable questions about *a deep praxis that can and does undo* the *world.* In lockstep with this discursive and practical work, I approach a few of those uncomfortable questions along the way to working through this book's various scenes of *animal* living.

Throughout this project, I sometimes prefer species over ontology, animal life over *being*, as *being* seems to bring so many unsettling hierarchies in its wake, though I do concur with Aileen Moreton-Robinson that "'being' is the metaphysical dimension of the ontological" and "the underlying reality of the world" while at the same time I recognize that this world we assume is not *the* world, but *a* world.[24] I focus away from *being* whenever possible—sometimes it just isn't possible, so I fail—because I want to loosen our (the human) hold on species as a *practice* (think "ism"), while simultaneously focusing on those moments when that ontology, as a conscious act of witnessing the self or being in the world, for the human, can prove an impediment to theory-making.

The "power" that Lorde writes about comprises the political life that peoples of African descent must encounter, live with, and live by. If we were to tell *an* other story about the political, as Weheliye suggests and as Deleuze and Guattari surely acknowledge is possible, then the political's necessary scaffolding and temporal frame could be opened up to other possible configurations. In various vocabularies of vulnerability, two giants of biopolitical critique have marked the political. I cite them both here: Jacques Derrida, "Politics supposes livestock," and Achille Mbembe, "Politics is death that lives a human life."[25] Both philosophical contributions come from the continent, though we don't often think of one of them in this way. Politics is indeed an abject state. Derrida reminds us that the civil society we so invest ourselves in is nothing without livestock; there is no livestock without the practice of management as a demonstrable effort that constitutes the "political" through which we produce *proof* of the human. For Mbembe, politics is death itself; human life is so circumscribed by the political that death is the only (life-)world where such life, any life can be evidenced. Hardly a script for living in *an* other world.

Donna Haraway, influenced by the work of Deleuze and Guattari, adds to this discussion by remarking that "the body is always in-the-making; it is always a vital entanglement of heterogeneous scales, times, and kinds of beings webbed into fleshly presence, always a becoming, always constituted in relating."[26] In feminist configurations of the political, the body is ever present, and it is most felt in terms of discourse in animal studies. In an earlier iteration of her analysis of species, becoming, thresholds, and crossings in the same monograph, Haraway points out the necessity for "remaining at risk and in solidarity in instrumental relationships that one does not disavow."[27] That "risk" is a kind of vulnerability not open to Black subjects; we are at risk, always, but do not exist *in* risk as a praxis. Think of this text as the breath you exchange with *an* other, and then think of that being as a horse, or a mollusk, or an ocean—all who find their way into conversation in Black and feminist texts from Joy Priest's *Horsepower* to Alexis Pauline Gumbs's *Undrowned: Black Feminist Lessons from Marine Mammals*. These vulnerabilities abound for us in the whole of every orifice that permits the occasion for being with/out Being, for living as *an* other.

When I open up the possibility for ethical relation, therefore, I conversely expose the possibility for spectacular failure as with Derrida and his cat in *The Animal That Therefore I Am*. I know, in the end, that every attempt to arrive at a discourse on the animal will leave me in the lap of the human. But there's no face lost in trying, right? I began this argument with a brief for the animal, a move that might seem out of place if not a bit jarring, because in the vocabularies of vulnerability applied to Black agents, we can recognize a constant worry about the descent into animality or, simply, becoming animal. For some, blackness is that shadow of the human waiting to bring itself back from the brink of animality; for others, blackness is *the* animal that threatens the blood/brain barrier that is the (absolute?) distinction between hum:animal.

What I want to do in the pages that follow is to map a relationship among hum:animal:blackness that doesn't always already see animal life as something to descend *into* or as descent itself. Animality is an animation of an existing imaginary. As Zakiyyah Iman Jackson observes, "Critical black studies must challenge . . . animalizing discourse that is directed primarily at people of African descent, and animalizing discourse that reproduces the abject abstraction of 'the animal' more generally because such an abstraction is not an empirical reality but a metaphysical technology of bio/necropolitics applied to life arbitrarily."[28] All mammalian life is animal life; species is an inhabitation that marks difference among, rather than between, thus elevating difference to a category worthy of remarking upon. In addition, I am looking for an inhabitation of vulnerability—something that Heidegger's formulation of the human's capacity to overcome cannot imagine—that is not *just* the negative consequence of enduring biopolitical regimes—freeing up a bit of space to think about the complexity of human being, the situation of the animal and the conundrum that blackness's affective life presents to a critical world preoccupied with a certain *ordering.*[29]

In short, we are *taken* by words every day. To unpack this arrangement among being, ontology, and species, my process is queerly aligned, inappropriate at times, and deliciously feral. In the first instance, I feel to start by sleeping with the enemy, taking a queer tour through Martin Heidegger's prescriptive documentation about *being.* His elucidation of the distinction still matters and troubles me: humans die, while animals perish. In the next section, I take Martin Heidegger to bed.

being
‾‾‾

on-tic (*adj.*)
>   Relating to entities and the facts about them; relating to
>   real as opposed to phenomenal existence.

af-fair (*noun*)
>   An event or sequence of events of a specified kind or
>   that has previously been referred to. A love affair.

>   What is human being?
>   **MARTIN HEIDEGGER**, *Being and Time* (2010)

Who but our dead Hannah Arendt can say that they have slept with Martin Heidegger? I am the twenty-first-century soulmate, pillow-talking my way through the landscape of complicated eruptions of being and doing, seeing and knowing. To be interested in Mr. Heidegger for a thoroughly left subject is to be like Toni Morrison's Sula, watching her mother burn out of *interest* rather than rage. This is the true mark of the sociopath.

In the fall of 2004, I—not yet comfortable in my own skin, not thinking animal quite yet, but human always—dress to see TimeLine Theatre's production of Kate Fodor's play, *Hannah and Martin*. I come to see people of Jewish and German descent make love, not (yet) war in the messiness of rising fascism. I am betraying a college oath not to touch, like Faulkner's Judith, any of the things that *he* had touched. I am taken by their clandestine love and cannot tell with which part of that phrase I am enamored: is it the love or the clandestine that so makes me shudder? In that theatre in the round— an experience known to me as a child in the seats at Washington, D.C.'s Arena Stage and even then too intimate—I pledge to return to H's work, not knowing that it would be animal, *not* human that would drag me there.

I have come to the crux of relation among hum:animal:blackness through the trope of the affair. A queer affair where "the question of existence is an ontic 'affair' of Dasein."[30] Love and accident produce and frame the theoretical and philosophical inquiry here. We proceed in a time before Jean-Paul Sartre attempts to answer Heidegger's existential temporal dilemma with yet another tome. We proceed with a line of thought that can only be understood through a constant tautology: the affair we are about to embark upon is defined by the adjective, "love," making an affair a particular crisis of love itself—an event worth remarking upon.

Our work is with the Stambaugh translation, rather than Macquarrie and Robinson, gendering our journey to the center of inquiries about the very constitution of the human, for at least *one* human. While time is of the essence here, literally, make sure you remember who the keeper of *it* is—it belongs to Mr. Heidegger and, while you are here, no one else. Before we begin (again), some ground clearing. Dasein as noted here will be defined as "being-there"—a being in its being and while there in itself, it contemplates its [own] existence. The possessive here is bracketed because self-possession must be accomplished by a philosophy of being in the first instance; work that has yet to be completed. The existential is the question of being itself (for Dasein?)—it is Dasein that provides the opportunity for philosophical inquiry—an opportunity whose temporality is not *just* a moment for historical conjecture, though that inquiry is an interesting one.

We proceed in the wreckage of a (clandestine) affair, wrapped in the security of the queerest of temporalities, basking in the understanding that knowing anything for certain would be a huge mistake on our part. The relationship I have with my very being is circumscribed by a lie taken for truth: "Being in the world belongs essentially to Dasein [the being of human being]" (24). But, historically speaking, I am a being outside of other beings (I am Black), so I move with stealth to a reckoning with what has traditionally been understood to be Dasein, whose member stands erect, always in a classic mimicking (or is that inhabitation?) of *seeking* behavior. As an animal, or perhaps a bitch dog, I skirt the outer margins of the order of things, looking for a place to rest my pillow-talking head. How to move through rough terrain with a "dialectic" now considered "a genuine philosophic embarrassment" (24). The possibility of exchange has now been taken off the table—more fodder for my understanding of the journey before us (forestalled, always) as one that reflects Genet's fine depiction of a late twentieth-century house of mirrors—the state and the revolution become one in the everlasting trope of the whorehouse. My lot is always with that bitch dog and her pillow-talk.

Before we can acquire "information about beings," we have to first challenge the assumption embedded in all hermeneutics of there never being a question about *being*. How to commence the gathering of information without first an understanding of whom we are targeting in our investigation? Thinking through "what is human being" requires us to think also outside the proverbial box called scientific method. Or at least, this is what Mr. Heidegger calls on us to do.

But first, at least a beginning. To answer the question put before us— one that will *not* be resolved through the kind of deduction contained in scientific method—Heidegger starts with "an enigma lies *a priori* in every relation and being toward beings as beings. The fact that we live already in an understanding of being and that the meaning of being is at the same time shrouded in darkness proves the fundamental necessity of retrieving the question of the meaning of 'being'" (3). While these beginnings seem to eschew measurement as a presiding framework for our investigation, there is the problem of example here—how are we to understand "being" at all outside of something against which it must move? The "darkness" and death ("shrouded") that he refers to signal the necessity for investigation, but they also contain the scent of something else. What we *know* is inadequate, surely, and made even more so by the fact that we, unbeknownst to us, have relied on such underexplored definition. We, in fact, are blind to who we are in the world. This new awakening, this inquiry produces another effect: we can become master of the self in a way never dreamed of. We can become all that we can be without even knowing that we don't know our being (or the being of others) yet.

The lover anticipates my call for clarity and assurance. He writes, "In working out the question do we not 'presuppose' something that only the answer can provide?" (7). As if in answer to this nagging question, but years later, Jacques Derrida follows up with his own pronouncement, "Politics supposes livestock."[31] Two philosophical traditions, coiled like a DNA strand, but one goal, surely—to get at the heart of (animal?) being—to understand our striving, our penchant to know thy/self. For Derrida, the answer to this question of being relies on a demonstrated and flawed management; for Heidegger, this knowing gets ahead of itself, it manages too, setting the circumstances of answering before it begins investigation. Perhaps Merleau-Ponty *is* right, the self's own perception is incredibly *overawed*.[32]

So perhaps repetition is in order here. As we travel through the first pages of Heidegger's inquiry into the (state) of human being, we see the nervous iteration out of which hum:animal being tumbles. "It is said that 'being' is the most universal and emptiest concept. As such it resists every attempt at definition. Nor does this most universal and thus indefinable concept need any definition" (2) and again, "The question of the meaning of being is the most universal and the emptiest. But at the same time the possibility inheres of its most acute individualization in each particular Dasein" (37). Wow, such a fragile and underwhelming conquest he will make. He is the lover that we practice upon, rather than wed. Is *Being and Time* a primer for how to become love's bitch? I will get to this much later on, but first to the *animal* before us.

Dasein is a being whose gait and intellect are constantly stumbling. Dasein has no assurance in itself that does not always already falter at the onset. A lover with shaking hands betrays his devotion and unbeknownst to himself uncovers the terms of his own dismissal. "Dasein is a being that does not simply occur among other beings. Rather it is ontically distinguished by the fact that in its being this being is concerned *about* its very being. . . . Dasein always understands itself in terms of its existence, in terms of its possibility to be itself or not to be itself, stumbled upon them, or in each instance already grown up in them" (11). An unusual fool, this Dasein, but a crafty one whose measure of (him)self is brought forth as a possible lie.

As if to solidify the point of this staggering ineptitude, Heidegger then offers: "Dasein has proven itself to be that which, before all other beings, is ontologically the primary being to be interrogated" (12). A being who cannot know itself knows itself as the primary *one* to be interrogated. Nice. We differ from nonhuman animal life because "Dasein tends to understand its own being [*Sein*] in terms of *the* being [*Seienden*] to which it is essentially, continually, and most closely related—the 'world'" (15–16). Ah, the world. At this point in our pillow-talking Martin is beginning to bore me, he is sleeping on the job, and I am phenomenologically *bent*, in that British sense of the word, and he is reminding me that "ontology is possible only as phenomenology"—being can't survive as a politic, it needs a place to inhabit, a geopolitics worthy of its promise as a framework for its own living.

like for as : an antinomian crisis

> To tell you how I came to be free, first you got to understand what bondage was like for me. How it attacks the senses. The sound of it. The crack of the whip like thunder. The feel of it. Like you could barely take a full breath. The taste of it, like all your teeth made of copper. The smell of it. The fadin' stench of everybody sold away. And the look of it. *Every eye turned down to the ground, away from the horror.*
>
> **"MINTY" [HARRIET TUBMAN]**, *Underground* (2017), dir. Anthony Hemingway

The infamous scene of a near-lynching in director Steve McQueen's 2012 movie adaptation of Solomon Northup's kidnapping into bondage published in 1853 as *Twelve Years a Slave* lasts only 2 minutes and 54 seconds. Figures 1.1 and 1.2 reproduce two images from that sequence to illustrate some of the features of Black life's precarity and, in turn, how such precarity marks the animal's presence, not as descent, but as coequal disenfranchised subject. Joshua Bennett sees this potential for mutual engagement in *Being Property Once Myself* where, at least in literary texts, we can find "alternative models for thinking blackness and personhood *as such* in the present day."[33] Blackness has (always and already) in its peripheral vision the life, the situation of the animal. I want to ask here too: can it be a "slave" narrative if the man in question is actually not just free(d) but a free-born subject? But to ask such a question assumes that all of the enslaved are not free, at least to themselves. Which begs an answer to yet another question: is all freedom a matter of laws or even individuals? My point or points here are that the question of Black freedom continues to telescope—one question collapses into another as the condition for human being—to echo Weheliye's brief for Black studies—is constantly reset, repackaged, given the ebb and flow of circum-Atlantic tides and global capital.

....

Northup, as Platt, is not twice freed but born free—of free Black parents—so his encounter with slavery reverses the signal trope of the Middle Passage, placing his captive life *here* rather than *there*. *His precarity is more twentieth century than nineteenth century.* But I get ahead of myself. In the first scenes of Northup's capture and travel south in the film adaptation, we are treated to a discussion among Northup and two enslaved men. In their whispered conversation about how to survive, how to live and whether to fight, one reminds the others that "survival's not about certain death, it's about keeping your head down." And Northup's reply is "I don't want to survive. I want to live."[34] So the terms are set in the film's beginning: that the tension between "surviving" and "living" is a question at the heart of what enslavement *is* and means. The question that screenwriter John Ridley seems to want to open is an *ethical* one—as enslaved character after enslaved character weighs the tension between surviving and living. In a conversation with Eliza, who will not cease weeping over the loss of her children, an annoyed Platt angrily cautions her to be quiet. A heated dialogue ensues, and in response to Eliza's question about Platt's refusal to openly grieve for his own children and about the plantation owner Ford's favor for him, Platt retorts with "I survive!" And Eliza's reply is that he is no better than "prized livestock." She then asks, "So you've settled into your role as Platt, then?" When Platt grabs her and demands that she not accuse him for simply surviving, she corrects his misunderstanding by saying, "I have done dishonorable things to survive and for all of them, I have ended up here. No better than if I stood up for myself." As with the scene of Platt's near-lynching, this exchange is the fiction of the adaptation and not the narrative itself, bringing us closer to the uncomfortable span between the lives of the enslaved and the *survival* that produces a future for the African-descended. In addition, what accompanies this scene is a lesson in the difference between "niggers" and other African subjects—the first are born and bred in captivity and will not fight, the second group has potential for revolution. It is a lesson that will become instructive for Northup as he, Eliza reminds us, slowly becomes "Platt." The ethical questions that haunt Eliza and produce the death of one of the two enslaved men whom Northup conspires with briefly on board the steamboat are at the center of this adaptation.

In the published 1853 narrative, the scene wherein the carpenter and day laborer Tibeats tries to lynch Platt does not result in such an extended stay at the end of a rope. In Northup's original account, he is tied, the rope is placed around his neck, and he is delivered to the base of the tree, but his hanging is forestalled by the appearance of the overseer, Mr. Chapin, who runs off two of the off-plantation thugs who accompany John Tibeats in his act of revenge for the literal whipping that Northup gives him.[35] In both movie and narrative, Northup escapes his extralegal death penalty.

The McQueen version is more brutal—it brings our Mr. Northup to the brink of death and at the same time suspends him in the foreground in the first instance and in the second, in the background of quotidian life—a woman prepares dinner (figure 1.1) in one screen shot, and in another, children are at play (figure 1.2). The backgrounding and foregrounding point toward the temporal nature of the near-lynching scene—the open-air abattoir of slavery revealed, hum:animal stretched before living and dying; the ever-present threat of being strung up produces as well as preserves the distinction. While there are no companion/ate nonhuman animals that we can see in this scene, an earlier moment with dogs and children in the same field drags itself into the wake of this hanging. The scenes appear almost idyllic, until like a Kara Walker silhouette, the figure in the background *and* in the foreground becomes legible to our seeing.

The cruelty of Northup's predicament is heightened by the work and play that take place around him, as he suffers unto (forestalled) death. In this scene are two kinds of death: one *extralegal/state sanctioned* and another *social*, where the body of the one who has transgressed the law—descended into an animality represented through violent disregard for the rule of law, law of the master, status of the enslaved, as is the case here—is displayed for all to see while at their quotidian lives. The bodies in this 2 minute and 54 second sequence complete daily routines under the constant threat of death; in this case it is wise to go about one's business, to obey the unwritten law of the slavocracy: that any attempt at ethical action will be met with brute force. "Every eye turned down to the ground, away from the horror." This cruel pageant of quotidian life is disrupted when a Black woman steps quickly into the frame, gives Northup water, wipes his face, and retreats. Perhaps she is that new-world subject that Hortense Spillers speaks of toward the end of her groundbreaking 1987 essay, "Mama's Baby, Papa's Maybe: An American Grammar Book." I will return to this in a bit.

Does violence that opens the body for all to see its sameness have an aesthetic? If it did, then it would be this 2 minute and 54 second sequence

1.1 Northup (Chiwetel Ejiofor) near-hanging in the background in this shot of the cabins of the enslaved on the Ford plantation before Northup is purchased by Epps. *12 Years a Slave* (2013), dir. Steve McQueen.

1.2 Northup blurred in the foreground, still hanging precariously from that tree. *12 Years a Slave* (2013), dir. Steve McQueen.

where Platt is almost lynched and which lies at the heart of the McQueen adaptation of *Twelve Years*. Having beaten a white man with some status on the plantation, it is clear that Platt will pay for that particular act of self-preservation. In the next scene, the spectacular beauty of a day in the Louisiana sunshine provides the backdrop for the lynching that almost was, as Platt dangles from the rope, his toes precariously planted in muddy loam as he struggles to stay alive. The beauty of this scene is cut through with shots of Platt's struggling feet as—in the background of that weeping willow or stronger oak—enslaved children, women, and men, white children, women, and white men go about their plantation life.[36]

His potential death must be witnessed by us all but actually seen by no one—the world white supremacy has created, to paraphrase Charles

Mills, must indeed be invisible to itself. Northup's struggles at the end of his rope—pun noted—remind us of the desperate flailing of pasterns and hooves in the abattoir. I am not the first to make this observation of blackness's relationship to the animal in the scene of rendering flesh from bone, disarticulate parts ready for consumption. Charles Burnett gets at this nicely in his brilliant film *Killer of Sheep* (1977), a film I will treat at some length in another section of this book.

A similar sequence opens up the space among hum:animal:blackness in Burnett's classic. In juxtaposed scenes of children at play and preparing sheep for slaughter, Burnett deftly comments on the shared space between quotidian life and the possibilities held open by the presence of the slaughterhouse among us. I want to argue that this space can be read in the service of affective life. If we do not mark the animal as worthy of destruction here, if we hold open the possibility for community in the midst of such a disaster as the killing floor, then we might be able to think through Burnett's own commentary on the possibilities of (human) beings and revolutionary space. The like-for-as moment in Burnett's film puts pressure on the work of the slaughterhouse, reminding us of the parallel between becoming *meat* and becoming *animal*. We wouldn't be able to treat human beings like *meat* if the work of the slaughterhouse were not ever present in the background, turning the horror of the detention camp, the killing floor, or the strange fruit of a dogwood tree into the simplicity of the quotidian's constant presence. This like-for-as situationality is understood most succinctly by Kari Weil when they note "the postmodern turn to animals . . . is part of this ongoing reassessment of Enlightenment ideals and a concurrent effort to give new definition to the human not as a being opposed to animals, but as animal."[37] Thought on antiblackness would remind us that such shifts in language do not address what subtends the possibilities for animality or blackness as cocreated concepts in the first place. The *world*—just a world, really—might be registered in a series of hierarchies, but what is still left at issue is not that these hierarchies exist but what manner of relation/relating might come forward to contest them and how? This moment where ethical relation seems to best ontological ones is in "an attempt to recognize and extend care to others while acknowledging that we may not know what the best form of care is for *an* other we cannot *presume* to know."[38] I am intrigued by the word "presume," as it assumes a set of criteria imposed on a situation where knowing is obscured by presumptions of race, sex, or species that then become operable as racism or sexism or speciesism. The trick is to get rid of the presumptions and their organization and therefore to grow both our consideration and its capacities.

Returning to McQueen's epic retelling, instead of thinking of Northup's treatment as being *like* (that of) an animal—the very meaning of the phrase leaving open the possibility for disregard, for something outside the self—we might be inclined to think of Northup's being treated *as* an animal (thinking with Weil's observation above)—a semantic ordering that holds open the possibility of ethical relation, of relationship, of, as Donna Haraway reminds us in *Primate Visions, kin.* I am not proposing that we consider "kin" in the same problematic way in which humanity claimed its great ape cousins: so much of us; so much like us that they are worth saving. What I am proposing here is that we reconfigure—perhaps that alternate assemblage that Weheliye invokes—the grounding that holds the potentially of connection as an always already troubling decline. What I am looking for here might be that negotiated space—something the late José Muñoz once called, after Gramsci, *hegemony.* A relationship not set in line with the (perfect) order of things, but one in which two beings in close proximity (a precarious concept as well, by the way) create the possibility of *an* other world(s). Thinking through Heidegger's work with Dasein—the being of human being—Matthew Calarco notes, "Only human Dasein is capable of relating to beings *as* beings—a tree *as* a tree, a dog *as* a dog. This 'as' structure, which marks the uniquely human opening to world and Being, is something forever barred from animal life. And it is this 'as' structure that the animal is deprived of, that the animal lacks, and that renders the animal poor in world."[39] I am attempting here to mind the gap and close it too, preying upon the condition of the distinction—at least in Heidegger's terms—while at the same time leveling the playing field, offering the possibility of beings *as* beings to one *an* other. I want to remake that "as" for hum:animal relation.

But Platt's hanging conjures up more than just the presence of bare life—life that exists for another by being reduced to its biology, life *managed* by its opposite (which never really seems to get settled upon with any real conviction in philosophical discussions). This bare life is also a life in partnership, animating the role that bare life plays in the everyday. For Agamben, the bare life that represents sacred man ("a life which may be killed but not sacrificed") is, ironically enough, "an obscure figure in Roman law."[40] Bare life is snared by a state of perpetual laws, and the nonhuman animal's presence represents the constant flagrant disregard for the law itself. My purpose here is not to argue the fine points of the biopolitical as a paradigm but to consider how—since Agamben's notion of bare life is wedded to a particular historical reality (the Holocaust) and because animal and Black life surround and outlive the longevity of such historicity—we might find ourselves asking what the human really is or does in this situation which stands as particularly *antinomian*. In many ways, McQueen's version of the narrative substantiates the basic underpinnings of what bare life is. *This* Northup can be slaughtered/murdered/killed, but he cannot be sacrificed. This is precisely the predicament of the enslaved: as property (someone else's life) they can be killed, but because they are property under the law, they cannot be *truly* murdered by anyone, really. The ledger will remark upon the loss of profit, the balance of debts and obligations, but the *narrative* of the taking of life—the story that one could argue *makes* life itself—is an inherent impossibility. There will be no crime of murder for which someone can be charged, stand before the bar of the law, do time; the crime here is in the loss of valuable property.

In this system of laws that blackness stands outside of, the extraction of flesh is real. In the adaptation of Northup's narrative, Tibeats reminds us, after his humiliation at the hands of an exasperated and wronged Platt: "I will have flesh and I will have all of it." This is perhaps an attempt to render the words of the narrative in reel-time; those words recalled by Northup are: "He [Tibeats] was my master; entitled by law to my flesh and blood."[41] His return to the plantation to get the pound of flesh owed to him is thwarted by the overseer Mr. Chapin, who runs off Tibeats and his two accomplices with the following words—largely true to the narrative itself: "Ford holds a mortgage on Platt of four hundred dollars. If you hang him he loses his debt. Until that is canceled you have no right to take his life. . . . There is a law for the slave as well as for the white man."[42] But I am interested here in the "flesh and blood" as this alignment of words produces an entitlement that at its heart is about issue, generation, and perhaps genealogy. And to return to Hortense Spillers, the problem posed by "Mama's Baby" is that this organic issue is never secure in the male but originates in the organic life of the female. It is her flesh (and blood) that is of great consequence in the flesh and in the system of laws that holds her responsible for making him a slave in the first place.

The conditions of the slavocracy give rise to all manner of bootstrap legalese—the matter of laws is always already fungible and the matter of Black freedom is always a fugitive enterprise inside such a broken and on-the-spot jurisprudence. I am not the first critical ethnic/Black studies critic to point out this conundrum. Moreover another question obtains: Can

Black freedom be attained or be different from that freedom called "emancipation" within a system of laws? And *whose* freedom exactly? What is its gendered meaning? A conversation between Edwin Epps, who becomes Platt's owner to settle a debt, and the Canadian carpenter Bass, with whom Platt works on the construction of a building on the Epps plantation, exemplifies the precarity of laws. Epps tries to cajole the taciturn Bass into a drink and respite from the heat. Bass is not interested in rest or the system of enslavement that Epps engages.

BASS: Quite frankly, the condition of your laborers . . . it is horrid. It's wrong, all wrong, Mr. Epps.

EPPS: They ain't hired help, they're my property.

BASS: You say that with pride.

EPPS: I say it as fact.

BASS: This conversation concerns what is factual and what is not. Then it must be said that there is no justice or righteousness in this slavery. But you do open up an interesting question. What right have you to your niggers?

EPPS: What right, I bought 'em, I paid for 'em.

BASS: Of course you did, and the law says you have a right to hold a nigger. But begging the law's pardon, it lies. Suppose they pass a law, take away your liberty, making you a slave? Suppose?

EPPS: That ain't a supposable case.

BASS: Laws change, Epps, universal truths are constant. It is a fact, a plain and simple fact that what is true and right is true and right for all. White and Black alike.

EPPS: You compare me to a nigger, Bass?

BASS: I'm only asking, in the eyes of God what is the difference?

EPPS: You might as well ask what is the difference between a white man and a baboon.[43]

It is the nonhuman animal that stands in the chasm between Black and white, as mediator between the law of God and the laws of men. As the baboon—seen by Epps in a New Orleans market—solidifies the boundary between white and Black, it brings to a smirking Epps a sureness of mind. Its impact is that to consider the matter of Black freedom we must consider the life of the nonhuman animal and its distinction from "our" selves, as a matter of justice. Or put more succinctly, correcting this grave error in the alignment of discourse around ontology and species must be a matter of justice, not a matter of laws. So what are the acts of justice that the narratives (film and text) can support? That Black female who breaks into the scene of Northup's own near-death as a symbol of the insurgent potential to disrupt the work of the abattoir—of the place that renders flesh from bone, turning what was once a living being into meat? Perhaps. If bare life is biology and not living, if we can interpret Foucault's biopolitical as "not a space of life, but a spacing of life," then when does the biology end and the living begin?[44] We seem to be Heidegger's ticks spaced out in a forest waiting for the warm body to arrive. What are the temporal possibilities for foreground and background in this space-ing?

Just as the one woman breaks into the scene of the slaughterhouse's reckoning, the only realized threat of flesh torn from bone is that of Patsey— beaten in both narrative and film adaptation—as Northup/Platt remembers the horror as "She no longer writhed and shrank beneath the lash when it bit out small pieces of her flesh. I thought she was dying."[45] In the end, his break from plantation life—from the condition of unfreedom bestowed on him by two men never effectively prosecuted for their crime—is also his break, I would argue, from this new-world subject, this female subject whose revolutionary zeal and unfleshly demeanor occasion the survival of our Northup, and the masculinity that so intrigues McQueen and perhaps fuels his somewhat brutal adaptation.

flesh and bone

> These niggers are human beings.
> **BASS**, from Solomon Northup, *Twelve Years a Slave* (1853)

In the summer of 1987, two texts that would become central to how we see ourselves in the world in the African-descended imaginary broke into our theoretical consciousness. Each spoke of the flesh, and each reconstituted the organic matter of that new-world Black female subject. For Hortense Spillers in "Mama's Baby, Papa's Maybe," this subject, an ur-text for an American grammar of new-world being, was a different matter altogether. Spillers writes, "Only the female stands *in the flesh*, both mother and mother-dispossessed. This problematizing of gender places her, in my view, *out* of the traditional symbolics of female gender, and it is our task to make a place for this different social subject. In doing so, we are less interested in joining the ranks of gendered femaleness than gaining the *insurgent* ground as female social subject."[46] Spillers opens up the space for "mother" to perform some gender-work and so, nose to the ground, I am now concerned with both the category "mother" and the shadow it casts over that thing called "reproduction."

In another register altogether, for Toni Morrison the flesh represented a similar grounding for recognition and revolution. In the Clearing scene in *Beloved*, Baby Suggs commands:

> "Here," she said. "in this here place, we flesh; flesh that weeps, laughs; flesh that dances on bare feet in grass. Love it. Love it hard. Yonder they do not love your flesh. They despise it. They don't love your eyes; they'd just as soon pick them out. No more do they love the skin on your back. Yonder they flay it. And O my people they do not love your hands. Those they only use, tie, bind, chop off and leave empty. Love your hands! Love them. Raise them up and kiss them. Touch others with them, pat them together, stroke them on your face 'cause they don't love that either. *You* got to love it, *you!* And no, they ain't in love with your mouth. Yonder, out there, they will see it broken and break it again. . . . This is flesh I'm talking about here. Flesh that needs to be loved. Feet that need to rest and to dance; backs that need support; shoulders that need arms, strong arms I'm telling you. And O my people, out yonder, hear me, they do not love your neck unnoosed and straight."[47]

Note here that for the most part, Baby Suggs's flesh is ungendered, and each and every part, rearticulated, could stand for any mammal, anywhere. The disarticulated flesh of a human being tied to the ground or a tree is reimagined in Baby Sugg's Clearing, and given the work of Katherine McKittrick to make that Clearing meaningful in Black geographies of female selves, the presence of flesh, loved and perhaps whole, is as much a matter of *place* as it is the place of matter. For McKittrick, Morrison, and Spillers, that matter is decidedly female. McKittrick outlines a process whereby "locations of captivity initiate a different sense of place through which Black women can manipulate the categories and sites that constrain them."[48] Years ago in my first monograph I took this discussion of "flesh" in Spillers and Morrison to be one and the same. Flesh, in my reading, became radical possibility in both texts. A reading that did not bear fruit in the decade to come, as flesh has been tied to the turning of the Black body into a machine, a Slave, a fungible commodity.[49]

Before I move on to present critical engagements with the encumbrance of "flesh" I want to sit a minute with Merleau-Ponty's particular attention to "flesh" in existential phenomenology. He observes: "The flesh is not matter, is not mind, is not substance. To designate it, we should need the old term 'element,' in the sense it was used to speak of water, air, earth, and fire, that is, in the sense of a general thing, midway between the spatio-temporal individual and the idea, a sort of incarnate principle that brings a style of being wherever there is a fragment of being. The flesh is in this sense an 'element' of Being."[50] This conjuring of flesh as element seems to align with Baby Suggs's flesh as matter—it is an "element" of being, but perhaps not B/being itself. Both authors—Merleau-Ponty and Morrison—broker a revised relationship toward embodiment, where flesh mediates, is perspicacious. As an elemental structure, flesh is interstitial, more like sinew than bone, more like kin than blood. We are done with fucking Heidegger—his ontology is useless to us. Merleau-Ponty is perhaps the better lover for our journey to mother-love, to some kind of gendered project of being/Being in the flesh—not matter but love, not mind but element—a constitutive part of being/Being but not its sum total.

I don't want to cite Merleau-Ponty as an origin, since he most certainly is not, but I do want to open up other possibilities of en*flesh*ment (*pace* Povinelli) that might accrue in thinking about the *condition* of being that we find ourselves in. Perhaps no other feminist thinker has devoted herself more to this otherwise thought than Elizabeth Povinelli, and while I turn to her reading of Burnett's *Killer of Sheep* much later in this book, I want to see her work on flesh, particularly in *Empire of Love*, as modeled after the trajectory that Merleau-Ponty, Morrison's Baby Suggs, and, yes, Spillers seem to share. At the beginning of that work, Povinelli asks us to think of flesh and discourse beyond their opposition in political theories of the self. To do so, she focuses on carnality (rather than corporeality) as a kind of mediation of flesh and environment. In this creative biosphere, she imagines other possibilities for *flesh*: "I want to show how the uneven distribution of the flesh—the creation of life-worlds, death-worlds, and rotting worlds—is a key way in which autology, genealogy, and their intimacies are felt, known and expressed. The dynamic between carnality and the discourses of the autological subject and the genealogical society is in this sense more like a skein than a skin—like a length of yarn or thread wound loosely and coiled together, a flock of birds flying across the sky in a line, or a tangled or complex mass of material."[51] Thinking of Povinelli's move to carnality and away from corporeality brings the *elemental* aspect of flesh to the forefront; brings an alternative materiality to the practice of *loving* that Baby Suggs insists upon. Moreover, for Povinelli "the governing metaphors of flesh" are "race, gender, sexuality" and we fear that this flesh "can never be extracted from its discursive conditions."[52] Is flesh a metaphysical relation or is it a political one? Is there an interstitial place where the flesh resides, somewhere between world(s)?

But the flesh that Spillers conjures in 1987 and that Morrison reimagines seems to have other trajectories in more recent genealogies of Black thought. In Afro-pessimism through a range of texts, flesh is the ordering of a Black self, a being dis-ar-ti-cu-lated to realize the task of enslavement: the rendering of Black hum:animals as flesh. Since this Black flesh has no body that coheres, it cannot proceed to matter in forms of worlding or as a materiality. Zakiyyah Iman Jackson affirms this reading of flesh and body in pessimism and in Spillers's oft-quoted paragraph about "body" and "flesh" by noting that her "'before' is often interpreted as affirming the notion that the biological matter of the flesh can and does exist prior to cultural inscription, but this is precisely what I am arguing against."[53] The other "before" that comes to mind here is the loss, the situation of kin disarticulated from place *before* Middle Passage, so that the originary mourning for African-descended persons bound for the catastrophe that was becoming the "New World" takes place on the continent and is carried forward to this place. We are taken more than once, as is a horse, broke for riding, twice removed from place and kin.

My query supposes that there is more than *one* theory or perspectival vantage of blackness to be reckoned with and that these theoretical outlines carry with them a contradiction—how does gender matter in a "feminist" discourse about a body that does not cohere? Spillers points to this problem in "Mama's Baby" when she realizes the (white?) feminist outrage that will occur when she draws attention to the connections between the terms "motherhood" and "female": "Motherhood and female gendering/ungendering appear so intimately aligned that they *seem* to speak the same language. At least it is plausible to say that motherhood, while it does not exhaust the problematics of female gender, offers one prominent line of approach to it" (78). She goes on to insist that "gendering . . . *insinuates* an implicit and unresolved puzzle both within current feminist discourse *and* within those discursive communities that investigate the entire problematics of culture" (78). This is a line of argument in Spillers that I will be tracking throughout this book, as the category of "mother" works itself into the hum/animal distinction and every aspect of what it means to carry oneself forward into the human.

In many ways, Spillers responds to that feminist take on gender "undecidability" with a refusal. Thinking through the Moynihan Report's inaccuracies, she writes that "the respective subject-positions of 'female' and 'male' adhere to no symbolic integrity. At a time when current critical discourses appear to compel us more and more decidedly toward gender 'undecidability' it would appear reactionary, if not dumb, to insist on the integrity of male/female gender" (66). She continues with an effort to restore "Power to the Female (for Maternity) . . . to the Male (for Paternity). We would gain, in short, the *potential* for gender differentiation as it might express itself along a range of stress points" (66). While this project is not concerned with a restoration of gender differentiation, I want to acknowledge that Spillers's work does not exclude queer readings so much as it grounds *gender* work in the capacious territories of reproduction; such a focus resides relentlessly in the category known as *female*.

The more feminists try to move away from the slippery slope of female reproduction, the more ensnared we become in the difference that gender makes. And in the worlds of Afro-pessimistic thought, and especially in Frank B. Wilderson III's first iteration of the discourse as a tool for theorizing blackness, we consistently lose *gender*. Yet, the mobilization of Black-life-unto-death is not without its gendered life—as the taken lives of Black "men" (#Blacklivesmatter) became juxtaposed to those of Black "women" (#sayhername). Twenty-first-century iterations of Black death in pessimism usually refer to a blackness flattened, ungendered, generalized, and so the matter of gender is subordinated to "the state's mobilization of Black death."[54] My question is what shall we make of this juxtaposition and can our discussion of gender be recognizable in a framework where gender is almost passé? Or is the violence of ungendering, following Spillers, another *particular* form of violence done to Black bodies? I think Wilderson and Jackson are right—critical theorists like Michael Hardt, Judith Butler, and Povinelli need to respond to the particular problem that blackness presents for their theorizing. At the same time, I believe that these projects are not the same project, as undoing gender is not the same action as the violence of ungendering, precisely because this specific action needs, necessitates the hold, the womb. Spillers wants us to pay attention to this difference and for this lesson to cohere, I am arguing, we need to understand what hum:animal is and does in the making of mothers and motherfuckers. I hope to provide some African-descended liberatory practices as models for this work in my examination of the MOVE organization's pathbreaking work on animal liberation in the next chapter.

The tension here is that the queer feminist critique of gender (Judith Butler) and its *undoing* does not get at the specificity of the violence of *ungendering*, a process which calls into account the ability to undo that which has been set in place. And yet we have this insurgent female social subject, not articulated through gender as it has been written in feminist critique, but as *an* other, nonetheless. And is it possible that this new-world (insurgent) subject, the Harriet of that generation and the next, might take her proper place in legacies of Black liberation?

This discussion of the *flesh* in relationship to gender intrigues me because it is the flesh *from* bone that makes the abattoir for the subject of my inquiry, "hum:animal"; it is the flesh disarticulated from bone that makes "meat" from non-hum:animal. But tracing gender in Black thought on Black death is like following a finger's imprint upon the water. The ephemeral nature of "it" marks a fugitivity in direct contradistinction to the fungibility of slavery itself. Even more importantly, how to reconcile our work on Wilderson's "Slave"—a condition of modern thought—with the knowledge that for Spillers, given the fact that the internal slave trade was indeed more reliant on female bodies than male, "the quintessential 'slave' is *not* a male, but a female" (73). My simple offering here is that we might be able to think through this conundrum of *rendering* in a situation where the non-hum:animal gets its due and the gendered nature of Black resistance *and* collusion might resurface as a possible query or even interest. And more precisely to "collusion," and to the difficulty of the next readings I will offer about the overseer's whip; about the one "before the lash" and behind it.[55] What I want to track here is hum:animal in the full circle of its ethical relation and to do this, to think through what being a Slave might mean, we must put our noses to the ground and look at both the persistence and the enormity of the *problem* before us.

If we scan through a rough selection of texts in Afro-pessimism, we find our "gender" bundled in with a group of investments—race, class, nation, gender, and sexuality.[56] Critics in pessimism are quick to point out the particularity of gender and race's "slip and slide"—and how difficult it is, excuse the metaphor here, to rein them in.[57] "Black flesh," for Wilderson, is what slavery "reconfigures the African body into."[58] For Hartman, Sexton, and Wilderson, "flesh" is produced under conditions of slavery where blackness is violently robbed of its ontology, of being anything other to itself but what enslavement has in mind for "it."[59] One of the remaining questions for pessimism is its concentration on a Heideggerian metaphysics, rather than the *il y a* (there is/are) of Emmanuel Levinas, whose inclination is toward the more literary.[60] I recall here that there is a tension in our interpretations of "flesh," one I resolved in my first book by thinking of Morrison's "flesh" as one and the same with Spillers's conceptualization. In this moment, I do not walk back that conflation so much as I want to offer that the *literary* version of "flesh" might be more promising than the theoretical one, as the literary creates a relationship to bodies that do not cohere but exist nonetheless. They exist in Baby Suggs's Clearing and out there (worlding perhaps) in some form of ethical rapport. It is the hum/animal distinction that Heidegger offers for ontology that so intrigues Black thought. But the possibilities of moving outside, or gesturing to an outside of his worlding contained in other metaphysical and phenomenological texts—like Merleau-Ponty's flesh in the belly of existential thought—don't find themselves at the table of pessimist ideas, though Calvin Warren's brilliant assessment of Heidegger's thought gestures toward "spirit" as an (elemental?) end to the corruption posed by the metaphysics.[61]

Another question that opens up here is what happens when the enslaved are emancipated? They do not go gently into a freedom in the flesh, as other human subjects might enjoy. Tracking the end of the metaphysics, Wilderson reminds us that "The Slave needs freedom from the Human race, freedom from the world."[62] It is precisely this contention *within* Afro-pessimism that so invigorates me—how to get blackness past a *human*ity that so signals a bankrupt status; and how to think the idea of Black freedom through the multiplicity of species, rather than an ontology produced upon the negation of the Black in a paradigm that is so faulty and centered on *human* life? I want to argue that a look at gender and hum:animal life might get us closer to that insurgence that Spillers refers to at the end of "Mama's Baby, Papa's Maybe." This is why I drag the literary and its imaginary into a set of *practices*, as this study is the first to focus on African-descended peoples caught in the act of *living* with animals. Many of the readings in this book, theoretical and otherwise, focus on praxis. While there is some attention to hum:animal imaginaries, I attempt to focus on created world(s) and bring these interactions to our collective understanding of what happens when this doing thwarts convention or, unfortunately, aligns itself with it.

So, we have a paradox, or perhaps a different ordering arising from criticism and fiction, between philosophically driven and aesthetically minded texts. For Morrison's Baby Suggs, flesh is reparative; for those who follow critical strands of Afro-pessimism, the flesh is created out of a wounded body. The only flesh that Baby Suggs can hold on to in the Clearing, then, would be one forever disconnected from a body that can be loved in that place. Following Spillers's theory of the domestication of gender, Wilderson gives ample attention to the difference that gender might make in his pairing of Butler and Spillers in a chapter on *Monster's Ball*. But even before that, we understand that the task to be performed here is an obliteration of white (female) claims to a gendered difference that does *not* serve the interests of race, more broadly.[63]

In a word, the problem of the Negro is not only a problem for thought, a process that Wilderson rightly observes in Frantz Fanon, "Violence is a precondition for thought," but the problem of the Negro is also a problem for gender.[64] Or to put it more pointedly, it is 2022 as I write this and we are still considering blackness as a universal whose gender (male) is assumed, at the same time that we see ourselves letting go of gender altogether as a determining factor in self-identity. How can we think *gender* in the space of negation of its claims on the human altogether?

More on the above in a few paragraphs. In steps along Wilderson's important study of Black films, blackness, and critical cultures, he continues to assail that gap between "Black being and Human life" a chasm that is "intuitive and anecdotal."[65] Any inquiry into that revolutionary grounding of blackness *in existing thought* would create the conditions for the dismantling of systems devised to hold "it" in place—for example, outside of humanity or at least human life—and would arrive at an ethic that is not sustainable for the whole of humanity, in a scenario where the specter of whiteness holds no possibility for blackness's promise except as shadow. If thingness belongs to blackness, if slavery turns Black people into objects, can some/thing some/one work some magic and get us back to where we once were as "Africans" before we were "Blacks"?[66] This before-middle-time is a temporality that supersedes what became of us (the tense is wrong here if I want to keep the promise of Patrick Wolfe's work in the forefront: the practices of (settler) colonialism represent a *process*, not an *event*) and returns "us" to something like that French feminist concept of women and the symbolic in the time before Oedipus.

Spillers seems to make this temporal shift more elastic, as she encourages and cautions us to understand that gender differentiation in terms of *labor* might not have cohered on the African continent either. If we think of this here and there temporality, then the array of ethical choices for us as (formerly) enslaved subjects opens up just ever so slightly so that we can see that it is not one choice made by another so long ago (*should I take the whip when it's offered to me?*) but a series of the same choices—ones that belong distinctly to a species who holds down the rights to *being* altogether. What is truly gripping about the work of *being* is that it conditions itself, perhaps following Heidegger, as a substance in and of itself, unable to consider any other kinds of life-living propositions readily available to it. This island-unto-itself fashions its world as *the* world, and entices us to *want*, at times desperately, to become part of it. These moments of hopefulness about entering this body politic—and Wilderson is right about this—produce an object that thinks itself a subject who consistently shows up a dollar short and a day late: the price of the ticket.

But back to taking that overseer's whip. The foundational and interesting question of slavery is one of ethics, *not* ontology—I am in agreement with Levinas here. As Jane Bennett reminds us, "No particular ethics or politics follow inevitably from a metaphysics" (84). This ethical dilemma is understood as a vital force indeed in Elizabeth Povinelli's *Economies of Abandonment*, where she maps a series of ethical predicaments predicated on Ursula Le Guin's conversation with pragmatist William James in the short story, "The Ones Who Walk Away from Omelas," released in the same year as Charles Burnett's film short *The Horse* (1973). While I found my own way to this question of the whip and the overseer before I came to Povinelli's paradigmatic reading, it bears thinking about. At the center of Le Guin's story is the suffering of a child kept in a closet, covered with sores and beaten periodically in exchange for the city's existence. For Povinelli, "the ethical imperative is not to put oneself in the child's place, nor is it to experience the anxiety of potentially being put in her place. Le Guin's fiction rejects this ethics of liberal empathy. Instead, the ethical imperative is to know that your own good life is already in her broom closet, and as a result, either you must create a new organization of enfleshment by compromising on the goods to which you have grown accustomed or admit that the current organization of enfleshment is more important to you than her suffering."[67] The footnote to this ghastly array of possibilities indicates that one answer is self-annihilation.[68] But if it's not fiction but lived experience, then the stakes are so much more present to us—the dilemma is not a philosophical one, but one born in enslaved experience that comes forward to us still in a question that needs to be asked and answered—one that Black feminism contemplates in Audre Lorde's poetry. That this self-annihilation comes forward in Povinelli's text about abandonment and exhaustion—"what can be exhausted because this exhaustion is necessary for the endurance of something else"—is instructive.[69] That it helps frame the impolite ethical question—not as a matter of philosophy (thought/violence), but as matter of action (doing)—that I must ask in this contemplation of Northup's life "choices" is an inevitability that has reached its own limit.

What whites and/or enslavers can do to African-descended people is, in fact, not an interesting question anymore—it has been asked and answered: pretty much any motherfucking thing they want at any time. The more challenging question about enslaved experience is not its afterlife—the effect of its ontological proofs on generations of those *left* behind—but its *contemporaneous* question that sits in the air between the subject of the lash and the maker of its distinctive crack: should I take the whip when offered to me? Not doing so will incur almost certain death. And so, the question of the life of some beings and not others, where life is not a simple and singular referent (MOVE organization), but that which can be turned into a differential hierarchy of *lives* in the plural comes to matter more.[70] We step over the ethical question (notice how I do not say "dilemma") into other modes of understanding.

Digital media scholar Ian Bogost sees this focus on "life" as limiting: "One type of existence—life—still comprises the reference point for thought and action."[71] This focus in *thing* theory cares not for the abattoir that turns flesh into meat, and thus destroys what *life* is or can mean. It is also not surprising, but still mind-boggling, that philosophical inquiry into the animal is so far still segregated. In readings across the speculative realist world—from the actor-network theory of Bruno Latour to the process-philosophy that might include someone like Karen Barad in the feminist science tradition— very little attention is paid to the trajectory of the "human" through almost four hundred years of its "modern" history; it is of no consequence to *the world* that philosophical inquiry grounds itself in. Charles Mills is right, the world that they have made is invisible to them. This is the outrage that so concerns us in Black thought. And again, there is more than one way to approach this runaway horse close to the rail. I want to resist the call to do *one* thing, and instead expand our ability to do many. The understanding that Bogost brings to his work on our experience of alien objects stands in subtle juxtaposition to propositions about life, which always already refer to the human. In a world where several centuries of the trade in human flesh/ being transubstantiated the meaning of thing *and* human, and I would venture to add substance itself, it is hard to see this boundary between "life" as human and all other things as absolute or important anymore. No one seems to be able to handle the disruption to the neat hum/animal distinction and its binary others that the work of slavery produced *in us*. Philosophy itself is indeed poor-in-world.

So, the question in the *afterlife* of slavery that comes forward seems to be an ontological one, but the one it leaves behind still sits in that place—like re-memory—and it brings itself forward as a foundational question of species-oriented selves intent on the work of collusion that not only produces systems of toxic taxonomy but also conditions us to recognize the human "machine" (Agamben) as a simple and necessary recursion. I am working on a theory of *being* that might be a theory of life instead, but without, as Wilderson states, the annoying rallying cry of white feminists *and* operation rescue workers. I am thinking with Kevin Everod Quashie's *The Sovereignty of Quiet: Beyond Resistance in Black Culture* (2012), searching for a stillness in the noise of the metaphysical hold, a letting be that is far more interesting than the violence of great apes going about their business, though I will get to that too in this text.[72] I am looking for something out of the man-centered (yes, I said that) work of ontology, that can take on a feminist brief for mother *and* female that might make it through the quagmire of gender (dare I say reproduction) that we find ourselves in whenever we get to the embodied nature of being. I believe I might fail miserably, but I am taking direction from *the animal* in all her dis-tinc-tive parts. I have moved *as* animal for a decade or more, attempting what my MOVE counterparts in animal liberation also failed to do. But we try, nonetheless.

In closing these ruminations on flesh and bone, I return to that insurgent Black female that Spillers ends her 1987 essay with—if "she" doesn't obtain, if gender is *felt* through the African American male's experience of that "motherhood" denied, then what portion of this pessimistic journey through Black "life" makes this new-world subject *female*? The work of gender is never done, and so I want to take a little time with gender in the next section as I return to Platt's "relationship" with Patsey (the new-world subject?) and oddly enough, Jane Bennett's work with reproduction in *Vibrant Matter*.

"what will become of me?"

> There exists a vital force inside the biological organism that is irreducible to matter because it is free and undetermined agency.
>
> I believe that encounters with lively matter can chasten my fantasies of human mastery.
>
> **JANE BENNETT**, *Vibrant Matter* (2010)

In Spillers's 1987 essay, the play of gender and family is so imbricated as to make the matter of Black life determined by its reproduction, "outraged" but still reproducing. Why must such a revolutionary entity, this female insurgent, be tied to her *familial* mode of being—father lacking and mother dispossessed? Whither queer sexuality in such iconic *reproduction*? In essence, not only is this outrage still readily apparent as all around us the reproductive life of blackness is assailed, but also *life* is brokered in blackness such that the purposefulness of our freedom is somewhat enmeshed in the claims we can (or cannot) make over our issue and its/our future. Often in queer studies work this attention to "family" is repudiated as heterosexist, where "the coupling of man and woman becomes a kind of 'birthing,' a giving birth not only to new life, but to ways of living that are already recognizable as forms of civilization."[73] It is clear to me that reproducing this tension between queer and not-so-queer investments is counterproductive to the work that Spillers is trying to perform. The capacities attached to male and female matter greatly to the making of the enslaved *and* the futures they imagine. This is the mess from which other forms of *living* emerge, and Spillers wants us to unpack this hot mess first to see which terms cohere and which ones make no sense in this arrangement of bodies in their primal scenes.

In his most substantial examination of gender through the prism of queer theory in *Red, White & Black*, Wilderson offers that he concurs with Hartman's assessment that the performative is an underwhelming category of analysis "because it is impossible to divorce blackness from captivity, mutilation and the pleasure of non-Blacks." For Afro-pessimists, the challenge to predominantly white theoretical work is what form(s) of blackness step out from the yoke of these annihilations to participate in this boundary-breaking *agency-producing* performance? Wilderson cedes the territory of feminism to whiteness, bypassing a host of Black queer feminist texts in his assessment of Butler's work and that of white (queer) feminists in general. His critique is geared toward whether gender obtains without a "body" to house and perform it in—how does a Black person get to a *body* in an ontological arrangement where such a thing has been evacuated from the landscape of possibilities? The body in a feminist text gives us "a capacity for spatiality [history] and temporality possessed universally by all." Wilderson wants to know "what 'event' . . . reinstated Black corporeal integrity . . . so that philosophers and film theorists . . . could imagine Blackness as possessing the capacity to be staged in dramas where . . . value reifies as gender?"[74] It is a question that Black feminists have held open for critical theory for decades, and so Wilderson's pointed critique and assessment of (white) feminist claims of the body's capacity for performance as absurd are produced within a long line of critical Africanist dissent. So, what to do with that *female*, who without signification, signifies still?

This is indeed a thick stew of notbodies, political agencies, and violence. I do not know if all feminisms, including Black feminisms, would hold up to, could hold up to Wilderson's wholesale critique of the feminist project, but I do see some fissures that are worth noting. To see the Black body at all, one would have to engage a "murdered corpse"—which/who "is not relational because death is beyond representation, and relation always occurs within representation."[75] Anyone who can say that hasn't spent vast amounts of time in a US South where haints abound, people talk to ancestors, and modern-day spiritualists share a meal with the dead. Perhaps the most spectacular statement in this line of argument is that "the terrain of the body and the event of sexuality were murdered when the African became a 'genealogical isolate.'"[76] In the work of M. Jacqui Alexander, Alexis Pauline Gumbs, and Katherine McKittrick, in the ongoing project of Donna Haraway, and nestled in the new materialisms is a gesture toward a mode of relationality that cannot be represented; some world making simply cannot be seen, cannot be made to be seen. This work must be *felt*.

I want to take some time with vital force and the *agency* that it brings to the forefront to think through and perhaps *with* this deep challenge to the ways in which "the human" and its embodied tyranny has captivated our imaginary. If flesh can be elemental, if it can be a kind of thought-in-action rearticulated in a Clearing of Baby Suggs's ordering, then the agency of that being once considered human, never obtained if not long gone, is indeed of interest to us and to a mode of Black feminist thought that is not *explicitly* engaged in Wilderson's text. I am tracking with that insurgent *female* subject that Spillers has informed us is surely out there. I am also arguing that strands of Spillers's work escape the neat ordering that Wilderson confines them to—they contribute to the messy project of articulating Black being and *life* in a theoretically bound world that cannot see beyond its own embodied representations.

The objective here is not to argue the fine points of blackness's ability to be seen and felt in the world/a world (or any other); instead, I am curious about where and how gender obtains and/or *matters*; about whether there is agency *in* insurgency; and about this flesh called to us through *fact* and *fiction* (which is the same medium through which Wilderson finds his craft). To this list of inquiries, I reiterate a previous one: in Spillers's insightful essay, what is the purpose of couching our predicament as Black beings in the language of family and generational begetting? Whither reproduction indeed. A particular kind of gendered *enfleshment* was conceptualized in the slavocracy as "issue." This is an awful simultaneity of events: a problem, a coming out, a child or children of one's own and the act of supplying an item for sale, at least definitionally speaking. It is *she* who "gave birth to the commodity and the Human" in Wilderson's opening articulation of his project.[77] In my view, it is this weighty responsibility for a Black future that Spillers wants to unpack. It. Is. Simply. Too. Much. To. Hold. *Issue* is a circumstance therefore tied to what *gender* is and means in the slavocracy; issue is what it is to be a female in that world. It is a strange cohabitation in the flesh, the carrying of the rule of law, the making of some vital force not irreducible to matter, but mattering nonetheless. And deeply. There is no Black life without insurgence—in Wilderson this is a necessary violence that has specific aim; in Spillers it is an insurgent life that occurs outside the frame of argument. In essence, Spillers seems to go to the territory as she breaks the feminist prohibition against an ordering that takes the life of *an* other in its enfleshment seriously as *life*—a theoretical preoccupation, I would argue, that is produced in Black liberation struggles in the 1970s and to which I will return in just a bit. We argue that the life of the mother is paramount in feminist praxis, but we also maintain in more nationalist struggles that the life of the Black child is a future that cannot wait.

There is tension for sure, and I do not seek to resolve it. Rather I want to mind the gap it creates in narratives of flesh, ontology, and, eventually and perhaps now, ethical action. After all, Wilderson reminds us early on that the dilemma he parses is an *ethical* one: "What are we to make of a world that responds to the most lucid enunciation of ethics with violence?"[78] That sentence makes me want to cry in the beauty of its truth and I am grateful to Wilderson for putting our Black thought—crazy thought even—to paper.[79] One of the solutions is to simply "give life itself back to the Slave."[80] But *what in the world* (and I can hear my grandmother's voice in my childhood ear asking me this on the daily) is "life itself"? My "what in the world" frames the Black feminist project in a vernacular utterance that contests always the neat boundary between the world I inhabited in my murdered *body* and *an* other world my grandmother wanted me to pay attention to and find *a way of living* in. Hers was a Clearing of sorts.

This is where the work of Bennett comes into the frame because the problem, stated by Wilderson and illuminated by countless critical theorists, *is* "ethico-political life" and how can that centering on life be efficacious if humanity or homo sapiens is the only life worthy of consideration?[81] So the questions abound: what is *life* and what might be an *ethical* approach to it? What is Black female insurgent *life*? Does or can *life* have gender? How can thinking *otherwise*, to borrow a phrase from work across the spectrum of critical ethnic studies—from Kandice Chuh to Tiffany Lethabo King— produce an "ethico-political" project we can get behind?[82] I return to Northup's narrative in print and reimagined in celluloid and the question that Patsey's *life* and *living* seem to leave in the open.

Freelance writer and white southerner Katie Calautti became obsessed with her own "attempt to track Patsey's life after Northup's departure in 1853."[83] Though she conflates the book's title (*Twelve Years a Slave*) with the film's (*12 Years a Slave*), her laborious strivings to find our Patsey produce some rather bizarre tellings like this one of a trip to Bunkie, Louisiana: "In this town, everybody knows everyone who knows something about someone from someplace. The Louisiana welcome is a deep, cozy rabbit hole—I'm not entirely sure I've yet dug my way out."[84] Southern life, a repository for blackness, is a cloying quagmire of collapsing temporalities, making a rabbit hole a Black (w)hole.[85] To find that insurgent female is a journey worthy of *Alice in Wonderland* and Calautti's quest begins to mirror the very structure of colonialism's eye.

In *Twelve Years*, Northup describes Patsey in the following manner:

> Patsey was slim and straight. She stood erect as the human form is capable of standing. There was an air of loftiness in her movement, that neither labor, nor weariness, nor punishment could destroy. Truly, Patsey was a splendid animal, and were it not that bondage had enshrouded her intellect in utter and everlasting darkness, would have been chief among ten thousand of her people. She could leap the highest fences, and a fleet hound it was indeed, that could outstrip her in a race. No horse could fling her from his back. She was a skillful teamster. She turned as true a farrow as the best, and at splitting rails there were none that could excel her. When the order to halt was heard at night, she would have her mules at crib, unharnessed, fed and curried, before uncle Abram had found his hat. Such lightning-like motion was in her fingers as no other fingers ever possessed, and therefore it was, that in cotton picking time, Patsey was queen of the field.[86]

Patsey is an uber-hum:animal whose intellect in Northup's assessment stands separate from her animal life, even when there is clear evidence in his bifurcated assessment that Patsey's intellect is in the *doing*. A being stripped of intellect exists for the taking of others—it is an old paradigmatic understanding of animal life *and its difference* that permeates Western thought and brings Patsey to the doorstep of Northup/Platt's field of vison. The manner of remarking on Black female *insurgent* life is therefore an ambivalence cut through with contradictions in a knowing which cannot be easily put to paper. Given the parallels in the text to Stowe's *Uncle Tom's Cabin*, it is not a stretch to see this description of Patsey as a thickening of Sojourner Truth's own narrative description of *her*self and how Northup's as-told-to tale that functions as an autobiography might have borrowed from Truth's narration of her life, as intellect comes into her narrative *after* she reminds us of the doing: "I have plowed and reaped and husked and chopped and mowed. . . . I am as strong as any man that is now. As for intellect, all I can say is, if a woman have a pint, and a man a quart, why can't she have her little pint full?"[87] Truth signifies on gendered difference, sending it up in a litany of proofs that contradict their quantification (pint/quart), therefore rendering them as qualifications that can and will be rightly assessed. Master narratives of doing and having for human being were thick on the ground in the 1850s as the slavocracy faced its eventual dismantling and the flurry of Enlightenment-driven treatises choked printing presses and libraries with arguments for or against the hierarchy of men.

This hierarchy of men unfolds in Northup's narrative through the figure of the whip, as maker and marker of status. The moment of rendering flesh from bone—a space psychically managed by the abattoir—conjures another scene from McQueen's adaptation of Northup's narrative. While the previous scene of Northup's hanging is lengthened and brutalized (one could say to sell tickets in the theater), the second scene of the whipping of his friend and confidant Patsey is produced in contradistinction to the narrative itself, as a more violent scene than the narrative conveys. In *Twelve Years*, Northup writes:

> During my eight years' experience as a driver, I learned to handle the whip with marvelous dexterity and precision, throwing the lash within a hair's breadth of the back, the ear, the nose, without, however, touching either of them. If Epps was observed at a distance, or we had reason to apprehend he was sneaking somewhere in the vicinity, I would commence plying the lash vigorously, when according to arrangement, they would squirm and screech as if in agony, although not one of them had in fact been even grazed. Patsey would take occasion, if he made his appearance presently, to mumble in his hearing some complaints that Platt was lashing them the whole time.[88]

Solomon Northup's *Twelve Years a Slave* is a work of *creative* nonfiction. We must remember that when we read; we must remember that when we see its translation onto the screen. When we think about the violences under slavery, we immediately conjure an imaginable scene of Black and white subjects locked in perpetual rage against one another. I have no doubt that this is the central plain of slavery's institutional life. But what this scene's attestation—that Platt's whipping was or is different from Epps's—does for us is more of my concern as a scholar with a brief for Black feminist work. We reiterate slavery's violent scene because we are certain that this nation is continually trying to erase it. But its reiteration does nothing to move us toward closure. As Faulkner once said, "Was IS." And if you think this is going to be a conservative rant about how we should be over such scenes and their repetition, you are wrong. What I am driving at here is that when this ordering is gendered in such a way—a scene where Black men *beat* Black women to *survive*—then the action seems to be delivered to us in ways that are soluble, in terms that produce its erasure. It must be un- seen through a skillset catalogued *to undermine exactly what is being done.* Northup's narrative secures in the foregoing description of Platt's "dexterity and precision"—think *machine* here—the possibility of sabotage in slavery's literal instrumentalization. Platt's precision is what is at stake in this ritual- ized beating of a Black *other.*

To drive home this point, I turn to an observation. During the celebration of our department's fiftieth anniversary, the University of North Carolina campus was in the throes of dealing—and badly—with its legacy of the Confederacy. We were particularly enmeshed in attempts to rid ourselves of the statue known as "Silent Sam," placed on our campus in 1913 during a fiery speech by local manufacturer Julian Carr, who bragged about beating a Black woman in public that very day. In conversation at our donors' lunch, an alum ventured to talk about the controversy. When another alum defended the presence of "Silent Sam" on our campus as our collective heritage, I ventured to ask him about what meaning the beating of a Black woman in public might have for the presence of this not-so-very-artful piece of art on our campus. I will never forget what he told me in his red-faced rebuttal: "What happened to that woman is of no consequence to the presence of that statue on campus." How can the beating of a Black woman be made to matter in the face of the red-faced thing called "heritage"? *Every eye turned to the ground away from the horror.*

Returning to Platt's cinematic hanging, while he might be figured as Billie Holiday's strange fruit, he is no stranger to those around him. Platt's struggles in slavery's abattoir captures an intimacy, a familiarity that reminds me of something that French philosopher Jacques Derrida once said: that war is a gift from your friends, not the work of strangers. Part of me wants to believe that someone surely would have found a plank of wood to place under Platt's feet to give him those few inches needed to move closer to the living. In this twenty-first-century adaptation, the complicity that the scene demonstrates, the work of silence among his community of *friends* is what *also* holds our attention and is both Ridley's and McQueen's objective: to put pressure on our ethical relation. To remind us that ethical relation is not only made in joy but also realized in the catastrophic moments that produce hum/animal, over and again. In this moment, the lynch mob literally fades and we have perhaps the signal truth of slavery: to defend the self or attempt to defend another is to risk certain death. It is perhaps a necessary risk if enslavement is to end—think Audre Lorde here—yet, such necessity might produce a possibility for a collective future, but it does not forestall or help us with the *individual's* strivings or our sense of how to belong to that community in *blackness.*

But something else even more troubling haunts the margins of the film's and the narrative's central storyline: Platt's main goal is to return to his family. His hope is to separate himself from the community of the enslaved and become reunited with his *biological* life. This perpetual desire in narrative and film stages the relationship between Black community and Black family as one of contestation. And in this moment, the crucial lesson of the film is revealed: Black community must be forsaken if the Black family is to prevail. It is a thorny *issue,* but one that must be considered seriously as the message of McQueen's feature. What makes slavery survivable here, at least for Northup, is that it has a before and after marked by the title's temporal surety: *Twelve/12 Years a Slave.* We can eat our popcorn in peace, knowing the nightmare filleted before us has a beginning, a middle, and an end. The political work of narrative and film is to instruct us in how to forgo our ties to community and reconstitute ourselves into that vast American dream heralded as the biological family. This necessity to belong to *proper* family is evidenced toward the film's end when Northup is finally collected by a family friend and climbs into a wagon headed for New York. As he moves toward the wagon, Patsey calls out to him, "What'll become of me?" In the feature film, he looks back, but only briefly, thus holding her life's future in his companionate gaze momentarily. But in the narrative, he simply ends the paragraph and begins another one with: "I disengaged from her and entered the carriage."[89] McQueen wants to hold this Black female insurgent subject in the possibility of ethical relationship that the narrative itself cannot sustain. It is the same insurgency that McQueen wants to mark when a Black female figure, *not* Patsey, brings Platt *née* Northup water to sip in an attempt to ease his pain during his protracted near-lynching. There is something in insurgent femaleness that a twenty-first-century diasporic Black subject like McQueen wants to look upon intently, wants to pull from the wreckage of Northup's attempt at *auto*biography.

In the aftermath of Northup's reunification with biological family, one has to ask: what becomes of the Black subject, the Black person who has no tie to such a thing? This is the question—the queer question—that Patsey's life (in and beyond Northup/Platt's framing) opens for us and for that *Vanity Fair* author, no matter how imperfectly. I too want to know about Patsey's feeling, want to hold it in at least some momentary regard for the work ahead. And even more directly, what becomes of the Black woman, left behind on a road with her back barely healed from lashes inflicted by the same man who now walks toward the wagon heading north to reunite with his *biological* issue? Is not Patsey's issue (Black future?) his as well in the community of the African-descended? This too is an instructive moment. It should give us pause. As Northup recalls after Patsey's protestations and query: "I disengaged myself from her, and entered the carriage. The driver cracked his whip and away we rolled. I looked back and saw Patsey, with drooping head, half reclining on the ground; Mrs. Epps was on the piazza; Uncle Abram and Bob and Wiley and Aunt Phebe stood by the gate, gazing after me. I waved my hand, but the carriage turned a bend of the bayou, hiding them from my eyes forever."[90] This moment of eyes *not* seeing or the scene of enslavement in *all* of its familial relations, being hidden by a bayou, points toward the assemblage of things nonhuman that Bennett wants/needs to address as actants. Thinking about other beings as actants at the site of slavery's ethical life is worthy of consideration. This *not* seeing seems to be the lot of human being in the *face* of a violence and an unfulfilled ethical promise/commitment to its unmaking. Northup leaves Platt behind and moves into his *auto*biography; leaves Patsey in a suspended animation at the end of a coil of leather that Platt-becoming-Northup-again is also implicated in as maker and marker. *Her* predicament is the question lodged at the heart of *Twelve/12 Years a Slave*. The insurgency is both in other *matter* and in the tale itself.

If in fact the gestures of the horrific are molded by the ordinary, then the cohesion of the eyes cast down and away from Platt's refusal of his *made* family for Northup's reunification with his biological one, then this act of turning away is as unsettling as the opening of Patsey's back just four chapters earlier—a relationship that is shortened in the film version, at least episodically. The question then becomes: *Is the insurgent being, this new-world female social subject (much more interesting than gendered femaleness) the "thing" that needs to be left behind to move a certain kind of blackness to its fruition as freed/modern subject? Is the pessimism riddled with the* effect *of such a terrible ordering? Is finding the way back to the human, always already an impossibility metaphysically, bankrupt but necessary anyway, not to prove a point about whiteness's* hold, *but to prove a point about gender?* And here we are back to that feminist reading where "value reifies as gender." While gender certainly accrues and cannot be brushed aside, I want to put a bit of pressure on what gender can do in a space where the *human* is not the only agent worthy of interest or interests. I offer an exchange of layered images: the flayed back of a Black woman for the back of a horse or maybe a mule. A central question in slavery opens up a flawed hum/animal distinction that subtends the lot. We struggle at the end of our rope here. The driver cracks his whip on the back of the horse suspended at the end of a knot of leather connected to that female (en)slaved through violent gesture and some of us step into the *future* (the provenance of the male gender and therefore stolen *for*/held captive *by* the male gender too). A *time* promised to us in the belly of the enslaved, forestalled always and an insurgency of matter, a kind of living, *an* other. Destiny, like our Patsey, unknown.

In both narrative and movie adaptation the scenes in which Patsey's life seems to be of some consequence to Platt are moments of her literal disarticulation. I want to return to that moment when Platt is forced by Epps to take the whip and beat Patsey—I want to return to the ethical dilemma of "the Slave" referenced in Wilderson's work. What indeed is the ethical dilemma of the enslaved? For Wilderson it is a call to recognition that the only way to resolve the contradiction of Black life itself is through the taking of Black life. And, I would add, this is not such an outrageous contention if we take into consideration the work of *confederacy* in the slavocracy—for it is collusion produced as coercion in its *future* reimagining that makes the system work—beat a life to save a life and narrativize such action as a necessary evil nestled within a corrupt system. The voice of this confederacy is loud and clear: "Come with me if you want to live" and is predicated on and subtended by the same confederacy that produced hum/animal distinction.[91]

We are to have compassion for Northup's plight, rendered to us as an autobiography that would not occur if all the makings of its very substantiation were not exiled from it, in pieces. I understand that the ethical life of the enslaved is an impossible conundrum *and* a cruelty as that ethical action so central in the look of *an* other is reconfigured as negative existence for the enslaved. Framed as a matter of hum/animal difference, though, the space that opens up in this narrative is one in which the insurgent Black female cuts through, leaving a temporal occlusion in this scene of our undoing; forcing a bit of warm air up above the cold air. In this moment, the taking of Black life as one's own life, remembering Lorde, is the antidote to a confederacy that exposes the lie of difference and precipitates human being's undoing. In many ways, stuck between the necropolitical potentiality of whiteness's reach and the impossibility of blackness's fruition, collusion mediates. Always. An insurgence could be the realization that the occlusion is not the anomalous event but should be/should have been normative praxis all along. It is the difference between poetry and rhetoric.

I turn now to a particular kind of *embodied* temporality that the Black future represents, a kind of exchange between mother/mother-dispossessed that constitutes the core of that insurgency Spillers might be referring to—what is the matter of this Black female *life*? Is it an *insurgency* of new materialisms we need to take more note of? At one point in a discussion of the various and conflicting views about vitalism and human life in a chapter entitled "Stem Cells and the Culture of Life," Bennett casually remarks "I do not think that there is any direct relationship between, on the one hand, a set of ontological assumptions about life or matter and, on the other hand, a politics; no particular ethics or politics follow inevitably from a metaphysics" (84). In fact, what becomes of ethical life is a nonstarter, and I think there is agreement on this count in Wilderson's work where the *ethical* question of the Slave is met with violent response. But if we remember, at least in spirit, the "unthought"—first gesticulated wildly in Fanon and reimagined in Nahum Chandler's *X: The Problem of the Negro as a Problem for Thought* (2014)—then we might find that the central idea of the Enlightenment, to keep pace with my pessimistic colleagues, was indeed to unthink the human as any other embodiment *outside* of a propertied, white male. Our first gesture, then, is to leave the human alone; it is a worthless shell for understanding who (politics) and how (ethics) we are. If there is a politics or an ethics emerging from the metaphysics, it is truly *un*ethical, which is not to say that ethics or politics don't "follow" but that they cannot be understood collectively in the positive at all—like the body that cannot cohere—instead, this form of living is a constant disarticulation of what can be considered as ethical or political. What I find useful in an animal studies approach to the question of the ethical or the political is that the machinations of homo sapiens ought not and cannot be the only actants, to borrow from Bennett, that determine what life or living *is*. The moral tenets that subtend our ethical commitments are in and of themselves faulty. And in fact, this expansion of the field of possibilities for consideration of hum/animal difference makes for a much more engaged Clearing. I want to mark that slight difference here—that the having (of an ethics) is a positive statement that doesn't quite cohere in ontology, but which marks the place of an ethical life nonetheless. Might this be the *trace, an* other that haunts the boundary of Derrida's *The Animal That Therefore I Am*, which among other things attempts to track the incoherent loop created by our attempts to make hum:animal (dis)articulated matter?

I will get to Derrida later. For Bennett, the central question of her book as a whole is whether materiality possesses agency as affective life in relationship to hierarchies of human endeavor and even over and above them? While it would be reductive to attempt to summarize the fine distillation of philosophical arguments over vital force, soul, and matter, it is important for my purposes to think about her central question: "Can materiality itself be vital?" Central to this task—the task of making human being *matter more*—is the following contention that Bennett sees as a cornerstone of "the culture of life" hypothesis (one that she critiques): "Humans are not only organic, unique, and ensouled but they also occupy the top of the ontological hierarchy, in a position superior to everything else on earth" (87). Damn. Building upon deliberations from an earlier chapter, Bennett's analysis sees the distinction among *human* life, *a* life, and *matter* as important to a thoroughgoing discussion of what's at stake in our understandings of what "life" itself might be, or I would contend *can* be, since we are always working with *being* and *potentiality* (of life). This uniqueness of the human in culture of life ideology, as a theologically determined distinct autonomous self—autobiographically inclined like our Northup—is endowed with a vitalism from the divine, a remnant of the old theology that still lives within the Enlightenment's ontological proof. What I am pointing out here is the uncomfortable space of Northup's culpability in our collective response to the "quintessential slave." Is the only ethical response available therefore possible only for white subjects? Is it possible to make something (ethical) out of nothing (violence)?

The inherent violence of arguments about how to value life—especially *unborn* life—comes forward in Bennett as a particular problem, and I would also argue, as a fundamental problem for a feminist inquiry which then meets a Black nationalist response in the future of the child (un/born). This violence that Bennett exposes is much like the violence cited by Wilderson in the making of the human. She asks, "How can love of life coexist with love of violence? How was this strange link between care and conquest formed?" (88). The pessimist's answer would be that it is simply inherent in the ontology. And Bennett's analysis is susceptible to this critique since she believes that no ethics or politics can come from a metaphysics. Bennett's specific question is about the evangelical advocates of the sanctity of life and their unsettling acceptance of war as a necessary violence to preserve this rather *ordered*, though nonsensical (one must take life to preserve life) approach to life. What I find intriguing within exceptionalist claims about the "human" is the extent to which these believers in "soul vitalism" understand that "Man is the most vital . . . in the sense of possessing the greatest degree of freedom and capacity to act in ways that cannot be reduced to their situational or environmental determinants" (87, 88). Ah, the provenance of men. This "freedom and capacity," to reach back to the beginning of this chapter and its analysis of Wilderson's pessimism in particular, is only attained through violence and at the expense of *an* other, so that the condition of freedom is mired in unfreedom. This is a central tenet of the pessimism, but it cannot be applicable to the condition for blackness always.

If we take Wilderson's assessment of Black freedom as a condition necessitating violence, and couple this with what we learn from our foregoing discussion of *Twelve/12 Years a Slave*, the condition of autonomy and therefore freedom is not necessarily forged in ontology or an ontology with a purpose like a hierarchy of Black and white actants, to borrow a word from Bennett. This Black freedom—a temporality forestalled and literalized—is forged in the belly of the mother, mother/dispossessed. Instead, like Bennett, I want to see this provocation called human being coexist with actants, one of which for her in this chapter is "the ultrasound images of unborn fetuses" (88). In this arrangement, the unborn fetus becomes interesting not as a political tool in a hierarchy of valued forms of human living (the abortion/not abortion lockstep). The unborn fetus becomes interesting for its potentiality among a constellation of other beings whose potential is imbued similarly, and this constellation is only viable, let's say, through acknowledged relation. New materialisms doesn't necessarily unmake the settled ground upon which "race" is made to be coherent. It always already exists in these hierarchies of being, to rehearse Kyla Tompkins's query about its positioning on the playing field of ideas; new materialisms remind us that the bayou that occludes Northup's vision is something more than a utilitarian obstacle or literary device that momentarily produces limited vision.[92] What a theory of more present actants does offer us is the parallel critique of a violence inherent in structures of care, while also dislodging *the potential* in the form of the human's reproductive capacity, and a potentiality in forms-of-living-as-themselves that are not necessarily placed in a hierarchy of relation that needs to be *represented* to be understood or felt. As Bennett notes in another chapter, "What dangers do we risk if we continue to overlook the force of things?" (111). The problem and potential here are to unmake the violence necessary to preserve *life*, and this query is not a political one at all, but a recognition that sits both within and outside of human being as *an* other and its potential.

Said *an* other way, to say that a human body does not cohere but then to posit a future toward which a kind of Black insurgence (femaleness) directs itself is to recognize the potentiality of life not as political life, tied to the problem of *issue* above (in chattel slavery and in *Roe v. Wade*), but to preserve the potentiality of Black being as an embodied insurgence, female-having, mother-(dis)possessing. For if we continue to define *issue* as law of the father, then the possibility of escape, of insurgence in the *now* becomes forever forestalled by a recursive inevitability that my issue will be like me: chattel. Given the vital force of *things*, *objects*, *others*, and the extent to which Spillers is right to call out reproduction as a potential crisis for feminist thought, the terrain is indeed steep but fruitful nonetheless.

And what about that vital force so argued over and attested to—is it only available to *female* gender in the form of *an* other organism (the fetus) with the same potentiality for sex/gender whose cohabitation is ever-changing and representative of a founding *being with* that is the experience of all mammals? Embodied reproduction is not only its male and female parts but also the host of other actants who cocreate. Is reproduction the only means by which the capacity of gendered flesh (the only gender is female gender, as man is a universal), is made real and can gain that insurgent ground that Spillers attests to in that 1987 article? It appears that our arguments over abortion might come down to simple arguments over the potentiality (fetus) for *female-ness* to matter to us—that is the unsettled *issue.* I am saying nothing new here about women's bodies or arguments *over* them. But what might be possible is to couple the potential that lies beyond the human—the lives of other species—with that revolutionary potential available to that insurgent "female social subject" and to create a mash-up of something that is altogether fugitive—not because it has escaped some place or outcome, but fugitive, because it exists alongside and *in* "an array of bodies" (112) taking its own flesh, to follow Morrison here and loving it hard. What a queer little thing she must be.

In the last chapter of Bennett's book, she offers, before a reading of Guattari's *The Three Ecologies*, "Vital materiality better captures an 'alien' quality of our own flesh, and in so doing reminds humans of the very radical character of the (fractious) kinship between the human and the nonhuman. My 'own' body is material, and yet this vital materiality is not fully or exclusively human. My flesh is populated and constituted by different swarms of foreigners" (112). Tracking back to Bogost's brief for *Alien Phenomenology*, the thing that is considered outside the human might not be so *alien* at all. In this regard, I think that Kyla Tompkins's analysis of the "new materialism"—what's so new about it?—is warranted. When I read Bennett or Bogost, I think back to Baby Suggs's words in the Clearing, and it is not difficult to imagine the rearticulation of blackness: not human, but consisting of parts once rendered flesh, parts not distinguishable from other forms of living, and in a place *elementally* defined by a world-ing outside of human-ity's constructions/interventions or hot mess.

Even at the moment when the biological becomes us, is inside us, when we realize that to be human is to be made up of so many other life forms that then equate to the entity we know as human, we understand such a moment of absolute confluence through a narrow metaphor of relation that solidifies the one thought-constellation on this earth that is so deadly: the family. If I go so far as to tweak Wilderson's point about relation as both blood family and what can be represented, then the biological materials that forge meaning in a future we cannot obtain, but do nevertheless, worry the boundary of not gender but femaleness. Platt leaves the made community of slaves to become whole again in biological family, because as Bennett reminds us about our own *bio*-sphere, "Proceed politically, technologically, scientifically, in everyday life, with careful forbearance, *as you might with unruly relatives to whom you are inextricably bound* and with whom you will engage over a lifetime, like it or not" (116; emphasis mine). How is one to relate to relatives who we are told are not human but actants, a part of us, through a paradigm in which blood-relation then again matters as an interpretive framework through which to seek/see kinship or ethical action? Femaleness matters certainly, and while I have been trying to have a brief for gender, I find that what is left is a calling for a femaleness that is fecund and infused with the being of so many actants, whose futures depend on *her*.

Ontology mires us in a series of proofs and even experiences that so crowd the work of Being that I doubt it will be easy to get beyond them, though some have tried. When Bennett asks us to "picture an ontological field without any unequivocal demarcations between human, animal, vegetable, or mineral" (116–17), I wonder why this is an ontological field. Moreover, what should I care about this world where the human is no longer an integral central part in itself, if this world-making is informed by not one single word written by an African-descended person over three hundred years of argument? Why must our bodies be reimagined, but the theory that makes them so remain oddly within the same genealogical coordinates? In closing, Bennett notes something "too close and too fugitive" (119) and I wonder, if she sited that new-world female subject in her periphery, dragging her flesh behind her in an arc and act of magnificent desegregation, would she pause? Like our Platt née Northup, Bennett finds: "I am, for now, at the end of my rope" (122).

collusion

When I was younger and learned about slavery, I remember talking among friends and thinking that I *would never, could never* be a slave. In our imaginary incarnations as enslaved beings, we pictured ourselves as Tubman revolutionaries, as mighty Toussaints, as radical abolitionists. Shortly after seeing McQueen's celluloid version of Northup's temporally fixed experience of enslavement, I had dinner with friends of friends, both of whom are vegan. In the course of a discussion about meat eating, one of them remarked, "I'd rather die than eat meat." I thought about that remark in the context of the film I had just seen and I smiled. We are all little revolutionaries when the time comes. When the time comes.

I was born in a segregated hospital. It wasn't until having children (albeit only briefly) to feed, clothe, get to school, and shepherd through this quotidian life that I realized how much (de)segregation had contoured my very being in those late sixties and early seventies. We did not arrive late to anything. I never had the wrong shoes or socks or other meaningless accoutrement. We were always "tight." My mother marched me through a newly desegregated world with military precision. We could not afford to misstep. People were watching us. People, some of whom were related to us by birth or marriage, were waiting for a divorced woman and single parent to fail in every way. My mother was a mighty Harriet in those days, but not because she thwarted the system always—sometimes she did not. She was mighty because she kept us alive. She struck when necessary, coiled and ready, but for the most part, we flew under the radar.

I soon learned that my efforts to desegregate would not end with a traditional bildungsroman advance into adulthood; the work would be ongoing and isolating and along the way I would see and understand that collusion keeps the animal in check, always. Collusion helps systems of power run smoothly, and the question of Black freedom, of emancipation itself, is caught up in the question of Black death and that distinction between hum/animal. In this regard, the pessimism is spot-on; the only way to preclude the possibility of the expiration of Black life is for some of us to die, in the perhaps desperate hope that some-one-of-us, to echo James Baldwin, will surely step up with the refusal.[93] Revolutionary action—a particular inheritance of Spillers's embodied female social subject created in part by new-world avarice—requires us to walk away from that particular set of distinctions that cast human life above.

other.

animal.

life.

Stepping outside the sovereign's (I will get to that entity in this book's last chapter) system of laws, this new Black female insurgent can indeed be sacrificed, as much as she can live. It is a death that defies the remnants of the social, calling upon the materiality in one's own life and that of others, making a mockery of the political's instantiation.

This explication of scenes from Northup's narrative and the film adaptation of his life opens us up to other avenues of exploration in discourse at the *threshold* called "hum:animal." My aim here is to offer that as Spillers's essay opens up the possibility of *ungendering* in the hold of the slave ship, it leaves us with a reproductive conundrum in its fourth and final section—what to do with the following: the daughter, an African American male who inherits, and that "female social subject" who does not and cannot obtain in the gendered ordering we are used to in the aftermath of slavery. If we focus on ethical relation and revolutionary potentiality, then we see Black subjects, vulnerabilities on display, capable of producing important interventions in our consideration of animal life. I am tracking now to that consideration.

2   companionate : species

We are training each other in acts of communication we barely understand. We are, constitutively, companion species. We make each
other up, in the flesh. Significantly other to each other, in specific difference, we signify in the flesh a nasty developmental infection called
love. This love is a historical aberration and a naturalcultural legacy.
DONNA HARAWAY, *The Companion Species Manifesto* (2003)

Whether this [death] is due to the terror and strain which they under-
went at capture, or to being confined in cramped cages, I cannot say.
But the fact remains that not more than half of them arrive safely at
their destination, despite our utmost care.
CARL HAGENBECK, quoted in Joanna Bourke, *What It Means to Be
Human* (2011)

Life lurks in the zone of indiscernibility of the crisscrossing of differences, of every kind and degree.
BRIAN MASSUMI, *What Animals Teach Us about Politics* (2014)

distinction

The hum/animal distinction is inundated with vocabularies of
flesh. The hum/animal distinction is caught in a web of regulated
belongings—family, race, culture. All cohere when the boundary
between human and nonhuman is breached, willingly, and therefore queerly, through pleasure. One of the above epigraphs is taken
from Donna Haraway's now classic manifesto. Haraway's work reminds us that the questions we ask or the meaning we derive from
them cannot take place in a species-bound ordering that looks so
much like the very one we are trying to deconstruct. In other words,
Haraway observes that the narrative of "embodied cross-species sociality" might afford an opportunity to remake what stands as the

political and the ontological, a prohibitive ordering of living that depends upon the human (its cognition), but as several animal studies critics have shown, rests upon that primary *distinction*, hum/animal. To be distinct is to be out. standing. in. your. field. To be a nonhuman animal worth recognition is to do . . . something very similar. In drawing together two strands of thought—one taken from Deleuze/Guattari's "becoming with" as a gesture of other sociopolitical worlds and the other taken from the feminist ethic of care tradition—Haraway's position muddies the matter of distinction, as neither theoretical standpoint is adequate to the task of knowing what the animal sees, thinks, and, to follow Derrida, *regards*.[1] I think the key-word in the phrase, "embodied cross-species sociality" is "sociality"—what forms of sociality with hum:animals are considered "embodied" or "cross-species" enough to garner recognition but not revulsion or outrage? What forms stay within the boundary of the order of things? What is "sociality" here, and how can it be realized in animal worlds? How can it be realized in hum:animal belonging? Is the standard always already a *human* rather than *nonhuman animal* standard, one where the doer is more important than the being-done-to?

In order to shake the sense of ourselves as being who we are in what we are, I offer the following: We are on a planet called Earth where water-based life is the norm, but if we took the essence of water as polar molecule, and perhaps investigated the possibilities inherent in say, another polar molecule, then we might be just as happy in some other embodiment as an ammonia-based being, rather than a water-based being, and thus attendant to the cultures created by that liquid form. Shulamith Firestone, Haraway herself, and human biologist Anne Fausto-Sterling all exposed the gendered-culture nature of scientific inquiry.[2] And there is no greater science out there than that which focuses relentlessly on the human. One of those sciences—and Louis Althusser was right to investigate the possibilities of this point—is philosophy.

But even philosophy tried to rid itself of its own (human) reflection, at least practically, through the early animal studies work of a few graduate students studying together in England.[3] In 1971, they published *Animals, Men and Morals: An Inquiry into the Maltreatment of Non-humans.* Stanley Godlovitch, Roslind Godlovitch, and John Harris were all influenced by Ruth Harrison's (in)famous critique of industrial farming and its impact on Britain in *Animal Machines* (1964), published in the same year I drew my first breath. The great Peter Singer, now a bioethicist at Princeton University, was asked to write a review of *Animals, Men and Morals* for the

New York Review of Books. The title of that review was "Animal Liberation," and he called their stunning collection of essays "a manifesto for an Animal Liberation movement."[4] In that review, Singer begins with a standard separation of church and state: "We are familiar with Black Liberation, Gay Liberation, and a variety of other movements. With Women's Liberation some thought we had come to the end of the road," indicating that the idea of an intersectional liberation movement was a thing of the future at the writing of his important review.

What these late-twentieth-century activists and scholars puzzled about was whether or not we could move our discussions about morals and ethics—but mostly ethics in the end—to consider the condition (welfare) and singular purposefulness (liberation) of the nonhuman animal. From this opening in philosophical inquiry, the work of animal studies and its three nodes—hum/animal distinction, welfare/rights, and food cultures/studies—were established and continue to hold some attention and share theoretical ground with one another. In very few places along the highway of this rich body of work on the problem of *species* in human intellectual inquiry, does Black thought become a consideration or an optic (except for in the most dreaded comparisons that focus on Black persons being treated *like* animals and therefore, denigrated).[5]

And yet, two figures and one revolutionary fringe group emerge early in this decades-long inquiry, at least in the United States, to rethink our relationship not only to the category of distinction but also the very idea of ontology (being) and species in which such distinction is held. I am thinking here of Dick Gregory—famous for his civil rights activism and his food systems political work, and Charles Burnett, L.A. Rebellion school member and director of two pivotal films about hum:animal relation, the short *The Horse* (1973) and the feature film *Killer of Sheep* (1977).[6] I am also thinking of the MOVE organization and the "pro-animal rights worldview" that helped to get them bombed by the Philadelphia police in the spring of 1985, over a decade after their founding. I return to Burnett in another chapter. This chapter focuses on that period in the mid-to-late 1970s that sparked a revolution in hum:animal relation that became animal liberation and then animal studies in its more academic incarnation—an incarnation that has, for the most part, wholly ignored key animal-focused aspects of Black liberation movements, even though those radical organizations provided the kindling for the revolutionary claims of PETA and other organizations.[7]

One of the slippages that rattles me in my decade-long research in the field and practice of animal studies is the slippage, much like that of gender in our engagement with the (Black) human, between groups/species of animals. Rarely do philosophers take on the work of distinction among animal types, many—except for Haraway and Vicki Hearne (authors I deal with here as well)—seem to have no dealings with animals beyond domesticated dogs or cats, have no dealings with animals at all (Heidegger is a good example of the latter), or do not stretch themselves beyond their own relationship with "pets" to investigate some other knowledge about animal life.[8] Becoming with is a vulnerability, one that surrenders *life* to *an* other in a momentary glimpse of what might be possible if we followed Audre Lorde's advice about being willing to sacrifice the self in exchange for a future for our children. In essence, it is rarely a feral cat or dog, only a captive cat or dog, that is the subject of inquiry in animal studies. More to the point here and perhaps interesting, but not all that consequential: it is the cisgendered male philosophers who have the least contact with nonhuman animals, and it is the cisgendered women—Donna Haraway, Vicki Hearne, Kathy Rudy, Vanessa Woods, and Temple Grandin—who get down in the dirt with sheep, dogs, horses, and cows. While philosophy has vision for hum:animal life, feminism seems to have a practice for the *doing*.

Reading across rather than vertically in the archive and the canon of studies in hum/animal distinction, I am amazed by how distinction in and of itself is the *motive* behind all manner of discretion *and* discrimination.[9] Like other critical theorists and even Afro-pessimists, Lisa Lowe offers that "the modern distinction between definitions of the human and those to whom such definitions do not extend is the condition of possibility for Western liberalism, and not its particular exception."[10] It is in the spirit of that declaration that I attempt to wade into the vast archive of (mis)understanding and perception of MOVE's philosophy for a species-oriented rather than human-focused planet.

What draws my attention to MOVE in Philadelphia is their consideration of the captivity of animals as a question well worth posing for the way humans live. As well, I was compelled by how their intersectional agenda—Black liberation/animal liberation—took radical turns that were not always already acceptable to a human-centered public. I want to stick with the term *animal liberation* rather than *animal rights* because I think it is a term more in concert with MOVE's work as an organization.[11] It is the same work that Derrida, Deleuze and Guattari, Hearne, Haraway, Wolfe, and Rudy turn themselves to, but you won't find MOVE members or the L.A. Rebellion films of Charles Burnett or the internationally renowned food systems work of Dick Gregory among their inquiries. This is more than an oversight, it is the constitutive enmeshment that a certain center of animal studies has with its hierarchy of ontology, rather than the brief it might be able to make about *species* and their intersectional living.[12] With its focus on ontological claims—and I'd like to thank Margo Crawford (UPenn) for bringing this into sharper focus for me during an MLA panel discussion—and with blackness being so far outside the vision of an ontology made for, by and about whiteness, it is no wonder that the work that we do to challenge such systems often goes unrecognized for the most part.

It is this claim to ontology *over* species in Haraway's naturalcultural assessment of the late Yale English professor and trainer of dogs and horses Vicki Hearne's work that makes for a huge difference between Black cultural modes of naturalcultural formation and the *dressage* (following Derrida) of workers/trainers like Hearne or Haraway. Hearne, as Haraway notes, had a particular disregard for "animal rights," and so she was more interested in the *doing*: "Hearne sees not only humans, but also the dogs, as beings with species-specific capacity for moral understanding and serious achievement."[13] For Haraway, Hearne's legacy for emergent naturecultures is that the possibility of hum:animal interaction and connection is produced when training (dressage) is evident. For my work, Hearne's emphasis on *training* reproduces one of the tensions in *work* with animals, as the rewards of *communication* emphasize a decidedly *human* vantagepoint—the hierarchy is still masterfully in place, and the animals at issue (human and otherwise) come to one another in a worlding that is not in contradistinction to the distinction, but an outgrowth of its *naturalcultural* state. And yet, as I will argue, MOVE's family believed in training (dogs, not roaches or rats they cohabited with) and so their hum:animal living engaged in routines of discipline (and pleasure?) that articulate qualities of relation but perhaps not ones that produce absolute freedom for either.

A philosophy more in tune with MOVE's purposes here—with their practice of hum:animal liberation—would be that of Giorgio Agamben. He authored deeper investigations into the "state of exception" and finer understandings of biopower-after-Foucault (matched only by those of Achille Mbembe), but he is also the author of the following question in *The Open* that stopped me dead in my tracks on my way to thinking about the animal: "In what way can man let the animal, upon whose suspension the world is held open, be?"[14] Even in this pithy book, you have to move through a lot of philosophy, and get bored (again) by Heidegger (see chapter 1), in order to come to his startling revelation: what if we just let the animal "be"? Imagine that.

This letting be and letting go is the chief grounding for MOVE's approach to the question of the animal. My brief here is for blackness and its imprint on a naturalcultural legacy that is anything but what it says it is. It is not *natural* for Black people to do anything with animals, and there is no *cultural* referent for doing this work beyond a historical fixity (enslavement) that prevents the work of hum:animal:blackness from being seen, though Joshua Bennett's work in *Being Property Once Myself* illuminates and shatters this silence, at least on the literary front. "This is a story of biopower and biosociality," Haraway reminds us, but the hitch is that when overly determined racialized bodies *do* "biosociality," the stakes are much, much higher.[15] In blackness, attempts at "biosociality" end in death; in whiteness, we have an assortment of things to do with cute little puppies (I'll get to that in the next chapter) who grow up to be great agility dogs, or companions, or heelers, or herders or . . . [16]

Therefore, let us consider MOVE and what they *did* with animals. Theirs is a philosophy for living that I want to argue had real and tragic consequences for their lives as Black people *doing* animal liberation. In fact, much of the literature about MOVE actually misnames their practice of being with animals—they were not a group overtly concerned with animal rights so much as their stance on animals in captivity was a measure of their *practice* of obliterating through action, the hum/animal distinction, and the modes of *enslavement* engendered by it in the sociocultural fabric of living.

This *being, becoming*, and *doing* all point toward providing a kind of theory for that "unbridgeable gap between Black [animal] being and Human life" at the center of Frank B. Wilderson III's text on cinema. Wilderson's insistence, however, that the African-descended being is, at the Middle Passage, an object, a Slave who cannot be, can never be a *subject* is a *property* of human being that cordons off and reifies both species itself and the distinction between hum/animal. This particular mode of *life* or *living* for blackness is unsustainable. What MOVE allows us to see is the condition of enslavement for *all* beings and through their experience of radical practice, they offer a way to challenge our own focus on the human for blackness, while also providing, through their struggles to define their own reproductive lives, a way to tacitly anticipate Spillers's revolutionary work. In particular, Spillers's insistence that a culturally defined gender difference does not cohere for Black *female* subjects whose reproductive capacity is a tool for the continuation of the *objectivity* of blackness is daunting. Nevertheless, there is that *insurgent* Black female new-world subject that follows us, that we are following along the edges of Spillers's own assessment.

A note before I begin: as I write this, Delbert Orr Africa, Janine Phillips Africa, Janet Holloway Africa, Eddie Goodman Africa, Mike Africa, Chuck Sims Africa, all part of the MOVE 9, incarcerated for forty years for the death of a Philadelphia police officer in the first siege of a MOVE residence in 1978, have been released (Merle and Phil Africa died in prison). This contemplation of what MOVE was trying to accomplish is a small homage to Black genius, and, yes, its total *liberation*.

MOVE something

The House of John Africa is Built on the
Foundation of Life.
SIGN OUTSIDE MOVE HOUSE IN 1978

MOVE members are . . . life feeling people.
LAVERNE SIMS, MOVE Commission Hearings

To sadistically exploit, impose on any one form of life is to, in fact, exploit, impose on all forms of life.
MOVE DOCUMENT, date unknown

There is a self-evident (if complicated) difference between the word *motherfucker* spoken in a kitchen and the same word broadcast over a loudspeaker.
ROBIN WAGNER-PACIFICI, *Discourse and Destruction* (1994)

5:27 p.m. May 13, 1985. 6221 Osage Avenue, Philadelphia, Pennsylvania.[17] *Six adults, five children and some animals. Sixty homes in cinders. A radical natureculture movement. Some other kind of animals. A policing force. Some more animals. Equivocating public opinion. Some fewer animals.*

The group called MOVE came to life in the early 1970s and was started by handyman Vincent Leaphart. In the Powelton Village neighborhood where he lived, he was nicknamed "Vince the Dogman" because of his affection for dogs.[18] Leaphart lived in the cooperative housing project formed by Powelton residents when they won their dispute with Drexel University over its land grab in the area.[19] The other founder, who eventually turned ATF informant, was a graduate of the University of Pennsylvania's School of Social Work named Donald Glassey.[20] Viewing themselves as primarily a political group, MOVE's practice included animal liberation, antitechnology, and a form of vegan life that included a raw food diet. They demonstrated at pet stores, circuses, and zoos.[21] Many observed that they began as a non-violent, back-to-nature organization. Most believe that it was the continued violence meted out on MOVE members during their several arrests that caused them to take a turn toward self-defense and a confrontational style. Part of their naturecultural vibe was that "the babies did not wear diapers but defecated in the yard along with the animals that MOVE kept."[22] In addition, "MOVE members ate mainly raw fruits and vegetable[s] and rejected cooked food in general," a practice that had its simultaneous arc in Dick Gregory's fruitarian regime.[23]

As sociologist Robin Wagner-Pacifici notes in the preface to her 1994 book-length study of the events that led to the bombing of the MOVE compound by the Philadelphia police, "If one were asked what the conflict was about, one would be hard-pressed to answer with ease or confidence." She continues by observing that "the MOVE conflict was a strange hybrid, a charged space at the intersection of race, modernity, class, nature, urban life, and culture."[24] In this sense, the tragedy in Philadelphia some three decades ago is a microcosm of that naturecultures paradigm that Haraway gestures toward in her tiny manifesto, *The Companion Species Manifesto: Dogs, People, and Significant Otherness* (2003). Haraway's body of work on the animal maps a skin-deep biogeography of hum/animal distinction and practices, steeped in an ethics of care. This care manifests itself as *curiousness*: "Caring means becoming subject to the unsettling obligation of curiosity, which requires knowing more at the end of the day than at the beginning."[25] Haraway's way forward settles in the comfortable realm of the intellect, and her practice is work, through training. This structure of feeling is entwined—knowledge and practice participate in that productive scale of human measure that seems to constrain the very point of contact it seems to engender. Processes of extraction *creep*, infiltrating the naturecultural bond, making knowledge the principle *object* lesson. For Haraway, becoming *with* the animal is a moment made possible through hard *work*. Obliterating the distinction is a matter of training, companion species become so to one another in the full arc of their *work* together—which is a series of practices that lead to some mutually fulfilling goal. And, much like Hearne, there does not appear to be room for companionate possibilities *without* the display of mastery (training/dressage) so common to a particular way of undoing hum:animal relation.[26]

Derrida grounds the rigidity of the distinction in the limited avenues philosophy has to open up the animal's consideration (or the consideration of animals). Samantha Frost's ambitious book *Biocultural Creatures: Toward a New Theory of the Human* (2016) gets at the problem of the human through a simple question, culled from a Nikolas Rose essay, of "how we should *live* as humans."[27] This question is indeed at the center of MOVE philosophy.[28] Although precarity is a bankrupt concept, several theorists, scholars, and activists have reveled in a fundamental belief in its efficacy as an explanatory category, even a mobilizing force for understanding planetary shifts in the population known as "the human." Reading the introductory pages of Frost's book, I come in contact with (our) vulnerability: "The accretion of political and economic injustices creates specific forms of vulnerability to disaster for particular regional, national and subnational populations."[29] I understand that the "populations" described by words like "accretion" and "disaster" and "particular" can be understood to be: "homosexuals and transsexuals, comatose medical patients, people with physical and mental disabilities, racial and ethnic minorities, immigrants and refugees, prison inmates . . . the list goes on."[30] This is a list of everyone and no one at all, really. It is also a common critical practice to attend to proliferating vulnerabilities. While we are busy defining blackness as precarity, producing the only lens through which it can be known, we can fail to see blackness as elemental (Merleau-Ponty's "flesh") and foundational to a cocreated understanding of hum:animal life.

We will see that MOVE *practices* demonstrated another kind of being—forged in a reframed ethic of care, MOVE members reconfigured hum:animal and tested the limits of our *being* together, and they represent, I argue, one of the most profound challenges to who we are or more importantly, how we are organized (think distinction) through human being, as a category of practice in the late twentieth century. MOVE not only flirted with the distinction by raising their children in a manner unsupported by the dictates of modern life (an unbalanced form of living they called the "lifestyle") but also produced a *being together*, through other forms of training or even dressage (MOVE members believed in exercise and often took the dogs they lived with on runs and to the park) that produced a unique form of hum:animal companionate life (see figures 2.1–2.3) but did not open up to modes of progress or over/coming.

So, one could say that MOVE does not depart from some feminist methods for work in relationship to hum:animal contact, yet their methodology of walking their dogs and their own concentrated attempts at discipline and physical health don't translate into the same kinds of *outcomes* for hum:animal relation that the intensive training of dressage, eventing (my

2.1 Don Camp, "MOVE," *Philadelphia Evening Bulletin*, April 7, 1975. Special Collections Research Center, Temple University Libraries, Philadelphia, PA.

2.2 Don Camp, "MOVE headquarters," *Philadelphia Evening Bulletin*, May 19, 1977. Special Collections Research Center, Temple University Libraries, Philadelphia, PA.

2.3 Albert F. Schell, "MOVE supporters," *Philadelphia Evening Bulletin*, August 4, 1978. Special Collections Research Center, Temple University Libraries, Philadelphia, PA.

sport of choice), agility, or showing in general require. There are no ribbons or higher breeding fees from simple walks in and around the park; neighbors won't applaud you for not spraying for roaches or laying out rat poison or for allowing human child and dog feces to mingle and compost in your yard. Their labor was always already, nonreproductive, a refusal of overcoming in the strict understanding of the forward-driven capacities for *life* in evidence in human being. There is simply no advantage to such pointless husbandry.

In light of my arguments in the foregoing chapter—ones that trace the all-too-unstable trajectory of gender through modes of blackness housed in the belly of pessimism, I want to also think through what I found in the MOVE records at Temple University.[31] When you examine the early life of MOVE, you come to the conclusion that their struggle for hum:animal liberation placed itself not only at the nexus of the distinction but also at the border of what constitutes reproductive agency in a growing diverse bio-culture. I track and bring forward another form of Black femaleness. In each and every iteration of MOVE *being*, the Black mother can be seen and felt. among her children.

naked.

hum:animal.

What I am offering here is that the condition and possibility of Black mothering haunts the edges of the MOVE conflict—which is not *a* conflict, but several, manifested in the very meaning of duration: a long arc of state intervention and violence. The police brutality meted out on MOVE members took various forms—and one of them was a particular brutality aimed at Black mothers and their children. From MOVE's inception in the early 1970s to its bombing in 1985, we have to remember that not all interventions involved the police, but an ever-widening carceral state that included the work of child protective *and* city services.

In order to start the conversation about that Black female subject, *reproducing* or engendering a future in the final moments of Spillers's landmark essay, I want to start with a statement and then the archive. One could say, based on the rate at which Black women lose their children, that no children on the planet are to be protected more from the faults of their (Black) mothers than Black children. Period. And nothing points this out more clearly than two photographs taken during MOVE's early years that I hold in juxtaposition here (see figures 2.4 and 2.5).

The first photo is of a phenotypically white woman and a child at a protest against MOVE by Powelton Village neighbors.[32] Other photographs taken of the protest by the *Philadelphia Evening Bulletin* staff photographers

2.4 Anthony Bernato, "East Powelton residents protest 'MOVE' actions," *Philadelphia Evening Bulletin*, June 20, 1977. Special Collections Research Center, Temple University Libraries, Philadelphia, PA.

2.5 Frederick A. Meyer, "Police woman holds MOVE baby," *Philadelphia Evening Bulletin*, August 29, 1978. Special Collections Research Center, Temple University Libraries, Philadelphia, PA.

indicate that white neighbors bused themselves to city hall to complain openly about MOVE. In a 1985 transcript of an interview with Philadelphia Special Investigation Committee (PSIC) investigator Edward Scott, Charles Burrus notes that "the white citizens of Powelton Village had made complaints to the City concerning the MOVE members and their basic complaints were children without clothes, rats on the premises, and numerous dogs and other animals on the property."[33] Their concerns, as evidenced by Burrus, ranged from the MOVE children to other animals; a pendulum swing that indicates the proximity of hum:animal life to Black children and, by extension, their mothers. The first photo captures the racialized nature of the protest in two important ways: it demonstrates that whites in the city were indeed incensed by MOVE, and it also tells us that they were not shy about bringing their own reproductive lives to the table in such protests. What is it about Black liberation struggles that so threatens the possibilities for *white* women and their children, born or unborn? In the distinction hum/animal lies a profound problem of father-right, mother-love, and of course, racialized reproduction.[34] I will get to the problem of father-right later in this chapter.

The second photo has two arcs in my own emotional life in the MOVE archive. I came across this photo in the digital archive of the *Philadelphia Evening Bulletin* first and it floored me. How had I not seen this before? When I made my trip to Temple University, I had this photo on my mind, a constant presence in my work; it reminded me that something much larger was at stake in MOVE's revolutionary legacy. Something about this photograph touched me in the *now* and an explanation eludes me. For now I will say that the photograph of the Black woman and the MOVE baby is, of course, a form of surrogacy, as the Black officer of the state holds a MOVE child in a haunting juxtaposition—to one another, to the photographer, and to the existing archive of photos, especially figure 2.4. There is refusal all around. Can the MOVE debacle teach us something left over from the struggle in the flesh outlined in the previous chapter? Is the flesh always the place of slavery's wound and therefore natural counterpart to the "human"? Or is there something about a Black (insurgent) female subject mother-having-mother-right that forestalls this quite easy juxtaposition of "subject to object"?[35] What *are* the stakes for Black female reproduction—a constant carceral state, a surrogacy meted out in Black/face?

That reproduction in MOVE challenged the very notion of hum/animal distinction is clear. MOVE philosophy and practice centered hum:animal *life* and its potentiality for itself; MOVE waged a struggle to redefine (re)(productive) life that has profound implications not only for a practice of being with but also of letting go the very notion of species which keeps hum/animal politely in its place. Theirs was a kind of poetry in a world of rhetorics of dis-articulation. They *lived* a different story "in the flesh a nasty developmental infection called love" and were committed not to their own autobiography, an impossibility of writing, but to the biomythology of poetry in a rhetoric-filled world.[36] What remains to be seen in reproduction's afterlife? As the enslaved, Black female "subjects" marked their children for chattel and held them in the perpetuity unique to bondage. What to make of this historical reach that steals the autobiography of blackness itself?[37]

In fact, the archive demonstrates from newspaper clippings to police reports to neighborhood interviews that the community's involvement with MOVE focused as much on its Black liberation stance as it did on the viability of MOVE's reproductive family life. Interestingly enough, early media attention on reproductive practices within the organization focused on Sue Africa, one of the few white members in MOVE. In an article focusing on MOVE and specifically the birth of Sue Africa's second child, *Philadelphia Evening Bulletin* reporter Leslie Bennetts says that MOVE is a "radical interracial group" and describes the MOVE headquarters: "If you manage to get around the garbage, the barricades, the swarms of bugs, the dogs, and the people and make your way through the dark corridors of the dilapidated home, you will eventually find the back room with its clotted straw and its new resident."[38] Obviously, Bennetts is no fan of the MOVE way of living, and she and other members of the press continually refer to Sue Africa as a "spokeswoman" for the group, guaranteeing an elevated status for Sue Africa—a claiming of her right(white)ful place.

While that May 13, 1985, scene is etched in our collective national consciousness, my work centers itself on early MOVE philosophy and presence in the city of brotherly love. The standard approach to MOVE's philosophy is to see its detriment in its intersectionality—it was simply too diffuse and, at times, outrageous to garner a large constituency. In their book *The MOVE Crisis in Philadelphia: Extremist Groups and Conflict Resolution*, Hizkias Assefa and Paul Wahrhaftig note "we were hesitant about undertaking the research because the case appeared too bizarre, and it seemed unlikely that anything coherent could be learned from it."[39] But as Linn Washington, who covered the organization for the *Philadelphia Daily News*, observes: "[They began as] an insignificant protest against the caging of animals at the Philadelphia Zoo in 1972 by a band of boisterous, profanity-spewing radicals known as MOVE."[40] In a letter written to the PSIC in 1985, Ramona Africa observes that the criminal justice system in Philadelphia focused on them early on: "Innocent MOVE people have been given outrageously excessive bails by judges legally when we peacefully demonstrated at the Philadelphia Zoo, the Circus, Puppy Palace, the S.P.C.A. because of their cruelty to animals."[41] Interesting enough, at the same time that MOVE was protesting at the Philadelphia Zoo, the Pennsylvania legislature was contemplating a controversial piece of legislation known as "The Dog Bill," opposed by the Philadelphia SPCA because it sanctioned the use of stray dogs for medical research.[42] The early protests and rhetoric of MOVE were decidedly focused, in part, on animal liberation, pointing out in their philosophy in a document known as "The Guidelines" or "The Book": "The roots of this [mainstream] lifestyle are corrupt, diseased, and people as well as animals, have been viciously exploited."[43] In their own words, the MOVE organization organized itself around the following principle: "Move's work is to stop industry from poisoning the air, the water, the soil, and to put an end to the enslavement of life—people, animals, *any* form of life."[44]

Formed in the early 1970s, MOVE's animal/total species liberation stance was in effect almost a decade before Ingrid Newkirk and Alex Pacheco founded People for the Ethical Treatment of Animals (PETA) in my hometown of Rockville, Maryland, in 1980. In many ways, MOVE's stance on the animal in particular and species in general, concentrated as it was on "liberation" and not "rights," freedom from enslavement, rather than "welfare," was a far more radical positionality, I argue, than the one PETA espoused, since PETA's initial primary political agenda did not pertain to domesticated animals, but animals in service to science for the benefit of human being. PETA sought to free nonhuman animals *from* something. MOVE sought total liberation and in doing so, they also sought a method focused on *life*, a continuous process of being present, an inhabitation of being rather than *becoming* or *being with*, as each entails a kind of heretofore separation that produces the need for reintegration. Their way of life is strikingly radical and wholly missed in animal studies work.[45]

They did not see domestication as a singular achievement in hum:animal life, but one of the signs of a corrupt "civil" society.[46] An early (1975) print media piece on MOVE philosophy started with "Man and dog occupy equal footing at the home of MOVE."[47] In that same news piece, Don Africa intones: "'But life,' he says, 'is uniform. There is no difference between our life and the life of the tree out in the yard.'" And in yet another piece, this time in the *Philadelphia Inquirer*, Larry Eichel writes that "they also are philosophically opposed to zoos and aquariums."[48]

The MOVE philosophy is perhaps most starkly evidenced in a 1985 PSIC interview with Gerald Africa. Speaking of the events surrounding the barricading of the first MOVE residence in Powelton Village, Gerald Africa notes that one of MOVE's chief sticking points was the city's recommendation for the care of their animals, "[Gerald Africa] advised that the MOVE members had approximately 60 dogs living in two houses and that the city wanted the dogs to be given to the SPCA, which they totally rejected as they did not want their animals gassed."[49] In fact, from a review of early news reports on the MOVE organization, they were targets of police harassment *because* of their stance on animal life, in particular, as the city of Philadelphia as early as July 31, 1976, planned a forced inspection of the MOVE home because of neighbors who complained about the "60 dogs" living at the property and the "500–1,000 rats," "human feces and garbage . . . seen on the lawn."[50] But so much in the mainstream media about MOVE is about perception rather than fact and so the numbers above are unreliable, at best.

In a stunning departure in the 1985 Gerald Africa PSIC transcript, we find the following exchange:

> In a side discussion regarding the animals, Investigator Scott asked Gerald Africa if he thought 60 animals in two houses were too many animals for a healthy environment for children and adults, that these animals would present . . . a health hazard beyond human endurance. Gerald Africa explained that as the animals would leave their droppings on the floor, the MOVE members would immediately clean this up. He further explained that the animals were on one level and it did not present a problem to the MOVE members. He advised that they accumulated these animals by taking in stray animals and other animals that were left with them by neighbors and people in the community. Investigator Scott then replied, "Why weren't the animals spayed to keep them from reproducing?" In a hotly tone, Gerald Africa replied "Why weren't you spayed, you must understand MOVE is all about living." No further discussion was made regarding the animals.[51]

It is so clear from this interview excerpt that Investigator Scott has some very clear ideas about hum:animal cohabitation. But what arrests this moment of judgment is Gerald Africa's "hotly [*sic*] tone" and his counterpoint question about Scott's own reproductive life. The distinction between hum:animal life is not only exposed here but gendered. Since we all know that spaying is reserved for female dogs, and neutering is what happens to male dogs, it is interesting that Scott puts the reproductive onus on female dogs and Gerald Africa reminds him that such a technique could be/should be practiced on him. I don't think Gerald Africa's comments are meant to be gendered. Nevertheless, the gender-play here is of great consequence to my analysis, as it shores up societal notions of female bodies and their procreative force, while exercising such societal control in the service of a conversation about reproductive control between two men. A reproductive control that puts pressure on the scene of domestication—"a healthy environment for children" as a standard *for* life and its living. My observation here is that MOVE is always already about reproduction, and the hum/animal distinction that the group contested through practiced disavowal constantly produces the occasion for an assessment of MOVE's relationship to quotidian reproductive law (of the father). Human reproduction is the constant trace that follows after MOVE, dogging its every intervention into life in "civil" society.

To bring home this point, I now turn to three different incidents involving MOVE children and pregnant MOVE women. In April 1975, MOVE women—Consuelo Africa, Gail Sims Africa, LaVerne Sims Africa, Sharon Sims (Fox) Africa, Sharon Penn Africa, and Sue Africa—were arrested and detained at the 8001 State Road facility. Several, including Sue Africa, refused to leave unless all of them were released—four were pregnant at the time. Between 1975 and 1976, MOVE members charged the Philadelphia police with the death of four infants. In their own publication, MOVE members described a March 28, 1976, confrontation with police:

> Janine Africa was trying to protect her husband Phil Africa when she was grabbed by a cop, thrown to the ground with 3-week-old Life Africa in her arms, and stomped until she was nearly unconscious. The baby's skull was crushed. . . .
>
> Police denied that any beatings took place or a baby was killed, and claimed that the baby probably never existed because there was no birth certificate. To prove the death to a doubtful media, a few local politicians and photographers were invited to a dinner at MOVE headquarters, after which they were shown the baby's body.
>
> Charges against the six MOVE men arrested in the attack were dropped when it became apparent that MOVE neighbors could give eyewitness testimony to the baby's murder.[52]

The brutality of police, the viewing of the baby's body, and the claims of MOVE members about their murdered children are noticeable across a range of archival sources.[53] Here we see a plethora of state-sanctioned meanings being proffered against the insanity of MOVE's attempts to circumvent them. The dead child exists in ever-expanding telescoping acts of being disappeared: no birth certificate, no baby; no police beatings, no baby killing. No accounting for the moment where Life Africa expires. Their protests at school board meetings, use of profanity and bullhorns, and finally brandishing of weapons on the front porch of their Powelton headquarters led to a police barricade of MOVE headquarters in March 1978; and on August 8 of that same year, a confrontation where nine members of MOVE were arrested and later incarcerated for the killing of police officer James Ramp. A death that MOVE claims was actually caused from friendly fire, not MOVE bullets. Nevertheless, a day later, their home was bulldozed by the Philadelphia police, then under the Frank Rizzo administration.[54]

One story among the alleged killings of MOVE babies by the police is the most harrowing and involves Alberta Africa's forced miscarriage while in police custody. Accounts by Ramona Africa, LaVerne Sims Africa, and William Africa essentially tell the same story: "When Roberta Africa—who was pregnant n. [*sic*] made it clear that she was pregnant—was arrested and taken to the roundhouse [Eighth and Race] where she was drug out of a holdin cell, held down on the floor by four huge male cops with her legs spread eagle while a Black female officer named Robinson kicked 5' Alberta Africa repeatedly in the vagina until Alberta's unborn baby bled out of her."[55]

The above account is gruesome, and it occasions a reprisal of my first question—"Would you, could you, take the overseer's whip when it's handed to you?"—which brings forward Patsey's life. In addition, I want to take a moment here to reach back to a discussion of Haile Gerima's *Bush Mama* (1975) in Wilderson's *Red, White & Black*. In a chapter entitled "Cinematic Unrest," Wilderson notes that while Gerima's is "a work of fiction," it opens up with an actual scene of Gerima's film crew being stopped and harassed by police. Pursuant to his work on the pessimism, Wilderson understands that both the filmmaker *and* the lead female character, Dorothy (Barbara O. Jones) are "beings for the captor" and are in a "state of open vulnerability—given Blackness as the always already available prey of civil society and the state."[56] I would like to think about my work on MOVE as a complement to Wilderson's idea that films like Gerima's and Burnett's (*The Horse* and *Killer of Sheep* in particular) showcase "blackness on the move" during a decade of intense cultural production (mid-1960s to mid-1970s). Briefly, Gerima's film documents "L.A. ghetto life" and the radicalization of its main character, Dorothy, who kills a policeman when she walks in on him sexually assaulting her eleven-year-old daughter. She is involved with a Vietnam veteran T.C., who is wrongly incarcerated, and at the end of the film, she is carrying their child. Dorothy is eventually incarcerated for the killing of the cop and is in turn brutalized by a guard while in prison.[57]

In fact, two moments come together in this work: the beatings of pregnant women by the police *and* women attempting to protect their children from being assaulted or brutalized in the same manner; such experiences were ubiquitous during a time of movements for liberation. Scholar Allyson Nadia Field writes of a similar sexual assault in Chicago, reported on by the Black Panther Party newspaper in 1973.[58] But there is something *in* Black feeling that Wilderson leaves behind in Gerima's incredible film. At the end of the feature, Gerima's Dorothy speaks directly to the audience, in a scene from her own home, but with a voiceover that is clearly from a Dorothy who is behind bars. This scene shows Dorothy in her living room with the poster over her right shoulder of an Angolan "bush mama" revolutionary with a baby on one arm and a gun in the other.[59] The scenes of Dorothy in her prison cell losing her baby precede the actual scene of her daughter's rape, so that the temporal and causal elements of the film are shifted. As the after and before are collapsed—recalling the temporal collapse of background and foreground in McQueen's *12 Years a Slave*—we watch overlapping images of Dorothy in her cell, of her killing the police officer, and of her daughter's sexual assault in a harrowing montage, a static interrogative voiceover repeatedly intones, "Do you understand? Do you agree?" All against the background of Onaje Kareem Kenyatta's music. In these scenes, it is the first time we see Dorothy without her signature wig, something she remarks upon as she stares into the camera with her hair locked/twisted up and she delivers the last words of the film. In many ways, her monologue opens up the possibility for something other than death *in* blackness, for Dorothy to be more than the sum of her *parts*.

Dorothy's is an epistolary leave-taking—a love letter to T.C.—and I cite it here at some length because of its rich complexity:

> Dear T.C., I was just thinking about the night they said that you did the crime. You remember it was the same night you had the real bad nightmare. Why didn't they believe you was here with me? Ole rif-raf me. You don't even look like the man they said did it, but you still doing the time. So much have happened T.C. T.C., they beat our baby outta me. They wouldn't let me see nobody, not even a doctor for ten days. We got to make changes T.C., so we can raise our kids with both of us at home, so things go right. I been blaming myself all this time, 'cuz things wasn't right. I thought that I was born to be poor, be pushed around and stepped on. I don't want Luanne thinking like that. I can see now that my problem is a place I was born into. A place with laws that protect the people who got money. Doctors and hospitals for people who got money. It's evil and wrong. I have to get to know myself, to read and to study, we all have to so we can change it. So we can know how to talk to each other. Talking to each other is not easy. I know you in jail T.C. and angry, but most of the time I don't understand your letters. Talk to me easy T.C., 'cuz I wanna understand. It's not easy to win over people like me. There's a lot of people like me we have many things to fight for just to live. But the idea is to win over more of our people. Talk the same talk, but easy T.C. You remember when you used to ask why I always wear a wig, all

day and all night, when I eat, when I sleep. T.C., wig is off my head; wig is off my head. I never saw what was under it, I just saw on top: the glitter, the wig. Wig is off my head, T.C. T.C.?

I love you,

Dorothy.

Another scholar of the L.A. Rebellion, Morgan Woolsey points to the "epidermalization—the denial of interiority" to African women in particular, and it is clear here that Gerima's Dorothy touches on this in her monologue.[60] The fact that Black *life*, and its *interiority*, does not matter is not lost on her, but her attention is focused on this interiority and a conversation she wants to have with T.C. There is a sweetness to her request, a request for him to be "easy." It is a moment where the Black interior breaks into the frame and we are reminded that a scene of Black care is compromised (but not broken) by T.C.'s arrest—ironically, for being in a place he was *not* because he was actually being comforted by Dorothy after a nightmare. A scene of comfort, exchange, and possibility unavailable to those outside the existing frame—a frame that becomes multidimensional in these last celluloid moments. The potential scene of their domestication is brought to heel before police violence which cannot/does not recognize that moment. Moreover, this Black female interiority is enmeshed with the lives of children, as potential or otherwise, telling another story of life's insurgent possibilities. With my queer studies hat on, I can see the value here of making sex/intimacy public, creating a potential for democratic space and "contact" that disrupts categories of difference in public intimacies as acts that Samuel R. Delany participates in and wishes for in his evocative *Times Square Red, Times Square Blue* (1999).[61] The democratization of a public intimate connection is the only mechanism for liberation that can produce *community*. Dorothy brings this work from the bedroom to her audience as she entreats T.C. to be "easy."

But the conversation that Dorothy seems to want to have with T.C. is twofold. It harkens back to the moment of Black intimacy missed by an overwhelmingly racist public, but it also suggests some tension, some moment between them that needs illumination. Caught between the need for approval from him ("T.C.?") and her desire to state something important about the revolution—that cannot be handled (handed-down/Spillers) by him alone, Dorothy appears to us as the *insurgent* subject here. She is clearly incarcerated when she delivers this monologue, but in the scenes of her in jail, Gerima is careful not to depict Dorothy behind bars. In this final scene with the camera focusing first on the poster, then on Dorothy and with its temporal shifts, we have a Black female subject standing outside a system of subjugation, producing the quiet manifesto that is her insurgence.

My text is always already suspicious of the move to see blackness as a kind of interminable vulnerability, and furthermore, a vulnerability that sustains a gendered being in the course of our opening up but does not/ has not reconciled itself to Spillers's initial claim of that ungendered space of Middle Passage and beyond. Can it be that some attention to gender is always already an outdated mode or practice and that to *find/found* this moment in hetero-reproduction is somehow backward-feeling for a queer studies bent on *trans*forming the field? Perhaps. But it is clear to me that this is the chad that is left hanging in Spillers's theory of new-world-Black-formation. But my intention is not to move through a protracted analysis of Gerima's brilliant feature to disprove Wilderson's surrounded/sounded-in blackness response to cinema—his is a cogent and daring take on what representation *cannot* see.

The echoes of Gerima's *Bush Mama* in MOVE member claims about the beating of Alberta Africa are hard to ignore. Blackness is certainly on the move and the most powerful symbol of its movement—at least in one direction—is the combined blood of baby and mother on the floor of the penitentiary—a moment that is "fictional," after all. What indeed is the psychic life of this moment in a period of great Black revolutionary impart? For Wilderson, this moment and white response to literal Black power demonstrates a gap between white and Black: "How do we explain a white political cinema genuinely anxious about government corruption, the integrity of the press, a woman's right to choose, the plight of turtles and whales, or the status of the public square, and a Black political cinema calling for the end of the world?"[62] In the end, their cinematic dilemmas are not only disparate but white radicalism looks a lot like some hallmarks of white supremacy; I don't disagree with this contention. But I am compelled by the way in which this mama/baby dilemma leaps from celluloid to broadside, from "fiction" to a constant refrain at the center of MOVE's early confrontation with the police. Moreover, Wilderson's portrayal of concerns for "turtles" and "whales" in white political cinema overstates the reach of whiteness and undervalues the ethical dilemmas that are the focus of his inquiry. But this is almost too obvious and certainly not unique to Wilderson; you can find this sentiment—this relentless focus on the "human" as a white category that proliferates planetary concerns only and for white people (and their benefit)—in almost every aspect of Black thought.

I want to reach back to Baby Suggs in that Clearing from the first chapter of this book—to remind us of the remarkable work Morrison does to fuse hum:animal belonging, to undo distinction, at least in its *parts*. Wilderson tells us, at the end of his analysis of Gerima's classic, that "the film invites us to ponder the image of Dorothy beaten and alone in her cell and the battering of her womb as the a priori captivity and sexual destruction that distinguishes Black women from the women of civil society."[63] I would say here that while the distinction among *women* in this society is most definitely racialized, I am offering that the scene Wilderson rests upon—Dorothy's demise—is not quite the potential that the film settles on, in the end.

MOVE's politics gesture toward a space where the human, at the pinnacle of an ordering of all life on this planet, could at least enter a zone of sustained and even relentless questioning. It is no longer *that* we live—(through) suffering—but *how* we live—that will potentially structure that Black revolutionary moment we keep gesturing toward, one that also encompasses that insurgent potentiality in Black female form. This insurgent entity, or its psychic life, produces the occasion for claims of harm to MOVE children. The connection between MOVE mothers and their children and the constant police brutality they experienced comes across in the trial of John Africa after his extradition from Rochester, New York. On the stand, Delbert Orr Africa detailed MOVE's claims of "'police atrocities' against women and children."[64] In yet another account, John Africa sobbed, "You got our babies. You got our women."[65] John Africa and Alphonso Robbins were acquitted of bomb-making charges even after Donald Glassey—former member of MOVE—turned state's evidence to escape a marijuana conviction.[66] In the course of MOVE's political life in the city of Philadelphia, thirty children were taken by social services in two states—Pennsylvania and Virginia. If you add the number of children MOVE claims were killed by the police in advance of May 13, 1985, the total number of children killed by the state is six and the number of miscarriages through beatings numbers four. The figures are staggering and point toward a perception not only about MOVE but also about *all* Black women and their children.

In a *Philadelphia Evening Bulletin* piece written months after the bulldozing of the Powelton Village MOVE headquarters, Adrian Lee notes that one of the caregivers at the Stenton Child Center where MOVE children were taken noted, "It had all been done with love. I know that's not what you were expecting to hear, and sometimes, thinking about MOVE, I don't believe it myself. But I've cared for a lot of kids in this place, and I know those who are accustomed to love and those who haven't had it. It sticks out in everything they do. And as long as I remember MOVE, I'll think about it. It made that much of an impression on me."[67] The Child Center caregiver speaks against the overwhelming negative public opinion and reporting about MOVE members either neglecting (through malnutrition) or using their children as shields during police operations. In a parallel life, reporting on the MOVE animals seized in the August 8, 1978, police raid, Eric Hendricks, spokesman for the SPCA, observed "all but one of the dogs were 'very friendly. Usually this is an indication of being treated well by humans.'"

Even more poignant perhaps is the index to Robin Wagner-Pacifici's detailed study of the May 13, 1985, incident. While one can search for "children" and find some notations, there is no entry for "mother" in her index. In the context of children, she notes, "Neighbor children were viewed as different from MOVE children and the repercussions of their perceived ontological difference spread widely through the neighborhood and the city administration to the plan and the operation of May 13."[68] In one account from an Osage Avenue neighbor, MOVE children were described as "cattle," which leads Wagner-Pacifici to say that the MOVE children "are portrayed as animals. Not wild, savage animals, rather 'cattle,' domesticated and dumb."[69] While the purpose of this chapter is not to examine the May 13, 1985, debacle, it is clear from PSIC reports and Wagner-Pacifici's meticulous examination of its findings that "animal," "domesticated," "wild" and yes, "motherfucker" (elsewhere in PSIC documents and in her book) contribute together to some great drama in which mother-right and father-having are contested, and also where something of the distinction imposed upon hum:animal rests as an arbiter of that relationship.

In a stunning conclusion to her examination of discourse in the late MOVE conflict, Wagner-Pacifici offers: "On the other side, as in some surrealistic painting of melting clocks, it is a story of a house that underwent a strange transformation. It grew a bunker; the doors and windows were boarded up with logs. It was a house that was itself in a state of terror. It was a house with children, those mythical creatures of this romance about civilization. But if this house was no longer a home, perhaps the children were only 'children' and a bomb could break the spell."[70]

I am not sure how to even respond to such an ending. Instead, I counter with the following photograph—one of my favorites—from the archive, one that sets us on a cusp in our journey to know MOVE philosophy, MOVE women, and, yes, their children: hum:animal (figure 2.6).

"The house of John Africa is built on the foundation of life." Indeed. Here, perhaps the beginning of the next tragic MOVE chapter, the hum/animal

2.6 Jack Tinney, "MOVE house," *Philadelphia Evening Bulletin*, January 19, 1979. Special Collections Research Center, Temple University Libraries, Philadelphia, PA.

distinction alive only in the reflection of the car taillight; a quiet moment as a MOVE member stands on the porch of their newest home, looking directly at the camera. A welcome or a warning, we will never know, but somehow all of the nomenclature comes to bear again—what is "wild," what is "domesticated," and who exactly are MOVE's "children" after all?

"it's a beautiful day in the neighborhood"

Heidi Feldman reminds us that MOVE's incarnation wasn't solely in Philadelphia but elsewhere in the state and country. In an impressive undergraduate senior thesis (Swarthmore College, 1987), Feldman notes that over the course of their political activism, MOVE was subjected to state intervention from social workers and police across several locations: the Powelton Village house at 33rd Street, a MOVE house in the Church Hill section of Richmond, Virginia, the Osage Avenue organization home, the McIlvaine Street house in Chester, Pennsylvania, and the Flint Street residence in Rochester, New York.[71] That early MOVE interaction with the police centered upon their animals is corroborated by Lucien E. Blackwell (majority whip of the Philadelphia City Council): "The MOVE members said the police department also had stopped them on the street on several occasions while en route from a meat market where they had purchased horse meat for the dogs. They said that the police department would seize the meat and many hours later would return the meat with no comments at all. The MOVE members said they were afraid to give the meat then to their dogs as they feared it was tampered with."[72] In this same memo, Blackwell outlines a decade later that the "animals on their premises" provided the occasion for police intervention. Time and time again, the MOVE effort to work hum:animal relation is met with harassment by the Philadelphia police, Licenses and Inspections, and Children and Youth Services. Some question why MOVE didn't simply attempt to relocate to a rural property more conducive to their way of life. There are two competing, but important, answers to this question: (1) MOVE wanted to confront and correct the mainstream lifestyle where it existed in its most potent form: urban areas, and (2) MOVE feared that attempts to purchase property in a rural location would isolate and remove them from the public eye, therefore making them a target for state-sanctioned violence.[73] Given what happened with the Branch Davidian compound in 1993, it appears that MOVE's fears were not entirely unfounded.

One of Feldman's interviewees, a Powelton Village neighbor named Ron Whitehorne, remembers early MOVE philosophy as "their whole rap was like . . . real revolutionaries are in touch with themselves and are dealing with their lives, and they went into their whole rap about diet and lifestyle."[74] Whitehorne later formed Powelton United Neighbors, one of the many neighbor's groups and also recalled that the tension between neighbors and MOVE in Powelton was more intense than the conflict they created and the divisions they fostered on Osage Avenue. Unlike her brother, Whitehorne's sister Susan lived just a few doors down from the MOVE house and notes that the most frightened neighbors were "particularly people with children, who were afraid because of the fact that they knew MOVE had weapons, or it was reported to have weapons, and the harangues and the language and all the things that the kids were exposed to, the fear of rats biting children."[75]

The Quakers come up across a number of engagements with MOVE during their history with the city—in *Philadelphia Evening Bulletin* photos, in the negotiation for the purchase of a MOVE property out of the city/state boundary (in Virginia), and in negotiations between neighbors and MOVE on 33rd Street. One Quaker-led neighborhood organization put out an informational flyer detailing the different community groups and approaches to MOVE in the neighborhood. The "Tuesday Night Group" flyer from July 9, 1977, highlights the viewpoints of seven community groups, with MOVE among them. I quote from two of those groups here to demonstrate the range of opinion about MOVE:

> They have maintained an unsanitary, rat-infested building within our neighborhood; they have strewn garbage and human excrement freely around their building, causing a health hazard and an incredible stench; they have maintained within their building 30–60 unlicensed and uninoculated dogs; and they have abused their own children through malnutrition, exposure, and threats to kill them as hostages. Two years ago, several hundred of us petitioned the city to take action to alleviate this problem. Many times since then, individuals and groups from our community have demanded city action. No action was forthcoming. (Powelton Civic Homeowners Association)

> We support MOVE's right to life and freedom and free speech, and demand an end to their harassment as well as our own. There have been many conflicts between neighbors and MOVE's lifestyle. But neighbors' objections to rats and garbage are not the reason for the present confrontation. The main issue in this situation is clear—police abuse and brutality. MOVE has gained considerable community support by speaking out on an issue that demands

the attention of all residents—police abuse in our community. (Concerned Citizens to Insure Justice for MOVE)[76]

Regardless of neighborhood sentiment about MOVE, Carolyn Sounders in Chester notes that the house that MOVE bought in Powelton Village was "right in the middle of the white community."[77] This is perhaps why mayor Frank Rizzo sought to exacerbate tensions with a barricade of the block where MOVE resided after members of the group had brandished an automatic weapon.[78]

A few years after taking up residence at 307–309 North 33rd Street in the Powelton Village section of West Philadelphia, the MOVE organization was the subject of a 1976 documentary produced by WPVI, the local ABC affiliate. In a scene from that work featured in the 2013 documentary *Let the Fire Burn* (dir. Jason Osder), the commentator's voiceover about the group considers their way of life "revolutionary" and notes, as the camera rolls over MOVE members breaking up the concrete sidewalk around their property, that members were doing so "in their vigilant effort to maintain close contact with mother earth." Osder's excerpt from the station's segment on MOVE reproduces the part where the camera pans to the right and focuses on two young white men (YWM), one of whom questions a MOVE member:

YWM: But you have to have some kind of standard for your organization here.

MOVE MEMBER: Yeah, life.

YWM: But you are not animals.

MOVE MEMBER: Why not?

YWM: I don't want to be personal.

MOVE MEMBER: But no, wait a minute. Why not? We are animals because our reference is no different than the reference of animals. There's is only one reference and that's Life. That's what MOVE is about. Life, Truth. That's our religion. (7:33)

For the YWM in the video, the standard of "life" equates to "animal"—it is a stunning equivalency and belies so much of what subtends ontological paradigms. In that world, "life" is understood as a hierarchy of living, and for MOVE, that world corrupts "Life, Truth." The MOVE member's response to *not* being an animal is "Why not?" The YWM backs out of what he fears is an argument that has turned "personal." The exchange captured by the film is a rare glimpse into the ideology of MOVE and how it confounds the very idea of the human as a standard for living in civil society. But MOVE's contestation is not merely a challenge to civil society but an undoing of its signature organizing principles; sacred to this political collective is the sense of the self as distinct from animal life. MOVE disrupts that quintessential belonging.

Moreover, the YWM above initially expresses a sentiment that is reflected in interviews with Powelton residents; John Whitehorne recalls during their several meetings with neighbors about the MOVE presence on the block, "You had to have a perspective of some kind, and you had to draw some lines."[79] While his remark particularly engages what he feels is the flawed Quaker approach to community building where everyone has a voice and all are equal, it does demonstrate that neighbors and, yes, passersby were confounded by MOVE's multivalent, yet simple platform: LIFE.

In another interview, this time in the women's publication called *Hera*, two years later and two days before the Philadelphia police barricaded (March 13, 1978) the block where MOVE set up its headquarters, William Africa explains their philosophy: "Our belief is life. We advocate revolution for the purpose of clearing up life. Man has taken life and re-formed it, like taking an apple and turning it into a piece of gum. As he does with all life. We understand that civilization as man has built it is wrong. That it's not working—that's why people aren't satisfied."[80] In the same interview, Africa states that the organization is also not into "blowing things up," because terrorism "doesn't solve problems. . . . We're not about destroying life"; in addition, he notes that MOVE does not advocate for "lesbian [word missing] liberation." He also sets forth the MOVE approach to marriage, children, and family, indicating that "because it is all one family, everyone helps in raising them."[81] While much of the interview questions are answered by William in the beginning, the newsletter's interviewers (I. Lacey and K. Moore) turn to the difference that gender makes in the MOVE household. Muriel Africa answers the question put to them both: "What's the role of women in MOVE and how much control do you have over your own life and how you live?" Muriel Africa responds: "Our role is the same as the men's. No matter what we do, everything here is equal. It's not like a man's revolution and the woman in the house. The womens is out and doing the same thing as the men do. I work just as hard as the men do. They clean just like we do; they watch the kids just like we do; so there's no difference." Note the similarity among texts: Muriel Africa's brief story, Northup's description of Patsey, Sojourner Truth's public statement, and even Spillers's note on African cultural practices in "Mama's Baby." In each one, the African-descended female is doing *ungendered* work. For the most part, Muriel affirms that since equality is the goal of MOVE organizational life, women's liberation is perceived as unnecessary or superfluous under conditions where roles are performed without *gendered* restrictions.

There are several moments in the above WPVI documentary exchange that are extraordinary—the first and most obvious is the openness of the Black body to critique by any white subject. The next moment of this exchange is the negative pronouncement about animality—the MOVE members are NOT animals—a recognition of the "human" that produces the legitimacy of hum/animal distinction. It is a call to belonging in human family—a belonging that MOVE members constantly rejected. This Black "family" is simultaneously negated through the ability of said "family" to be interrogated and held as suspect by anyone at any time. The purpose here, at least discursively, is to separate the MOVE member from his belonging with/to the "animal" with the promise of a false legitimacy tied to *being* human. Such a pronouncement secures the humanity of the (phenotypically) white subject, who has the power to name, but this power is demonstrated in a distinction between hum:animal, rather than blackness and whiteness. If the MOVE member can respond and uphold the legitimacy of the distinction, the human family can get on with its business. Their work with animals has spanned the whole of its incarnation as a movement.[82] My critique here is legitimized by what precedes the exchange excerpted for Osder's 2013 documentary—the above youth points toward the yard and *first* asks: "Who is the father of the baby over there?"[83] So, the question that opens up the consideration of the animal is one in which paternity matters. The answer to the question is not forthcoming, at least to the YWM's satisfaction, as the MOVE member notes that "all MOVE people don't live in headquarters." The MOVE member deflects the question of paternity with his answer. The hum/animal distinction then becomes a measure of assessing familial relationships; one legitimated in this culture by the ties of a (white) father to his children. That the MOVE principals are uninterested in (1) the distinction and (2) the legitimate ties to paternity confounds their "visitors."[84] The MOVE member's insistence upon a "single reference" being "life," a vantage point available to all "animals," is a kind of blasphemy in the face of established hierarchies of being.

But what this exchange brings to mind, at least for this project, is the way in which the question of the distinction nestles within it the illegitimacy of Black *issue*—one that Spillers indeed points toward in her work on the "flesh" explored in an earlier chapter. If indeed this new-world female subject, who arises in the flesh out of a Middle Passage itself confounded in a situation that is *father lacking*, what practices of Black (family) life can emerge that can challenge such an arrangement? I want to offer here again that it is near impossible to unpack such possibilities without also tackling the predominant ordering that has so set this planet's teeth on edge: hum/animal.

Something curious arises in this video—a moment where a contradiction (and the MOVE platform is peppered with uncomfortable irresolution) or a problem for the coherence of MOVE family is exposed by Phil Africa. Looking at the camera and speaking to the murder of Life Africa (March 28, 1976), he reminds the viewing audience that "had the mother been Sue [instead of Janine] Africa, she might not have been swept aside so easily by the police." In my view, after looking through the copious PSIC papers that speak to MOVE's presence in Philadelphia for the years 1972 to 1986, the legitimacy of Black women as mothers is one of the central turning points of MOVE's legacy in the city. A legacy that cannot be understood unless we are first willing to contemplate how the question of the animal is brought to bear for MOVE's radical intervention into the limits of civil society, and that society's myriad of dependencies on distinction as a particular mode of living.

So, to LIFE. This embrace of "life," is not unique to MOVE. While the reach of this tenet across a range of Black liberation struggles in this country is outside the scope of this project, one can see its manifestation in other creative, Black revolutionary spaces. Ajulé (née Bruce) Rutlin, poet and member of the BAG (Black Arts Group) in St. Louis, Missouri, provided the liner notes to the release of a BAG recording of Solidarity Unit, Inc.'s *Red, Black and Green* free jazz album, created on the evening of the day that Jimi Hendrix died (September 18, 1970, released 1972; see figure 2.7).[85] He writes:

> The Red, Black and Green Solidarity Unit is a group of young Black muse/icians who are cool would/could walk and talk real hip about some down city shit, dig? All the way down! No mistake They are poor and savage realists who have survived the deadening effects of civilization . . . they resent the intrusion of machines . . . protest the suffocating neglect of spiritual values . . . the unchallenged rule of hierarchy . . . ossified hearts . . . polluted minds. This muse/ic is not imprisoned in squares and plastic symmetry. It is beyond the rule of ticking monster clock, *the beat of the slave driver's whip.* DEATH to the "Star," "Superstar"! and "Kapitalist individual." LIFE to the Black people, poor people, the unfortunate—the group![86]

2.7 Album cover, Solidarity Unit, Inc. 2008 Eremite reissue. Photo by author.

RED, BLACK AND GREEN
Solidarity Unit, Inc.

Theirs is a rhetoric of *life* borne out of the despair of Black death, it is a method aside from/in spite of an ontology that provides its own proof for Black annihilation. Theirs is a kind of living "beyond . . . the beat of the slave driver's whip." I argue that it is no accident that the whip is referred to here. An iconic implement that secures Black experience across centuries, it calls attention to several iterations as both the master's mind and a tool for division in Black life, as these "poor and savage realists" want nothing to do with the "Kapitalist individual," with the driver's whip in his hand. It is "LIFE" beyond what we know of as "civilization" and its "machines."

While BAG's participants did not express an explicit relationship with hum:animal, Rutlin's philosophy is unmistakably intersectional and designed to focus on "LIFE"—a tenet that comes up in MOVE's written documents about its own organization. In their account of the blockade that led to the March 1978 bulldozing of the first MOVE headquarters, members remark, "On March 16, 1978, the police set up a blockade around the house and shut off water lines. Those inside included pregnant women, nursing babies, children, and animals."[87] It is clear from their self-writing and their rhetoric that they have a brief for the vulnerable and that "pregnant women, nursing babies, children, and animals" form a group ("the group!") on par with *an* other. After two months of the blockade, the MOVE headquarters was stormed by police and "MOVE adults were forced to hold children and animals in their arms to keep them from drowning."[88]

In other scenes in the WPVI documentary, naked MOVE children walk among dogs and each other while MOVE adults espouse the tenets of their philosophy, working out a companionate thesis in the real time of nature-cultural life that Haraway indicates comes into existence "from the middle 1970s" (figures 2.8 and 2.9).[89] The tragedy of the MOVE bombing was exacerbated by the deaths of five children in the fire—children whose innocence was the subject of much discussion among the city's administrators. I move back to that earlier quote from Wagner-Pacifici's study of MOVE: "However one slices it, neighbor children were viewed as different from MOVE children and the repercussions of their perceived ontological difference spread widely through the neighborhood and the city administration to the plan and the operation of May 13. . . . The exact ontological status of these children was contested theoretical terrain. Were they kids, plain and simple . . . ? *Were they feral children, growing up wild in the middle of civilization?*"[90] In fact, images of animals, domesticated or feral, dog (pun intended) fact-findings. The irony of Wagner-Pacifici's need to *differentiate* is that African-descended children in the Osage Avenue neighborhood who are not MOVE children get to inhabit their humanity in relationship to other Black children who are arbitrarily perceived as actants in the drama that leads to their deaths. The only alternative to civilization is to be feral, these dichotomous wild/ domesticated, feral/civilized couplings dot the landscape of possibility for hum:animal in the place where MOVE emerges. The MOVE organization is part of a naturecultural revolution, true revolutionaries, insurgents even: 141 demonstrations; 97 court cases, 8 community meetings and 193 arrests. In testimony before the PSIC, district attorney Ed Rendell noted that "their stated goals, [that] they were a back to nature group, were frankly a bunch of bull."[91] For Rendell, MOVE could only be a Black revolutionary machine designed to tear down the civilized fabric of a predominantly white city he helped police. A civilization predicated not just on the difference between Black and white, but one adjudicated by hum/animal's prescriptive nature.

On the thirtieth anniversary of the bombing, Gene Demby, reporting for NPR, remembered:

> When I was growing up in Philly, if you went to a large enough Black cultural event, you would see signs expressing solidarity with MOVE, so I had the sense that MOVE was part of the political life of Black Philadelphians. . . . MOVE was actually a group that was hard to pin down ideologically. It was hard to tell if they were a cult, it was hard to tell if they were a political organization. They ate raw food, they were anti-technology, they protested

2.8 MOVE child and dog. Temple University Urban Archive. Series 1, Subseries 1–2, WPVI News Footage—Public Affairs Presentation of WPVI-TV, "Visions of a New Day. MOVE," written, produced, and directed by Ademola Ekulona, recorded May 15, 1976, airdate June 13, 1976.

2.9 MOVE child and dogs. Temple University Urban Archive. Series 1, Subseries 1–2, WPVI News Footage—Public Affairs Presentation of WPVI-TV, "Visions of a New Day. MOVE," written, produced, and directed by Ademola Ekulona, recorded May 15, 1976, airdate June 13, 1976.

outside of the zoo and outside of pet shops, because they were pro-animal liberation.[92] They often ran afoul of other Black radical groups in the city. MOVE made it a point to be uncategorizable.[93]

Could it be that MOVE's agitation for animal freedom pushed forward the cause in some small way in this country? What I want this exploration of MOVE's animal liberation ideology to accomplish is to challenge the sustained idea of MOVE's incomprehensibility by placing them in a historical context that is intersectional and in line with a movement among other African-descended peoples to take hum:animal seriously.[94] Significantly, perhaps, for the arguments in the earlier section of this book, the sole survivors of the state-sanctioned bombing were an African-descended woman named Ramona Africa and a nonbiological child named Birdie Africa, née Michael Ward. Both fugitives; one an insurgent.

motherfuckers

Philadelphia was familiar to me—my cousins and my beloved uncle and his wife lived there before their move to the suburbs of Villanova in the early 1970s; my mother and I traveled to the city often. On one of those trips, I remember a billboard on the highway: "Vote for Rizzo and keep the Niggers in their place." It was my first sense that those things you could say but shouldn't say about Black people in private were actually perfectly okay to say in public—every day, all the time. By the time I got to college and white girlfriends waxed nostalgic about their cross-country trips, I had learned not to talk about the billboards, or finding a bathroom or searching for a place to eat. I looked at road trips with trepidation. There was no American wild into which my bottled spirit needed to be released; I was just fine with it intact and under my watchful eye. So, when I heard about the bombing, saw the smoke on the television on May 13, 1985, I understood *how* Philadelphia could arrive at that point. I was overly familiar with the city's biography.

As stated earlier, MOVE's first catastrophic run-in with the police came over a decade before May 13, 1985. In August 1978, after a months-long blockade of the group's residence and an attempt to move them to a farm, there was an exchange of gunfire that led to the death of one police person; the next day, the residence was bulldozed to the ground. Wagner-Pacifici's study focuses on discourse and discursive methods in the public inquisitions and the self and community articulations of the group. She notes at several junctures in her introduction to the case that MOVE participants challenged prevailing notions of "domesticity," and that, in particular, definitions of what a child *is* played heavily in the discussions in the postapocalyptic moment. Moreover, Wagner-Pacifici observes that "I cannot say, for example, that because the police and the district attorney and the mayor had moments in speeches, warrants, and so forth in which they use the term *terrorist* to label MOVE, that the labeling process *caused* the choice of weapons and strategies taken by police and fire fighters on May 13."[95] Those of us invested in the interrogation of anti-Black racism, pessimism or no, would probably argue with Wagner-Pacifici's assessment of *cause.* It is clear, however, from the writing and the work on the word "terrorism" itself, that this is a pre-9/11 study. Nevertheless, a case can be made that MOVE and the state-sanctioned and often disorganized discourse around the group solidified and created our post-9/11 views on "terror" in the United States. Wagner-Pacifici demonstrates that the discursive platform upon which MOVE acted out its mission included "unstable" nomenclature that ran from "malcontents" to "nonconformists," "code violators," and, yes, "terrorists."

In the first iteration of MOVE's confrontation with the police (1978), a five-month blockade included negotiations for the group to move to a farm outside the city, negotiations that at one point involved the Quakers.[96] The inhabitants of that second MOVE house used loudspeakers and the term "motherfucker" to harass neighbors and the police: "You mother fuckers don't give a fuck about black folks in South Africa cause you don't give a fuck about black folks here in Philadelphia in this mother fuckin country."[97] Audre Lorde once provoked a disapproving public when she and a friend "exchanged the word 'fucker' for 'mother' in a whole day's conversation, and got put off the Number 5 bus by an irate driver."[98] Ironically enough, the work of MOVE members to make profanity good again was echoed in the Philadelphia police commissioner's instruction to the bomb making crew—"to get them motherfuckers"—a statement that was fervently denied in PSIC transcripts.[99] While the group believed that one of their nodes of resistance to mainstream life was through profanity, Wagner-Pacifici notes that MOVE's claim that they were "a family and a group with civic virtues was rejected by putting forward opposing images of MOVE's bestiality, its unsanitary cohabitation with dogs, cats, and roaches, and raw meat thrown outside for the animals."[100] How cohabitation becomes bestiality or sex with animals is beyond me, but it is clear from archive records that the city's fears of MOVE included suspicions of the group's *collective* desire.

But other evidence in the local media demonstrates that the failure to domesticate "pets" like dogs and cats was not the only concern of onlookers. As one Philadelphian remarked to a *Philadelphia Inquirer* reporter: "Leaphart had an uncanny calmative effect on young children and wild animals."[101] The evacuation of Osage residents before the MOVE bombing serves as an eerie prelude to the evacuation efforts before Hurricane Katrina in New Orleans, as residents of the Osage and Pine neighborhood were told to leave their pets at home—many left food and water out for them. On Mother's Day 1985, African-descended mothers of human and nonhuman animals left their homes so that the city of Philadelphia could finally "get those motherfuckers" for blaring the word "motherfucker" from a loudspeaker mounted outside a second-story window. At the time the conflict began, with Police Commissioner Gregore Sambor's announcement, the conflict moved from the city of Philadelphia to the generalized and universalized rancor of "America:" "Attention MOVE. This is America."

The police ran out of rounds, and yet there were no automatic weapons found in the home on Osage Street. Audio from the stakeout squad video that day has one officer saying, "They won't call the police commissioner a motherfucker anymore."[102] Toward the close of Osder's film, after we find out that Mayor Goode left politics in 1991 and all of the replacement homes were condemned in 2000 for shoddy construction, the narrative goes back to footage of LaVerne Sims testifying before the PSCI. As she speaks, she breaks down so that her words are barely audible: "In the beginning MOVE people were the most happiest bunch of people you could ever know; we were a family, peaceful, loving. In the beginning MOVE was harassed a great deal, we were beat, many many times, we were jailed, many many times, and I'm talking about a people who have feelings, who are no different than you or I."[103] Her grief is palpable.

The position of "family," the role of the mother is sent up in a peculiar moment that Wagner-Pacifici recounts. After testimony during the PSIC inquiry about whether or not one of MOVE's members, Louise James, was beaten by her son, Frank, former member LaVerne Sims asked the chief counsel to the commission: "Mr. Lytton, am I to assume that the bomb was dropped on the MOVE people because Frank beat his mother?"[104] It's a cheeky inquiry and one that exposes the gendered roots of anti-Black hysteria: no one is going to bomb you for beating your mother, and no motherfucker is going to get up on trial for doing *that* either. And yet, this beating of a "mother" as inconsequential is not lost on me as a parallel to my observations about the same in the preceding chapter. In closing her chapter on MOVE's motives as an organization, Wagner-Pacifici, quoting Pierre Bourdieu, observes that their "incoherence" caused a kind of "metaphysical fury." Yes, at the level of ontology, MOVE was a thorn in the side of the great chain of being. But more than that, the particular way that MOVE carried out its sense of itself as an organization of "feeling people" who would not, could not abide by that hum/animal distinction made for a more concerted break with onto-logical understanding. Their claim was not for participation in the category of the Human; their claim was for *relation*. The work of relation is to change the perspectival terms of relation altogether so that lover/loved and other/object dissociate themselves from a hierarchy that can be managed, sustained, and then replicated. They want to stop the *real* motherfuckers. They were, in the end, truly "cultural deviants."[105]

In her review of the commission hearing records, Wagner-Pacifici aptly observes that MOVE's neighbors often pointed out that its members, includ-ing its dogs, lacked "domestication," a difference that Wagner-Pacifici sees as differences in approaches to life that then become valued through nor-mative stereotypes, and a difference that African-descended peoples could not benefit from when the city torched their homes as well. I want to offer that the "incoherence" of MOVE's platform (frustrated by their own con-tradictory claims, no doubt), rests in our inability as a culture to see the intersectional value of their stated goals for living, but also the importance of their desire for living in the context of issues that were perceived to be outside the scope of "Black" desires. How have we missed the opportu-nity to assess what could be the first US-based movement to challenge the necessity for, efficacy of, the hum/animal distinction in US history? How to think through MOVE's contributions to animal liberation in a discursive and visual field that cannot see. them. at. all?

It is in the embrace of hum:animal that blackness rejects the "life" brokered for us by the conditions set forth in the Middle Passage and the dictates of a social contract otherwise known as "civil society." Through a refusal—to borrow from Shana Redmond—to uphold, to recognize, or to tolerate the distinction, blackness returns itself to the possibility of *life*. Redmond reminds us that "a refusal of self, a series of conscientious and sustained acts that condemn individualism in the service of complicating, developing, articulating and protecting a radical whole" constitute what it means to *refuse*.[106] By turning the Black body inside out, MOVE confronts the limits of the "human," a condition organized and mandated by civil society

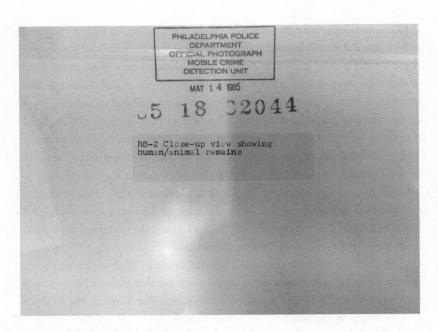

2.10 Back of photo exhibit from the PSIC archives. Photo by author.

for its particular purpose: to keep blackness so very much in contestation and/or competition with the animal that we will not even attempt what has already been defined as an impossibility: to confront the very grounding of the distinction and its reliance on so many disarticulations. As a movement, MOVE tried and failed to accomplish this. But I hope I have demonstrated here that their revolutionary experiment in animal liberation is *the closest* we've ever come to being open to species and carried by their embrace. It is a condition of being that cannot be achieved through *dressage* or *work* or even *care* (though the trace of all three are present in MOVE practices)—none of which are an ethics in and of themselves.

· · · · · · · · · · · · · · · · · ·

In the end, "hum:animal" life occurs in death.

Hundreds of photos of a scene of mass murder unearthed. What we lost in the fire . . . 2,500 records—and that was just one house—a sonic library held, caressed by blackness. An untold number of nonhuman animals—many of them left inside when residents were evacuated that morning and told that they would be able to go back to their homes later that evening. Now a charred mess. The house of John Africa and eleven of its residents.

The photo of said remains (figure 2.10) is unremarkable, one can barely see the outline of anything worth regarding—the photo is the record of what the caption on the back says it is, nothing more. "R8-2 Close-up view showing human/animal remains." Without distinction, but still distinct. Entwined. Species. Companionate.

MOVE's work in hum:animal life, its insistence on pointing out who the real motherfuckers were in the room, produced a spectacular brief for Black mother[fucking] insurgence and all its female parts.[107]

3 diversity : a scarcity

In distancing ontology even further from epistemology, we lose the capacity to provide political critiques of epistemologies, for we lose access to what is outside, to the outside of knowledges, to what they leave out, transform, or cannot know.
ELIZABETH GROSZ, *The Nick of Time* (2004)

Arguably, modernity has cost existence its diversity, has drained the earth's capacity to maintain life. . . . Modernity sustains, in the brief compass of this text, the disappearance of animals as a constant state.
AKIRA MIZUTA LIPPIT, *Electric Animal* (2000)

There are probably genuine students of animals and communication in the laboratories—but how do you enter into a contract about talking with a being you are going to kill?
VICKI HEARNE, *Adam's Task* (2007)

scarcity

Diversity moves against the grain of distinction, and so might (perhaps) be a necessary stopping place after our exploration of MOVE's vanguard challenge to *distinction* itself. Each of the epigraphs above points to the way in which *diversity* is important to all endeavors, whether that endeavor encompasses ethno-identities in an academic setting or something as expansive as the biosphere. I want to stay with the juxtaposition of epigraphs here because there is great overlap, if not a yawning gap among them.[1] For Grosz, taking existence seriously would entail a movement toward the outer edge of the known world and propel us into new epistemologies and a much-needed diversity of knowledges, worlds, and others. What both Grosz and Lippit inadvertently point toward is the recognition of diversity as always already about a simultaneous having and not having, about existence and extinction. If one recognizes diversity only at the moment that its waning (extinction?) becomes apparent, then what diversity really reminds us of is scarcity; scarcity almost always engenders panic.

Panics produce rescission and preclude the possibility of expansion. In times of panic, we can err on the side of excess.[2] I finish this book at the edges of another global pandemic which has sparked two public health crises: one relatively new to us, the virus known as SARS-CoV-2, and the other more familiar, the ongoing violence of racism. In these days, we are coming to know what human being is *for*, how it means, and what it needs to do. The questions of diversity that I hope to lay open here are ripe in this age of COVID-19, the disease caused by the above-named virus. To start I will say this: scarcity holds no brief for the relentless lack of abject poverty or hunger; its place is strictly bound by the condition of having in the first order of things.

When Lippit proclaims, "modernity has cost existence its diversity," I cannot help but think in terms of what modernity or whose modernity Lippit refers to. Modernity, at least in much of philosophical thought outside of critical race theory, is rarely understood through the system of peonage and slavery that arguably made it possible.[3] Modernity in epoch time is certainly the blood, bone, and sinew of Black and Indigenous being, since "it" was carved out of the flesh, a property or element of being whose vital force is endemic to our "modern" capacities for life. One could say that Lippit's claim about "modernity" works only if modernity's stabilizing actor is a certain kind of human being, someone endowed with the power to make scarcity ebb and flow as well as to control our definition of it. On the other hand, exempting whole swaths of peoples from their accountability in humanity's overcoming—its acts of extinction—presents a powerful and dangerous conundrum for those of us interested in matters hum:animal. While no one wants to be accountable to us (the marginalized), how do we become accountable to one another as *an* other and, yes, to that great biosphere which makes and, yes, in this pandemic moment, breaks human being?

Modernity's model of scarcity does produce a constant evacuation of the animal—framed here in this project as an/other—whose disappearance is assured as a "constant state." I want to acknowledge Lippit's attempt to blur the distinction hum/animal. The grand project in the philosophy of the Enlightenment—and here the pessimists are right—arranges a place for blackness as the antithesis of being itself.[4] But words like "modernity" soften the blow, produce blackness as a *potential* partner in the project of becoming—one in which the self's own scarcity is reified over and over again. Scarcity models require enormous amounts of *work* to maintain; the project of producing an/other while subjecting "it" to constant erasure is exhausting.

In fact, all of the epigraphs for this chapter are mindful not only of philosophy as an Enlightenment project but also of the subject (as a certain kind of being) of philosophy itself. Reading Cary Wolfe on Jean-François Lyotard's musings about the "inhuman," I am reminded of the way in which we continue to think of the philosophical subject as a universal entity, struggling ungendered (but male) unraced (but phenotypically white) with the larger problems of hum:animal being.[5] The subject is actually revitalized through a sustained and arbitrating knowing that must insist upon its own reiteration; a reiteration that tends to put human being, and more often than not *a particular kind of* human being, into its center. The subject representing "difference"—a "being" understood through some forms of Black thought as an "object" in diversity's game—is always already thought of as excluded from the means of production, and if you will, from any and all authorship in regard to epistemic investigation. These assumptions about its/our relationship to language, freedom, even life itself, abound in philosophical and theoretical work.

Having participated in "diversity work" across a number of college campuses, I come to this framing discussion of diversity and scarcity with no small amount of frustration about the nature of that work. In diversity work on college campuses, Sara Ahmed observes that "the diversity world is shaped by the failure of diversity to bring into existence the world it names."[6] In a similar mode, modernity's reliance on scarcity or a constant disappearance of the animal, reflected also as one's-own-self, produces a backward drag on the definitional force of modernity. Its Enlightenment project has always already been to produce modes of power in sameness, while all along heralding a coming community (think "dominion" here) that is recognizably "diverse."[7] Diversity becomes a machine for the recognition of whiteness and its attendant feeling. Our work in the diversityverse is to attend the affective life of predominantly and culturally white institutions. Indeed, there is no there there. In fact, what we have is "ethnocentric monoculturalism," a construct that produces visionlessness among white colleagues—who do not notice their own "ethnocentric beliefs, values, and assumptions."[8] So . . . first, how do you work with some*one* to see some*thing* that is invisible to them *and* even if were to become apparent, it would still be some*thing* they would not want to see at all? In Sara Ahmed's *On Being*

Included: Racism and Diversity in Institutional Life, she writes, "It is hard to get whiteness recognized by those whose political agency benefits from it not being recognized" (152). The double invisibility here is lethal: white cultural norms remain invisible and Black achievement is a nonstarter at best, an oxymoron at worst. In the end, diversity is not a field of difference in which we all are out standing. Instead, it is a reflection of hum:animal's steady and simultaneous erasure.

When and what colleagues do see is often a reflection of the self. Allan deSouza writes: "A white faculty member welcomed me to a new school, saying that we are the same because she has a Native American grandmother, with the insinuation that this ancestral legacy made her, and hence the department, *already* 'diverse.'"[9] And the confusion around what diversity is, means, or does institutionally isn't completely attributed to what "white" faculty members think. In an email to me, a Black male faculty member once claimed that the fact that they hired me at his prestigious southern university meant that the department wasn't homophobic. I had heard the same logic applied to the presence of Black faculty on campus—no matter how few our numbers. We were evidence of a step in the right direction, even if that step felt like a push over a cliff into an abyss. But this is precisely how scarcity *labors* in diversity work. I argue that the scarcity in diversity *is* its primary work and that such work is a form of violence that words like "microaggression" or even "white fragility" don't quite capture.

Ahmed understands efforts to combat institutionalized racism on college and university campuses as an instantiation of the institution as an organism with feelings. She writes: "The organization becomes the subject of feeling, as the one who must be protected, as the one who is easily bruised or hurt. . . . There is an implicit injunction not to speak about racism to protect whiteness."[10] Like its counterpart, the corporation, the university is a (human) being, endowed with all of the benefits of the social contract which ties (human) being to forms of governmentality.[11] But again, like the questions raised above about the subject of philosophy, I worry that as the "college" gains the attributes of (human) being, then the relative distinctions that obtain and the centrality of white subjects in the very diversity work that assumes an/other object, all of a sudden comes much closer to the kind of sustained erasure—that constant state—that Lippit so astutely exposes.[12]

The field of animal studies has long eschewed sentience as a standard or necessary capacity for the recognition of nonhuman animal life. Relying on the ability to *feel*, relying on *sense*, is a problem for animal studies because it yokes animal liberation to modes of being related to the category of the human. In this scenario, "its" being is predicated on, traffics in a kind of sameness that is a demand useful only to human being. Again, the turn toward the recognition of difference is filtered through a belonging that intentionally narrows its scope. Feeling becomes the provenance of those with the capacity to master its affective life. In institutional space, *becoming animal* is no longer the verdant imaginative expanse of Haraway or Deleuze, but rather a space of exclusion formed against its ready alternative: the happy space of comingling and becoming. Feeling in institutions is a whitewash.

Whiteness functions as a character in its own science fiction scape, exists in its own protected biosphere, and is capable of maintaining its vibrant matter from inside an incredibly nimble forcefield. This connection between biospheric ecologies of being and the diversity world becomes even more charged if we were to concentrate on the *other* meanings of the term "diversity." Diversity also describes a kind of antinomian crisis, a "contrariety to what is agreeable, good, or right; perversity, evil, mischief" (OED). This might explain why so many of those "diversity" positions in the academy are funded from that all-too-familiar pot of "discretionary" (discretion is tact and confidentiality) monies: under-the-table deals that provide for services of a salacious nature; mischief. Discretionary targeted opportunity hires instantiate the sense of diversity as a smutty business. If we set this third definition of the term against Lippit's ordering of diversity as a biospheric process couched in a fundamental act of disappearing, we might begin to think that a human-centered discourse about diversity is fundamentally at odds with the kind of diversity needed to fuel life itself. And it is. Both the project of sustaining diversity within the institution and the call for increased "diversity" at any given moment (nick of time?) seek to put human endeavor over and against nonhuman animal life. Diversity work, at least institutionally, produces a necessary and persistent alignment between nonhuman animal life and those who are underrepresented in such spaces.

In the academy at least, you know you are "diverse" when your vulnerable populations do not exceed a certain number. In addition, you can resist the number of "minority" full-time employees if you make the case that there are not that many qualified people (think scarcity) out there to fit the bill. To reach back to Lippit's point about modernity and diversity: modernity allows us to hold open the possibility of the animal's disappearance as a "constant state." Recognition of this fact could bring us closer to Lyotard's sense that humanity is becoming "inhuman"—we are moving away from rather than toward the light. I could fall back on Lyotard's sweeping theoretical gesture here if I were able to understand to what/whom "humanity" actually refers.

Which brings me back to my earlier question about modernity in Lippit. In essence, are "we" having the same conversation at all here? And more to the point, is the possibility of "the same" even applicable when the prevailing constituencies are so marked on one end (we know who the vulnerable are) and so assumed (when I see it, I know what it is) on the other?

This problem of constituency and definition plays itself out, as I note above, in the university. Diversity does other work for us institutionally—it allows us to continue to think so myopically about what diversity is that we fail to utilize the differences of opinion already seated at the table.[13] Does diversity work to ensure scarcity, or to bring the biosphere into its fullness? Is diversity just another occasion to practice bad faith? I will end this meditation on diversity as scarcity with an anecdote that helps, I hope, to bring home several points I have been plotting.

When I was an associate dean at the University of Illinois Chicago, I attended a meeting of the affirmative action officer's (EEOC) roundtable of Chancellor's Committees representing various underrepresented groups and diverse constituencies on campus: Latino/a, Black, LGBTQ, etc. I came to the room as a representative of the LGBTQ Caucus. It was a lunch meeting and I arrived about ten minutes before we were to proceed. I nodded hello to a few people I recognized and noticed several folders of information placed around the table with name cards in front of them. I secured my boxed lunch, located the folder and place card with my name on it, and sat down in the chair in front of them.

At some point before we began, the assistant to the affirmative action officer got my attention and said, "I have a folder here for you." A bit puzzled, I responded that I had located the folder with my name on it, so all was well. She still seemed a bit perplexed, if not agitated, during the light banter among representatives of the different committees as they gathered their boxed lunches and claimed their places at the table. Right as the meeting came to order, she said to me, "You are [insert more appropriate African-descended sounding name], right?" I replied that I was in fact Sharon Holland, that my folder was in front of me, and that I was good to go. She still seemed perplexed but at least she relented. It was clear to me what had just happened, but I think it was a mystery to her until the meeting moved forward and another visibly Black woman walked through the door—revealing that she was the representative of the Chancellor's Committee on African American issues, not I. The assistant saw me as Black and assumed that I was representing my African American colleagues. She was so persistent in her belief that even after I informed her that I was sitting before the folder with *my name* on it—obviously, I know my own name and how to read it—she remained bewildered. I couldn't possibly represent an LGBTQ constituency at that meeting. Needless to say, I didn't stay on that committee for very long after the incident. To be fair, there were other factors at work here—one was the extent to which representation and diversity dangerously overlap in academic institutions, another was the extent to which the LGBT constituency at UIC had for some years maintained an all-white representation so that collective expectations and assumptions made it logical that a phenotypically white representative would take *my* seat at the table.

If diversity is something we seek so that knowledges, to echo Grosz, can be brought in conversation with the machinations of ontology, then how do "we" foster the beginnings of that recognition? New knowledge challenges human being at every committee table across the university and at every moment as we encounter *an* other life. But how might we acknowledge these efforts at institutional *and* global climate change as a simultaneity? Climate is both something like weather and the pulse of a place on the ground. When diversity represents a scarcity that is affirmed by the rhetoric of the university and its agents (that would be the "we" here), then we become profoundly restricted in our understanding of how it actually works to maintain some life over others, to echo Lippit. And this indeed is the diversity work that we do on college and university campuses: we preserve and maintain some lives over others. This might be one of the central reasons why saying "Black Lives Matter" creates a visceral reaction in white-aligned people—as it calls out the true objective of inclusive society: to create a condition for Black life where scarcity is the norm and where matter matters not.

The terms at play—diversity, scarcity, and even modernity—all have their groundings in somewhat disparate intellectual/epistemological communities. Ultimately, the relative value attached to any term in any location is difficult to assess. There are many conversations taking place, to be sure, but only a few of them "count." And theorists across disciplinary boundaries have been speaking to the problem of the centrality of a single inquiry in theory for decades—critical race theory scholar Richard Delgado took on the problem of citation in law journals in the early 1980s; Avery Gordon and Christopher Newfield took on Walter Benn Michaels's syllogistic and often essentialist rendering of racial practices; Charles Mills has offered a devastating critique of "white supremacy" and philosophy; Satya P. Mohanty, Paula M. L. Moya, Michael Hames-García, and others launched an intervention into theory with postpositivist readings of canonical texts and political theory; Robert Warrior has rearticulated Indian intellectual traditions while, Craig Womack has promoted a radical separatist approach to critical thinking in Indian country; Hortense Spillers interrogated the category of "woman"/gender before Judith Butler's *Gender Trouble* made its debut; and scholars like Lindon W. Barrett, M. Jacqui Alexander, Mike Hill, and Kandice Chuh have taken the centrality of terms like "blackness," "whiteness," or "Asian American" and offered innovative and often brilliant readings for new formations of knowledge. But the mainstream, as Merleau-Ponty suggests, "glides over these things and does not touch them." These inquiries represent *a* world to be sure, but not *the* world.

Once seen as evidence of what makes "us" strong, diversity brings us diminished returns—it saps the strength out of a once vital ecosystem. No wonder academic institutions have made a mockery of the term "diversity"—a diversity misrecognized by all of us through conservative nomenclature as "identity politics."[14] In its institutional form—as an administrative rhetoric—"diversity" no longer speaks to our strengths but our weaknesses. Diversity articulates our failure to transcend, mires us in the corporeal, makes the body more important than the "mind," and therefore flows against the higher ground of the ivory tower's intellectual objectives. This is perhaps why the feminist in me gets nervous when folks are eager to leave the body behind, or say that it does not cohere, because it carries and (sometimes) sustains life, literally and figuratively. And if the mind, at least from the standpoint of the humanities, is the focus of our endeavors, then the body re-*minds* us, calls on us to alter both space and time in the service of its constitutive parts. Following upon Baby Suggs's devastating and clear calling out of bodies and parts to *flesh* in Morrison's *Beloved*, I return to this *meta*theme of disarticulation, the hanging death of hum:animal flesh throughout this chapter.

In the meantime, it appears that in the move toward interdisciplinarity, there are more disciplinary boundaries than we could have imagined. We wield the absoluteness of the differences between and among critics as readily as we understand the divide between human and (nonhuman) animal. This project bears the marks of an ongoing frustration with our inability to speak to one another about the challenges that diverse epistemological registers bring to the table of ideas. What would it mean for us to really speak to one another, to change the way we think and write, to engage in the process that is biodiversity, at its most literal iteration, where disparate presence is a measure of healthy relation? In the age of the subjectless critique, who or what is or can be the subject of theory? What *being* would dare try?

What I have offered here is a reading of diversity world campus cultures as a microcosm of other struggles for the category of the human; I have attempted to create a conduit between animal studies and this *other* culture to demonstrate how much they are in lockstep with one another. Diversity world culture cannot be adequately assessed inside the confines of human being, as it relies on the same species-oriented methods that have sustained biospheric extinction events as a norm; it is set up to legitimate processes of failure as a constant state. My next engagement returns to the work of my first chapter, reassessing the distinction that is hum/animal, and opening the question of lines of descent, of genealogy as a hallmark of knowing something about *an* other.

the known world

If one were to chart the very interesting career of blackness from the interstitial space of the Middle Passage and beyond, you would find a historical accounting that carries the weight of an ontological proof. Black beings' accountability to the hum/animal divide is marked by the status of being nonhuman—having been one among the animals, among those who "perish," rather than "die," according to Heidegger—blackness makes its mark on the animal in very convoluted ways. Part of the point of this project is to tease out the way in which blackness matters (or not) to what I am calling hum:animal studies, a method of studying the animal that tracks with animal studies but takes a decided turn toward the unknowable. I have a suspicion that the rhetorics that hold blackness at a distance in the discourse on the hum:animal sustain both what and who is central to the inquiry itself and the *political* position of blackness within such investigations.

I want to take a moment here to mark in some detail the specific and early origin of this project. Edward P. Jones's novel *The Known World* (2003) is essentially the story of an African-descended slaveholder in fictional Manchester County, Virginia. The novel gleaned no small amount of criticism for its focus on Black slaveholders and its unflinching look at each character's flawed ethical compass. It is this quality of the text—its opening of slavery's field of vision vis-à-vis its masters, that brings to mind the painful and somewhat controversial stakes of what diversity does, and how diversity marks not the inclusion and equity we seek but the myriad of problems its presence creates for what is *known* or even possible. In this regard, the movements here will run alongside the opening argument of this chapter, as diversity as scarcity and not abundance will give way to the proliferation of *it* as a kind of problem for rethinking an overdetermined historical landscape.

Much like Faulkner before him, Jones produces a complex genealogy of white and Black and their African-descended enslaved, whose issue crisscross what will become the United States. The work of genealogy is crucial to the project of whiteness and its overcoming; quoting Ruth Frankenberg, Sara Ahmed notes that in institutional diversity work, antiracist praxis often leaves white liberals "without any genealogy."[15] What besides the history of racism and oppression *is* whiteness anyway? Antiracist work strips white subjects of their biographies and exposes them to perishment, rather than optimalizing them for the work of dying; diversity work, creating and managing *an* other, returns their rightful genealogies to them, allowing white subjects to remain out-standing-in-their-field. The resistance to antiracist practice might best be explained through the work of animal studies. Human being most desperately needs a biography of note in order to die a proper death. Perishing is for other *animals*; to perish is to be taken by a world made by others. A world whose making is produced by a racial hierarchy; to perish is to truly flirt with and succumb to a naturalized racial order *made for other nonbeings to experience*, one embedded in a hum/animal distinction that persists.

....

The Known World's central characters are: Henry and Caldonia Townsend, Black holders of the enslaved Moses, their overseer, and his wife, Priscilla; William Robbins, the white owner of the largest plantation in the county of the enslaved; and Augustus Townsend, Henry's father, who is consistently ashamed of his son's slaveholding. The story also encompasses the free Black population of Manchester, the enslaved/freed issue of Robbins, and the lives of nonbiologically related enslaved, in particular Celeste and Elias on the Townsend farm, and their counterpart, Alice Night, characterized as a woman broken by slavery, but whose life as an underground railroad conductor is spectacularly revealed to us in the novel's last pages.

At the novel's opening, Moses eats dirt, lies naked in a "patch of woods" and masturbates while his master, Henry, dies (July 1855) not too far off from where Moses finds his pleasure.[16] Much of the story travels back and forth in time; the world of the novel unfolds as the bulk of the story occurs sometime between the 1840s and 1860s, while temporally, it also anticipates a future in which the physical novel emerges. The shock of its environs is perhaps best detailed by Moses's case:

Moses was the first slave Henry Townsend had bought: $325 and a handshake from William Robbins, a white man. It took Moses more than two weeks to come to understand that someone wasn't fiddling with him and that indeed a black man, two shades darker than himself, owned him and any shadow he made. Sleeping in a cabin beside Henry in the first weeks after the sale, Moses had thought it was already a strange world that made him a slave to a white man, but God had indeed set it twirling and twisting every which way when he put black people to owning their own kind.[17]

The last words of this excerpt—"their own kind"—point toward the community of African-descended people rather than the enslaved. These words set the stage for Henry's ceaseless ethical trespass in the novel. Indeed, Katherine Clay Bassard notes, "That Henry grows up in a system where property relations are recognized above family relations constitutes the construction of his identity and his world."[18] Faulkner's imprint is all over the novel, and Henry and Moses sleeping on the floor together is straight out of "The Bear" in *Go Down, Moses*.[19] In many respects, the novel is a catalogue of how the slavocracy warps humanity's moral compass; it asks and attempts to answer that thorny question that lingers from the first chapter of this book—what indeed to do when the overseer hands you the whip? Should you, could you, to save your own life, beat a Black woman to near-death? Should you, would you, lose yourself in the *doing*? What is the cost of keeping homo sapiens alive to its own self and its *others*? If there is a metaphysics for the *human*, it is most certainly in a *separatist* state; making its live-li-hood a world, but certainly not, *the* world.

At its core, the novel understands that the principal ethical terrain—if ethics are what you do and what could be called a moral life is something altogether unattainable in the face of such a great system of persistent and violent injustice—of slavery is a messy, deeply imperfect enterprise and that no one escapes its investment in the capacity for human cruelty-in-capitalism. Morrison does remind us, after all, that "they came for the cash, too."[20] *The Known World* also understands that relationships of power shape the world we see, that the ants crawling around under a rock, to paraphrase Lauren Berlant, are in fact a village and a force; it is *a kind of knowing* that we cannot/will not see. Unseeing is willful, concerted, and, yes, strategic. Merleau-Ponty tells us that the self's own perception is such a very flawed thing, and the work of opening up to other worlds is perhaps beyond the tiny scope of myopic human endeavor. The known world, to us, is a world of scarcity, rather than diversity. Diversity *is* the worlds all around us, but for our limited perception, hidden in plain sight. Given the above stakes and the messiness of human endeavor, it is hard, ontologically speaking, to envision a category of human one can actually have some hope of or desire for being part of.

This problem for human-being-under-slavocracy—which becomes the inheritance of human-being-under-Enlightenment and thus its puzzle to solve—brings itself forward at the end of what is certainly a lavish spacio-political novel. The enlightened cannot escape the backward drag of the slavocracy. In a chapter where Caldonia visits the quarters of the "plantation" left to her after her husband Henry's death, Moses has run off and Elias is overseer. During this episode, Caldonia is visited by a Hartford, Connecticut, insurance agent and we are subjected to the following ordering:

> "So," Topps [the Atlas Insurance agent] said as he finalized everything, "there will be no protection at this time on the perishment of your human property." "Perishment," or natural death, was a word the people at Atlas used very often and no one used it more than the widowed Topps, who saw himself as one day ascending to an important position at the home office in Hartford, Connecticut, and looking down over the land and dispensing wisdom learned from years toiling in the wilderness of the uninsured. The word perishment had been thought up by a man at the Hartford office to try to convey the fragility of human life, especially that of slaves, and to try to get across to a customer the utter need for Atlas's policies on those lives, slave or otherwise.[21]

Humans die, while animals perish. Someone has obviously been reading his Heidegger. The extinguishing of human life has manner, method, sound to accompany it; it even has afterlife. Animals have no such luck; they perish displaying a limitless incapacity for consciousness in the face of the grim reaper. Jones's brilliant refiguring of this popular Heideggerian proposition is extremely lucrative for my study.

In this known world, insurance flattens difference in kind—"slave or otherwise"—pulling distinction into the murkiness of difference in degree. If we uphold the Hartford office's distinction (hum/animal), human being becomes animal being in an astonishing disregard for the master's attempt to separate certain carriers of humanity from its imposters. The collapse here, the space where distinction has no obvious utility, returns us to a bi-ologism. The effect of perishing is that the life of the enslaved and that of the non-enslaved are indistinguishable in the insurer's lexicon; in Jones's cosmos, then, the condition of human Being is figured as "slave or otherwise" and is predicated on the term "uninsured." The uninsured inhabit a "wilderness"—perhaps an alternative kind of open? What better way to become chattel than if someone has a lien against your very life? Here, perishment speaks to the "fragility," the vulnerability of human life, remarking on the artificiality of the separation between "slave or otherwise," returning humanity to its condition in the open with the animal. The worlding here belongs to capital. Moreover, the reiteration of the root word "perish" provides job security and the possibility of ascension on the corporate ladder for this particular agent. The profit margin grinds all human Being into meat. (Where is Larry Flynt when you need him?) What if the endpoint of chattel slavery is to make humans, property, to produce *and* conceal a kind of universal perishment under the guise of differential deaths—where one dies (human) and the other perishes (animal)? Perishment in *The Known World*—as a shared condition for "slave or otherwise," and as a familiar trope of hum/animal difference—evacuates *dying* from the territory of "human" experience. Property is forever the twist and turn of not only Black life but all life, at least in this Atlas agent's schema.

A note on the text: Caldonia Townsend, as Black female enslaver, appears not to be the insurgent female subject that we've been looking for. She is no emancipator, and throughout the novel she is, indeed, hard to get to know. The world that we can see and know in Jones's complex novel is very much a collection of worlds, each of them warped and bedazzled by someone's convoluted attempt to stay unsullied in the midst of the slavocracy's atrocities; to practice good faith in a bad faith economy. No one escapes, and the worlds here are rich in what cannot be seen—the known world is flattened by the ethics of the slavocracy and the only clear-eyed keepers of a way forward, of other worlds and their possibilities, are revealed to both reader and one Black enslaver at the very end of the novel.

And then there is also that clear-eyed dog . . .

In a letter to Caldonia, his sister, Calvin explains why on his way to New York, he has stopped in Washington, D.C. While the story that occasions his delay is surely about the novel's dramatic conclusion, there is another from before, brought forth in these last pages that gives pause. Gay and in love with his sister's husband (Louis), we learn midway through the novel that Calvin's trip north is guided by the memory of a dog in a photograph of a family in New York whose gaze to the right of the frame—to something other than the terrain of the photo itself, to other worlds beyond the one he knows as circumscribed by slavery's reach—fills him with melancholy. Jones explains: "The feelings for Louis had been there for some time, but it was two months ago that he knew it was all hopeless and that to save himself he had best take himself someplace else."[22] Two months prior to Henry's death, Calvin goes swimming with Louis and when the two lay down next to one another on the bank of the creek, Calvin "had noticed a tiny pool of water and sweat that had collected in a small depression at the base of Louis's neck. . . . Calvin had wanted to lean over and drink with his tongue from the pool."[23] His desire to see New York is bound up with his *desire*, and it reeks slightly of dog. It is an odd thing to find a companionate species vision here; its thinking outside-the-box nestled inside the hope and longing of a queer subject, thinking queerly too, perhaps about that beyond.[24] So, Calvin arrives in D.C. with the dog's vision on his mind, only to find his vision—his *historical* one and therefore, his autobiography at least— amended even further.

In the dining room of the boardinghouse he finds himself in, Calvin witnesses two stunning pieces of art made of clay, cloth, and paint—both by Alice Night. The story gathers from the edges of the two maps—one without persons but a county, the other a farm nestled in that same county with persons depicted. As he *reads* what worlds unfold before him, he is hailed first by "Moses's Priscilla" and then by Alice, the woman whose first and subsequent appearances in the novel lead us to believe she has lost her mind in slavery's terrible labyrinth. He writes to his sister that upon seeing Priscilla, "I knew in those few seconds that whatever she had been in Virginia, she was that no more."[25] The language moves from "whatever" and "that" to something beyond the page that cannot be captured, like the dog's vision; a world, but not *the* world. But a world with the potential to remake the larger-than-life one that seems to dominate. The fear of the enslaved transfers to our Calvin, who stays on in that small boardinghouse filled with fugitives and, yes, insurgent women. His fear is now "my history," and he speaks of being "cast out."[26] What to make of the self's own history, one's autobiography subjected to the worlding of an enslaved other and a dog?

Calvin ends his letter by cautioning his sister to remember his fear when she addresses her reply to him. Figuratively, our Calvin does go to the dogs— he inclines his head to the right and his search for what on earth that dog might see brings him to *his* history, now reframed in *an* other's act of creative worlding. This autobiography is also touched, handed/handled by the *female*. If to perish is to be taken in the open by the world (a world) created for you, then the condition of the human ("enslaved or otherwise") under the slavocracy is surely one of perishment. It is the dog's vision coupled with that of the enslaved, one that is considered "like" the dog in the first order of things, that produce world and therefore *die* being in the world rather than just of it.

What I am offering here is that Jones, often criticized for focusing on African-descended enslavers, utilizes this particular subject position to say something profound about human being and the hum/animal distinction that subtends it. Calvin's moment of reckoning is suspended in a knowing so absolute, a knowing kept (quiet as it's kept?) by two insurgent, not just fugitive subjects, witness to the fact of the world that brought him forth. This moment reminds me of that phrase that invokes the simultaneity in hum:animal *difference*, in Derrida's work on the animal: "And we should not exclude the possibility that the same living creature is at the same time follower and followed, hunter knowing itself to be hunted, seducer and seduced, persecutor and fugitive, and that the two forces of the same strategy, indeed in the same movement, are conjugated not only in the same animal . . . but in the same instant."[27] Calvin is a being at rest, no longer fugitive nor persecutor, settled in his desire (perhaps), having been brought "north" by the vision of a dog, now satiated (perhaps) in a moment of profound reordering. No small insurgence that. But I do note that the question of queer desire, satiated desire here is put in service of the enslaved and the dog; what could be queerer than a desire reoriented toward a different landscape of embrace?

So much has transpired in this moment in the novel—it is a denouement like no other and totally unexpected. We are introduced to the fact that the map is certainly not the territory. The world that is *known* to us is but a fragile overlay on many worlds, interconnected and, at times, beyond belief. The pall of the slavocracy covers Manchester County like a damp blanket in winter; in Alice Night's art, human and animal parts gaze outside the boundary/ies drawn by the supremacy of property *first*. These last "images" in Jones's novel return us to the world's bio and material *diversity*. A world of paint, clay, and cloth—evidence of something moving swiftly beyond the edge of a photo, a stand of trees, or possibly collective vision. What does the animal, human or otherwise, *see* when it looks at these many worlds, overcome by the pall of property? What if the animal responded, or more importantly, what if we reacted to and or engaged its response and, from that, forged meaning-making? Where can that dog's vision lead us? How might this world *respond*? The next engagement seeks to think through this *call and response* from the perspective of the closest cousin to human being, our brothers and sisters in the category of the great apes. When this meaning-making produces a response from animal life that doesn't necessarily suit us or our vision for corporeal wholeness, or the pleasantries of *being or becoming with*, then the stakes of diversity and its achievement become all the more precarious.

strategic dismemberment

No, no. That's not the way. I told you to put her human characteristics on
the left and her animal on the right. And don't forget to line them up.
SCHOOLTEACHER, from Toni Morrison, *Beloved* (1987)

Homo sapiens, then, is neither a clearly defined species nor a substance; it
is, rather, a machine or device for producing the recognition of the human.
GIORGIO AGAMBEN, *The Open* (2004)

Morrison and Agamben both note the way in which the very recognition of the human is produced through taxonomies. The necessary order taxonomy produces secures diversity and its constitutive *parts*. For Agamben, the *human* does not and cannot know itself outside of the machinations in play to produce it as worthy of recognition. Homo sapiens/human is a tautology of immense proportions. In short, one cannot approach the question of the human, let alone that of the animal, without giving serious attention to the science of delineation and measurement that secures the categories in the first place. Staying in this comparative mode, it is not lost on me that these taxonomies are *gendered* still, as the female enslaved and the universal man of Agamben's argument stand in stark contrast to one another as objects/subjects of inquiry here. Through what mechanism is recognition/knowledge obtained? As we investigate the terrain of hum/animal difference, we are forever haunted not just by a female, but a *Black* female. She haunts the boundaries of Merleau-Ponty's elemental flesh as well as the work on *flesh* as a matter-making practice under slavery in the rhetoric of pessimism. Her flesh is a substance that arises out of more than one Black Atlantic text and turns itself loose upon us, altering *being*, moving it toward *relation*.

Scholars of philosophy from Levinas to Derrida and most recently Matthew Calarco have taken issue with Heidegger's somewhat dogmatic view of hum/animal difference, with little account in any camp for how the category of the human remains so stable in the first order of things so that it can be utilized consistently in the service of proclaiming the animal difference.

Calarco also sees the dogmatism of Heidegger's pronouncements, reminding us that "*whether such a distinction between human beings and animals can or even should be drawn* is never raised for serious discussion."[28] I laud Calarco's book for its clarity—he puts his finger on the *power* that obtains from drawing distinctions, and like Derrida, wonders, at least implicitly, what the animal would say in their moment of regard for us—a question that is further incapacitated by the fact that the saying is always already all around us. The requirement is an active *listening* and/or *seeking* like our Calvin. This would require some kind of ethical terrain—some kind of insurgence, a chosen vulnerability that might be able to refuse assimilation, even at risk of one's own life. And even our Calvin, whose head is inclined in the direction of *animal* vision, is terrified that the truth of his carefully stitched autobiography will be found out, so he makes sure to caution his sister about his vulnerability in his letter to her.

For Levinas, the quibble with Heidegger is the centering of ontology over ethics; ontology in its rigid assumptions about living itself, precludes seeing the face of the (an)other and establishing that central ethical commitment. Despite his argument with Heidegger about metaphysics, Levinas cannot bring himself to recognize animals outside a conscripted and inadequate-to-the-task anthropocentrism (one that Agamben finds is "lethal and bloody"), noted also by Derrida and later by Calarco.[29] I will come back to this moment in Levinas later in this chapter. Ontological proofs presuppose a hierarchy that is unyielding and unending—how *being* engages the world by making or breaking "it" stands against how the ethical commitment of face-to-face engagement alters hierarchies, or at least before Derrida's reading of Levinas, it would appear to do so, even when his toolbox fails him at every turn.

Derrida's work *The Animal That Therefore I Am* lives at the boundary of hum/animal, worrying the distinction from all philosophical vantage points but never achieving hum:animal vision. It is startling and, along with work by Agamben in *The Open*, points toward the fact that the space between human and animal is no gentle pause nor polite interruption, but in the case of philosophical inquiry, it is a violence; and, *pace* Agamben, it is man against animals. Derrida's interest in the animal is both mythohistorical and material. Who are they to us in our fictions and embodied experiences of the world, and how can they matter to us? Along the way in his signature text on the animal, more than a few pointed sightings of them happen throughout his work: there are a few cats (well, maybe just one: his), a couple of dogs, several horses, and of course, monkeys. One could say that deconstruction is a relentless quest for our recognition of the inseparability of *life* (the house of John Africa is built on a foundation of *life*); it is at its most basic a discourse about *justice, universally applicable*. Deconstruction's motive force makes a lot of sense when we pair it with some basic facts about Jacques Derrida's life. He was a Sephardic Jew (Yahadut Sefarad), born in El Biar, Algeria. Though under French control at the time of his birth, Algeria (which gained its independence in 1962) is, after all, an African nation and so very few have thought of Derrida as an *African* philosopher; what's in a name, but our ability to do so? And how to do so in a space between continents where a geographical description morphs into a racialized one? Nevertheless, his outsider status as an Algerian person of Jewish descent perhaps forms his absolute commitment (though flawed) to and brief for *an* other.

In *The Animal That Therefore I Am*, Derrida views much of philosophical thought—a crisscrossing through Cartesian, analytic, pragmatic, and psychoanalytic genres—as inadequate to the task of centering animal vision ("Can one from the vantage of the animal see oneself being looked at naked?").[30] He remarks, somewhat playfully, "Descartes, Kant, Heidegger, Lacan and Levinas . . . everything in them goes on as if they themselves had never been looked at, and especially not naked, by an animal that addressed them."[31] He engages in the practice of substantive mis-reading—something Calvin Warren so aptly pointed out—that Black scholars and queer scholars (see previous sections of this book on "flesh") partake of in order to bring substance to their embodied experiences of worlding; experiences that often remain outside of traditional philosophic inquiry.[32] Since mis-reading is about judgment and interpretation, it simply signals the necessary work of dismantling forms of dominant knowledge, and in Derrida's case, a logocentrism at the heart of our grammar. It is the mis-reading that gets us there; it is the established interpretation—for Derrida this would be the bankrupt practice of *naming* animal life ("the animal") as separable from human life in addition to thinking of "the animal" as lacking response, only possessing of re-action, that produces the first mis-take.[33] In short, from Linnaeus to Horkheimer, Derrida to Agamben, philosophical inquiry has defined "the animal" as out-side of the limit(s) of the human.[34]

Agamben attempts to tackle the question of the animal by interrogating "the Open"—allowing being in the world (human) and being of the world (animal) to rest and even gaze upon one another. He tries to offer us a radical notion of that cognitive space and asks: What would happen if we simply let the animal be? What if mastery were not (human) destiny? Earlier in the same text, Agamben notices that this mastery can be understood as a kind of obsessive "overcoming"—"not an event that has been completed once and for all, but an occurrence that is always under way, that every time and in each individual decides between the human and the animal, between nature and history, between life and death."[35] In Agamben's formulation, overcoming is neither the epitome of human production nor the end of its historical arc; rather, overcoming represents for us the opportunity to acknowledge the phenomenological conundrum inherent in all being: *choice*. Choice here for Agamben is not the reserve of those with consciousness. In the Open, in the space where the animal is exposed to the human in a kind of suspended reciprocity, choice is a matter of relation, rather than a force (of law). This choice, perhaps gets us back to that question posed early on in this book's argument: could I, should I, would I, take the overseer's whip?

While there are reams of paper devoted to the hum/animal divide, at the time when I began this decade-long project, there were very few sheets that take up how the transatlantic slave trade might have fundamentally transformed the (philosophical) distinction between hum/animal while simultaneously altering the kind of inquiry we might make into such a separation.[36] To date, there is much company in this field, but little from the vantage point of hum:animal living. Nonwhite subjectivity in the space of the Middle Passage, moving betwixt and between, could represent the impossibility of holding that interstitial space inviolate—a point made by Hortense Spillers over thirty-five years ago. The focus on blackness and, by extension, Black being also entails seeing blackness as the thing that is acted upon. Blackness is exposed, in the open, neither in the world nor of the world, but unmade by the autobiographical reach of doers.[37] In another direction, the question of the hum:animal opens up to blackness in precisely the ways in which I have articulated it, so that blackness cannot be understood as being-becoming outside of its position in the Middle Passage. This articulation also has an ethical downside, as it posits blackness's particular overcoming within the neat confines of the human, so that our opening to animality is registered in precisely the Heideggerian terms that much of the literature on such difference seeks to contest. In many ways I want to limn that middle ground and its epistemological possibilities. I do not aim to keep to one epistemological register so much as I desire to animate and play with the assumptions inherent in theoretical discourse at the site of hum:animal. To limn this middle ground would be to consider sexual difference/gender as an operational component in the progress-oriented, overcoming represented by hum/animal distinction. How does hum:animal desire figure into this collapsed relation?

The importance of the hum/animal divide has been a staple of philosophical thought, and as Cary Wolfe observes, Jacques Derrida can be credited with thinking through—in a body of work that spans decades—philosophy's commitment to that divide. In fact, Agamben notes with a bit of hyperbole, "The decisive political conflict, which governs every other conflict, is that between the animality and the humanity of man. . . . In its origin Western politics is also biopolitics."[38] This pronouncement does a great deal of work, especially if you are a "man," a bearer of rights, one who both goes to war as well as produces the law that insists on its necessity. But the management of "bare life," as Agamben puts it, the achievement of humanity (history's end) through a suspension of animality in a post-Holocaust context could license the absenting of a racialized and gendered politic (an argument that Charles Mills and Carole Pateman would support), turning biopolitical concern into a dialogue among men.[39] Here, biopolitics simply supports as well as masks the central contest within the boundary of the human. One could be generous and say that Agamben is merely supporting my position by recognizing the humanity/animality of man as a central and therefore problematic conflict (a biopolitics) and abandoning the metaphysical imperative of qualitative distinction between animal and (hu)man. If this is the case, why not name, via example (and philosophy is most at risk when it ventures into the "real"), events or moments when the animality of man and the inefficacy of distinction loom large on the horizon of ideas?

If we take blackness as our subject between 1474 and 1834, can we now speak of the inquiry around the animal, the human in the same manner? Do catastrophic events change our focus? The answer would be "yes" for Mr. Davis, guardian of one of the chimps in the story I turn to in the next part of this chapter. Perhaps we falter when the lens is turned in our direction, because we can say to ourselves, as Judith Butler surmises in the aftermath of September 11: "There is no history of acts that is relevant to the self-understanding we form in the light of these terrible events. There is no relevant prehistory to the events . . . since to begin to tell the story a different way, to ask how things came to this, is already to complicate the questions of agency."[40] Butler is spot on about how *events* "complicate the questions of agency"; and she is as discerning in her accounts of catastrophe's epistemology as we are about most traumatic events: to have a "past," to have an auto/biography, is to tell *an* other story, to change the terms of the debate altogether. Instead of recognizing the devastation of 9/11 along a continuum of events, call them transatlantic slave trade, potato famine, and Indian removal, we isolate them, understanding what's at stake without a past or a future, but a continuous present that unfolds as if time stood still—we take space and occupy it, we displace people, with something called "strategery [*sic*]," and "the war on terror"—we are enmeshed in a Jamesian pragmatics.[41]

The hum/animal distinction has no real use for an assessment of the animal, in itself. Its building blocks are *difference*: capacity, language, and, yes, suffering, a collective discourse of opposition which comes ever close to animal life, but nonetheless, cannot *see* "it." It is an astounding lack of the very capacity that produces the dominance of the human in the first (and only?) order of *things*.[42] Derrida writes: "I am saying 'they,' 'what they call an animal,' in order to mark clearly the fact that I have always secretly exempted myself from that world, and to indicate that my whole history, the whole genealogy of my questions, in truth everything I am, follow, think, write, trace, erase even, seems to me to be born from that exceptionalism and incited by that sentiment of election."[43] That secrecy is a confederacy of sorts; this "exceptionalism" in regard to "the animal" is a problem for philosophy, and it is found more succinctly in Heidegger, where "the animal" is poor-in-world and Dasein is the particular expression of the human being of Being and is world-forming. To even think "the animal" is to remove oneself from the possibility of being an animal; that removal is both the insult and the impediment, right? The achievement of a recognizably *diverse* world would require the suspension of the boundary known as hum/animal *and* a subsequent acknowledgement of kinds of white power—whose practitioners are not always already white—that hold it in place. This dual dismantling is necessary but hardest to achieve.

We must remember that Derrida's investigation in his work proceeds by enjambment—our thoughts, naked before the animal and the following/being followed, bring about displays of gender difference, and at times connote (hetero)sexual desire.[44] One concept falls upon another as we nip at the heels of the animal nipping at our heels; we clearly try to fuck one *another*. But Derrida's concern is with the animal as it loops back to us, hails us, and *considers* us. What to make of that gaze and our inability to register its possibility in any philosophical discourse worth remarking upon? Unmaking the human, a category shored up again and again in philosophy and rendering it vulnerable takes a great deal of *force*.[45]

To be unmade, to stand in the open, facing *an* other as who and what they/we are is to rid the human of the juxtaposition necessary to make taxonomy matter, is to stage the warring debate between ontology and ethics. I would suggest that MOVE stages as a praxis the problem of ethics and ontology; theirs is a messy crosscurrent of being *and* committed doing and seeing. In all of the mighty theoretical texts I have marshaled to answer this question of hum:animal, there is no real place for letting be. Critics, philosophers, and erstwhile judges want something to replace the black hole that metaphysics will leave behind when it takes its leave of us. What if what is left (behind/following) is simply what there has always been, for MOVE, for Baby Suggs in that Clearing, for Calvin *still* (and perhaps satiated) in Washington, D.C.: a being *together* (hum:animal) indescribable as method in this world, but surely a concerted practice, always already *here*? A diversity of being and doing. The group. A collective.

While I might not always agree that blackness is an ontological negation in the metaphysics (not because I stubbornly want to believe in Black joy, but because there is a hitch in the paradigm's relationship to *gender* or a lingering femaleness that will not rest or go away), I also struggle to account for Black being in a system in which the ontology's violence produces *nothing* out of solid matter, and the practice of seeing blackness in an ethical face-to-face paradigm is always already unobtainable. Perhaps the answer does not lie in human thought, but in the thought of the nonhuman animal, unmaking hum/animal difference through acts of *strategic* dismemberment. It is to this simple and messy pleasure (?) of disarticulating *flesh* that I turn to. I present the following argument because of these foregoing, sometimes *elemental* pressures. In this next assessment, diversity hits the ground, running.

....

March 2005. In southern California—about thirty miles east of Bakersfield—a few chimpanzees are one chromosome away from making history. Several years before 2005, a husband-wife team relinquished their family member Moe to Animal Haven Ranch after a shocking incident involving a houseguest and a severed finger.[46] They had mounted an unsuccessful legal challenge to get their chimp back home with them in West Covina, California.[47] One of the signs held up by St. James Davis during a protest for Moe's return to them in 2000 reads: "'Moe' Belongs with his Family."[48] Five years later, upon arriving with a birthday cake to celebrate Moe's thirty-ninth, they are overjoyed to see the chimp. In the course of their visit, they notice that the door to the adjacent primate cage is ajar. No worries, they have that one chromosome that says "mastery." What unfolds next is truly horrific and bloody, as two of the male chimps at the rescue—Buddy, 15, and Ollie, 13—close in on the master and divest him of the following body parts: "all the fingers from both hands, an eye, part of his nose, cheek, lips, his buttocks [and his testicles]."[49]

There are several lessons here, and two of the most general kind are: *don't turn your back on the open door*, and *animals are dangerous*. The Kern County Sheriff's Department commander Hal Chealander remarked on the incident: "What provoked the chimpanzees was something from within the chimpanzees. Whether it was jealousy or some other primal factor, it was something within their own makeup that triggered this."[50] In another more comprehensive story in the *Los Angeles Times*, reporters interviewed "ape expert" Deborah Fouts, director of the Chimp and Human Communication Institute at Central Washington University, who said, "It sounds like people were showering a lot of attention on Moe, birthday cake and the like. . . . Perhaps the other chimps were jealous of Moe."[51] *L.A. Times* reporters Pierson and Landsberg reiterated Fouts's claim by surmising that "the attack may have been prompted by an emotion chimps may share with humans: jealousy." What these various media accounts do is assume the chimps' behavior is both similar to ours and something apart from who we are. When it comes to the animal's *response*, our interpretations equivocate. The landscape of opinion is sharpened by this chimp episode, where the *diversity* of opinion is widely and, yes, violently articulated.

There are several moments across news sources worthy of attention in this chimp response, but particularly in the extended pieces in the *L.A. Times*: the almost obsessive concern with the behavior of humans and their great ape cousins is evident as each story toggles from experts to eye witness accounts attempting to find the *causal* relationship among events leading up to the devaluation of Mr. St. James's human real estate. And that causal relationship is marked by distinctions—the height of the chimps as compared to human beings is noted in the copy and in dual diagrams outlining the places in the facility where Mr. Davis's dismemberment begins and ends (figure 3.1). But the most notable distinction is outlined in *Washington Post* reporter Amy Argetsinger's analysis in the aftermath of the attack: "For the ugly truth is that these kinds of attacks are quite common—in the wild, against other chimpanzees [*pan troglodyte*]. Males are highly territorial; if threatened, they will shred a rival's genitals, rip out his windpipe."[52] Boys will be boys indeed. Clearly the strike on the Davises while visiting their family member struck a nerve with human being. The struggle to understand what would make members of one's family pounce on one another—on a macrolevel, humans, and on a microlevel, the Davises—reproduces a fine line of distinction that is traversed multiple times in search of answers. In fact, the animal does respond, decisively with the mother of all bombs, taking out the reproductive life of his cousin, devaluing all that makes "human" in the first instance.

Powerful primates

State and Kern County authorities continue to investigate how two male chimpanzees attacked and injured two people visiting another chimp, Moe.

Chimpanzee
(Pantroglodytes)

Weight: 100 to 120 pounds

Height standing: 4 to 5.5 feet

Diet: Plant material, insects

Strength: About five times that of humans.

Lifespan: 55 to 60 years

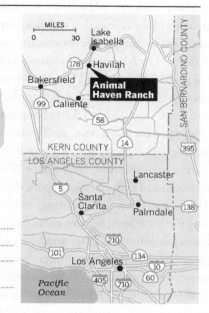

Where attack took place

This is an approximate layout of the area of the Animal Haven Ranch where six chimpanzees were housed before the attack:

❶ Four chimps leave through side of their cage. Moe and a sixth chimp stay caged.

❷ The four chimps enter the house. Owner detains two females, but the two males leave.

❸ Attack occurs by table where St. James Davis and his wife are celebrating Moe's 39th birthday. When the two male chimps are shot and killed by the owner's son-in-law, the two females run off and are later recovered.

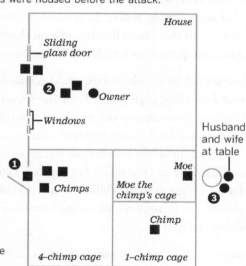

3.1 "Where the Attack Took Place," *Los Angeles Times*, March 5, 2005.

No small surprise then that research scholar and science writer Vanessa Woods also notes the Moe birthday party attack in her 2010 memoir, *Bonobo Handshake: A Memoir of Love and Adventure in the Congo*. Hers is a scientist's approach and she affirms that violence over territory, females, and rival males is consistent in chimpanzee community and that the cause of such squabbles is identical in *both* human and chimp social worlds contexts. As the life partner of primatologist Brian Hare, Woods conducted experiments among the bonobo (*pan paniscus*) great apes in the Congo with Hare for the better part of two years. Compared to their chimp cousins, the bonobo, with whom we share 98.7 percent of our DNA, are "female-dominated . . . they committed very little violence."[53] They also enjoy sexual contact with one another as a regular part of their sociality. The work of Woods and Hare is important to this study because of their questions about the members of the great ape category and specifically how human being, as a cousin to bonobo and chimpanzee among the great apes, became more *like* chimpanzees than bonobos in our social organization. As Hare and Shinya Yamamoto report: "Understanding how bonobos and chimpanzees diverged from one another can allow for inference about cognitive evolution in similar traits in our own species."[54]

In this scientific world, the extractive process often hinges on the usefulness of cognitive information about bonobos *for* their human cousins. And yet, with less than 3 percent difference between human and bonobo DNA, the *usefulness* cuts both ways here. Woods is painfully aware of the extractive nature of animal study. Before the account of Moe's birthday party bloodbath, she recalls that Hare's first research on chimpanzees in Uganda dealt with nine chimpanzee attacks. She then muses:

> Many animals kill members of their kind. A male deer might mortally wound a rival. Even rabbits fight to the death over territory. But a group of bunnies will not go into enemy territory to hunt down another bunny. They don't form a gang and hold down the victim and punch and kick him and break his legs and rip off his testicles and scream in cruel triumph. They don't drink his blood and tear off his fingernails. It takes a certain amount of intelligence to get the bone-chilling satisfaction of causing so much pain to someone else. It requires sophisticated emotions that resemble hatred and jealousy and spite.[55]

Woods is speaking to human *and* chimpanzee violence. The similarity among two species of great apes and their organized violence is astonishing. It should tell us that who we are as a species is less about qualitative differences among us in the family of great apes and more about articulating who we are through patterned and sustained practices, often violent ones. These chimpanzee strikes cohere on two fronts: reproductive capacity and heteropatriarchal force. You cannot bring entire communities to heel without interfering with their ability to engage in an embodied future. Reproduction must be managed and violently, if necessary. The difference that the bonobo make is that they are *queer* to the core, they do not participate in the management of parts and their competitive value, they acknowledge the place of the mother, the life that should matter most if they are to secure any kind of future for themselves.[56]

The illusion of human-ity at the apex of *being* itself is produced through practiced war. Reflecting on what marks difference among human being, I can see that racism is an organizing principle that is not a distraction, but a necessary war for obfuscating the potentiality of our species and its crucial *intersectional*—think *diverse* (ity)—life. In that moment when the violence that makes distinction is offered to us, when the whip is extended to us, can we (ethically) commit to a refusal, one in which our survival over that of *an* other is not secured? Can such a moment actually produce sustained life-in-as-future, rather than its annihilation?[57] What to make of an ethical life, a life worth living that does not support human being as its principal and principled subject? My concern here echoes Haraway's feeling: "Those whose social definition of identity is rooted in the system of racism will not be able to see that the definition of human has not been neutral, and cannot be until major material-social changes occur on a world scale."[58] I explore one of Haraway's most significant, in my opinion, and often railed-at publications, *Primate Visions: Gender, Race and Nature in the World of Modern Science* (1989) in the next arc of this chapter's argument.

....

A life worth living or a kind of living that Aristotle once posited with curiosity at its center. A living among the living, by the living and for the living, regardless of capacity or difference articulated in capacity, or being or language. Racist practice is the vain art of the terrified-to-know. A knowing manifest in that ontological terror that Calvin Warren tracks in his book by the same title. One that can be redirected if we incline our heads, track our vision ever so slightly off center and forge the beginnings of an ethical life. The ethical commitment that Levinas proposes, but ultimately fails at is a face-to-face encounter that lacks vision—it is human-centered and inept. To avoid war, one must signal something beyond the kind of simple cooperation that builds skyscrapers and produces vaccines; for the whole of our community of the living to survive, we must incline our heads slightly to some *other* in the shared terrain in which we are out standing, to some *other*, *an* other we cannot see or whom our science cannot hold. We must have vision without sight. This gesture perhaps returns us to that insurgent self.

Somewhere in this story of bonobo difference, and human striving is the story of the mothers—the Congolese women who bond with the bonobo babies and are the heart of the nursery at Lola ya Bonobo, and the group of bonobo females who organize to take care of and defend their young. Woods explains the bonobo female-centered society that she observes: "Most mothers defend their young, but rarely will five unrelated females flock to help them."[59] I am thinking here of the unrelated females in the MOVE organization and their children (hum:animal); I am thinking about what happens when a group of women/mothers steps outside of the order of things, and begins to think differently about, perhaps even reject the ontological grounding of (human) relation in *being* itself, a category that then births *becoming* as a possibility yoked recursively to the very essence of what it means to be *human*. A dog chases its tail, but gladly.

Cheeky, yes, to compare women, some of them Black, to great apes. Disastrous though for human being for us to consider our way of being (literally) as above reproach and as adequate comparison among a whole host of beings adjacent, invested and, yes, integral to our very matter-ing on this planet. By now you will have surmised that I am thoroughly uninterested in racist comparisons of African-descended people to apes that continue the logic of the *distinction* to the detriment of hum:animal. My observations around "like" for "as" in the first chapter of this book expose the dangers of this interest in comparison at the same time that the last chapter of this book briefly recalls being *like* and its impact on how blackness, how indigeneity, can be seen. In an essay on animal rights, Catherine MacKinnon observes that "the primary model of animal rights to date . . . misses animals on their own terms, just as the same tradition has missed women on theirs. If this is right, seeking animal rights on a 'like-us' model of sameness may be misconceived, unpersuasive, and counterproductive."[60] A reliance on "sameness" serves both to obscure African contributions to the lives of our not-so-distant cousins, curtailing our understanding of our relatives with a paradigmatic and violent chokehold, and for the purposes of my work here, most interestingly, to detract from what being *female* can tell us about hum/animal distinction.

I prefer to think with the mothers, the insurgent females, and the queers who follow just to the left of that hind, resisting the *auto* in autobiogra-

phy, moving toward a biomythography—a story we tell as we go along together, neither becoming or being with, but possibly, just possibly, always
insurgent. Diversity substantiates difference and produces its replication in
and through an ordering that eschews the *intersectional*. Diversity produces
the very scarcity it seeks, and in its wake, it drags gender and reproduction
as emblematic and value-laden aspects of its particular force in the world.
Now, one could say that this chimp strike reifies our male-centered and
reproductive inhibiting naturecultures. But what it does for this line of argument is point out the inaccuracies of our own settled notions of who we
are and how we come into our being together.

mother love

> Motherhood, while it does not exhaust the problematics of female gender,
> offers one prominent line of approach to it.
> **HORTENSE SPILLERS**, "Mama's Baby, Papa's Maybe" (1987)

> Deeds, as opposed to words, are the parents of facts.
> **DONNA HARAWAY**, *Primate Visions* (1989)

> In the end, if fate is just a roll of the die and you could be born anywhere, to
> any family in the world, if you look at the odds, who would you rather be?
> Most of the time, bonobos have no hunger, no violence, no poverty. And for
> all of our intelligence, all our *things*, bonobos have the most important of all
> possessions—peace.
> **VANESSA WOODS**, *Bonobo Handshake* (2010)

> Reproductive labor is the work necessary to the reproduction of human
> life—not only having and raising children but also feeding people; car-
> ing for the sick, the elderly, and those who cannot work; creating safety
> and shelter; building community and kin relationships and attending to
> people's psychic and spiritual well-being.
> **LAURA BRIGGS**, *How All Politics Became Reproductive Politics* (2017)

I sit and read through Donna Haraway's stunning, *Primate Visions* and take
note of the fact that the copy of the book now in my possession has been
"withdrawn from the London School of Economics Library." Cheeky that.
Nonetheless, since gender is on my mind, Haraway's book is essential in
teasing out how primatology evolved as a field in lockstep with gender and

race. She starts out by asking: "How do the terrible marks of gender and race enable and constrain love and knowledge in particular cultural traditions? Who may contest for what the body of nature will be?"[61] She is one of the cisgendered female researchers who speaks of "love and knowledge," and I have mirrored her approach to intellectual journeys in hum:animal with the beginnings of this project in "accident" and "love." It is at this point rather pedestrian in the course of feminist scholarship on science to understand the world of experiment and observation as an *objective* world; and yet, we continue to posit such fictions in our approach to that hallowed ground called "science." What we have is a diversity of players, but a field in which scaled value is the operating force. How can we get to the truth of what the animal said or does in the hot mess that is *scientific inquiry*? She continues: "Never innocent, the visualizing narrative 'technology' of this book draws from contemporary theories of cultural production, historical and social studies of science and technology, and feminist and anti-racist movements and theories to craft a view of nature as it is constructed and reconstructed in the bodies and lives of 'third world' animals serving as surrogates for 'man.'"[62] It is indeed a messy soup. For Haraway, the animal is relegated to that third world of othering, a provenance that is now surely passé, but one that beckons us to consider animal worlds alongside "human" ones— or at least to consider that the construction of animal and human might be one and the same.[63]

Woods's work is indebted to Haraway's *Primate Visions*, a work that infuriated primatologists and scientists alike because of its often meandering but also pointed critique of the history of anthropological science for its lack of attention to gender and race and for its naturalization of the white male subject at the center of scientific inquiry as expert and master of mastery.[64] It is a first and early attempt (1989) by a theorist to think with Foucault's paradigm of the biopolitical as a structuring logic for our approach to hum:animal, and in this regard it is a feminist classic.[65] But even to say this is to remind myself of Haraway's central point: that primatology, in particular, does not develop without feminist concern; to the contrary, "the marked bodies of race, class, and sex have been at the center, not the margins, of knowledge in modern conditions."[66] One of Haraway's central findings is that the shift in primate study that occurs sometime in the late 1970s, early 1980s, is precipitated by the work of women scientists like Barbara Smuts, trained in the new sociobiological studies and fixing their eyes upon female primates and their worlds.[67] As we move to untangle the knot of hum:animal we find gender surely, not as a byproduct—something left behind, a trace—of some prior system, but a cornerstone of existence *in difference*, to begin with. Gender breaks upon us as a simultaneity—something that Spillers tracks so beautifully in "Mama's Baby." Just as we cannot untangle gender-as-sexual difference from hum/animal distinction, as Derrida reminds us, we also cannot forget, as Spillers argues, "female" seems to track with "mother" for the foreseeable future, and together the two make up this complicated *gender* that feminists have come to know and love on. How then can a question of the human and the animal proceed without some attention to the *mother*? And if and when we do pay attention to *this gendered constellation* and its trace, reproduction, how might we find ourselves situated?

The strategic great ape strike that stands as a central concern in my previous discussion of it understands, as does Laura Briggs, that *reproduction* is indeed at the center of all politics. Politics constitutes cultural belongings and hierarchies of value. This monograph understands that primate strike as a core *political* act. Buddy and Ollie, teenagers engaged in making a point about what's *just*, speak to their great ape cousins in a mutual language, divesting their mark of the makings of the human and its point of origin. In a political system built on inequality, which is a violence in and of itself, the work of reproductive violence is the trace of all politics. Hum/animal life is articulated, I would argue, not just through ontological proofs that pertain to B/beings, or taxonomies that create something called the "human," but also through a much wider spectrum of ordering that puts pressure on the distinction and consistently calls to the foreground its gendered trace.

When we think about hum:animal life and its management—if management, to echo Derrida, is after all about *politics*—then we inevitably rely upon gender to do some heavy lifting—the reproductive work that Laura Briggs so eloquently points us toward. Work that remains so very meaningful, but invisible nonetheless. So, the Pandora's box that opens is in the messiness that is Haraway's signature, and in many ways, Spillers's too, as each of these feminist critics is liable to borrow from a number of disparate "texts" to make their central point: there is no signal or signature corruption or political system without the drag of gender in its wake. At the same time, *gender* is hard to track, slippery even, in its ability to matter in sex/gender on the one hand and through reproduction on the other. The best way to be successful, at least critically, is to produce a universal category (otherwise known as man) and to forget HER altogether.[68] That gender might still matter to us is upsetting, to say the least, having attempted to rid ourselves from it for the better part of a half century of feminist work. But the insurgence that Spillers sees in Black femaleness at the end of that important essay is one of the crucial persona (I use the Latin here purposefully)—fictive or once living—to and for unlocking hum:animal.

In truth, our knowledge of hum/animal distinction is bound up with gender and race, Haraway argues, so that the study of what is closest to human being in the "animal" world is not an inquiry that can proceed without attention to either. And yet, time and again, gender *and* race seem to not be able to hold together for any length of time in our critical analyses of hum:animal. In addition, when feminists commence to talking about mother. love., very little attention is paid to Black thought in general, and in Haraway's extensive study she takes note of the paucity of Black female primatologists and bemoans the pseudoracist science found in *National Geographic*, but we will not see her engage the thoughts or words of Black women in particular. They are a scientific rarity, at least professionally speaking. This persona, for Haraway, is truly a fiction, as the footnote to the following statement—"It would hardly do to address this specific 'white' dilemma, which has global consequences, with a woman of color, scientist or not"—reveals that Haraway's "woman of color" is the computer scientist character, Velma, in Toni Cade Bambara's *The Salt Eaters*.[69] But while I am critical of this move, I also note that Haraway perhaps follows in the footsteps of Black feminist critique that has as its object and proof a propensity to blur fact and fiction. We get there by any means necessary.

At the end of her lengthy exegesis in *Primate Visions*, Haraway returns to science fiction and the awakening of a new African-descended mother in Octavia Butler's *Dawn*. While there is no real-life character of this kind that can populate a (white) feminist theory about our deep species kinship, fiction is nonetheless a potent end point. While the queer child has no-future, and we can thank Lee Edelman for that, the Black child (the mother goes without saying?) not only is going to be all right but also is a necessity for species survival.[70] This species is no longer homo sapiens but something altogether new; a new materialism in the flesh. Perhaps what *reproduction is for* at the end of our investigation of the thorny signature that is the hum/animal distinction is to produce that rarity of *being* who(?) lives outside of ontology's temporal vacuum of competing no-thing-ness, chipping away at a boundary's constant reinvigoration.

If, as Haraway suggests, "In myriad, mundane ways, primatology is a practice for the negotiation of the possibility of community, of a public world, of rational action. It is the negotiation of the time of origins, the origin of the family, the boundary between self and other, hominid and hominoid, human and animal," then the kind of strategic dismemberment that the chimp attack that opens these musings points toward is indeed instructive.[71] What possibilities of community, of public worlds(s) or even rational action does great ape violence gesture toward? I am interested in this "primate" strike for its more literary meaning and terrible irony: each strike represents the valued difference between the human and the animal; each strike narrows the distance between man and animal; produces a reminder of an uncomfortable belonging. If the nose is the defining feature of the (human face), and the prehensile thumb is what binds us to the other apes (chimpanzees, gorillas, and orangutans) and reproduction is the sacred cow of human being's survival, then this was no random battery but a decisive blow—a bomb that falls with precision—the mother of all bombs. In this case, the letter has a destination and its arrival is punctuated by a spectacular and pointed delivery. In the above scene, the chimp, once part of the human family, now exiled, cannot be drawn back into "it"—he resists incorporation or at least civilizing behavior that is required for reunification. He resists civil society and its politics through a spectacular display of bad management. Or put another way, he eviscerates the human in order to become part of it again—creating another kind of togetherness, another way of being (together). Creating or opening up, to return to Grosz's words that frame the beginning of this chapter, another kind of *knowledge* about diversity. One we cannot bear to gaze upon. This view of ourselves is unflattering; it lacks *vision.* Our flesh is exposed.

Perhaps the question ought not be about which ape we emulate, so that we can somehow set the course of human history right. Instead, the question should be, as Grosz observes elsewhere, "how to expand the variety of activities, including the activities of knowledge production, so that women and men may be able to act differently."[72] Again, we have the tension between being and doing, between ontology and ethics, between male and female as at least partners in a *politic.* Whatever the philosophical register, the question remains: can the "thing" outside the human be reintegrated, without a substantial and violent tweaking of the system that once held it at arm's length? Violence makes this system, and only violence can end it—this is the turn toward the tautological that Wilderson's assessment of Black revolutionary film supports. Once the taxonomic shell game is revealed, then the question of reintegration is moot. What if there is just *life*, a single referent, and every other difference is simply beauty or function or awe? Unbeknownst to her, Rosi Braidotti reiterates a central claim in African American insurgent expression with the following proposition: "'life itself' as a form of active ethical citizenship."[73] Fusing discussions of the biopolitical, medical technologies, and modes of belonging (race, gender, nature), Braidotti steps into the space of doing rather than *doing to*, a less hierarchical call attended to in Black practical thought. So much of what makes human being elevated matter above their great ape cousins is brought low in this chimpanzee attack. The strategic nature of this strike turns animal magnetism—what draws us to another—into attempted murder. I am not unaware of the gendered nature of the above strike—and I'll get to this in my examination of the film *Equilibrium* (2002) in the next section ("puppies") of this chapter.

I want to end with the depart/ed testicles, with reproduction's (lost?) potential. The reproductive challenge starts for me with a footnote in Karen Barad's *Meeting the Universe Halfway* (2007) and extends itself into the pages of Jane Bennett's *Vibrant Matter* (2010). Providing the citation for her rehearsal of feminist criticisms of Simone de Beauvoir's feminist classic *The Second Sex*, Barad tells us that her chapter on biology may be "usefully meditated on by contemporary feminists in order to help recalibrate the possibilities for direct engagement with the body's biology."[74] Somewhere in this messy mix, ontology, ethics, and new materialism meet. Later, Barad puts a finer point on the problem of our engagement with the effects of power on embodied subjects. She notes that Bruno Latour has called for "a new parliamentary structure that invites non-humans as well as humans," but then she worries: "but what, if anything, does this proposal do to address the kinds of concerns that feminist, queer, postcolonial, (post)Marxist, and critical race theorists and activists have brought to the table."[75] First, we do not find out what those concerns are, exactly, yet they are marshaled to call out Latour for his myopic vision or at least its paternalistic parts.

This constellation of vulnerable others, in Barad, is invested with a plural concern that produces itself as an *affective* minority, when given the group's numbers, it would seem that if they have any *concerns* at all, they are certainly in the majority. What kind of politics construes these questions as a minority view, brought to an already constructed table, rather than culled from the principal table itself? But most egregiously, time and again, what stops us from reconsidering the hum/animal distinction with any amount of rigor is because of well . . . everyone else excluded from the category "human," outside the boundaries of the rational. This is infuriating and presumes that only white subjects (as Wilderson surmises in *Red, White & Black*) have thought about or cared about hum:animal worlds. This critical worry over what the folks in the balcony might say—and our persistent understanding of *that* world of worry as the only one in play—gives incredible purchase to the supremacy's will-to-power.

The central question about life itself is a thorny one, and it is not my objective to solve the feminist abortion problem or to determine through philosophical sleight of hand just what life means, is, or does. Though, I do want to offer here that Agamben's call for "letting be" and MOVE's practice of the same are more than instructive and noteworthy. My purpose here is simply to move beyond the blood/brain barrier of racialized thought around hum:animal and throw somewhat of a spotlight on those moments when the animal *responds* and when human being attempts to do things as hum:animal. In short, by thinking through gender and its relationship to the distinction (hum/animal) as foundational, we must also come upon the edges of reproduction's capacity. Its capacity is certainly at play in both Spillers's reading of an antebellum Black past and a Black future that can be articulated through femaleness. How might we as feminists (but not as other critics?) come to really understand the "body's biology"?

I return to Jane Bennett's discussion of "the culture of life" in evangelical belief. When life begins at the cellular level is the object of discussion, and in this conservative politics of life, former congressional representative Tom Delay notes that the objection to stem cell research is in "the dismemberment of living, distinct human beings for the purposes of medical experimentation"[76] Use of the word "dismemberment" catches my eye each time I read Bennett's text as does the "living, distinct human beings" part and I can't help but think (again) of those chimps and their strategic dismemberment, of the disarticulation made possible in the abattoir and at the end of the hanging rope; of how hum:animal is bound together in an interminable arc of dismemberment—a rendering unto meat/flesh that ensnares us all. In a "culture of life" argument where all life is supposed to matter, notes Bennett, it is strange to see the proliferation of processes of dismemberment and, yes, war. The distinction that matters here is *in* human being, but Delay is ignorant of the processes of dismemberment that always already accrue in the making of such a category of being.

Bennett tracks the *Evangelium Vitae* put forth by Pope John Paul II in 1995 and utilized by "non-Catholic evangelicals," as an enduring approach to the matter of "life." Her aim is to tease out, selectively, several distinctions among matter, vital force, freedom, and soul. The more theologically inclined believe in a soul, imbued with the particular power of an almighty who then sets the human self above others; the more scientifically engaged understand "the vitalistic nature of all being."[77] For those more inclined toward value-driven hierarchies of life, the public policy impact of maintaining and implementing a "culture of life" is staggering. For my purposes, the vitalist-scientifically driven version seems to be the most in line with "foundation of life" or "life as a single referent" ideas, where all beings possess a vitalistic nature—matter itself, hum:animal—such that the killing of another is not about moral code or sovereign right but requires concerted, even at times *tactile*, ethical relation, made not because of the dictates of a culture, seen and unseen, but from a comfortability with what one cannot know. It is the best use of our thinking selves and the most controversial. It is thinking through insurgence. It is thinking queerly every time. All the time.

It is noteworthy that each policy Bennett names is bounded by a gendered distinction. She writes: "The culture of life has been invoked to support legislation to keep a feeding tube inserted into a woman whose brain had ceased, to restrict access by minors to abortion and to outlaw certain modes of abortion, as well as to oppose federal funding for embryonic stem cell research."[78] All politics is indeed reproductive and therefore gendered politics, female politics. Is "female" gender at all or something altogether different? I think this might be the natural outcome of Spillers's assessment.

Reproduction fascinates me here and I spend time with both Barad's call to reassess "the body's biology," and Bennett's brief work with "culture of life" to put some small pressure on the problem of biological reproduction for theories of being that denote, always, the notion of the singular, autonomous individual—note the terms "living" and "distinct" from above that define human being. Note also the pressure such musings might put on that earlier explication of Haile Gerima's *Bush Mama*—Dorothy's ending monologue, the woman with child on her hip just over her shoulder might represent the *issue* that reproduction brings to the table of liberation's ideals. There is no way around it, so Dorothy writes a letter to T.C., and the scene of her reading this intimate communication to us drags the reproductive life and living of Black insurgent females into the frame. It ungrounds the autonomous subject in fiction and in life—as Dorothy's story is a fiction, but the bush mama's is not—asking us to see *an* other way forward.

Reproduction presents a problem for a feminism wedded to *an* embodied life, and an antiblackness that sees itself without a body that coheres. While this might seem like a good antiabortion argument, the focus here is not on the outcome of such recognition of *an* other inside or part of, or dependent on the self, but the acknowledgement that there are always other beings inside the psychic container we call self—helping us to think, feel, and act. Their collective being, which is our being too, is not a matter of debate limited to binaries of life or death or over/coming, but a matter of a nimble embrace of the kind of death structured by living, not as a singular substance, but one among many. Cocreating. This radical *intra*dependence is what *life* means in insurgent thought. Out of that *intra*dependence comes the insurgent, on a freedom quest, perhaps, decidedly female, who refuses the overseer's whip. Every time. All the time.

Might that container of life or self *counter* a Kantian proposition where the only benefit of anticruelty toward other beings is in the potential uplift of the human self, where the dispensation of justice is relevant only for its effect on human being?[79] This was certainly one of the considerations among early animal studies practitioners in moral and ethical philosophy where the proliferating questions were about moral reasoning in the killing of animals, and one of them was most certainly whether or not the maltreatment or killing of animals had a negative effect on human beings.[80] For example, the question "can the animal suffer" is saturated in the overvaluation of the human, *its* self-interest, and its capacity to world. It is a superfluous question that upholds a bankrupt standard. A consideration where not just some lives but all lives literally are matter (animate, animated, or inert) worth considering for their own sake, might lead to more fruitful grounding for the end of politics as we know it where the *political* is in and of itself a process of control centered on reproductive lives. To eschew the political or the "ethico-politico," as Povinelli and Jackson describe it—to shear ethical action from its political circumstances (always already grounded in the human), might leave a fissure in the order of things.[81]

In fact, it is the African-descended mother's situatedness, as bearer of children, as giver of ontological status, as the one who stands outside the law, that Spillers finds worthy of a lengthy and complicated exegesis. The purpose of the exegesis is not to answer but to ask questions—and so many abound at the end of Spillers's text. It has taken (Black) feminists decades to unravel their meaning. The question of life itself is always already situated in the embodied persona of the female. How she obtains in gender and as gender, as a substance (accountable to a world, mistaken for *the* world) is bound by difference mapped onto hum:animal. *That* story is not an autobiography, but a *bio*mythography that awaits us. Barad reminds us that "nonhuman creatures" in Beauvoir are simply "*slaves* [emphasis mine] to their biology," again reiterating as Haraway proposed throughout *Primate Visions* that our vocabularies of gender, race, class, and the animal are bound together in web-like formation; we pluck one string and the whole vibrates—this is the situatedness of science itself. Almost twenty years later, physicist and feminist scientist Barad offers, optimistically, "Agential realism takes into account the fact that the forces at work in the materialization of bodies are not only social and the bodies produced are not all human."[82]

Barad also notes that "questions of space, time, and matter are intimately connected, indeed entangled, with questions of *justice*."[83] But again, this question of justice is bound by the *giving*—as if life itself were not always already just. What is justice in the face of ethical life? Are they one and the same? Is one the goal, and the other its practice? And is the meting out of justice a matter of gendered practices, sedimented and long-standing? Brian Luke, writing for a collection of feminist ethics of care essays observes that "justice" and "caring" are different avenues of approach to animal liberation; one is the focus on fairness, interest, and claims, the other emphasizes connection, responsiveness, and "satisfaction of needs."[84] If we take the violence represented by the culture of life that Bennett so astutely remarks upon—to sustain the life/world of the embryo at the same time that this life/world is sustained by acts of war—then the question of what *just*ice is or looks like, for us and those chimps at Animal Haven Ranch—is always at the fore. The remaining question certainly is, though Derrida has answered it in part with his force of law claim and Wilderson has answered it in the revolutionary call of African-descended masculinity: can violence be a way through/toward justice? The question of the hum:animal sits squarely in the territory of what justice means and is. My next meditation on puppies explores this possibility of the ethical action that produces what is or can be considered "just." If we remember that *just* can be "exactly" and "barely," the possibilities for *just*ice are varied and several. And what of that "mother love" with which I began this part? The work of diversity is ostensibly to produce justice, as diversity provides the opportunity for justice at face value. From the vantage point of the human, diversity is a competitive gamble that sets the world on its end. This next exploration thinks through modes of justice in contestation.

puppies

The dusty boxes I explored on my research trips invariably disclosed disturbing, if not horrific, images and lurid descriptions of animal abuse through the ages—an emaciated, dying workhorse; a burned and beaten kitten; a macabre experiment that grafted the head of a puppy to its mother. As abolitionists had done before them, animal advocates devoted

significant organizational resources to countless publications, photographs, and lectures that emphasized the visual and often shocking aspects
of cruelty. They knew that sympathetic media coverage of the gruesome
and the dramatic sometimes reaped significant public and political support
and generated the momentum for change.
DIANE L. BEERS, *For the Prevention of Cruelty* (2006)

Justice requires suffering. Two tales, both of them entail no small amount
of truth telling. But each instructive for our attention to those puppies
and the matter of justice; of how to make justice happen in real time.[85] It
is time for dinner during pandemic, and my queer family and I gather in a
Durham neighborhood, a traditionally African-descended part of the city,
now being gentrified as was much of the city in the wake of the restaurant
boom of the mid-2010s. On their tiny street, my large truck is an annoy-
ance, but I am happy this time that I have parked it respectfully off the
road, and nearly into a drainage ditch and precariously close to a neighbor's
mailbox. I am always having to apologize. We sit outside as the meal is in
stages of preparation and we finger the place our masks used to be; I am
annoyed by a barking dog. I follow that obstreperousness to a cage on the
front porch of the house on a slight diagonal across the street. I am a bit
mortified. Is this usual? My friends explain that the dog used to be inside a
lot, and then, perhaps after a catastrophic failure of potty training, the dog
was placed outside, in the small cage. I asked them if they had spoken with
the neighbors and/or tried to intervene? They found themselves at a bit
of a loss, not knowing the neighbors' immigration status and not wanting
to call any kind of police. I wholly agreed, and it got uncomfortable when
one friend remarked that "Bobby" had a cat friend who came to visit, so
his situation wasn't all that awful. I quickly cut in with an irritated "let's
call cruelty, cruelty and not dress it up as something else because it makes
us feel better." Awkward; even good people when confronted with the clear
suffering of *an* other will resort to explaining it away; few humans act, as
animals, on matters of justice.

But as the conversation continued and the dog's whining bark accompanied us into the evening, I asked about the name for the dog and they said it
was a name that someone in the neighborhood gave him and it caught on,
so he became Bobby. Someone must be reading their Levinas. I was amused.
I remembered the now famous story that Levinas tells in *Difficult Freedom*
that several philosophers have dwelled upon with no small amount of relish.

It is a short piece, a tale from Levinas's time in a "forestry commando unit for Jewish prisoners of war in Nazi Germany."[86] He writes:

> And then, about halfway through our long captivity, for a few short weeks, before the sentinels chased him away, a wandering dog entered our lives. One day he came to meet this rabble as we returned under guard from work. He survived in some wild patch in the region of the camp. But we called him Bobby, an exotic name, as one does with a cherished dog. He would appear at morning assembly and was waiting for us as we returned, jumping up and down and barking in delight. For him, there was no doubt that we were men.[87]

Interestingly enough, this tale, "The Name of a Dog, or Natural Rights," begins with Levinas citing a biblical verse essentially about eating the carrion animals killed by other nonhuman animals. This lesson in "flesh" and violence is accompanied by Levinas's tale of the dog, Bobby, but this striving for recognition under the bounded category of the "human" is framed by two references to primates. The first concerns the "children and women who passed by and sometimes raised their eyes—stripped us of our human skin. [To them we] were subhuman, a gang of apes."[88] The terrible irony here is that had they been a gang of great apes, it would have been the women and children and not Levinas and his "rabble" who should be afraid. But we can't fault him for both the analogy and for not having access to the science that would come about more than a generation after his own, proving that, as Zakiyyah Iman Jackson observes of animality/blackness and their coevolution, his understanding of great ape difference was more likely racially charged.[89] Still, Levinas's focus on carrion, on the substance of embodied life that is produced as meat/flesh, sets up a kind of psychic prohibition, keeping him from engaging the full embodiment of hum:animal life. This focus on the abattoir's vision of being together clouds his own. In the same paragraph he speaks of his group as "beings entrapped in their species" and asks: "How can we deliver a message about our humanity which, from behind the bars of quotation marks, will come across as anything other than monkey talk?"[90] I want to be careful here, as I believe the quest for human-ity is so very different in the register of the camp than it is for the plantation. In the stories I recount or explicate here, what we have is a tale of staggering injustice from the great apes and their tail/tale-having monkey counterparts, to the Jewish men, to the women and children passing by, to that dog called Bobby. The possibilities of justice are precluded over and over again as stories about our two Bobbys cast about for relation that can stick in a messy morass of violent misrecognition. Why can we not simply act on the witnessed suffering of *an* other?

....

In a public lecture given at the University of Puget Sound in December 2015, I stood before a large audience gathered in a church and presented a portion of the argument of this book. I was still feeling full of the president's dinner, though I had finished my presentation. Satiated, I took my first question. The question is: "What do you have to say about the recent events in Charleston? People are saying that we care more about puppies than we do about Black people." The question refers not to the devastating massacre at Mother Emanuel in downtown Charleston on June 17, 2015, but to an incident that occurred some months later and went viral. In this latter event, a Spring Valley High School resource officer (why not name the school-to-prison pipeline directly here, rather than obliquely) throws a Black female student, still seated at her desk, to the ground.[91]

I was inclined to give a lie for my answer, knowing the kind of hellmouth that such comparisons of hum/animal difference often produce. Instead, I paused and decided to tell a truth. I noted that this dichotomy between Black bodies (young or old, queer or not, male or female) and the routine hagiography of the puppy is a false one. I also noted, quite frankly, that we care not for puppies at all and relayed two anecdotes: (1) A friend in veterinary school's Facebook story about her time in pathology lab, when instructed to take their specimen for the day, she moved to the area indicated and found a neat pile of dead puppies stacked up for students' easy access. (2) On the internet any time of the day you will see videos of homo sapiens setting kittens and puppies on fire or beating them to death, while someone obviously tapes such occurrences without stopping the perpetrators. I offered that this false dichotomy produces death for both subjects, as the lie of our society's love of puppies allows us to maintain the suffering of animals as a constant, and to believe that human beings suffer a worse death than nonhuman animals, when, in fact, their deaths are mirrors of one another and our values . . . well . . . are delivered to us backward as a compendium of falsehoods about how we live *together.* This is the "space, time, and matter" that Barad sees as dependent upon "questions of justice."

The falsity of our particular social configuration—a condition wherein the political gestures toward an array of evaluations and hierarchies which are then revealed to actually be false—is alluded to in the work of new materialism, and in the work of feminist science on "matter" and "mattering"—

think ethics of care. It is why I keep coming back to questions of the material world in relationship to hum/animal distinction. In Bennett's *Vibrant Matter*, she alludes to an argument in her second book, *The Enchantment of Modern Life: Attachments, Crossings, and Ethics* (2001). She notes that "the idea was that moments of sensuous enchantment with the everyday world . . . might augment the motivational energy needed to move selves from the endorsement of ethical principles to the actual practice of ethical behaviors. . . . The theme of that book participated in a larger trend within political theory, a kind of ethical and aesthetic turn inspired in large part by feminist studies of the body and by Michel Foucault's work on 'care of the self.'"[92] For Bennett, after Deleuze and Guattari, the work of the assemblage—the vibrant matter that does not hold to the distinction between animate and inanimate—produces the occasion to rethink, to "reinvoke" our moral and ethical proclivities. When one takes the whole of her theory into account, it becomes clear that the alternative she suggests for an *ethical* life in the midst of the political, is wildly possible once we understand that the pronouncements and attachments we have to what is right and what is wrong are so far out of sync with our *practices*, we might do better with a reoriented worldview.

If having a reoriented ethics requires a practice that also embraces the aesthetic, then violence, raw or aestheticized, is part of that aesthetic, is even normalized in the course of producing *just*ice. The trace of those chimps at Animal Haven Ranch, Bobby on the porch and Bobby in the camp, and the dichotomy of puppies and Black bodies all sit in the embrace of violence in *just*ice, violence as *just*ice. As I noted earlier, there have been perhaps enough arguments about justice and the law, about its achievability in a rights-based world, but what I am offering here is for us to step back, for us to consider our cousins and their sense of justice, for us to (re?)consider violence as a necessary component of what is or can be just. For us to take stock and see that the collusion required for the slavocracy to function *is* part of the hum/animal *distinction* that produces negative life outcomes for practices of hum:animal living.

To bring this argument home, to tarry in the aesthetic for a bit here, I move to a brief consideration of Kurt Wimmer's film *Equilibrium*. The film replicates studied relationships among race, gender, and hum:animal. Christian Bale (from *American Psycho*) stars as Cleric John Preston, who is part of the central administration of a utopian/dystopian society, Libria, where humans hope to avoid another devastating war by injecting themselves with a substance called prozium to curb all human emotion. The society is based on conformity, and in this monochromatic community, "Father" is a constant presence, overvoiced throughout the film with Hitler's Berlin as the backdrop for its set. In one of these many state-sanctioned lessons, we learn of Libria's promise: "Prozium, the great nepenthe. Opiate of our masses, glue of our great society. Salve and salvation, it has delivered us from pathos, from sorrow, the deepest chasms of melancholy and hate. With it we anesthetize grief, annihilate jealousy, obliterate rage. Those sister impulses towards joy, love, and elation, are anesthetized in stride—we accept as fair sacrifice. For we embrace prozium in its unifying fullness and all that it has done to make us great." Clearly, the work of eliminating sense is gendered work; feeling, converted to "sense offense," in Libria is attributed to what would be termed worth sacrificing: the female and, we will learn very shortly and soon enough, the mother in her wake.[93] Moreover, positive emotion—"joy, love, and elation" is her terrain, while negative emotion is a pathogen without origin, gender, or explanation. That "jealousy" is juxtaposed to "love" in Libria is particularly interesting, given those Haven Ranch chimps and the "love" of Mo's human parents. Libria is a place where diversity has been flattened, where scarcity has been allowed to ravage that machine called *the human*.

As a Grammaton Cleric trained in the martial-art-inflected "gun kata," it is Preston's job "to seek out and eradicate the sole source of man's inhumanity to man: his ability to feel." He finds pockets of resistance in the city and "the Nethers"—"sense offenders"—and executes their members and their cultural booty with Bradbury-like efficiency.[94] Eventually, our hero stops taking his dose of prozium, begins to feel, and becomes part of the resistance; but it is the series of events that precipitate the shift in his emotional landscape that most interest me here. Three of these events are aesthetically charged—whole rooms behind walls in the city and the Nethers dripping with objects: art, music, books, furniture, and culinary implements, all assembled perhaps to provoke feeling in sense offenders. There is no feeling without the memory of sense loosened by the arrangement of objects. How the culinary arts and cooking hold space in the frame of hum:animal belonging is the brief concern of a later chapter.

Early in the film, after a trip to the Nethers—a part of the body's landscape of unmentionables, the sacrum, the body's capacity—to investigate yet another cell of resisters, Preston is called to Vice Counsel Dupont's office. The Vice Counsel (played by Angus Macfadyen) inquires about Preston's uncanny ability to tell if someone is feeling. As Preston attempts to answer the question, the Vice Counsel interrupts him: "You're a family man?" When Preston begins to tell him about his two children, a boy and a girl, Dupont interrupts yet again and asks: "And the mother?"—provoking Preston even further. Without skipping a beat, Preston replies, "My spouse was arrested and incinerated for sense offense four years ago." Dupont asks, even though he knows the answer to the question: "By yourself?" Preston quickly counters with: "No, by another." Dupont then drives his point home: "How did you feel about that?" Preston: "I didn't feel anything." Finished with Preston, Dupont then asks, "How did you come to miss [your wife's sense offense]? . . . A nearly unforgivable lapse, Cleric." Once again, "the mother" and "another," two beings we have been tracking with hum:animal all along. The meeting is a kind of warning to Cleric Preston, as Dupont intones when Preston exits: "I trust you to be more vigilant in the future." Cleric Preston's breakdown, his descent into sense offense, precipitated by Dupont's question about "the mother"—shot by another, not himself— is augmented by yet another encounter with a woman in the city named Mary O'Brien (Emily Watson). After her capture and the incineration of her room and its affective life, they have a conversation at headquarters (1:17:30). Cleric Preston pushes the vial of perfume confiscated in the raid toward her across the sterile tabletop.

> **O'BRIEN:** Let me ask you something? [Pushing perfume vial back across the table and then when Preston reaches for it, she grabs his hand.] Why are you alive?
>
> **PRESTON:** I'm alive . . . I live to safeguard the continuity of this great society. To serve Libria.
>
> **O'BRIEN:** It's circular. You exist to continue your existence. What's the point?
>
> **PRESTON:** What's the point of your existence?
>
> **O'BRIEN:** To feel. 'Cuz you've never done it, you can never know it. But it's as vital as breath. And without it, without love, without anger, without sorrow, breath is just a clock ticking.
>
> **PRESTON:** Then I have no choice but to remand you to the palace of justice for processing.
>
> **O'BRIEN:** Processing? You mean execution, don't you?
>
> **PRESTON:** Processing.

All the layers of the relationship among gender, hum:animal, and their affective life come together in this short dialogue. The female sense offender
integrates the distinction of emotions offered to us in the film's opening
voiceovers; her explication of "breath" as "feeling" as another kind of temporality, outside mechanized ticking, gestures to a world whose life Preston
cannot know. She offers Cleric Preston some kind of nuance in the relation
between life and living. Their difference as citizens of Libria is not only
emotional—though we've already seen Preston forego his "interval [dose]"
of prozium—it is also existential. They possess the same language, but they
do not speak so that they can be understood by one another. And the shadow
of hum:animal difference haunts the edges of this world, where "processing"
has replaced "execution" as a working vocabulary, where *animal life* is described
as meat (pork, beef, poultry) so it can be readied for consumption.

Women and children come up again in the film in another crucial scene
in the Nethers, a region of Libria for dogs/puppies and human "waste." After
having executed his last partner Cleric Partridge (Sean Bean) for sense offense in the first scenes of the movie, Preston has been given a new cleric to
train—Brandt (Taye Diggs). While rousting yet another resistance cell—
fifty persons strong—in the Nethers they are alerted to "something out
back." The camera rests upon a large fenced area—inside are several adult
dogs chained to the ground by each of their pens. One of the attending soldiers announces, "These animals were defended by women and children;
we put them down easily." Brandt asks, "This isn't the first time we've seen
this. Why do they keep these animals? What do they . . . do they eat them?"
Preston ignores the question. And it is not lost on me that the "putting
down," here, first in reference to women and children, refers to hum:animal
life without distinction; the abattoir beckons always. In addition, the term
"easily" invokes ease of dispatch and compassionate/humane slaughter, a collective of oxymorons nestled in this new but very old model for civil society.

Brandt instructs the soldiers to "exterminate them." One by one the animals are shot, and among the sounds of animals whimpering and guns firing
and stylized violence, a puppy escapes. As the soldiers shout for Preston to
grab it and throw it back so that it can be exterminated, Preston lifts the
puppy to hum:animal eye level (figure 3.2).

The scene is a profoundly telling visual scape of our hum:animal dilemma,
and its constitutive parts. With the Africanist presence as the background
for the oft replicated representation of the hum:animal relationship, it would
appear that all of our hierarchies are in place. White folks really do care
for puppies more than human being. If we, however, consider the "putting

3.2 Cleric Preston (Christian Bale) and puppy survivor in foreground; Cleric Bryant (Taye Diggs) in background. *Equilibrium* (2002), dir. Kurt Wimmer.

down" of women and children, whom we do not see, the killing of the dogs and other puppies in this scene that we do see, then the one who escapes is not a symbol in a hierarchy of care, but a possibility for relation and regard. The face-to-face encounter with the puppy turns unethical slaughter, for Preston at least, into viable relation, but it does not erase or attend to certain hierarchies. In truth, the police state cares not for women, or children, or Black life, or puppies. Its entire focus is to produce unethical relation among constituents, precluding the possibility for the kind of practice of justice that turns *looking* into ethical action; that produces knowledge as a form of unknowing, from the *vision* just barely off the page. Preston, clearly now captivated and held in the regard of hum:animal vision, equivocates. He spares the puppy's life with the following excuse: "At least some of these animals should be tested for disease. If there's an epidemic in the Nethers, we should know something about it."

The puppy is the beginning of the end for Cleric Preston's devotion to Libria, and this montage of images is neatly arranged for our consumption as the quintessential scene of our puppylove and racialhatred. It also produces something else that we might see, how white female bodies, how "the mother" and later the child, stand in for negotiations of this space of hum:animal life. This configuration is ubiquitous in celluloid and digital dystopic dramas, as the Black family gives itself up over and over for the protection of the white mother and child in the second film in *The Terminator* series, and that is only the first instance.[95] The puppy is not more important than Black life in the film so much as it becomes a way to reconfigure and to mourn for the loss of the white mother. There is a hierarchy, but it isn't one based upon a situation of caring more or valuing less. Instead, the puppy negotiates that distance between the possibility for ethical action in the case of white mothers *and* the situation of ethical action in response to modes of antirevolutionary collusion. In the penultimate scenes, Preston returns to the seat of government to destroy it. He fights his way through a plethora of security forces using both gun and sword (therefore changing the genre of the martial arts flick) in order to confront Father, only to find that Father is deceased, and it is instead Dupont, the Vice Counsel, who is in control of Libria; Dupont is the one who first asks Preston about "the mother." The only person standing in between Preston and Dupont is Brandt, his former partner, whom he learns was planted by Dupont precisely for this moment.

The only phenotypically Black character in the movie who speaks, Brandt stands defiantly at Dupont's side, much like the character Stephen (Samuel Jackson) in Quentin Tarantino's twisted tale of the plantation South, *Django Unchained.* As a collaborator in the death of the mother, Brandt, like Tarantino's Stephen and like scientist Miles Dyson (Joe Morton) in *Terminator 2*, must die. In a sword fight that is brief and deadly, Christian Bale kills him with three swift strikes, one of them a final vertical strike down the face. Brandt falls to his knees with his back to us and our last glimpse of him is of a perfectly cut slice of his face separating neatly from his body. The potential for ethical relation is withheld from the phenotypically Black subject—thus placing Brandt outside the community of hum:animal insurgents, but also calling attention to his position as counterrevolutionary, and it is an unmasking/unmaking that brings forth a host of actors in this drama about ethical relation, mothers, and, yes, whiteness.

We are caught in the space of what violence is *for*: it prevents ethical action, always; it seeks not potentiality but death. The scene is even more astonishing, given that the publicity for the sci-fi vehicle highlights the relationship between the two men (figure 3.3): "In a future where freedom is outlawed outlaws will become heroes," placing the struggle for the end of human history—for the new-world order—in racialized terms and between Black and white. Capitalizing on the buddy-film genre—where white and Black agents keep law and order—the movie's advertising is of course misleading. This friendship is Derridean in nature: a gift of war. But it is also *gendered* by the killing of not one white mother but two. What makes

Cleric Preston a hero is solidified by the sense offence occasioned by "the mother" and his ability to produce *justice* as one who determines what stands for ethical commitment.

Now part of the resistance, Preston's next and last murder is of Dupont, who argues for his life with: "I'm life. I live, I breathe, I feel. Now that you know it, can you really take it? Is it really worth the price?" Preston's response is: "Definitely." And he kills him with a shot to the heart. This appeal to life, to his place as one who engenders, in the archaic meaning as a father who makes gender matter through *his* offspring, is against the definition of life put forth simply in this monograph. Dupont wants to suddenly appeal to their shared feeling, one supposedly rooted in a mutual begetting, but Preston reminds us that feeling is in the doing, and *justice*, even in its righteous call for *life* and *living*, can be corrupted by the law of the father and its racialized agendas. And so now, the substitute "Father" has no heart, and the Black Cleric has no face.

The next scenes show members of the resistance blowing up the prozium factories and taking the capital. In the mix are Preston's children, the male child, Robbie Preston (Matthew Harbour), smiling over a lesson on his school desk, and his daughter, Lisa Preston (Emily Siewert), smile on her face too, in profile with the rescued puppy licking her outstretched hand. Women and puppies.

The domesticated animal must be killed because it reminds us of the human (the sentient nature of being), or at least our capacity to express what we know of as "human" emotion. But the presence of the animal also ruptures the human. *Domestication*, is, yes, an act of mastery, but it is also a two-sided coin; it is also a colossal failure to master, really. What passes as sympathy for other beings in the film is in fact an inappropriate expression of that end—so that saving the puppy (who appears in the last scene at the feet of Preston's daughter), and passing it along to one's offspring, but killing the animal (the one who eats another) (Brandt), is an appropriate display of human being—and its ability to "overcome." This ending is no revolutionary moment, but a sedimented knowing about animal life—its human and nonhuman parts—hitched to a familiar script. Defacing blackness allows for the continuation of *a* human history, forever dependent it would seem on his/her annihilation, returning animal(s) to their proper place and severing blackness's connection to any kind of ethical life.

Moreover, it could be argued that Brandt's death revolves around the question of the animal—does he perish because he is Black or because he isn't a vegetarian? One very heavy-handed reading could be that Brandt perishes but does not die because he is defaced away from the audience—an audience whose gaze would put him in relationship with us: out in the open where the truth of Being experiences its final unconcealment. But the gaze here is a bankrupt measure of relation—the gaze does nothing to change the outcome for animal lives in the film. Nevertheless, the open secret of man's inhumanity to man is cast out of the new Garden of Eden where the puppy is given to its human family. In the end, blackness disrupts a founding equilibrium between man and animal.

On the other hand, the gendered nature of such strategic dismemberment cannot be ignored here, as these examples—the story of Moe and *Equilibrium*, Bobby and the puppy—revolve around male-to-male violence. Why did the monkeys choose the "father" and not the "mother" (Mrs. Davis, who fared better than her other half by losing only a finger)? In *Equilibrium*, the corrupting force of the errant female is placed under annihilation not by the father but "by another." As Cleric Preston experiences his return to "sense," we are treated to flashbacks of the events leading to his wife's incineration. Female bodies, like books, can be destroyed for the influence they wreak upon a population—their work is too generative for the automaton control required for citizens of Libria. Odd that the utopian future displayed in Wimmer's *Equilibrium* ends with the last chapter, "Paying the Price"—yes, diversity does have its price, but what is it exactly? Euphemism keeps us from examining the finer lesson of mastery every time. Strategic dismemberment indeed.

4 love : livestock

The animal is that from which the human tentatively and precariously emerges; the animal is that inhuman destination to which the human always tends. The animal surrounds the human at both ends: it is the origin and the end of humanity.
ELIZABETH GROSZ, *Becoming Undone* (2011)

I sit down next to the fire and discover my livery for the first time. It is in fact ugly. I won't go on because who can tell me what beauty is?
FRANTZ FANON, *Black Skin, White Masks* (1952)

When an animal gets sick here, they plug it into the wall.
HUSHPUPPY, *Beasts of the Southern Wild* (2012), dir. Benh Zeitlin

There is no good love that, in speaking its name, can change the world into the referent for that name. But in the resistance to speaking in the name of love, in the recognition that we do not simply act *out of love*, and in the understanding that love comes with conditions however unconditional it might feel, we can find perhaps a different kind of line or connection between the others we care for, and the world to which we want to give shape.
SARA AHMED, *The Cultural Politics of Emotion* (2004)

politics

In more ways than I can count, this thing called Black love has been packaged *for us* and on more than one occasion *by us* as a harsh and cruel thing. It is the forest that grows up between Sethe and Paul D in *Beloved* ("You got two feet, Sethe, not four"), or the ships at a distance in Zora Neale Hurston's *Their Eyes*; it is the kind of love contoured by the demands of the state in John Berry's *Claudine* or fractured by misogyny's consistent allure in Alice Walker's *The*

Color Purple. Loving correctly, without excess is to move through the world on "two feet," not "four." Proper loving is almost always never queer, at least if it is same species homo sapiens love; the queer love of hum:animal finds little vantage point in our fictions of being, it often possesses a diminished aesthetic life.[1] I hesitate to say that I am queering love, but I will admit to some disruption in an easy assessment of love's object. From the beginning of this project, I am always tracking *accident* before *love*.

Most recently critics like Joshua Bennett have returned us to the figure of the animal and the natural world in our aesthetic life, offering in his assessment of Douglass's engagements with hierarchies of being that there is an "unwieldy network of feelings that bind livestock and the enslaved together."[2] Moreover, Bennett's argument settles also on love unrequited and therefore counter to the liberating force we have often understood it to be. In a chapter entitled, "Cock," he writes of Morrison's *Song of Solomon*: "To configure love in such a fashion . . . is to conjure an expansive set of questions about the nature of kinship, about what it means to desire that which can destroy just as easily as it can make or mend."[3] Bennett is right that love contours kinship, that it makes and unmakes as a standard, what is possible for *being*. What love also creates is an affective trace; love inclines itself toward animal being-in-its-suffering and so the question that haunts this chapter's analysis is whether or not mutual suffering, built as it is upon a particular human quality and/or understanding of reciprocity, actually holds or makes durable relation with *an* other. I start first with love's failure in blackness, and then I turn to what it can and cannot recognize in its affective life as hum:animal.

In the last decades of the twentieth century, several Black critics invoked the very concept of "love" as a cure-all for what ailed Black community.[4] Love is something that we fail at, constantly. bell hooks (née Gloria Watkins) and Cornel West discuss the power of love in their 1991 co-authored text, *Breaking Bread: Insurgent Black Intellectual Life*. hooks dedicates the book to "transformative redemptive love between Black women and men," and Cornel West dedicates the book to his grandmothers. So, the book appears in the *wake* of homo sapiens gendered love that is not always tied to romantic affiliation, but where opposites must attract *and* where ancestral maternal lines have a psychic effect upon the making of Black intellectuals and their musings about love. In their second conversation of the text, each invokes beauty in the service of the political. Taking on aesthetic arrangements in various fashion magazines, hooks reminds us that "Black femaleness" is juxtaposed to the "White female body [that] always appears to be a signifier of 'natural' beauty."[5] I am interested here in the terms "femaleness" and "female" in hooks and how if we track back to Spillers and her sense of "gendered femaleness" and "insurgent ground as female social subject," femaleness can be that substance that is derived from the gendered scaffolding called "woman."[6] Femaleness is a kind of offal left over at slaughter of the category "woman," but where woman, as a political entity, has a chance to arrive at that insurgent ground through a process hooks defines as "self-love."

In answer to the problem of Black female beauty posed by hooks, Cornel West observes that "aesthetics have substantial political consequences. How one views oneself as beautiful or not beautiful or desirable or not desirable has deep consequences in terms of one's feelings of self-worth and one's capacity to be a political agent."[7] I am extremely skeptical of the viability of the political and its ties to agency, since the stakes for blackness in the realm of the political are so very overdetermined. Moreover, the autonomy of the self as sole political agent is at least complicated by new materialist endeavors articulated in earlier chapters. My question has always been whether or not the "political" (writ large) as that manner of species that can be seen, act, and be acted upon matters much in the end. I do, however, want to hold fast to something that Derrida proposes in *The Animal That Therefore I Am*: "Politics supposes livestock" (96). I will come back to this later.

hooks and West's collective vision of Black love comes forward as an "insurgency model" for Black intellectuals—one linked to and "permeated by the kinetic orality and emotional physicality, the rhythmic syncopation, the protean improvisation, and the religious, rhetorical, and antiphonal elements of Afro-American life."[8] Insurgency for hooks and West encompasses those "agents" that stand outside of the political, if the political is a category by which an entity demonstrates its force in the world. In the same church but different pew, feminist anthropologist Elizabeth Povinelli challenges the revolutionizing spirit of "love" when she places race and nonnormative sexual practices *in love* in direct relation and concludes, "True love works against the social as such even as it figures the social as a set of constraining surfaces, encrusting and deforming the true destination of the self."[9] Like hooks and West, Povinelli centers the "self'" as part of the matrix of love. In human terms, "love" begins with some kind of relationship to self—even if that self is understood as underrealized—in the first order and Black love/queer love works against a social world that has nothing to offer but constraint.

Later in *Breaking Bread*, the authors argue that Black insurgent actors find themselves through a "hybrid lineage [American, European, and African] which protects the earth and projects a better world."[10] In the end, their vision for Black love lives far outside—see "protean improvisation" and "kinetic orality"—the container (a conversation between male and female, men and women) they initially construct to house it. Where this love finds itself after it spills over, runs off the pages of hooks and West's provocative statement on Black intellectuals at the turn of the twentieth century is anyone's guess, but it does comprise the components and elements of *being* that are undeniably held in the possibility of Baby Suggs's Clearing or Merleau-Ponty's musings about what can be seen and felt. hooks and West produce an argument for Black love that encompasses a future through imagining "a better world" and that entails some form of protection that human being might provide for this place called "earth." The paternalistic approach to nature, as something separable and separate from our*selves*, produces our capacity for love as world-making, rather than letting go. In the end our "hybrid lineage" or *diversity* does little to contribute to a deeply reconfigured relationship to our biosphere.

Nevertheless, for hooks and West, Black love cannot be achieved without attention to the *self.* Self-love, with beauty's commodified aesthetic in the foreground, therefore produces the kind of efficacy necessary to build Black *political* viability. It is an old and odd rhetoric to be sure, but a necessary one in West's vision of Black (political) life. What if one does not desire, like MOVE members or perhaps even Platt's (née Northup's) Eliza, political agency? In theory, blackness's political agency in *a* world, in all of its aesthetic might, has the power to mark, to make injury to itself (lack of self-love), to others (fear of a Black planet), but it does not have the power to sustain, to create, or to participate in the worlds-making possibility that is love itself.[11] This is the question that Fanon asks: "Who can tell me what beauty is?" It is a question born out of great despair and fierce love, and is, therefore, beauty itself. The opening paragraphs of Povinelli's book on love demonstrate the extent to which love exists, but sometimes does not travel, especially when its loss cannot be marked across *social* worlds. She writes most candidly that she moves between "what would appear to be two very different social worlds: on the one hand, the social worlds of indigenous men and women living at Belyuen, a small community in the Northern Territory of Australia . . . and, on the other, the social worlds of progressive queers in the United States who identify as or with radical faeries." In charting a course between worlds, she notes, "The incommensurate nature of these social worlds and of the racial and sexual discourses that apprehend them make it difficult for me to do such normal things as express joy and grief in one world for the people I have found and lost in another."[12] Hers is an interstitial problem, much like that to which Hortense Spillers refers in her early piece from that 1984 Barnard conference in *Pleasure and Danger*, "Interstices: A Small Drama of Words."

I emphasize the word "social" above because I want to put some pressure on its efficacy—as the social often exists in what can be stated, known, recognized. These forms of linguistic, epistemic, and political life are what's at stake in our devotion to love. What do you do when you realize that your objective is not to be brought back into the space of the observable group, what then constitutes the political for you and *an* other? Answering Fanon's question "Who can tell me what beauty is?" with a refusal is absolutely necessary if we would like to see that insurgence take shape. Interesting that where hooks and West end up is relatively outside of the homo sapiens secured insurgency in love-making that they envision for the text. In many ways, the very idea of Black love shapes the conversation, but its boundary cannot hold as a purely homo sapiens event; even in a conservative text like this one, hum:animal breaks through the distinction while it is held away from the transformative power of love itself; a rabbit, for the greyhound, that can never be procured. This love's flaw, in hooks and West's formulation, first and foremost, must be ameliorated through the self's regeneration for the work of this fe/male love to cohere. I see two conditions arising from this reading of love. One is that this fe/male reunion is acquired through a kind of self-contained heteropatriarchy. Two is that for blackness, the very foundation of generative love proceeds from a sense that something in the self is broken and needs repair. And the salve is a binary form of relating that cannot hold if "improvisation" or "kinetic" energy are our touchstones.

I return now to a brief moment in Derrida's *The Animal That Therefore I Am*. Derrida notes—and this response is generated after a cursory reading of Descartes: "There is therefore neither socialization, political constitution, nor politics itself without the principle of domestication of the wild animal. The idea of an animal that claimed to break with this power to command beasts, to order the becoming-livestock of the beast, would be absurd and contradictory. Politics supposes livestock."[13] What does Derrida mean here? That politics is totally dependent upon our ability to domesticate the wild animal because this demonstrates a capacity to be self-governing, composed, ready for the world? Furthermore, the necessity of the wild animal's domestication to the very idea of the political can be seen most clearly, for example, in the New York Central Park rape case where Black and Latino youths were convicted and incarcerated for a crime they did not commit while politicians staked their reelections on the fact that they could govern this thing called "wilding" that the kids supposedly were engaged in. Subduing and/or mastering (Black/brown) beasts in the wild is evidence of one's ability to enter into that thing called "the political." I will demonstrate, hopefully, in the final chapter of this book how this "beast" and its governing is a fiction within European forms of sovereignty that then goes unrecognized as we move to think through the (im)possibility of sovereignty for forms of Indigenous living.

That last phrase from Derrida "politics supposes livestock" turns upon the idea of management, as now the wild animal is *live* stock, kept for sale. Think chattel here. Think of our current "farmer's market" where food as livestock is being managed but badly—as management now is more politically correct when it cannot be seen (Foucault is right about that panopticon) when the co-op storefront looks tidy and all the bad things—the kill shot, the offal sold in bulk, the hooves off to be boiled into gelatin—are out of the way of the "consumer" and replaced by polystyrene and cellophane. Animal protection lawyer Steven Wise reminds us that "Livestock husbandry was not just a way to make a living—it was a way of life."[14]

I return to a quotation used in the previous chapter in Derrida's lecture on the human/animal distinction and its philosophical trajectory through Levinas, Lacan, and Foucault, where he notes, "I am saying 'they,' 'what they call an animal,' in order to mark clearly the fact that I have always secretly exempted myself from that world, and my whole history in truth everything I am, seems to me to be born from that exceptionalism and incited by that sentiment of election."[15] For Derrida, to even think "the animal" is to remove oneself from the possibility of being an animal; that removal is both the insult and the impediment, right? It is a problem that opens up a space for further explication. When we turn our intellectual consideration to the animal, without regard to our being as animal, we confront a roadblock created by our own inquiry; we re-up the fundamental distinction. The question remains can we think a place for the animal's consideration that includes our own self-making? Regardless of whether or not animality/blackness share an origin in ontological framings of life's potentiality (being), we still must move even more to the space off the page. We do things to and with hum:animals, and the measure is in the doing, the gesture at the heart of approaching the ethical commitment of blackness to the animal and the contemplation of "animal" itself (who *is* the animal here, really?) in any arrangement of these embodied beings. My point here is simple: if to even think the animal is to do so at a pleasant remove, in a discourse that compounds the predicament of proximity being laid before us, then it is clearly time to reimagine the possibilities for hum:animal life in relationship to other identities-in-being. I now turn to consider Black love in another register.

(carrier) pigeons

The L.A. Rebellion in filmmaking spanned nearly three decades (1968–1998) and produced some of the most significant films on Black diasporic life. One could say that the L.A. Rebellion started at Los Angeles Community College (LACC), where its early filmmakers like Charles Burnett took courses in literature. Rather than report to the draft board during the Vietnam era, talented young Black men were looking for alternatives, so they registered at LACC and with fourteen units they could receive a draft deferment. While at LACC Charles Burnett, whose family hails from Vicksburg, Mississippi, began to read Thomas Wolfe and discovered James Baldwin and Ed Bowen, an equestrian/racing writer, and of course, LeRoi Jones before he became Amiri Baraka. Following the summer of 1965 Watts Rebellion, there was increased urgency to bring the resources of the university to bear on what was happening in the ethnic neighborhoods of Los Angeles. In 1968 at UCLA, African American assistant vice chancellor Charles Z. Wilson proposed several initiatives. Most importantly they wanted to "expedit[e] *creative* responses to legitimate issues that poor and disadvantaged minority students raised."[16] Governor Ronald Reagan was opposed to such measures and the initiatives went largely unfunded.

Burnett transitioned to UCLA's film program from creative writing at LACC. But the influence of his teacher Isabelle Ziegler encouraged him to start "getting into storytelling."[17] Like Octavia Butler in California and Purvis Young in Florida, the public library and, in Burnett's case, a long-standing job there in what he calls "the magazine pool" became central to the development of a capacious intellectual terrain.[18] One that he brings to bear in all of his films. Charles Z. Wilson and Dr. Elyseo Taylor's presence on the UCLA campuses demonstrates the difference that Black faculty make, as Taylor was the first Black faculty member at UCLA. His service in World War II and life abroad possibly helped to fuel his commitment to the diasporic lens for his students. Taylor began to recruit and train students of color in media production with a $17,200 grant from the Ford Foundation for his Media Urban Crisis Committee (MUCC) program, which trained

Black, Chicano, Asian, and Indigenous students at UCLA to use mass communication technologies.[19] What became the L.A. Rebellion was born, and Burnett was one of its first students as he served as Taylor's TA for the course "Film and Social Change," which is still being taught on that campus. Burnett stayed in the program for a decade (1967–1977).

Oral histories conducted with L.A. Rebellion filmmakers document the social and political effects of the Vietnam War, the Watts Rebellion (August 1965), and changing socioeconomic life in central Los Angeles.[20] The L.A. Rebellion was also part of a global Black diasporic movement among a generation of creative workers to tell their own stories and produce them for larger audiences. According to filmmaker Charles Burnett, whose early works *Killer of Sheep* (1977) and *The Horse* (1973) will be examined here, "I wanted to say something about the community, about the kids I knew, this whole distortion and life and stuff" and to produce "a rebellion against stereotypes and what had gone before." Burnett makes the first statement in the context of talking about constant police violence which he notes "was like apartheid." But Burnett's interest in animal life extends to his time as a child in Los Angeles, where he "raised pigeons," and laughing at himself, remarks that "people were going to parties, I was reading pigeon magazines."[21] No small coincidence that years later, Jim Jarmusch's *Ghost Dog*'s main character (played by Forest Whitaker) would also raise pigeons on a rooftop in Jersey City.[22]

Given Burnett's interest in *an* other species work, it makes sense that his first endeavors behind the camera's eye would be devoted to hum:animal life. But while his inclination toward hum:animal life was nourished by the LACC and UCLA, he also produced his films in the wake of public media attention to the lives of the cowboys and riders of the Black West. As early as 1966, two UCLA English professors, Philip Durham and Everett L. Jones, published two books, one scholarly, *The Negro Cowboys*, and the other a children's book, *The Adventures of the Negro Cowboys*. Interviewed by the *Los Angeles Sentinel*, one of several Black newspapers, the authors note, "Western stories are peopled by heroes who are tall, lean, and tanned—but lily white under the shirt."[23] Clearly Durham and Jones produced their texts to shed light on an unknown history and, as so many of these western films focus on Black male characters in the western saddle tradition, to bring attention to a wider range of Black masculinities. Doing so set these figures in direct relationship to settler colonial regimes and their heteropatriarchal entanglements.

In a 1970 series, *The Black Frontier*, Chicago's wttw produced four sixty-minute programs to expand public understandings of the West. As one news clipping from booking manager of the African American owned Lincoln Motion Picture Company, George P. Johnson's collection reveals: "Jim Kelly [a Black cowboy] and 8,000 other Black men were a firm wedge in the history of the cattle drive. They made up 25% of the unique individuals who lived the bronc-busting, whiskey-drinking, cattle-herding, weather-fighting life that was later twisted and polished into the myth of the fairy tale cowboy."[24] The wttw series launched in October of 1970 and in a November 14, 1970, review by Robert Lewis Shayon, he notes, "The series, if shown and studied widely, could do much to restore the cultural visibility of thousands of Blacks who shared the triumphs and defeats of westward expansion."[25] The review is clearly from a time before we became critical of our role in westward expansion or interested in the difference that gender makes. Worth noting is a stunning moment in the piece where Shayon observes that "the Blacks who settled the West all came from what sociologists today call 'the culture of poverty,' which presumably *breeds* individuals with low self-esteem and *mañana*-oriented lifestyles. If that is true, then one wonders from where the men and women of 'The Black Frontier' drew the inner strengths to help them survive and achieve in a socially hostile as well as physically challenging environment."[26] Interesting how the sociological insights about Black cultural life of the Chicago school make their way into a news story. Histories of enslavement and disenfranchisement are naturalized as a "culture of poverty," making Black subjects responsible for the violence of captivity and its hum/animal abattoir. But Shayon does get one thing right: "breeding" is central to the work of making differentiation matter and it is ubiquitous in discourse about horse hum:animal life, as my next chapter will attempt to outline.

Johnson's prolific archiving provides a window into the world that might have inspired Burnett's take on hum:animal:blackness. Other evidence that the Black cowboy was a figure that comes up as subject matter for student and independent filmmakers is taken from yet another clipping from Johnson's archive. In a November 30, 1970, review of Genesis III, an experimental shorts package, a short film by Ron Policy, Rod Whitaker, and Richard Cooris, all teachers of cinema at the University of Texas, is entitled *Cinemania*. The film is a send-up of 1960s films and features a gun battle with "a Black super cowboy, dressed all in white, who worries that the gun fight might lose him the Nobel Peace Prize for which he has been nominated."[27]

These shorts and popular cultural images of Black riders would have been known to Burnett during his ten-year stint as a graduate student at UCLA's film school. Moreover, public displays of Black male prowess and horse-man-ship could be seen as close as Hollywood Park, where a group of Black riders emulating the 10th Cavalry Regiment—the Black equestrian riders known as "buffalo soldiers"—would muster to celebrate their role as riders while also perhaps undertheorizing their part in one of the nation's deadliest acts of genocide against Indigenous peoples. As the clipping attests, "The 10th Cavalry is an all-Negro equestrian organization modeled after the original U.S. 10th Cavalry that was created by Congress in 1866 of colored troops. The 10th Cavalry distinguished itself throughout the territories of Texas, Arizona, New Mexico, Montana, Colorado, and Wyoming. The new 10th Cavalry is outfitted similarly to the famous 10th of a hundred years ago. It has 35 active members who drill twice weekly on their horses."[28] Hollywood Park was a thoroughbred racetrack in the Black neighborhood of Inglewood, California. This is where, toward the end of the film Stan, the central character in Burnett's first feature, *Killer of Sheep*, is most likely headed when the car he is driving breaks down on the side of the road.

About the creation of his second short, *The Horse* (13:50), Burnett observes: "I was using . . . a lot of literature at the time, like Faulkner and stuff like that, and I was impressed [by] his whole take on this—his southern depiction. And the images and symbolism, so, I wanted to do something very similar, so I made up this story about this horse that was hemorrhaging, that sort of was a symbol in many ways of the south and its changing, and things like that." The film was shot in Shannon, California, an area that "doesn't look anything like Mississippi or the south except for maybe like Texas, south Texas."[29] The 1973 short eventually won second place at the Oberhausen Film Festival.[30] Burnett clearly sees the horse as a figure for something else in the film, and my argument in this project has been that *animal life* (which is always already our own life) is not just a figure or metaphor for some*thing* else, for another, but a being of consequence whose life cannot be understood in the singular. Nevertheless, even though our approaches to animal life differ in regard to metaphor, it is possible to see in this short depiction of relationship among Black, white, and horse that the lines between hum:animal are not so starkly drawn and that the horse helps to guide, if not *world* the aesthetic and the affective life of the film.

The first long shot in *The Horse* is of two human figures, one clearly a child, and a horse in a very dry field in front of a rapidly dilapidating two-story clapboard house. Music from Samuel Barber's *Knoxville: Summer of*

1915 (for voice and orchestra) plays in the background. Despite the idyllic and hopeful notes in the piece, despite the trace of James Agee's now famous quote about his boyhood in Tennessee as a period of his life where he was "so successfully disguised to myself, as a child," the scene is menacing in its stillness. The second shot is of a pair of wingtips worn by one of the three white men gathered on the still-standing porch; two of the men talk to one another while the other paces back and forth. Elevated above the parched scene where the horse and a Black male child (Maury Wright) stand, the men converse and the scene moves to yet another white man, William (Gordon Houston) in a field rubbing his head. The next shot is of the back of that same Black boy, rubbing the belly and shoulder of a beautiful but undernourished dark bay horse (figure 4.1).

The scene is one of slow deprivation and hardship, with the fancy shoes and socks and the shiny coat of the horse the only measure of opulence in the film. In the midst of the boy's tender care of the horse's bites and his attempts to soothe, the scene cuts to Walter of the fancy shoes shouting to William, the white man in the first scene and the obvious owner of the horse:

WALTER (GARY MORRIN): William, I ain't got all shitting day. West? Lee? How long are you gonna stay out here? You gettin' way in the hell out here to see a damn old horse get put away. [And . . .] Where did that boy come from?

LEE (GEORGE WILLIAMS): That's Ray's boy.

WALTER: Why in the hell do we have to wait for some damn nigga? Any one of us could do it.

WEST (ROGER COLLINS) TO WALTER: Will is getting sick and tired of hearing your voice!

The creaking of an empty silo is the only background sound in this scene, attesting to Burnett's commitment to using direct sound. The Black boy leads another horse (a chestnut) back to what looks like a barn and we see them from a distance and from the rear, heads inclined toward the ground, signifying the chestnut's pending solitude as they are about to lose their *companion*. This depiction in particular points to the centrality of the horse as more than metaphor in this film. We are asked, in this journey from paddock to barn, to consider the *life* of the horses, and the affective world they cocreate with *Black* human being; this world-ing stands in contrast

4.1 Will Jr. and bay horse. *The Horse* (1973), dir. Charles Burnett.

to Burnett's purposeful framing of white vigilance over property. If this is a scene about a "changing" South, a transplanted Faulknerian Mississippi, then the euthanizing of the horse and the characters who have come to witness this act are significant. There is no real way to bring about justice without accountability, and the gallery of white men, not at all in alignment with one another (consider the above argument among them) provides more than a few vantage points from which to understand this hum:animal drama as not quite the sum of its parts. If the porch is judge and jury, the relationship of whiteness to civil society is undone by the presence of William, who is clearly in alignment with both Ray and his son. Hum:animal life is set in juxtaposition to an order of property before life itself. The ethical turn here is in the taking of life as a form of care and, yes, justice rather than in the kind of judgment of a waning regime of power.

In the next shot it is dusk and before the barn we see a cross and behind it a car driving down the road. A Black man gets out—it is Ray (Larry Clark, also the assistant cameraman), the boy's father. The boy runs to him and Ray lifts his son off the ground; their embrace reflects that interiority and affective life between the African-descended that Dorothy remarks upon in the final voiceover of Haile Gerima's *Bush Mama*. If the goal of the

L.A. Rebellion is to tell a different story about Black life, then the embrace of blackness in both films, and Burnett's extension of that embrace to the touch of the boy's hands on the horse's body, unsettle the prescribed place for blackness in representational space. The horse that they are to euthanize is part of the interior *life* of blackness, is bound up in it in ways that lie beyond the frame that Burnett attempts to capture. William is the one who produces human being in the film, as he brings the mark of its species dominance: the technology of the gun. Yet, it is a dominion to be used in the service of hum:animal relation. Even the signs of the human's supremacy in the film genuflect toward our entwined relation. Will retrieves the gun from the back of the car, loads it, and hands it to Ray. All four—horse, men, and boy—walk out of the shot. The boy stands with his hands over his ears, waiting for the gunshot. Just when he lifts his head to look, Ray fires. When it comes, the sound is loud, final, and concludes the scene. The boy flinches as we flinch.

I return here briefly to Frank Wilderson's assessment of *The Horse* as set in a "barren landscape." Perhaps the ailing horse lends to this observation, but if one takes species into account or moves outside the world that rigidly defines the human as its marker and maker, then the assessment of the landscape as "barren" offers us a decidedly narrow point of view. The scene is always already teeming with species life and also figures this *lack* as decidedly female as there are no cisgendered women in the film. Hum:animal potentiality shifts the terms of our reading altogether—the landscape is not a palimpsest for our creative life, but an ethically charged space of our own awakening *in* it, an argument that Dunning so exquisitely makes in her introduction to *Black to Nature.* In my reading of possibility in hum:animal worlds, I want to push back on the *fact* that "the horse is just an alibi and the boy and the spectator know it."[31] The pure representational force of the horse for Wilderson is jarring; its bare life separable from their living and their letting go. I am interested in the two events taking place, one in which property is at issue and the other in which life is at issue. I am also thinking about Burnett's own words about *The Horse* and its representation of a changing South. I am not attempting to create a counterpoint to violence in the "joy" of hum:animal living (this is indeed a sad film on so many levels), but I do want to leave open and call attention to the space that the relationship between hum:animal in the film opens for us to witness, if not engage.

The opening scene of the men on the porch is composed as if the viewer were at an auction, one staged for the selling of Black and animal bodies—a conflagration of parts and beings that is purposely juxtaposed in the film. It is a staging reminiscent of Alice Walker's attempt to see human experience through the psychic life of a horse pastured in a field next to her home in the short essay, "Am I Blue?" The "white" horse, "Blue" is, at first, alone. After a few months, he is put with a mare to mate. The lonely Blue tastes companionship and then faces loneliness again when the mare is removed, his purpose having been accomplished through her conception. Walker observes, "If I had been born into slavery, and my partner had been sold or killed, my eyes would have looked like that."[32] For Walker, the horse is imagined as a symbol in an essay that is a meditation about freedom and American cultural practices. The horse's animal life is evacuated for her own affective turn: "my eyes would have looked like that." The vision here is utilitarian, as the suffering of *an* other, produces *its* othering through our renewed and somewhat settler colonial accountability to it.

The affective life of human being's relation to *an* other is a problem for hum:animal in animal studies work that has been mulled over since the mid-1970s. The question goes something like this: is the life of the animal capable of being regarded by us for its own sake, rather than in our conceptualization of its capacity to suffer (like us)? Walker's essay gestures toward animal life but does not produce hum:animal belonging, as the suffering of the horse is stolen to produce the affective life of Black pain, rather than the ground upon which the horse's freedom can be understood or potentially produced. Suffering actually articulates the very remove that sustains hum/animal difference, and it is always already suspect as a kind of neoliberal engagement. The question is not whether the animal can suffer, but instead whether we have the right to utilize capacity as a grounding for/of our engagement. This question that comes forward in animal studies is a profound one, as it engages not what there is to know but what cannot be known *and* how to act on that impossibility as a potentiality that far exceeds what relation means at this point. What I am offering here in this brief explication of Walker's work is that there are ways to talk about hum:animal life that open these worlds and there are also ways in which we fail to render that life *visible* at all. In Burnett's film, the horse provides the occasion for whiteness and blackness to communicate. The horse mediates the scene of capital's transmutation—from horseflesh to horse meat, from human life to bare life. But, in Burnett's spare narrative, the relationship between human and animal fails to be limited by the solely representational. For Burnett, the affective life between human and animal—even in the midst of the taking of life—outstrips the claims of the market with its raised platform, and its wingtipped dandy.

In Charles Burnett's first feature, *Killer of Sheep* (shot in 1973, but not released until 1977), Stan's world is one where "politics presupposes livestock"; he is the one in charge of managing livestock unto death. But I want to reflect upon Burnett's work with hum:animal life in the context of Derrida's statement that "the idea of an animal that claimed to break with this power to command beast, to order the becoming-livestock of the beast, would be absurd and contradictory."[33] If this is the case, then Burnett's *Killer* most certainly breaks with this power to command, represented as an absurdity in Derrida's ruminations about hum/animal worlds. Human being that refuses mastery over the animal is an absurdity, yes, but what becomes of Black bodies who *refuse* in this web of management and mastery? Is the animal always already only a symbol of Stan's ability to master? Or is his presence at the end of the film as the killer of sheep, rather than the solely factory floor sweep of the film's first frames, significant enough to bring forward this question about *relation* in the film?[34] I am suggesting that the animal in *Killer* troubles the critical outcomes for both questions asked here.

What is it about the killing of animals in Burnett's early films? James Naremore notes that "the slaughter of an animal is a key element in the film [*The Horse*], functioning chiefly as a kind of metonymic illustration of a society in which the cruelest, most psychologically damaging work is assigned to the poorest and least powerful."[35] The horse is not being slaughtered but euthanized, so the choice of words is strange given the circumstances where two Black humans, one white human, and two horses carry out their relationships with one another, participating in some kind of visible ethical collective. When we cast relationships among beings in static relational terms, especially where power is concerned, we often then see their being together in scripts that circumscribe our readings. Nevertheless, the taking of the lives of nonhuman animals is as central to Burnett's earliest work as his concern for Black communities of struggle—if these two entities can be entirely set apart from one another.

In *Several Friends* (1969), there are two scenes that bring together the argument I make above about the West and animal slaughter. The film opens with all of the principal players in a car; on the way to their destination, they encounter a drunken parking lot fight. The spectacle draws a number of onlookers, significant among them, a Black man and woman on a horse in western saddle. It is as if horse and humans stop to comment on the ridiculousness of the fight—in this moment, Burnett comments on a ubiquitous horse culture in urban Black Los Angeles. In another scene, about midway through the 22-minute short (8:33), we find ourselves witness to chickens being slaughtered and prepared for meat. The scene lasts for almost a full minute as a chicken is killed, parboiled, plucked by hand *and* machine, and carted off by the butcher. In the very next shot, Andy's wife places a raw chicken in butcher paper on the counter and begins to prepare it. The parallel between the killing in one scene and the disarticulation of the carcass in another—of labor in and outside the home, of male work and female work, of public and private—all point to the taking of the chicken's life. The chicken's disarticulation is part of the work of *politics* in the film and necessary to its gendered articulation, as the political and its gendered meaning is defined for Derrida, by the presence of livestock. In this scene Burnett collapses male and female *work* by juxtaposing it and sends up *domestication's* gendered practice as connected to the abattoir.

Hum:animal life is richly detailed in another L.A. Rebellion film, *The Cutting Horse*, by Larry Clark (2002), and the tension between gender and domestication is evident in this later work. Though it comes outside the boundary of L.A. Rebellion–era films, Clark served as director of photography on several films throughout the era. Clark's *The Cutting Horse* follows the protagonist Ray Wilson and his return to train champion cutting horses on the farm he left fifteen years ago. Early in the film, we have a similar scene of a horse out-of-context when he rides a paint into a bar. As in Burnett's 1969 endeavor, horse and human appear on the scene as non sequitur witnesses. At one point the narrator offers: "Horses are swift and graceful, but when they die, they become a pile of putrid rotting flesh and bones. There is nothing sadder than dead horses except an unwanted pregnant horse on death row, waiting to be turned into dog food. Occasionally a good horse could be found among discarded horses, but you have to be somebody who can see the potential that lies beneath the mud, manure, and flies caked on the poor animal." Clark's narrator refers to the horse as being on "death row," a condition that turns slaughter into something else, inching us ever closer to hum:animal. Just a few lines later, the narrator reiterates the earlier sentiment by saying, "broken-down pregnant mare."[36] While Clark's concern with animal life is different from Burnett's, the work of breeding, domestication, and gender blur in hum:animal stories.

Killer is a spare black and white neorealist film about a Black worker named Stan (Henry Gayle Sanders) in one of South Central Los Angeles's many slaughterhouses (Solano Meats) in the 1970s.[37] Many critics have engaged the meaning of Burnett's choice of labor for the film. It is obvious that the kind of work that Stan performs has contributed to his depression, manifested primarily through his sexual alienation from his wife (Kaycee Moore) and from his family, more generally. Stan's first words in the film speak to his state of mind. Naked from the waist up, Stan crouches under his sink, performing repairs in a kitchen that holds interminable DIY projects. As Cecil Grant's "I Wonder" fades in the background, Stan stares somewhere off-camera, saying: "I'm just working myself into my own hell. Can't close my eyes. Can't get no sleep at night. No peace of mind." When his friend Oscar suggests that he kill himself like Johnny Ace (d. 1954) because it would make him a lot happier, Stan thinks about it for a split second and in this instant, his daughter (played by Burnett's own niece, Angela Burnett) appears over his shoulder in a dog-face mask, with her fingers in her mouth. The brief scene of her looking at him, he looking at her, her looking at us, is riveting and disturbing, and mediated by the gaze-less gaze of the bizarre dog face (figure 4.2). His reply to his friend is in the negative ("No, I'm not going to kill myself"), but his response is witnessed by his daughter's sudden presence, and it appears from his furrowed expression that he is concerned that she is there during his exchange with Oscar. I can't help but think of Audre Lorde's words in "Power" that capture the imperative to kill the self, rather than one's own children. So much happens in these first ten minutes in the film as Stan prepares to go to work in the abattoir: a perhaps cheeky exchange about suicide, the presence of children both in the home and outside at play, and Stan working at home before going to his day job.

But the film is also a story about the possible lives of Black masculinities, as the male children at play in the opening scenes of the film engage in a series of injurious games with one another (throwing rocks, attempting to push an abandoned railroad car over the body of a child who voluntarily puts his body over the tracks), interrupted by Stan's son (Jack Drummond) heading home to retrieve his BB gun. On his way, he encounters two men jumping a fence with a television set—when an older neighbor notices the two, one of the men threatens him with a stick. When the boy arrives at his home, Oscar hails him as "Killer" as he walks toward the back of the house to look for his gun; upset that he cannot find it, he grabs his sister by the mouth of the dog-face mask, sure that she knows its whereabouts. His father runs him off as the sister wails. *Killer* is a spectrum of masculinities that continue throughout the film, and part of Stan's quest is to wade through these possibilities. How can he inhabit his own life in the wake of capital that circumscribes it and through rigid modes of being that produce *him*? The presence of the dog-face-mask-wearing daughter and the bodies of sheep

4.2 Stan's daughter in dog-face mask. *Killer of Sheep* (1977), dir. Charles Burnett.

and the Judas goats who lead them to the killing floor, I argue, draw another map of possibilities for Stan—possibilities that question the "human" as an appropriate container for a self-determined life or for all life that matters.

Moreover, her stare, the dog face, and the hand in her mouth confuse the boundary between human/animal, adolescence, and childhood. It is clear that Burnett wants us to understand the fraught connection between blackness and the animal, as the animal gaze is a literal mask, a literal silent film through which father and daughter speak, or at least catch sight of one another. It is also a very heavy-handed way of pointing out just how much the animal means to one father and his family, at least in terms of their livelihood. In the end, the scene speaks volumes to the principle emotional action of the film: Stan is being slowly demoralized by his work on the killing floor of the abattoir.[38] Playing dominoes with his friend Bracy, Stan and his friend sip tea and coffee, respectively, from delicate teacups. He asks Bracy if the steam from the cup on his cheek reminds him of anything. His friend tells him "nothing at all," casting him a sardonic look. But Stan smiles and notes that the steam against his cheek reminds him of "making love." This nostalgia only elicits laughter from his friend and a crude joke about women and malaria. Once again, Stan is out of alignment with gendered expectations; his softness is a quality that the culture of the film cannot seem to reckon with.

The next scenes are of Stan at the abattoir, cleaning up offal and readying the assembly line. While the first scenes that open the film are of boys at their games and men in conversation, Stan's departure from the Solano Meat Company is cut with sounds of children singing the nursery rhyme "This Old Man." We are treated to a typical domestic scene of his wife preparing dinner and fretting over her face's reflection in a pot's lid; his daughter sits on the floor playing with a phenotypically white doll singing to Earth Wind & Fire's "Reasons." This scene of relative joy prepares us for the overwhelming silence between Stan and his wife at the dinner table—she breaks the tension first, asking with concern, "Don't nothing ever make you want to smile?" If we remember the above scene and the steam from the teacup, we know that indeed, something does. He just can't make a transfer of his feeling to communicate it to her. The kind of love he can recall in companionate masculinity does not seem to translate from one community of intimates to another. She tries to encourage him to rest, but, without a word, he rises from the table and proceeds to work on their hopeless kitchen.

Another trip to the abattoir and a return home brings two friends, Smoke and Scooter, to their front door. The two men attempt to entice Stan to help them with a murder plot. His wife interrupts their conversation on the front steps and asks Scooter, "Why you always want to hurt somebody?" His response is to give her a lesson about "nature": "Who, me? That's the way nature is. I mean, the animal has his teeth, and a man has his fists. That's the way I was brought up, goddamn me." He then says, turning toward Stan, "You be a man if you can, Stan." Then Stan's wife steps forward, arguing with the two about that last comment. In the ensuing monologue, she says, "You talking about an animal, or whatnot, you think you in the bush some damn where. You here, you use your brain, that's what you use." When she finishes, Smoke observes that Stan has worked "his whole damn life" and doesn't even have "a decent pair of pants." The characters in this drama are ambivalent about place—Stan refers to the South as "down home" in the early moments of the film, but at the same time the juxtaposition of Los Angeles and elsewhere—a south they come from is everywhere in Burnett's film—is marked unevenly. The South is a home-not-home and the difference between hum/animal life, using your "teeth" or your "brain," is geographically located where being "here" and not "there" creates noticeable difference. The South, therefore, is a marker of hum/animal difference, being "there" is like being in the "bush" and we know this when Stan closes the scene by chastising his son for using the word "Ma'dear" to refer to his mother. Stan tells him, "You're not in the country anymore."

One of the most cited scenes of the film, and its most frustrating from the vantage point of the progress narrative, is when Stan and his friend Gene purchase a motor and remove it from an apartment at least two flights up from the ground floor. After a protracted and arduous scene, they finally place the motor precariously in the back of Stan's truck, which is parked on a hill, only to pull away and find that the motor easily slips from the bed of the truck and hits the pavement, ruined when the engine block cracks. In *Economies of Abandonment*, Elizabeth Povinelli marks a space where the machinations of European democracy forge a relationship with the colonies where the future for some is a looming potentiality (never attained outside of the constant othering that defers it indefinitely) rather than a time in which such promise is guaranteed. One of the burning questions I have for Povinelli is this: Is there a temporality we cannot know as past, present, or future? If other worlds and otherwise exist, how might they betray that neat arrangement of *time* illuminated for us by a broken clock that keeps on ticking?

Nevertheless, to describe this temporal problem, Povinelli offers:

> My argument is that specific, if mobile, figurations of tense, eventfulness, and ethical substance aggregate harm in such a way that its ethical and political demand is dispersed and dissipated. But this book is also interested in how alternative social projects are able to open a space in these assumptions as they endure this dissipation—and more, to become more than merely persistence. As a result, I make use of an alternative glossary that seeks to illuminate ways that alternative social projects aggregate life diagonal to hegemonic ways of life.[39]

This description could pertain to a host of Black liberatory projects and social movements, and it is perhaps why she turns her attention to L.A. Rebellion filmmaker Charles Burnett as she casts about for purchase with her argument about *endurance* in particular. The social project of all Black life could be said to live at a less-than-right angle to the world created for its existence. But what to do when that life is not merely symbolic but evidence of *an* other life, a together-living housed in the touch of beings, through work and, yes, play? This is what I believe is the fundamental question of Burnett's labor with animal life—at what point do these life-worlds become hum:animal, indistinguishable from one another in the entanglement of their *affect*? For Povinelli, endurance is "an aspect of existence": "Internal to the concept of endurance (and exhaustion) is the problem of substance:

its strength, hardiness, callousness; its continuity through space; its ability to suffer and yet persist."[40]

Povinelli's evocation of the film's narrative of persistence stems from the following assessment: "The harrowing nature of the film is the vertiginous precipice of Stan's being and becoming as the viewer comes to understand that *the only thing separating Stan from the sheep is his will to persevere.*"[41] Returning to my discussion of suffering above, the outcome for Stan in Povinelli's reading is for him to realize that familiar phrase "kill or be killed." In order to have the human prevail, the animal must constitute the mark of difference, must embody suffering's limit *for* human being. But what if Stan's quandary isn't how *not* to be like the sheep, but bound up with the *life* of the sheep itself? What if his notion of care is not legible to anyone around him—an illegibility that Povinelli thinks about later as "the time they are in is a time no one wants to recognize"—except perhaps his daughter, who shares the blank hum:animal stare with him and so understands that his dilemma is not to be easily *overcome.*[42] That *overcoming* is the tidy balm of a civil rights dirge mired in the rights of the human. In noting the ethical turn and animal studies, Kari Weil defines it as "an attempt to recognize and extend care to others while acknowledging that we may not know what the best form of care is for an other we cannot presume to know."[43] What if Stan is searching for the best form of care, in the space left open between the bio*political*'s engagements? What if Stan's query were a *Black feminist* query? What if that search gestures toward *an* other opening that holds no interest for critical theory or for late liberalism's still contentious capital?

The dangerous *persistence* in Stan's deliberation is in the kind of labor that does not accrue to mastery—that moment that Derrida marks as an absurdity: any animal that has the opportunity "to command beast, to order the becoming-livestock of the beast" cannot give up on such a moment, for it defines what *politics* is and by extension the capacity of human being. And to engage *politics* entails taking that overseer's whip or making that kill shot. Our Stan certainly negotiates, *does* the work of ferreting out an *ethical* approach to his situation, which is the transformative work at the core of Povinelli's sense of ethical substance. What I want to offer here is that Stan's *work* might seem daunting in its enduring performance, but I want to mark that this is hum:animal work and Burnett maps its quiet way through Stan's everyday as he stares not only into the face of his own future, his daughter, with the dog-face, but also stares into a space beyond the camera's eye, seeking alternative vision, seeking a world that makes room for hum:animal living. A world not bound by the man/machine model.

As if to shore up this claim for a more nuanced, if not radical read of the film's quest to bring us to an alternative interiority, Alessandra Raengo writes that the "only (tentative and partial) access to Stan's mind . . . occurs in the slaughterhouse sequences, where he arguably appears most active. Yet it is the status of the sheep—suspended between the literal (Stan's job), the figural (insofar as they stand in for the coerced violence that encroaches on him), and the reference to a rich film history tradition . . . that acts as a virtual archive of possibilities for Stan's personal and political actions."[44] The animal as hum:animal is a politic, of sorts. If Raengo is right about Stan's general *feeling* in *Killer*, then we have to take seriously that he derives pleasure from his work with animals even as he begins to contemplate what *being with* under the conditions of a different kind of *labor* might mean for him. How can he *work* differently? How can he let go? How does the film allow him to do so and how might we begin to see that work, though it is mired in a discourse about living which finds no temporal *location* for this *ethic*? This dislocated temporality can be seen in the scenes not only in Burnett's films but also in Larry Clark's *Cutting Horse* (2022), where the horse breaks literally into the space of everyday living, inserting the equine self into the frame of human life, making it hum:animal.

This larger picture that Burnett helps to shape is what Raengo seeks to engage. At an earlier point in her chapter, Povinelli argues that the film arises during the same period in which PETA, Earth First!, the Animal Liberation Front, and the Earth Liberation Front came into being. Interestingly enough, we see that the film is coterminous with a discourse about the earth's potentiality (in ruin), but are we allowed to see the film as *directing* that discourse on the animal and its liberation? Could we see *Killer of Sheep* as not only coterminous in but also contributing to, if not defining, this discourse? If we place MOVE as a precursor to PETA, if we perform a bit of autocorrection when we insert the standard names attached to consequential hum:animal futures, then the space of blackness opens up to contemplate affective lives of hum:animal being. Stan's ethical dilemma and its work might seem more than mere substance as a sign for something embedded in human being or a particular stand of critical theorists out(standing) in their field.

Eventually, Povinelli asks, "And how do we explain why some people keep on getting on while others do not? Why, in *Killer of Sheep*, does Stan persist beyond the point of exhaustion for other people in his neighborhood? Muscle and will, effort and endurance: what do we imagine are the social origins of these practical concepts? How are they a part of the technology of power and the ethics of substance that should interest us?"[45] To be fair,

Povinelli, like so many of the theorists I engage in this book, is investigating one particular aspect of human being forged in the belly of philosophical thought and not always attendant to when and where that thing called blackness enters into the framing of our questions. She wants to lift the efforts of Indigenous friends in Australia and those of Stan from mere futility into *an* other arrangement—where "their reflexive action [comprised of "ethical substance"] exists within a given organization of power that continually throws them in the vertiginous gap of being and becoming and failing to become."[46] In many ways, the striving *is* the figuring out of this relationship, the reassertion of presence in the face of erasure; what I offer here is a sense that contemplations of hum:animal life create an ethic in some other place where ethical substance has a more promiscuous becoming.

In Burnett's *Killer*, scenes of a depressed and sexually frustrated domestic life are cut through with scenes of animal slaughter. There is little room in criticism to make the point that it is the killing of animal life that bothers Stan in *Killer of Sheep*, rather than solely the lack of overcoming or an ability to get ahead. Povinelli defines the action of the scenes in the abattoir in the following manner: "The slaughterhouse is Fordist in its mode of production, racist in its stratification of skills."[47] As I noted earlier, in *Killer of Sheep*, Burnett withholds the kill shot until the very end of the movie; it is there that we finally see Stan actually point the gun and deliver death to the expectant animal (figure 4.3). Povinelli seems to interpret his job in the abattoir from earlier scenes of Stan sweeping and cleaning buckets of offal, while phenotypically white men perform the job of butcher, but in reality he has one of the cleanest jobs in the factory: he hangs and shoots/stuns the animal, preparing it for the throat slitting, skinning, and dismemberment that is arguably the worst part of the Fordist machine.[48] It is at its closure that the film acquires its title. In addition, this naming comes on the heels of a somewhat cheerful domestic scene where Stan appears to be able to relax with his family. The tension seeps out of the film once the animal is literally put down.

Whatever the work of the film, it is clear that much of Stan's labor is cerebral while much of his physical labor—working on a hopelessly dilapidated kitchen, moving a motor from one place to another, walking away from connecting with his wife—is perseverance rather than progress. What we do know is that Stan (killer of sheep) is preparing sheep, not lamb, for slaughter and consumption. In essence, even the market toward which his labor is directed is a second-tier market for both products: material and meat.

In her explication of the film, critic Paula J. Massood remarks that "Stan's dehumanizing and bloody job" is a result of "literal capitalist violence."[49]

4.3 The kill shot. *Killer of Sheep* (1977), dir. Charles Burnett.

In many ways, the relationship between blackness and the animal for Massood is figured through the violence of capital and its regimes of suffering, as in Walker's discussion of the lonely Blue. The violence of killing animals has its motive force in the demands of capital, rather than human endeavor. What this reading does is narrow the essence of the dilemma Stan finds himself in—one that centers both upon the killing of animals *as work* and his relationship with animal life in particular. In an interview with Burnett in the wake of the Rodney King trial verdicts, Belgrade native and film scholar Aida A. Hozic notes that Stan's "existence is as bounded by invisible threads of hopelessness as that of the sheep that he is forced to kill each day."[50] Again, the affective relationship between Black being and the animal is rendered in terms of "force," indicating that if Stan had a choice he would not be the killer of sheep. That Stan shares something with the sheep is undeniable; that Stan understands that something as bound to his *labor* is up for debate. The animal in Hozic's reading is a symbolic stand-in whose parallel helplessness is doubly precarious as it relies on the helplessness of someone who is also othered. The psychic life of the film is to try to move us toward envisioning something else altogether: *an* other.

Interestingly enough, Massood, like Raengo, sees the slaughterhouse scenes as filled with ease of movement apart from the rather static domestic ones. Does Massood mean to suggest that Stan is happier at work, that he likes killing sheep, or that his remove from a feminized domesticity frees him to be him*self*? My point here is not to answer this question—in fact, relationships with animals, human or *otherwise*, at least from the vantage point of the film, are always already laced through with doubt, worry, and, yes, regard. Stan must sit with the affective life of slaughter, his own and that of the animal *other* (who is that exactly?), and I believe Burnett's point is not to resolve what in real life is impossible to resolve without self-annihilation. But even as I write the sentence before, I come to its end and want to erase every word because I understand that the contemplation of one's own death in the face of the death of *a being* considered less than the self, or at least a proper sacrifice in exchange for one's own life is a terrifying outcome to consider. But such an outcome is indeed part of the picture in *Killer*—it is the work of making hum:animal matter. Killing sheep is eating Stan's living alive, he *must* find something outside the boundary of work and labor. Burnett's beautiful film is a mapping of his journey, and that journey, I argue, is a much more radical one—one that brought the members of MOVE to a similar conclusion. *Life is a single referent.*

But there is another way in which capitalist violence is marked in the Hozic interview when Burnett talks about his childhood in Los Angeles:

> When I was growing up in LA . . . people had the prospect of owning their own homes. It was not a dream, it was possible. All that now seems just impossible, particularly for Blacks. There was this exposé about banks not lending money to Black people who certainly qualify for the loans; these institutions help create these all-white areas, these Black islands, and then they wonder 'Why? What's the problem with these people?' . . . There are all of these underlying ownership and housing laws which prevent interracial contacts. For instance, if you look at deeds on a lot of homes in Los Angeles, you will find that they stipulate that the houses cannot be sold to non-whites, and that is what makes the racial situation in this city so volatile and so precarious—the problem is there, but people do not want to confront it, they want to maintain the illusion of the melting pot.[51]

Burnett pinpoints the consistent economic disenfranchisement of Black peoples, a fact realized, almost offhandedly, through the language of an "exposé." The "literal capitalist violence" that Massood alludes to is not just present in Stan's current occupation, it is a historical constant. This indicates that what Stan struggles against literally cannot be depicted in the film; we must receive it *drylongso*, as an act of *being* manifested in the everyday. As Massood argues, "Stan labors but he will never get ahead."[52] His line of work is not just a mirror of the affective life of capital. I would argue that his affective life is bound to an entwined commodification of hum:animal, as a being to be reckoned with and, yes, to be managed. The killing of sheep in the film is interminable; scenes of sheep going to slaughter appear never-ending. Thinking through the animal in *Killer* might provide the occasion to rethink the human, as the idea of getting ahead, of overcoming in some way is central to the distinction between human and animal, at least philosophically speaking.

Given these observations, I would like to open up another possibility here—one that includes the capacity for another kind of Black love, a queer love, if you will. I read the constant reiteration of hum:animal relation in Burnett and in Black life as a call to think through both our attachment to the human in our explications of blackness and the ways in which our attachments, our love, can take an improper object, can venture beyond a self that must survive. In the end, I am not entirely convinced that Stan wants to be a *political* animal.

livestock

March 2010. I am on my way to the mare's field with Alyx behind me. When we arrive at the gate, the cacophony of crickets and frogs counterbalances the absolute calm of a Carolina blue sunset happening just over our shoulders. The gray mare "comes round" so that I can say goodbye and hand her over to her friends. It is some seconds before I realize that something is wrong. Alyx lurches backward with a whine; I am still puzzled, although I now realize that my body seems to be working in slow motion. Alyx catches my eye and it finally dawns on me: we are being shocked by the electric fence. I yank the metal end of the rope from the fence and call her to me, just close enough to remove the steel chain from the three loops in her halter. She spins and just before she turns she looks at me as if to say, "What on earth has gotten into you? What was that *for*?" (For several weeks after she will give me that same look each time I remove the chain around her nose and turn her out.) But in that moment, I cannot respond to her; my pulse is thready and I am exhausted from the ride, the cool-out, the mucking, and, yes, the electricity between us.

5 horse : flesh

It's a carnival-like atmosphere filled with runaways, addicts, desperate lost souls and the rich people who employ them.
SYLVIA HARRIS, *Long Shot* (2011)

Sir Philip and his daughter had the lure of horseflesh in their very bones—and then there was Raftery, and Raftery loved Stephen, and Stephen loved Raftery.
RADCLYFFE HALL, *The Well of Loneliness* (1928)

He seemed already to be rearing back, every inch of his flesh revolting before that icy vision.
JAMES BALDWIN, *Giovanni's Room* (1956)

Nowadays we can hear tell of black jockeys, the ones who became famous. But where are the stories of all enslaved black servants who worked with horses, who wanted to mount and ride away from endless servitude?
BELL HOOKS, *Appalachian Elegy* (2012)

traffic

It is appropriate, no doubt, that this book's penultimate chapter finds itself at the center of my passion: horseflesh. No other sport or indulgence or animal magnetism places its currency so very close to blackness than the work of the track, the traffic in flesh, horseflesh. Sometime early in this waking nation, not quite on the verge of a republic, America's sport was born on the back of at least one quarter horse mare and between the legs of more than one enslaved man. The patch of ground was sketchy footing, to say the least, and the crowd was gathered to see the spectacle of flesh, horseflesh.

I was asked recently by an undergraduate equestrian, still green on that college green that we have all imagined roughing up a bit with the thunder of our horse's hooves—I was asked about women, sexuality, and riding. On that day, she was passionate and so wanting to connect in our virtual paddock. How could I help her make these connections among the objects of inquiry she loved—women, horses, sexuality? As I unfolded what I have learned about horses, women, sexuality, history, and philosophy, she discovered that I was perhaps telling a familiar story about this South we both inhabit, but not one readily known to the white women who occupy the barns that dot the North Carolina landscape that is etched in my DNA, some six generations back. In many ways, this Old South, packaged by a term called "southern," can be found in its female hum:animal parts on the road from the local horse park to some daughter's mother's barn.

To move us in the direction of this relatively untold story—a connection between past and present *practices*—a detour to prove a point. Trolling through Amazon and looking for all things "south" in preparation for my work with the journal I would eventually retool, I came across this gem from 2013, *Better Off Without 'Em: A Northern Manifesto for Southern Secession.*[1] Midway through what is both a highly opinionated rant and a pointed and somewhat astute critique of our southern climate, Chuck Thompson takes a trip to Laurens, South Carolina. In the town square he finds himself in owner John Howard's Redneck Shop and observes, "Howard cuts the price of the Klan uniform to $100 if I agree to buy $25 worth of other white pride shit. This includes an instruction booklet of secret rituals titled *Kloran: Knights of the Ku Klux Klan*; an embroidered patch featuring a swastika and inscription 'Master Race Member in Good Standing' and another reading, 'We Must Secure the Existence of Our People, and a Future for White Children'; and bumper stickers that proclaim 'I Endured a Year of Black History Month the First Day,' 'Never Apologize for Being White,' 'Forget Tibet, Free Dixie!,' 'Public Warning: Children Left Unattended Will Be Sold as Slaves,' and 'If I'd Known This I'da Picked My Own Cotton.'"[2]

While the catalogue of racist paraphernalia doesn't surprise, it is interesting that it incorporates an acknowledgement that extends to both the presence of slavery among us and to some kind of *future* for children that erases that very market-driven economy of the flesh. I know one of those signs very well because from 2011 to 2015 during my time in community at a North Carolina barn, I confronted an iteration of it. Every day. The version at my barn held no warning, just a declaration: "Children Left Unattended Will be Sold as Slaves." A few points of clarification here: my barn was an all-women's space, many of them degreed, some with two groups of alphabet clusters behind their names. We were an educated lot for the most part and many of us "adult riders." I didn't see the sign on my first visit. On that day, I spent little time at the meeting place where we would gather for barn notices and trash talk, community, and horse love. The next week, while unloading the gear from my truck, I saw it, paused, and decided to push on. For me, at that moment, it was a joke right? Just a harmless joke; I knew then that the sign and what was printed on it would become the reason why I would have to leave the beloved community. Eventually but not now. Now was for sore pasterns and poultice from a jar, no doubt long ago crafted by African ingenuity; now was for the smell of leather and termite-infested wood, and the embrace of a cat named Killer slowing my roll on a cold day by tangling his legs between my own.

No one wants to leave the beloved community—its embrace is a beautiful thing. Over time I acquired a horse born and raised in North Carolina, whose birth name is Sherah with Joy, but who came to me as Annie—a mare with an attitude to go with her fiery copper color and her "star, broken strip, and snip" of white on her forehead. I brought her to that barn and we got to know one another under the lie of our belonging. In truth, I said nothing, did nothing about that sign. I kept my *sometime* feeling to myself. I knew already that some iconography sticks and that when you lift our proverbial cultural rock to reveal not just ants, impolitely disturbed, but a scene in which white people are called to account, the cost is tremendous. I had the courage to ride an ornery mare over green-as-grass and maiden fences and carry her down dirt roads in Klan country, but I had no desire to speak to the woman who owned that barn—someone I grew to like very much and who made a good home for me and my mare—about the sign above the gathering place. I was a coward who simply wanted to ride.

If we are looking for the white women who hold the dream of the Old South's failures in their mind's eye, we need look no further than the discussions of breeding and stock, buying and selling, and, yes, luck and love, that occur during any given and ordinary day while grooming, tacking, and going about the business of riding our horses. As one unsavory character in novelist Jaimy Gordon's prize-winning saga of the backstretch, *Lord of Misrule*, remarks: "If Breezy don't cripple him, maybe some young ladies' riding school will buy him cheap. He's a nice horse, ain't it? Good manners? . . . So maybe he gets a few more years of trail rides and virgin twats around his neck. It ain't a bad life."[3] When horses fail at the track, they more often than not find their way between the legs of girls and women in local barn cultures, long on the desire to ride but short on cash. This is not a send-up of my decade-long sojourn atop the sturdy legs of thoroughbreds and quarter horses; these are not stolen observations betraying a community that at times nurtured me and at others made me feel my blackness and my difference in profound and, yes, shaming ways. This telling is intended to consider the full arc of *horseflesh*, the being that bell hooks so aptly notes is "a dynasty of flesh/roaming in the mind's eye."[4]

Instead, what I offer, hopefully, is a reading of just how very enmeshed these worlds are; hum:animal traffics in *flesh*. The readings offered here are a call for a recalibration of work in the field of "southern" studies. My method comes not out of that "new southern studies," which seems like more of the same, but follows after that *dirty South* that details the genesis of a place built by blackness, messy and ratchet, bitter and sweet all at once. My work here follows *that* strand of insurgent blackness. Given that the hunt seat comes from that African-descended hum:animal relation that stretches back to the early 1770s in the South, I argue that it is impossible to have one without the other and that a look at how this world is under-stood and scripted, in fiction and in fact, might lead us to see the *how* of the animal's responding. Might we begin, like a horse, or that dog in Edward Jones's novel, to incline our heads otherwise? For example, if we open our understanding of how "quare," to borrow from E. Patrick Johnson or how a particularly southern sexuality is *constituted* in this place, might we also begin to think of our quare-ness outside the boundary of co-constituted humanity? Might we incline our heads to how these captivating beings have shaped what practices are engendered between our legs, after all? The traffic in flesh points toward relation
and human overcoming
and failure
and reproduction
and, yes, blackness always.

This writing is also the recognition of my place as an African-descended person whose lineage helped to found the sport that gave rise to my desire to move with horseflesh over obstacles and up wooded trails in a lazy sum-mer stroll, flanked by women whose company I enjoyed immensely. These women living and riding in the South with whom the joy of friendship is buttered, like good Sunday morning ho-cake, with the sour-mash of our en-meshed historical relations cemented in the trade in flesh, which continues on, all around us, unabated. I am lucky now to be at a diverse barn where

I am seen and felt; where my hum:animal life unfolds in a community of like-minded people.

That young female student, passionate about women, horses, and, yes, sexuality, was shaken by my revelation that the scaffolding we shared and trafficked in had a history so saturated in blackness, that it even contoured the very connection she sought to illuminate. How did women, horses, and sexuality become so entwined? How could we ride and jump and rub and muck and fall without the trace of blackness in our wake or on our minds? When I ventured to say that given my knowledge of the histories of the sport and its dependence on enslavement for its making, I surmised the following: that young white girls wanting to ride most likely were prohibited from the barn and its culture precisely because of the presence of (enslaved) Black men in its aisles, stalls, and feed and tack rooms.[5] Most likely it was not until after formal emancipation and the Jim Crow tactics that kept the sporting dreams of Black people from bearing fruit that it was perhaps deemed "safe" for white women to participate in barn culture to the extent that they do now—such that I have never been at a barn across three counties in the state where there have been more than one or two male riders at a time. In the North Cack, barn culture is ruled by females.

To drive home this deep suspicion about where the rudiments, the practices of enslavement continue to flourish, it is perhaps no surprise that in thinking about horseflesh and barn culture, taxonomies of being and modes of supremacy, I came upon the story of one Jim Farrands, imperial wizard of the Invisible Empire of the Knights of the Ku Klux Klan, who apparently used $375,000 of Connecticut Klan money to purchase an "83-acre horse farm six miles from Sanford, North Carolina, in Lee County."[6] Over a decade and a half of hum:animal relation in barn cultures brought me to Southern Pines, a half-hour's drive from Sanford. Among the woods that dot the periphery of pastures and paddocks and the sounds of horse tails swatting at flies and mares calling to their foals are the manicured stadiums, dressage arenas and the cross-country courses and the mostly white women, some of them females, who call these places home.

So, what do these "females" have to say about this world in the genre of fiction dedicated to the love of horseflesh? My work situates itself in the worlds depicted among three novels, Jaimy Gordon's *Circumspections from an Equestrian Statue* (1979) and *Lord of Misrule* (2010), and C. E. Morgan's *The Sport of Kings* (2016). The latter two novels concern themselves with the traffic in horseflesh, the "family" created by the culture of the "backstretch," and/or the blood family impacted by the quest for perfection in that trafficking.[7] All stories about the hunt seat—whether they depict lovers of the sport galloping across the steeplechase yards in Ireland and England, situated precariously in the low-stakes end of the racing world in US claiming races, or imagining the heart of elite racing on a Kentucky green—have one thing in common: the relentless obsession with the trade in flesh. A trade that finds itself at the track, in the barn, or on the course. But what the fiction produced from such a culture is rife with is the traffic in sex, flesh, and race that can challenge if not alter our prevailing notions of the how and why of certain *southern* supremacies.

Before we get to the twenty-first-century incarnations of cisgendered women's track inspired fictions, I want to attempt a literary genealogy for these kinds of tales, and for this trajectory, Jaimy Gordon's novelette *Circumspections from an Equestrian Statue* (1979) comes to mind. The personification of the statue and some cautions about its discourse with us propel the ridiculousness of this short work and its *commedia dell'arte* flavor.[8] Readers are introduced to an array of characters, centered around the real-life figure of General Ambrose Burnside, appointed by President Lincoln to command the Union Army of the Potomac, but who failed spectacularly at the battle of Fredericksburg and is described in Gordon's account as an "overdecorated fat-wit" by his mother-in-law, Mrs. Bishop (same in real life and in fiction).[9] The novelette is a comedy of errors, some of them grave, some inconsequential. In this tale, the legacies of the Confederacy—overinflated seditious generals, the perpetual subjugation of Black peoples whether by laws or the coercive rhetoric of obligation, and the reproductive work needed from the bodies of white women to cement it all (stature, subjugation, and propagation)—make for very interesting reading at the *tale* end of a project; this project on the relationship among hum:animal:blackness. I want to make clear here that I focus on white women in these narratives not because Black women's bodies don't matter in the reproductive schema of the slavocracy. Rather, I am intending to trace race, sex, and gender in stories centered around equestrian life. I am also attempting to mark the ways in which this genre of fiction produces forms of accountability for white female characters in relationship to their Black counterparts—accountability that focuses so heavily on the management of animal life as both a political engagement (and thus I work against my argument in the previous chapter) and an ethic.

Gordon's work mines the extent to which modes of torture and propagation are quotidian—endemic to cultures of the United States where seditious acts are passed off as heritage and female bodies, and here horses, and

Black subjects are arranged in a sordid tapestry of relationship to produce the veil that hides the unethical conspiracy among us. One of the most obvious statements about our collective national confusion about what the Confederacy is or does can be seen in the number of times that the word "General" is substituted by "Colonel" in conversations between former Union soldier Ambrose and Confederate sympathizer Dr. Wishey.

Gordon's story is bookended by the Civil War and the rise of gynecology, embodied in the character of Dr. P. Mariam Wishey, close enough but not quite to the notorious antebellum physician and torturer of enslaved Black women, J. Marion Sims. The drama unfolds during a dinner party in the drawing room of our General Burnside in 1866 as he entertains guests, the Reverend Woodbury and his wife Pamelia. Proving once again that Simone de Beauvoir was right to call marriage a contract between men for whom women are the language, the occasion for the story is General Burnside's concern over his otherwise "healthy" wife's inability to produce an heir. He invites southern expatriate Dr. Wishey, father of modern gynecology, from Liverpool to Providence, in order for him to examine his wife, Mrs. Mary Burnside. Of course, Mary is ostensibly unaware of the pending examination, which is characterized with the following exclamation: "How on earth were these things done! These investigations into the serpentine channels and mossy cavities of one's wife."[10] Like Faulkner's famous statement without question (mark), "So it's the miscegenation, not the incest, which you cant bear," which hangs in the air toward the end of *Absalom, Absalom!*, the scheme that arises is for Dr. Wishey, already obsessed with Mary from a photograph taken of her and sent to him by the General/Colonel, to perform his *practice* at the bequest of the good retired soldier.

These *practices* grow out of a particular southern culture; this pattern of control was endemic in antebellum enslaved life, as historian Marie Jenkins Schwartz observes: "The peculiarly intrusive nature of nineteenth-century medical therapies marked important new ways in which the material and emotional terrain of slavery expanded through the antebellum era."[11] In addition, she notes at some length the circumstances under which the increased medicalization of human beings owes a debt to practices engendered by the overseer's whip.

> Through the antebellum era, owners more and more turned to medical men, who they hoped would identify the cause of barrenness and provide a cure, help ensure that enslaved women would bring a pregnancy to term, assist at the childbed in difficult cases, treat complications from childbirth, surgically

repair reproductive organs, treat cancerous and other tumors, and provide advice and assistance for all the diseases of women. By securing the aid of physicians, owners hoped to extend their mastery over slaves to include not only social relations, but also bodily functions related to human reproduction. Doing so would ensure not only a well-ordered plantation for the present but also a secure future for generations of slaveholders to come.[12]

While Schwartz's research pertains to Black enslaved female bodies, what Gordon's novel addresses in fiction clearly represents the simple fact that the culture of slavery produced regimes of power that circumscribed, while not being circumspect. As Christina Sharpe reminds us, in the *wake* of these miseries, how can any life go *unmanaged* outside such a terrain of terror? A terrain constructed for use on the enslaved, but necessary also to the management of white femaleness itself as a counterpart to the *problem* being readily observed. In short, the female body is turned inside out by the apparatus of *care*. And, as Schwartz reports, as medical practices gained currency, it was not uncommon for a white enslaver to employ the same physician for his "family, black and white."[13] *This regime is indeed the speculum of the other woman.*

Gordon's novelette is rife with quotidian sexual violence and sexual inuendo, casually recalled with the narrator referring to "[Dr.] Wishey's very small fingers," and the Reverend describing his wife "as a sort of passive whirlwind idling on its back in a bedroom, while one by one the men it was cut to fit dove into its turning center."[14] It also has its queer parts, where Mrs. Burnside "dressed as always in pink," and the deceased nephew, Freddie Ballou, haunts the General/Colonel, having departed from the battlefield "up in a pink balloon named *Providence*."[15] Pink is for the flesh of (white) women and the nephew's ascension; pink represents a certain kind of invagination, the sexual threat here is to be turned inside out—dressed in pink, up in pink.[16] We learn early on that the purpose of Wishey's visit is to manage the reproductive life of Burnside's marriage. We learn also that five years before his visit Dr. Wishey wrote to the General/Colonel: "Colonel Burnside should know that women exist whose organs are so confused as to their purpose on earth that no amount of prodding—e.g., the Wishey incision of the *cervix* and *os* in the management of female sterility—can recall them to their proper usage. Was Mrs. Burnside much given over to fashionable spectacles? Going out at improper times, seasons, hours? strenuous dancing (waltz, polka, etc.)? champagne, creamed dishes, oysters, jellies?" In his reply to the good doctor, the General/Colonel sends along an "ambrotype" of his wife, in order to prove that she is "not ill, seems bursting with animal health and is a regular soldier at the dinner table. . . . She delights in her bed—let her please herself—that's all she will say, or her mother, Mrs. Bishop, either."[17] This epistolary exchange concerns "proper usage" and "animal health." The *process* here is for the restoration of what is deemed appropriate and healthful in the mind's eye of two men, both of whom are made into improbable ethical actors by the confusion of their loyalties (Union/Confederate) and their outrageous entwined intent to "examine" the General/Colonel's wife in order to control her reproductive life. Moreover, the constant reference to non-human animals as horses (for the Reverend, "his reins would freeze") or as things in relationship to them (for the General/Colonel, "was the size and shape of a light artillery piece whose horse had gone down") continues the parallels so obviously drawn elsewhere in *Circumspections'* hum:animal life.

It is clear that no small connection is out of the question for Gordon, and this is perhaps the novelette's strength and the reason why Gordon's works have garnered a small fandom. The comic tempo of *Circumspections* is only outdone by her underground fantasy classic, *Shamp of the City-Solo* (1974), published five years before *Circumspections*. To be circumspect, by definition, is to act with deliberation, wary of imprudence. This novelette is anything but careful. Gordon sends up almost every drawing room or parlor convention, demonstrating the perniciousness of domesticity itself, but a domesticity that traffics in animal parts and pseudoscience, reproduction and forms of masculinity, invention and theft. The *science* of racialized and gendered regimes of torture perfected in the antebellum period, forms of American ambivalence in our collective relationship with whiteness and the theft of Black invention through modes of obligation and servitude, are all the "stuff" of slavery. Gordon follows the history of the real General Ambrose quite closely, showcasing the relationship between General/Colonel Ambrose and Robert Holloway, his coachman in the novelette and a free Black person from Virginia and his personal valet in real life who was captured for seven months and held in Richmond by the Confederate government. When he was released, he purportedly skipped a visit to his wife and son and headed to reunite with Burnside in North Carolina.[18] Were they lovers or was their mutual devotion born out of the fabric of collusion, coercion, and theft that was the slavocracy? There is room to speculate that the odd and awful mixture above is the stuff out of which the narrative of this novel is forged. Like McQueen's twenty-first-century query into nineteenth-century ethical possibilities in the midst of the slavocracy, Gordon puts similar pressure on the kaleidoscope of slavery's *effects*.

Bookending the series of circumspections from a personified, though not animated statue is a series of "miscellaneous views" that speak to a culture that embraces a male gaze and produces spectacularity from difference. Among those slides or "views" for the stereopticon is one of "ENG AND CHANG, THE ORIGINAL, AND DISTINGUISHED, SIAMESE TWINS" which allows Dr. Wishey to imagine himself "an oriental potentate" looking down on his own estate with settled assurance.[19] This parallel confidence maps onto the bizarre affective landscape of his own medical machinations in administering to women. He admits that before administering to the General/Colonel's wife, Mrs. Burnside, "he had found the organs of women, when forced to look at them, primitive and weirdly fluid in their geometry, like certain sea polyps."[20] In her study of Chang and Eng, née Bunker, Cynthia Wu deftly argues that the twins, who ultimately settle in North Carolina (what is it about the North Cack?) represent to an emerging nation a mix of anxieties about the unity of the nation along with the invasive "scrutiny by medical professionals who had honed their skills on the social underclasses."[21] On the first count, Wu later explains that "racialized conjoinment" "compelled conversations about managing a polycultural public, either through negotiation or through coercion in order to build an abstracted concept of 'nation.'"[22] And that "medicine . . . is a forum that entertains multiple voices, weighs and balances competing interests, and opens up space for debate even as it implicates itself in hierarchies that unevenly privilege and subjugate physicians, patients and laypeople," while she also notes that the Bunker twins and other public medicalized bodies "inform what gender, domesticity and the sexualized dimensions of kinship formations in the United States" mean and do.[23] In short, operationalized public and private space, spectacularity and intrusive technologies, sedimented racialized histories and loyalties, reproduction and the (dis)abled bodies that it depends upon for its propagation are all bound to one another. And Jaimy Gordon is ever-conscious of this particular "American" soup. Perhaps the novelette's opening address to its audience is the best advice for how to think of its series of conjoined political realities: "We are not of the family, but there is no harm, as long as we ourselves are invisible."[24] Gordon creates an omniscient presence out of her audience—one "not of the family"—at the same time that she construes us/them as interlopers under an imperative of silence.

These clusters of aestheticized tension that Wu reminds us of and Gordon professes to also have their parallel in visual cultures. American racing itself, depicted in the aesthetic of Swiss-born Edward Troye's (1808–1874) canvases, is ubiquitous with images of African-descended peoples. In thinking about what lies beneath, what stays "seething with our presence," to reassert Toni Morrison's claim about blackness and the American aesthetic of the nineteenth century, I took a cursory look at sporting art in the digital world and came upon a 2018 auction of one of Troye's works, *Richard Singleton* (1834).[25] In this brief video, Bill from Sporting Art Auction presents a rare opportunity for us to own this painting, named for South Carolinian US Army Colonel Richard Singleton and previously held by Paul Mellon. As Bill takes us through the painting's history, he recalls another one, not of a horse alone, but one of a horse posed with three Black figures. Troye's portraits, honoring flesh (horse and human) are one of the few places where the historic contributions of African-descended peoples to the sport of racing are on display.

In Alexander Mackay-Smith's *The Race Horses of America, 1832–1872: Portraits and Other Paintings by Edward Troye*, the painting is captioned as "Capt. Willa Viley's *Richard Singleton* with Viley's Harry (trainer), Charles (groom) and Lew (jockey)" (figure 5.1).[26] Mackay-Smith notes that "Captain Viley, having purchased Harry for $1,500, is said to have given him his freedom, paid him $500 a year to train the Viley horses, and to have continued this annuity even after Harry was too old to carry on as trainer."[27] You see this quite often in accounts of enslaved subjects laboring for mostly white others—some accounting of a high price paid to demonstrate this *care* and an obligation extending beyond the time of capture—as if such information dissipates the sting of unfreedom, the constant desire for it, and the incredible loss of generations of Black creative genius to a sport from which we could take no lasting financial gain. I want to reiterate here that the goal of this project isn't to argue for our economic advantage but to think through the kind of *relation* between hum:animal that is crafted by racehorse men and in turn what gets left behind in this *trace*. Troye would go on to capture the great and unusually tall for a jockey African-descended Cato and Wagner in 1839 (figure 5.2), in the race that would set the stage for the Derby's emergence some thirty-five years later.

The contribution of African-descended peoples to the sport is remarked upon in Carrie Mae Weems's *From Here I Saw What Happened and I Cried*. One of those thirty-three toned photographic prints is "Riders & Men of Letters," depicting an African-descended subject in the attire reserved for horse trainers, echoed in the paintings of Troye. By combining two qualities of talent, the rein and the pen, Weems gestures toward not only the necessary skill of physical work but also the making of an artform *and* an imaginary

5.1 Edward Troye, *Harry Lewis, Charles, and Lew Readying Richard Singleton,* ca. 1835. Oil on canvas, 24-1/2″ H × 29-1/2″ W. Virginia Museum of Fine Arts, Richmond. Paul Mellon Collection. Photo: Katherine Wetzel. © Virginia Museum of Fine Arts, 85.645.

5.2 Engraving based on an 1839 Edward Troye original. Joseph Napoleon Gimbrele, *Cato and Wagner.* Engraving on paper. Clark Art Institute, 1955.1809.

5.3 Catherine Dawson side-saddle on a pony with two dogs, signed "Edward Troye, fecit 1850." 27″ × 36-1/8″. Yale University, Mabel Brady Garvan collection.

both of which create the psychic life and pool of knowledge engaged with horseflesh. Such a visual and textual reference in Weems gestures toward Arna Bontemps, *God Sends Sunday* (1931), a novel that pairs the story of horseflesh and blackness, and later, gender in its secondary life on the stage as *St. Louis Woman* (1946), Bontemps's collaboration with Countee Cullen.

In roughly two decades of Troye portraits, rarely do we see a portrait of a seated rider, or of young women or girls, though there is one 1850 portrait of a young girl, Catherine Dawson, sitting sidesaddle on a fourteen-hand pony in pink riding gear (figure 5.3).[28] The pinkness of Dawson and her outfit and the pink of the General/Colonel's wife and nephew provide a metaphorical continuum about gender, riding, and, yes, a certain kind of "flesh" that shows itself in Gordon's most acclaimed work—a work of what I call *track fiction*—*Lord of Misrule* (2010), winner of the National Book Award. In another of Troye's paintings, Catherine Dawson's brothers are depicted with two dogs as well, and the healthy strokes, almost rounded in the sister's mounted portrait, stand in contrast to the angular, finer, almost triangular lines employed in the painting of brothers John and William. Horseflesh is what dominates Troye's work, and the angular brushstrokes produce the deprivation that is the racer's life where horses and their starving riders are as commonplace as the denial of freedom. In the midst of these taut lines emerges the fattened *pink* daughter, readied for us and enfleshed.

In her review of Gordon's book for the *Washington Post*, Jane Smiley, who writes about the track, observed that the novel gives readers "a sense of being steeped in a specific and alien world."[29] Smiley once captured this world's gendered landscape with a comment on a quote from the great trainer Henry Blake, who quipped "Today, most of the horses we get are in the second group—strong horses spoiled by weak handling, often by women for whom the horses are too powerful and too strong." Smiley follows up this citation with, "Thirty years later, his observation still obtains."[30] Gender is not only a *politic* in barn culture, it is a. way. of. life., determining potentiality of horse and human.

Jaimy Gordon's later equestrian-based fiction is no Jane Smiley racetrack.[31] Hers was the dark horse win in the 2011 run for the National Book Award, yet few critics have written about the novel and few took note.[32] The novel draws from a collection of characters in her 1995 short story, "A Night's Work," and is told from the perspective of both horses and humans. It starts with Medicine Ed (Edward Salters II), owner of a "half-caved-in Winnebago," referred to by Joe Dale Biggs (one of the track's many bookies) as one of those "old timey negroes," a "conjurer" and grandson of

Eduardo Salters, "greatest jockey ever known in South Carolina, born in slavery, killed in a match race in 1888."[33] Can Gordon's haunting use of poetic racetrack diction and the voice of yet another Black groomsman/trainer tell us anything about how blackness and the horse script one another, rely on one another in some small corner of the planet where human meets animal again and again? Medicine Ed is seventy-two when the novel opens, a groom and quasi-trainer poised at the dustbin of the great sport of racing, and he rises to stake a horse named Little Spinoza along with "the he-she trainer [Deucey] and the lost college girl [Maggie]."[34] Every character depicted here is far from the tony Derby that Americans celebrate almost every spring since that first 1875 run on May 17 in Louisville. That was a race won by Black jockey Oliver Lewis on Aristides with its new track and Jockey Club, a consolidation of money and breeding and, yes, race that would see the beginning of the end of a long line of Black "jocks" by the 1902 running of the Derby by James Winkfield.[35]

Jaimy Gordon's racetrack, Indian Mound Downs, perched on the edge of the Appalachian Mountains, in 1970 is the backstretch of "claiming races," where horses and their humans find themselves after winning at high-stakes races is out of the question. Hers is that hum:animal iteration of the dirty South. It is a track settled upon an outrage of deterritorialization and desecration of the dead. Gordon claims to have pulled her characters from a stint she did as a young twenty-something at a racetrack mucking stalls and grooming horses. It is a world unapologetic about its situation—settled on an Indigenous burial ground, twice rehabbed. It is a place that sovereignty forgot.

Into this world of hot walkers and poultice makers, stall muckers and grifters, walks Maggie, girlfriend of Tommy Hansel, owner of what the Irish might call a "yard" but a rundown one at best.[36] Immediately, Maggie is not like the others in the barn, and all at once, so very much like the women you see there. Gordon writes: "For all her stamina as a human girl she knew she was lazy and unambitious, except for this one thing: She could find her way to the boundary where she ended and some other strain of living creature began. On the last little spit of being human, staring through rags of fog into the not human, where you weren't supposed to be able to see let alone cross, she could make a kind of home."[37] In many ways, *Lord of Misrule* is a novel that stands at the heart of the distinction, where hum:animal life and its possibilities are mapped into/onto life at the track. This geography is different and not quite human at all. Everywhere in this work is the sentiment expressed by Smiley earlier that on the track: gender matters. As Maggie rubs Pelter back to life, she notes, "She was glad there was no man around just then to tell her to show that horse who was boss" (25).

There are many characters in the novel: Two-Tie (bookie and Maggie's uncle), Joe Dale Bigg (stable owner), his son Biggy, Deucey Gifford (groom/trainer/owner), Gus Zeno (mobster), Joe D'Ambrusi (mobster), Suitcase Smithers (stall man), Kidstuff (blacksmith), Alice Nuzum (exercise girl and sometime jockey), Jojo Wood (jockey), and Tommy Hansel (owner/trainer and Maggie's boyfriend). But the central tension exists among Maggie, Medicine Ed, the four horses (Mr. Boll Weevil, Little Spinoza, Pelter, and Lord of Misrule), and the races they run. Each chapter is told from the interiority of a character or from the omniscience of a narrator, too lazy to put any of the dialogue in quotation marks, so we have to know the diction of each character in order to understand who's talking. It makes for a labored reading and a devil of a plot structure, but worth it for the sheer brilliance of Gordon's characterization. When she introduces Deucey, for example, the writing is crisp and the dismantling of the human is vivid and precise: "She was a dilapidated hull of a woman with wrestler's muscles and a bulge at the waist of her filthy undershirt that could only be what was left of her breasts" (23).

In the first fifty pages, it is clear that Maggie, much like the General/Colonel's wife in *Circumspections*, is to be controlled from the inside out. We are first introduced to Tommy's relationship with Maggie through his sex with her: "She is so small in the middle that you can pull the jeans down to her knees by opening just the one button with a soft pinch of two fingers, and look out now if she doesn't let you do it, without even opening her eyes to ask who it is, the slut, golden straw sticking in her dense fuzzy hair, thorning the kinky pigtails" (35). On the backside of the racetrack, human being sleeps with animals, and straw piles conceal hum:animal bodies in slumber and in ardor, and sex is part of the trade in flesh, always. Maggie is no fool, though, and understands her fear of Tommy, referring to him as "feline" and thinking that "there was something odd about his hands. They curled backwards behind his wrists, hiding themselves, as if they knew they were not to be trusted. She knew, herself, that they did not always mean her well. They knew how to do many things, or rather, they knew how to do one thing, how to tame animals, but this they did from a whole forest of angles, and always on sufferance, for under their gentleness was threat" (58).

The hum/animal boundary is no longer distinct nor absolute in the narrative terrain of Gordon's shedrow. Hum:animal flow in and out of one another and senses collide so that human embodiment itself is a constant question mark and producing difference *or* distinction becomes pointless. As Maggie's uncle, Two-Tie, muses about his gangster colleagues during a friendly "all-night" card game, "It was the low nature of their appetites that tangled them up in one species together, various breeds of dog as they were" (68). It is a place where Two-Tie's dog Elizabeth gets to think out loud: "Inside all of that free space in her brain she was completing a philosophy of the world wove together out of all the smells she had ever smelled. . . . She was history minded" (75). While this is not the becoming or being togetherness of the *care* tradition evidenced in Woods's bonobos or Haraway's agility dogs, it nevertheless gestures toward something more remarkable, perhaps. To have a history is to have an epistemic claim on life as we know it. Gordon's world is riddled through with hierarchies of hum/animal that fail to parse, even as the text goes about *naming* those hierarchies as salient.

This is instead a landscape riddled with the afterlife, the wake, as Christina Sharpe would put it, of the slavocracy. A world like Northup's that no species, alive or dead, *survives.* In many ways the only one who lives outside this quagmire of slavery's collective *affect* is Two-Tie, who remarks upon this world, having been ruled off the racetrack for nefarious activities, from a single vantage point: "Getting ruled off the backside for alleged conflicts of interest and unsavory associations after Mickey went to jail for the dirty bookstore was humiliating and at first inconvenient, but he began to realize in due course that it was all to the good if what you were trying to do was see the whole world of half-mile racetracks and the people and animals that lived on them as one world, and not just a big, all-over-the-place, unseemly business" (76). In the end, Two-Tie is murdered for his vision of this hum:animal world.

In this world, "taking her" figures as intimate relation for Tommy Hansel. The languages of sexual violation, enslavement, and horseflesh mingle and cocreate on our journey to that last and significant race. The worlds of enslavement are open to *everyone*—for Medicine Ed's ancestors, Maggie's predicament with Tommy Hansel (Medicine Ed calls her "a slave" at one point), the racetrack and, yes, the horses. Little Spinoza's section focuses on his late gelding, and it is in this section that Maggie engages again in the art of "rubbing" horses and steps into that tradition, "But she sensed a thread had been dropped somewhere, the route to some secret heart of this business had been lost. She didn't know anyone who literally rubbed a horse, not even old Deucey" (109). So she asks Medicine Ed, who fills in the blank of history, noting that the tradition dated back to Europe and racehorses and the rubbing that made the horses "dry and warm." The rubbing is an "erotic synapse of z's from the ends of her fingers into his bones and muscles" and she wonders, paragraphs later, "Why did she like doing this so much? How was it that she could bear these hypnotic repetitive tasks at all, such physical primitivity in the service of some other living organism?" "Was she some kind of born slave herself, a prostitute in a temple, a hierodule?" On this ground of care and touch, the erotic life of human and horse can be engaged, as Maggie tells her recently gelded equine friend, "Take my word for it, a sex life would have been far too hectic for a boy like you. What you need is a world that's just a whole lot of different flavors of good. . . . Spinoza, she whispered, I know you won't see this—sex is a kind of slavery at best . . . you as *you* get burned away" (110–11). The erotic life of this world cannot disarticulate human/horse desire; the two pull toward one another, setting each axis slightly off its center. In Gordon's cosmos, characters like Medicine Ed remember their desiring selves awash in horseflesh, as at one point, he recalls a mare named Broomstick and how "at night he liked to drink and lay down in the stall with her in the good smelling straw" (178).

Whatever it is that's lost on this backstretch, it stays just beyond a fingertip's reach. There are so many ways to be "a slave" in this novel's intimate life. The turning point in the novel doesn't occur with the last race, but comes when Joe Dale Biggs, who has claimed Maggie's Pelter, convinces her to get into his car and then doses her with an animal tranquilizer—acepromazine—making it clear that "when I entertain a lady I like her to be completely in my hands. If you follow me" (195). Maggie escapes on Pelter's back and runs into her uncle Two-Tie coming up the drive when she falls off Pelter at the end of the fence line. He collects his niece and later, when he confronts Joe Dale Biggs, he is murdered by Biggs's son, Biggy.

Throughout the novel, Gordon plays with hum:animal being. Tommy is referred to as "faintly simian," and Maggie also recalls herself as "that monkey" when in a flashback she observes:

> Once in a pet store she had brushed inattentively by a cage and the small monkey inside had snatched her by a shirt button and would not let go. She pulled backwards. The monkey had eyed her with all the grave desperation of his boredom and twisted the button tighter. She pried at the monkey's fingers with her fingers, but it was clear she would have to do him some violence, break his little fingers one by one, to get free. She finally had to rip apart her blouse. She didn't mind. She was moved. She knew she was that monkey. (198)

Gordon thwarts the possibility of animal difference at each turn, giving us instead an ethics of recognition that doesn't necessarily turn on an ethic of care—because the caging and selling and using of animal life is never *care*, but instead a twisted *approximation*. At the close of the novel, two of the horses die, another is retired, one goes away in a van after wreaking havoc on the track. Maggie returns to writing "Menus by Margaret" for the Thursday *Winchester Mail*, and it is surprising that in this text and in Morgan's *The Sport of Kings* food cultures are produced as a principal way of domesticating women, as the job bookends Maggie's time in the novel, rendering her life at the track a momentary blip in an otherwise serene life contemplating "MANY LIVES OF WORLD'S OLDEST BEAN" (21). The last voice in the novel is Medicine Ed, who remembering Maggie, the "frizzly hair girl," "had taken sometimes to rubbing Pelter up with cloths . . . and sometimes when they walking the shedrow like now and eye-balling each other like now, he was careful to remember into the horse that the Mound has claimers at 1250 too. It's still another place left for them two to go, even if it is down" (294). Somewhere in *Lord of Misrule*, past and present make themselves known to one another, the African-descended groomsman and the "frizzly gee-whizzing white girl" are inheritors of the sport of kings in a double helix of exploitation and race and sex and love. A hot mess for a hot walker. Margaret's or Maggie's exploits in food point toward another trajectory for hum:animal life: we are what we eat. Always. And the way we eat, what we eat drags domesticated hum:animal life into constant and communal orbit.

to market, to market

Since when has a person's eating habits been a crime punishable by death?
RAMONA AFRICA AND MOVE WOMEN

DURHAM, NORTH CAROLINA, 1971

It was disgusting.
Sulfur. Iron. Ammonia.
Brown eggs. Boiling water. Clorox.

Going to the farmer's market with my Nana was like visiting some earthly version of Armageddon—cleavers raised high in one corner, a crate of eggs perched on the tailgate of a battered Ford in another; blood smeared on hands, aprons, and implements. Cracker voices loud and annoying; tobacco spat two inches from my feet. Old men—Black and white—cackling at the seriously terrified look on my face. My grandmother pulling me along down one stinking aisle after another.

> "Not that one—the one in the corner. Tell that little man of yours not to splinter the backbone like the last time—it makes the chicken no good for the table."

> "How many? You don't say? Is she poorly?" ("Fair-to-middling, I believe.") "Bless her heart. I'll be thinking about you both. Now give me some of those string beans and peas. Deliver to my place after three, I've got things to do this morning and I don't want them sitting on the back porch in this heat."

> "That one's got great feet; how much did you say? Mm-hmm. Same as last year. When do you plan to . . . ? That would be just fine. I expect in two weeks it will be just perfect."

Although I spent most of my late teens and twenties pursuing every manner of personal food activism—from vegetarianism to veganism—I have since returned to the complete food chain—my inner omnivore. As I look back upon those dreaded visits to the farmer's market with my grandmother, I would give anything to be standing there in the runoff from animal slaughter and the steam from the boiling pots of chicken holding her soft arthritic hand and listening to the lesson she was trying to teach me: Shake the hand of the wo/man who kills your food for you; have a conversation with the planter who has raised the same heirloom beans for generations and knows how to cook them; be thankful in a world filled with famine of mind and body that you will never go hungry so long as someone cares enough to feed you, to show you how you are fed.

. . . .

The piece above is the beginning of a reflection on my early memories of foodie culture. My experiences in the farmer's market of the here and now—hipster queer farmers and bearded local beer producers; lefties with green grocery bags and kids with strollers more expensive than some people's monthly mortgages—bears little resemblance to the terror of offal that was the market of my youth. In fact, the farmer's market of my memory does not jibe with what came to be known as the mostly "white" food-focused slow-food movement that has been part of the Triangle for over two decades. In these circles in which I travel—made up of activists and industry folks, farmers, and foodies—there used to be a constant lament for the low numbers of people from underrepresented groups in our ranks. Given the revolution in food that followed in the wake of the establishment of the BLM movement and intensified with the killing of George Floyd (may he rest in peace and power, still), I have heard and can recall all kinds of historical reasons why this is so.

This lament parallels that of animal rights activism where studies show "less than three percent people of color" are active in the movement.[38] Most recently Julie Guthman—guru of West Coast food studies—notes "many of the discourses of alternative food hail a white subject and thereby code the practices and spaces of alternative food as white."[39] The editors and authors of the timely collection *Cultivating Food Justice: Race, Class, and Sustainability* (2011) indicate that the problem can be cited among the three approaches to food: food security (health/nutrition issues), food justice (slow food, alternative fair trade, labor community based/youth movements), and food sovereignty (food is about culture, not just nutrition; defining "sovereignty" as about self-governance, deep rootedness, and community narratives of self and place). While editors Alison Hope Alkon and Julian Agyeman point out that authors in the collection use "a variety of theoretical lenses including environmental justice, political ecology and critical race theory," it is noteworthy that intersections of race, class, gender, and sometimes the body do not include the category of sexuality.[40]

One critic who does intersect with sexuality in her approach to that thing called food studies is Elspeth Probyn, who observes "paying close attention to the sensuality of eating—the very queerness of sex and eating—may allow us to think about other forms of living ethically."[41] This same chapter includes a discussion of the results of a focus group of vegans and vegetarians. At one point, Probyn remarks, "The ways of spreading their message varied, with some arguing that by being with animals one is compelled to rethink eating them. In a somewhat slippery analogy, the point was made that being with animals was like falling in love with someone, say a Negro or whatever and realizing that 'oh they're like us.'"[42] I do not know where to begin to unpack this particular part of an otherwise compelling book on what I will term "food theory or theories of food," but the presence of the "Negro," its close proximity to "whatever" and the "animal," not to mention the "like us" analogy, is more than "slippery," it speaks volumes about the paucity of theoretical work geared toward discharging this loose configuration of connection among "Negroes," "animals," and "us." Moreover, the absolute binary created by the terms "Negro" and "vegan" in the focus group that Probyn alludes to also points toward the solid erasure of African-descended voices in the creation and meaning of vegan practices.[43] I want to argue that this destabilizing constellation is still operable when we are confronted with a certain history of the African-descended and their relationship to America's kitchens.

Thankfully, this problem of race in food studies is in the midst of a reckoning, as the Southern Foodways Alliance debacle during the COVID-19 pandemic and the rise of BIPOC voices in foodways in general has shifted the conversation in the field. In particular, I note the special issue of *Gravy* under the excellent editorial eye of Cynthia Greenlee in the fall of 2020 and the Netflix miniseries *High on the Hog* based on the book by the same name. Both publications move the work on *food* and Black lives in this country beyond the recognition of civil rights struggles and toward the complexity and ambivalence of a culture of eating and being with animal life.[44]

This chapter is dedicated to pulling apart the connective tissue—the sinew of "whatever," "animal," "us," and of course, "the Negro." "Whatever" is a nice beginning because it constitutes that which can be tossed aside—think offal, if you can—and that which must be emphasized—W-H-A-T-EV-ER. On the other hand, the animal here is always in lockstep with the Negro, threatening to consume him/her, or better yet, envelop "the Negro" in the cloak that is fur instead of skin. And then there is the "us"—that category of human who always invokes the collective over and always already against "them." Look! A Negro! What-EV-ER. Given this constellation of meanings and misapprehensions it might be appropriate to wonder what kind of work the word "species" really does? I am with Agamben here: homo sapiens is "a machine or device for the recognition of the human."[45] The above constellation also subtends the casualness of the connections among the four entities, the conversation, punctuated by "whatever," proceeds as if no response is expected because a suitable "answer" has been procured through an epoch of historical relations. Here the relationship between those who respond and those who react is mapped out in a dreadful assemblage.[46]

la bête noire

> La marquise de Coetlogon prit tant de chocolat, étant grosse l'année passée, qu'elle accoucha d'un petit garçon noir comme un diable, qui-mourut.
> **LETTRES DE MADAME DE SÉVIGNÉ**

I love chocolate cake.[47] As a home cook who entertains often, over the years I have made my share of them. Recently, I was looking for a quick and decadent chocolate dessert in my vintage cookbooks and settled upon a flourless chocolate cake—the varieties of which can be found across European/Western cuisine. I have made Italian and French, vegan and vegetarian, and northern and southern versions of the confection. In short, combine nuts (in some versions), eggs, oil or butter, sugar, and chocolate with some kind of leavening optional and you get a wonderful, delectable—"I can't believe it's not butter"—cake.

On this particular day, a quick search on Google for the culinary marvel produced a recipe on Epicurious.com with the following description: "This phenomenal take on a classic flourless chocolate cake lives up to its translation, 'The Black Beast.'" Pause. Just when I was enjoying myself, I am confronted with the long arc of history—with the when and where I enter of it all. What does *that* mean, exactly? If we track across several dictionary examples of *bête noire*, we have the term defined as "an anathema" or "a person or thing strongly detested or avoided" and I am told we are largely to thank the French for its wide circulation beginning in the mid-nineteenth century. In common parlance, the French term *bête noire* refers to the thing that one most desires but fears nonetheless. Think abjection here. The stuff of blackness is always made up of the bittersweet, is it not? And that this term that defines the most salient of kitchen challenges—a simple flourless torte—produces one's sense of mastery and craft ought to give us some pause indeed.

Moving back to the dictionary definition of *bête noire*, back again to its first part—"a person or a thing." This precarious teetering between personhood and thing speaks to the heart of the matter here and to the kind of questions I would like to ask about this slippage from colonial slight (Black beast) to culinary phenomenon (black beast, or the beast). The biography of the beast and its relationship to the sovereignty of the self will be the subject of chapter 6 of this book. To continue, how does such a term find its way out of the wretchedness of a colonial practice and its damning lexicon to become a culinary phenomenon? We can say much here about literally "eating the other" in the colonial frame, about what it means to take the beast in—to ingest "it" (person or thing?) and enjoy. Perhaps this is my own "whatever" kitchen moment, as I am called upon to make a choice: get dinner to the table on time, therefore inserting bad history lesson into slot A, so to speak, or rethink bad history lesson, and by extension, the guest list, altogether. A similar quandary is addressed in Kyla Tompkins's work, as she challenges us "to shift food studies attention away from the what of food to the how of eating. . . . I hope to point to the fact that the what of food is in part determined by the material and symbolic processes that brought food into contact with the mouth and the digestive system."[48] For Tompkins, the role of food goes far beyond what we eat, politically speaking, constituting discursive and representative interventions that literally create our relationship with the alimentary tract itself.

But the questions here are legion: In eating this fine, rich substance, are we dragging the course of human history along with it? Is taste subject to more than the vicissitudes of our salivary glands? Am I a racist if I love flourless chocolate cake, let alone make it for others to consume? Much of the work in this project is speculative, as it engages not just the how and why of it all but also the perhaps—the possibility of thinking through a problem that has a less than material answer. This focus on phenomenon—on speculation and possibility—led me to contemplate the origins of the name, *bête noire*. We could perhaps begin with Frantz Fanon in 1952, "I came into this world anxious to uncover the meaning of things, my soul desirous to be at the origin of the world, and here I am an object among other objects."[49] Here is that same tension between embodied personhood and juridical thingness—what is a person to do when one realizes that in fact, one is "an object among other objects"? It is a logic of negative relation—or a reductive sameness—that produces in Fanon a move toward self-evisceration, cannibalism (maybe one and the same), and of course, thoughts of the beast, a being whose trembling is infectious. The next question to ask is an even more vexing one: what are those "other objects"? One can certainly infer from his prose that the "other" here is hum:animal, but other objects in this piece are more vaguely referenced. They are the "whatever" of the initial observation—a shared being, perhaps, but no language between them to make the selves known to one another.

We have always thought of this relationship from one perspective in critical Black studies. The image here is of the Black (human) being separated from his humanity (I use a gendered term here purposefully). But the mirror here has two reflections—it cuts both ways—as the thingness of the Black human evolves so does the thingness of the others around IT. My work in this particular chapter revolves around this little twist in the negotiation between person and thing, and how such a negotiation tends to linger in that space where consumption, bodies, and beasts circulate. In the end, I am interested not so much in how the Black beast becomes a delicious cake, so to speak. So, I am very sorry to disappoint you here—the jury is still out on that one.

I am, however, interested in how this becoming—this movement into thingness—is framed in such a way that all beings in this new lens on (non) personhood become things as well. In this new configuration, what I am seeing around me as a colonial/postcolonial subject is that the other is also the other to me. This relationship to other persons/objects is negotiated in much of philosophy as a relationship that revolves around the figure of the face. I come face to face with you and am forced to recognize YOU—in capitals. This recognition is usually the stuff of what philosophers like Emmanuel Levinas term "the ethical commitment." In recent theoretical work on the hum/animal distinction and sentient beings, there is much debate about the form—the face—that this recognition takes—is the face a necessary component for recognition? Can the ethical commitment be formed without it? Can we see another without a face and sense its being-ness, nonetheless? Kelly Oliver, reading Derrida, observes that he is "adamant that an extreme ethics allows that we can never know from where—or from whom—we will hear an ethical call."[50]

All of these questions are important ones as I trace the mysterious permutations of this ethical commitment. But chief among them is a nagging sense that the ethical commitment inherent in that relationship between self and other is utterly broken in Frantz Fanon by the colonial experience—an outgrowth of enslaved experience, but not necessarily an improvement upon it. As scholars we tend to focus on a certain set of human relations that attest to this brokenness—that between Black and white, for obvious example or between persons in Black community (mother/son, father/daughter, sister/brother, neighbor/tenant, etc.).

So now we have three ideas floating around here: (1) Who/what are those others/objects that the Black figure suddenly finds himself among in Fanon's formulation? (2) Are ethical relationships important to connections between humans and/or things? And finally, (3) Is the relationship between self and other, at least for blackness in the colonial/postcolonial frame seriously broken and beyond repair? In the course of researching this project, I began to link these three questions to the presence of underrepresented groups or at least commentary on the presence of underrepresented groups in food studies work in particular. Because so much activism and scholarship in food began with the ethical treatment of the animal, I began to meditate on the absence of a focus on ethical relation to the animal in Black studies work. This is not to say that Black persons have not involved themselves with animal life in ethical ways—it is just to say that we often don't find Black studies critics thinking through those ethical relations beyond the symbolic. How to talk about animal life, not as figure, but as *life*?

Think of that opening farmer's market where food as livestock is being managed but badly—as management is more politically efficacious when it cannot be seen, when the storefront looks tidy and all the bad things are out of the way of the consumer. In many ways slavery became less politically efficacious because its poor managerial practice became so out in the open, was so evident and ultimately embarrassing—especially in the visages of the enslaved.

But I digress—think of these terms and of foodie culture's management of the marketplace, and of the presence of "livestock" in what constitutes "politics." The irony of this is that animals raised for today's farmer's market are kept at some remove from their relationship to livestock—think "free range," "grass fed," and "happy chickens"—at least in our imaginary. Slow food/human/animal, dragging blackness in its wake, perhaps will find itself now cognizant of the problem: how to eat a flourless chocolate cake or anything else ever again with the same kind of relish.

food is fodder

> In the eating encounter, all bodies are shown to be but temporary congealments of a materiality that is a process of becoming, is hustle and flow punctuated by sedimentation and substance.
> **JANE BENNETT**, *Vibrant Matter* (2010)

Before my foodie digression where I dredge hum:animal, rather than drag (though there is that too) it, I was working out sex/gender, race, and the connections between Black men and white women in the fictional life of the racetrack. It is fitting that C. E. Morgan's *The Sport of Kings* connects the Ohio River Valley and Kentucky's bluegrass—if the first territory can be seen to hold the fictional life of Toni Morrison's freed and enslaved and the latter is the always already of a place in a time warp of sorts. *New Yorker* reviewer Kathryn Schulz writes that the novel's "central preoccupation [is] . . . the way that African-Americans have been forced off track, literally and figuratively, to the psychological, political and material advantage of whites. The resulting book is enormously flawed, ceaselessly interesting, and strangely tremendous, its moral imagination so capacious that it overshadows its many missteps."[51]

The first scene that greets us at the beginning of Morgan's epic narrative is a primal one; it is of Henry Forge running from his tyrannical father, "sic semper tyrannis," who eventually crops his son.[52] The offense—allegedly kill-ing the bull of a neighbor—matters not as much as the hierarchy of living beings and things that the novel's opening salvo seeks to solidify. Henry's father John remarks, "I don't care that you killed an animal today. An animal is just unthinking matter. I'm not sentimental about that. But you didn't just kill an animal, you destroyed another man's property" (10). What ensues next is the story of how Forge Run was built by Samuel Forge, ancestor to Henry some seven generations back who elects to travel with "a bondsman he had bought for $350 on Richmond's Wall Street" (14) who becomes a "favorite slave" and whom he brings along "instead of one of his younger brothers—to properly scout a land only dreamed of, to protect Forge's life at the expense of his own, and to amuse him" (17). Property doubles back upon itself, it is a begetting that proliferates. Along the way it also cocreates, sharing the proper vision of "a land only dreamed of." The stuff of "race" in the US imaginary constitutes the bizarre entanglement of shared vision *out-side* of properties of "unthinking matter." Samuel and John and now Henry Forge perhaps are the inheritors of this vision, not singular, but built upon the purchase of property *fit* for the task at hand, and therefore they are re-liant on that property's compliance or the dream will surely fester. When "the strange family of things" gives way to "the spirit of lesser animals," we learn that the "slave" that ancestor Samuel brought with him was indeed "smart with black magic and a very fine cook" (100).

In Morgan's cosmos, property supersedes all else, making a mockery of words like family, love, or home. And the lesson bound in the slavocracy's ledger is handed down to Henry, much like Faulkner's Isaac McCaslin in *Go Down, Moses*.[53] John Henry tells his son, "Henry, you're always hijacking a principled conversation with nonsense and daydreams, and it's a result of spending so much goddamned time with your mother. . . . Real knowledge begins with knowing your place in the world. Now, you are neither nig-ger, nor woman, nor stupid. You are a young man born into a very long, distinguished line. That confers responsibility, so stay focused on your learning" (22). The dream of a distant founding Forge father is now be-come "daydream" and "nonsense." Indeed, Henry's education is to under-stand the potency of race and sex and place, and how they interconnect. On women, John Forge continues, after a statement about "well-educated men" and "white niggers," "I wouldn't say that they're naturally intellectu-ally inferior, as the Negroes are. They're not unintelligent. In fact, I've always found little girls to be as intelligent as little boys, perhaps even more so. But women live a life of the body. It chains them to material things—children and home—and prevents them from striving toward loftier pursuits" (23–24). Reproductive capacity is the cornerstone of slavery's law; a body "chained" to the material world, inefficacious in a world of "loftier pursuits." But the comparisons here are among blackness and a whiteness that is gendered and classed; white maleness is the law, and its issue, Henry Forge, is its shadow. The materiality of blackness (regardless of gender) and white femaleness sets the stage for an *en*fleshment in the novel that will have profound consequences for the story that unfolds.[54]

To witness John Forge's education of his son is to survive a series of racist and misogynistic maxims, which include the inevitable comparison of African-descended peoples to monkeys: "One smart monkey can find his way out of the cage, but that doesn't make him any less a monkey. And naturally, the other monkeys follow suit. They never realize until they leave the cage that they were warm and well-fed in the cage" (25). The intensity and surety of John Forge's claims on racialized and gendered life are so brutal in the book's beginning, the reader is educated along with Henry into this one moment of blood-borne belonging: "regardless, all the tangled roots of his inherited heart grew forever in the same direction: I am his" (25). Henry Forge's education is to get comfortable with being owned in blood and by inheritance. It is a profound education that leaves Black persons, white females, and even Henry in the materiality of bodies that assume kinship with other nonhuman animals.

The worlding of the *human* in *The Sport of Kings* is far different from that of hum:animal. In effect, the literature and visual culture I examine here testify to whom the human truly belongs. What I want to offer is that this world that is structured as separate and apart is unsustainable as human being's settled place; human being and its overcoming constantly bleeds off the page of its own creation. Modes of being and doing in horseflesh reflect the inefficacy of this *human* world and the desperation of its grip. The struggle for the legacies of enslavement—its lexicon and particular grammar—finds itself in fictional observations of *horseflesh* that makes and marks gendered and raced difference as a kind of corrupted *knowledge* at every turn—it is work unaccomplished without the drag of animal life in its wake.

It is while visiting a neighbor's farm with his mother that Henry's passion for horseflesh is awakened for the second time. The first time is in the book's opening scenes of young Henry fleeing his father's wrath with their farmhand named Filip sent to collect Henry on a Walker called Martha White, a horse named for the white girlchild whose likeness still brings us down-home southern cooking—yet another stolen legacy.

I want to take a minute here to trace how these three things: hum/animal distinction, food, and the stolen labor of blackness combine in an animal studies framework and how Morgan's novel, with just a quick nod to the name of a horse, opens up so much more for us to ponder. So much of the work of hum/animal distinction ignores the global investment in enslavement such that the distinction almost has no bearing, no *effect* whatsoever on the way in which such taxonomies of being inform that thing called "race." In addition, we are taught in southern foodways that the way to take care of our understandings of "race" and "region" is to pay a persistent nod to the regrettable legacy of slavery as we mind our butter beans and sweet potatoes, black-eyed peas and biscuits. The Martha White brand of superfine flours and grains holds a likeness of the founder's daughter at three years old (figure 5.4). This likeness is reminiscent of Troye's painting of Catherine (that I speak to below), in that the face is more like a Renaissance cherub. White femaleness enfleshed in hum:animal that continues its legacy of representing the diminutive qualities of flesh, whether through fattened youth or the angular starvation of adult riders, grooms, and trainers represented in his work.

That "Martha White" is both a horse and the *figure* of a stolen legacy of African-descent in our nation's foodways is no accident in Morgan's novel. Southern foodways, while acknowledging the contributions of African-descended peoples and their white (mostly female) counterparts, also holds within itself a narrative of northern aggression and southern victimization through extraction captured most vividly in John Egerton's classic *Southern Food: At Home, on the Road, in History* (1987). Of the period after the Civil War, he writes:

> When the war was over, the differences between the victorious North and the prostrate Confederacy became more pronounced, and the enormous chasm separating the two regions would keep them divided for generations to come. A century after they and the Northern colonies had joined forces to throw off the yoke of British rule, the Southern states found themselves returned to a colonial status, this time under the rule of the North. For another hundred years, the South would languish as a poverty-ridden backwater, an economic dependency of the expanding, industrializing North.[55]

In this chapter of Egerton's book, "Pass and Repast," what comes to the fore is a contest of winners and losers where the Confederacy and its violences are shrouded by the more potent injustice of a northern yoke and a colonial one at that. What is so arresting about the words "the enormous chasm"

5.4 Martha White
Flour tin.

is the extent to which African-descended individuals north and south of that Mason-Dixon line traveled often to visit relatives as *their* north and south was not so great a divide to brook crossing. It is not surprising that Egerton can write so blithely about such a miscalculation of status for the Confederacy. It is precisely how "lost cause" ideology comes to stand in for the methods and manner of the slavocracy so that the Confederacy's violent sedition looks like a reasonable and necessary form of (legal) state violence. One of the particular and useful violences of slavery's four-hundred-year legacy is to extract the labor of Indigenous and African-descended peoples and their work in kitchens and barns as *labor* and not art, as the selling of flesh by command, rather than the making of worlds hum:animal. The point here is to upset the rather neat binary that keeps us from seeing enslaved genius as anything but what we have been trained to see. This is perhaps why the African-descended coachman of Gordon's *Circumspections* continually appears with *his* invention at his feet or elbow—as a constant reminder of how African-descended ingenuity is an insurgence; worlding as it crafts a life for itself in relation to *an* other.

In the year 1606, settler colonialist George Percy made a few remarks about Indigenous peoples and foodways. While going about my work team-teaching and prepping for a class on food studies, I found his comments described by scholar David B. Quinn in 1987 from Percy's own travelogue of the Virginia plantation in 1606. His remarks made their way into the pages of Nancy Carter Crump's 1993 essay on the Albemarle region. Percy remarks: "It pleased God, after a while, to send those people . . . to relieve us with victuals as bread, corn, fish and flesh in great plenty . . . otherwise we had all perished."[56] In that moment, I want to pause—to work out the assumptions and the grounding of food/ways in so popular a narrative of Indian aid and Euro-despair, but I cannot because such a movement quite possibly takes us outside the work of food studies itself, so I must create another way to think through this moment of want and excess, fiction and fact.

I approach my work with caution but find myself again in the land of beyond when prepping for the graduate section of a food studies class that I am team teaching with another senior colleague—I come upon Elizabeth Wiegand's 2008 *Outer Banks Cookbook*—a work very much in kinship with Percy's travelogue written some three hundred years ago. This cookbook encourages us to discover the land that time forgot; travel here is both temporal and visceral—I am engaged in a project to eat the other, to participate in modes of consumption that replicate certain points on the scaffolding of white supremacy. But its content is subtly defensive almost, as Wiegand reminds us in a section entitled, "The First Outer Banks Tourists" that "These visiting Indians [Machapungas, Mattamuskeets, and Poteskeets] were the first to enjoy a seasonal visit to the Outer Banks, taking home their catch and undoubtedly good memories, just as today's tourists do."[57] In essence, sovereignty and land among tribal peoples are understood in the same grammar—they are tourists to one another as white settlers are tourists to these islands as well—and the violence of being held captive or having ancestral lands stolen is subsumed under the benign discourse of a vacation or holiday. The same scenario manifests itself in Nick Park and Peter Lord's aminated film *Chicken Run* (2000), where the hen named Babs, who is part of a concentrated animal feeding operation (CAFO), refers to those chickens taken to slaughter by constantly asking if they are going on "holiday."[58]

Later Wiegand notes that the first of several voyages to settle the Albemarle Sound resulted in contact with two Roanoke natives—Manteo and Wanchese. I learn later through Jace Weaver's *The Red Atlantic*—celebrated at UNC's food studies conference in the spring of 2015 with his keynote for that event—that each was of different though not distant tribal peoples, and each had diametrically opposed relationships to colonization. Published a mere seven years before Weaver's book, Wiegand's accounting of contact in the Sound notes that the English who first came to what would become Roanoke Island "took back two fine specimens of Wingandacon—Manteo and Wanchese."[59] These "specimens" now mirror gateway cities to the Outer Banks—a metaphor of two contested relationships to what we now refer to as settler colonialism. Feast or famine, food or flesh?

A few heartbeats later and after the famine of war, we find ourselves in what Wiegand notes was "the Freedmen's Colony" established on the north end of Roanoke. Near to the truth, *A History of African Americans in North Carolina*, published in 1992 by the Division of Archives and History, North Carolina Department of Cultural Resources, does mention "refugee communities such as James City (near New Bern) and on Roanoke Island."[60] At the close of the war, Wiegand observes "all property seized by Union forces [was returned] back to its owners. The freed slaves had no claim to the small plots they had worked for several years. Most left and went back to the mainland to find employment. The Freedmen's Colony was abandoned and disappeared—another 'lost colony.'"[61] With two lost colonies behind us, one predominantly white, the other of African descent (and another consumed by us, literally), equivalences of race and kind settled—for now—I return to Egerton's book. But not before noting that these lost colonies will come up again in our evaluation of Toni Morrison's novel *A Mercy* and the stakes of both sovereign(ty) and beast in that text.

Egerton offers readers a picture of the southern kitchen that emerged in the post–Civil War era. It is a space where Black and white cohabit, albeit unequally: "The white woman lived with the burden of a reality called defeat, the black woman with the disillusionment of an abstraction called freedom. Everything was changed—and yet, nothing was changed. The black woman was still poor, the white woman, more often than not, still had property and status but not much money, and so was poor too. The old domestic and maternal roles to which women of both races had been confined since colonial times remained in force."[62] And then, "With far less money for food and with no access to the expensive imported products they once had used freely, these white homemakers and the black women who cooked for them were thrown back on their own resources."[63] A close reading of this particular moment in Egerton's work reveals representations of Black and white women that endure. They live in a world separate but equal, as they forge a mutual ingenuity that births a cuisine. The work here happens in spaces controlled by white visions of the afterlife of slavery: Black women don't have their own homes to make or model or build, and their interiority, though available in Black-owned newspapers and other archival spaces, is withheld from us to usher in the making of a racial order that conceals a bitter bondage repackaged as familiar and necessary interracial co-constitution. And the myth of the interracial moment here is that these women were more likely to be cousins than blood strangers, and so there is belonging here, not born of necessity but of blood—an open secret in the kitchens of reconstruction and the Jim Crow South. Somewhere in this reconstructed world, Black women remain servants to white female capital and the ingenuity of blackness, though titled as Egerton remarks in a wave of cookbooks acknowledging Black contributions to southern foodways, remains underfunded. I would call this a consortium of southern competencies—knowledge and practice that conceals and obfuscates that those systems, though cocreated at times, still traffic in *distinction*. This is perhaps why the word "southern" leaves a bad taste in my mouth; we are only southern because settler colonialism made it so. The word conjures the necessity to repackage violence as a shared endeavor called heritage or tradition, marked by a distinction, a difference in the blood, that is hard to maintain with any certainty. Maintaining the fiction of our *inter* in the racial produces a scenario where distinct racialized beings are cooking together, rather than one in which cousins work together in the kitchen.

Returning to Morgan's opening pages and the scene of the mare named Martha White and Filip and Henry, the description of Henry and Filip is cut through with the body of the horse, a character in this childhood moment of reckoning. As the young Henry repeats the facts in a series of numbered lessons gleaned from his father's broken education, Henry observes of Filip: "*Number five, This race was a species of property. It says so in the ledgers.*"[64] What on earth is a "species of property" but a category of finer distinction among other *things* that are considered such? While the law of the white father prevails at Forge Run, its undoing is foretold in the novel's beginnings and will be mapped out by the work of horses and their humans.

In fact, John Forge's lesson to Henry about avarice and greed stems from the difference between husbandry he finds redeemable and husbandry he finds degrading. On the neighboring Osbourne farm, the land has gone from tobacco to horse pasture and Henry, fleeing yet another scene of domestic strife—first his own and now the forced sequestering of Mr. Osbourne by his wife as he detoxes from his morphine addiction—comes upon a round pen and witnesses the brutal breaking of a filly. The protracted scene ends with: "The sound she made was unmistakably broken; even Henry's virgin ears could hear that" (32). At this point Henry is sixteen and he comes upon his love of horses through the brutality that educates him and that puts its best foot forward in the making of horseflesh. It is unclear what "virgin" stands for here—whether his own sex or the experience of the horse breaking. "His eyes swerving back to the horse, who stood breathing hard, finally allowing the breaker to stroke her, huge eyes cast groundward in search of a self spalled to bits on the round pen floor" (33). Henry sees the "ruling strength of the breaker's body" and notes "a man and a horse were a perfect pair" (33, 34). In Henry's mind, his difference from his father is the fact that he wants to turn Forge Run toward the work of horseflesh, but this relationship is crafted from "a self spalled to bits." Henry's is a broken dream from its inception—as the psychic life of the mare broke for riding and "spalled to bits" haunts the edges of the story being laid out for the reader, and the tale becomes more about how she regains her footing than about how the Forges make good on the promise of mastery.

Henry's growing fascination with horseflesh leads him to eventually tell his father that he'd like to raise horses instead of corn on the family farm. The conversation results in the usual dejection over the patriarchal lessons of father John, and Henry retreats to his mother Lavinia's bedroom where, lying next to her, he laments, "Haven't you ever just known something? I *know* something" (39). On the edge of his mother asking him *"Tell me what you know"* (40), the narrative of Maryleen, the Forges' Black cook, follows the scene of mother and son contemplating what it is to *know* and comes before Henry's lesson in the ruin that is the traffic in *horseflesh*. The true knowledge of events in the Forge household is the provenance of Maryleen.

It is here that the novel's attempt to get at the interiority of Black femaleness produces its most curious life. For Maryleen is the pent-up frustration of a host of Black women, part Dovey Johnson Roundtree in the story of her stay at her teacher's house, where she learns to cook, part Francis Watkins Harper in her poetic commentary about the shortcomings of the male gender during reconstruction.[65] In fact, we learn a few pages later that Maryleen "found men repugnant" (44), and it is this axis, the suspicion she has of men and the worlds they make, that produces Maryleen as a free agent of sorts in the novel's early sections. But unlike those other cooks in kitchens, Morgan feels to give Maryleen an interiority that speaks to a quality of Black female ingenuity and gendered freedom. At the same time, as we shall see, this difference in freedom cannot endure, as the lessons of the kitchen circumscribe hum:animal.

In this story of how Maryleen came to Forge Run, we are told that "She wasn't here to child rear, or make nice with some white lady, or play the role of kitchen slave to the pink toes and the Filips of the world. She was here to cook. And she was exceptionally gifted at it" (41). The pinkness of white females is juxtaposed in this story of Maryleen's genesis with her refusal to use sign language to communicate with Lavinia, taking offense at Filip's instruction for her to do so and asking rhetorically, "After all, didn't they train dogs with hand signals?" (41). Again, understandings of domestic life, and training and dogs come together to shape and define Maryleen's existence at Forge Run. Maryleen's comment stays with the ordering of things, as hum/animal is produced through the linking of persons with a disability with dog training. Like John Forge, she is not only clear about hum/animal and its constitutive parts, but also cognizant that any proximity to animal life muddies the grounding of a proper species-driven alignment.

Right before the scene of marital infidelity unfolds, we also learn that Maryleen eschews her college acceptances to cook with her teacher, Miss Martin. While she seems to have given up book knowledge for something more practical, Morgan is quick to remind us that Maryleen also consumes "her Shakespeare, her Dickens, her Dunbar and Hughes." She has chosen craft rather than the evidentiary work of acquiring formal knowledge, and part of the tension in the novel exists in the extent to which its characters take the lessons printed in texts and apply them to their real-world circumstances, sometimes disastrously.

In what seems like one last attempt to wrest his son from the salacious pursuit of indignity in horse farming, a practice that does not produce right racial balance, John Forge drives Henry to the edge of the Osbourne farm and asks him what he sees. It is clear that their vision differs, as Henry sees "[nature] manicured into silence" (50). The multiple forms of silence employed across contiguous scenes is significant. Morgan writes:

> It was during the baking and cooking, when Miss Martin's conversation dwindled from current events to gossip to occasional rumination to companionable silence, that Maryleen's mind became suddenly, startlingly free, and she realized it was here she could make her home, in this deep quiet, regardless of whether it was in some white folks' house or in her parents' home, where her father did nothing but read his Bible and ignore her, and her mother was sleeping every moment she wasn't working. Silence was freedom. (42)

Maryleen's silence is unhoused, finding no space in blackness or whiteness; instead, Maryleen's is a "deep quiet"—and I am remembering Kevin Quashie's work in *The Sovereignty of Quiet* where we are reminded that "The inner life is not apolitical or without social value, but neither is it determined entirely by publicness."[66] Both silence and quiet, at least in terms of the women in the novel, hold space for a kind of interiority. This different kind of sounding is the space wherein a gendered domesticity moves at the edges of a backward racial order; it is also where the machinations of flesh find their resting place.

Maryleen's silence, Lavinia's deafness, and now the silencing of nature itself call to mind the extent to which horseflesh makes for the end of knowledge as John Forge knows it, as after bringing Henry to the Osbourne farm to caution his son against such ruination, Forge remarks, "Henry, the education I'm purchasing for you is to keep you on the established path" (49–50). To traffic in horseflesh is certainly to veer from this set course. At the same time, Henry refers to his father as a man who is "withholding answers like scraps from a bitch" and Henry knows he is that bitch. When John and Henry are on deck in this family saga, everyone else matters less as they matter more. Later when Henry has his own family and his wife, Judith, leaves him for another man, she will tell their daughter, Henrietta (of course), "We're trained from childhood to behave like dogs who sit and stay and wait for scraps" (117). Training, *dressage* produce hum/animal.

For the senior Forge, the travesty of the neighbor's horse farm is not just its "ostentation" (50), but how the work of creating horseflesh is counter to the taxonomies of race, sex, and class that Forge attempts to engrain in his son. Forge goes on at some length about what whiteness means to blackness. Watching "a Black man stooped over his mower as he traced the outer edge of the fencing," John Henry tells his son, "Watch how he slouches around without any dignity whatsoever. Born colored but made a nigger by being caught up in all this—and he knows it. . . . The black race has always depended upon our guidance to steward them into lives worth leading. A colored man uses his place of employment as a school to learn the best of what white society can offer" (50). For John Forge, the physical *aspect* of a Black body exists in the arc of whiteness's stewardship, not nestled in the situation of unfreedom that is Jim Crow Kentucky. John Forge sees what he wants to envision in a space, and even though his son errs toward horseflesh, he too sees what he wants to see, as we will soon find in the novel's next chapter.

The potentiality for white power nestles in its ability not only to manage lives but also to manage them *into* the right vocation. In Henry's father's epistemology, there are no Black women, just white men and the white women and Black men who need to be schooled by them. The story that Morgan tells scripts horseflesh and Black women into categories of the *beyond*; the former is indeed in contradistinction to the education into management, or a proper life, that Henry is to receive, and the latter is a quiet that John

Forge cannot fathom. Between these two *lives* in the text is the potentiality not for flight but for insurgence. Henry's attempt to merge his father's "education" with horseflesh will prove disastrous, but not quite in the way in which his father foretells. At the heart of this management is the unpredictability of the beast, nestled or coiled not outside but inside—this will be more apparent in my analysis of sovereignty in Morrison's *A Mercy* in this project's next chapter. John Forge is right about one thing: relationships with animals determine one's humanity, but he is wrong to believe that all of these machinations exist outside of the animal's (human or horse) *response*.

Morgan's first chapter, "The Strange Family of Things," is apt nomenclature for this moment of revelation of competing knowledges in the novel. Henry's Kentucky is the Kentucky of 1950s segregation and politicians like Robert Byrd. In a discussion of desegregation with Henry, John Forge's narrative of racial hierarchies from "hillbillies" "temperate Negroes," "crackers," and, yes, even a horse emerges: "It is quite easy to imagine the equality of all men when you sit on a high horse and don't have to walk among them in the fields. Indeed, everyone appears the same height from that view. But demount the horse and it soon becomes apparent that there are not merely masters and slaves by happenstance, but that these divisions are inherent and unavoidable" (55). It is a scene, much like so many between (overseer and master), father and son, where knowledge becomes mere rhetoric in the face of *fact*. In this scene, John Forge uses his relationship with Filip as a test case, referring to him as "weaned with a bottle of whiskey," "only five years my junior," "an uphill struggle" and "my biting dog" (55, 57). But this knowledge of Filip's character is assailed by Henry's knowledge, siphoned from his encounter with Maryleen soon after she discovers Filip and Lavinia's indiscretion in the kitchen pantry.

As John attempts to destroy Henry's dream of horseflesh, so Henry destroys John's dream of taxonomic management by telling him of Lavinia's infidelity. Henry is abruptly dismissed from his father's study and the scene ends with his father's sedan "like a big black cat" rolling down the driveway. Filip does not show up for work the next morning. The narrative takes a turn to consider the taking of Black life through extralegal lynching. This is also the moment when Filip becomes Filip Dunbar, and in his full name we become aware of his fuller story, "Filip Dunbar wasn't what his mother used to call the Christmas babies, the ones killed at Christmas, his mother born out of the foul pussy of slavery on a Jessamine County farm, where horses now run" (59). Reproduction, race, horses. The fetid life of the slavocracy spills forth into the present of the novel with great frequency and in this instance, its work is juxtaposed to the freedom of a place "where horses now run." This section soon gives way to Maryleen again.

Her gift of keen observation lands Maryleen again in the aftermath of Filip's abrupt and lucky departure from the town of Paris, Kentucky. As Morgan attempts to speak to the state-sanctioned killings of Black persons, Maryleen's narrative eschews Filip's disappearance for several pages, focusing instead on *why* Maryleen didn't hear of his departure: her refusal to go to church since she was thirteen, her parent's absence from services because of her father's Christmas flu and it being "hog-killing time." Again, Morgan emphasizes Maryleen's exceptionality: "She wasn't the black race and didn't answer to it; she was Maryleen, and she wasn't nearly as stupid as most folks, black or white" (60). Maryleen's exceptionality is carried over into the space of making the most of the hog-killing, including the use of the refined fat—"leaf lard"—of the hog. Maryleen, in the equestrian fiction discussed here at least, stands in contrast to Gordon's Maggie, as both make their home in food, albeit differently. Morgan's Maryleen tells us: "Most of the pig couldn't be used right away, but she was now set for a year of deep, bold flavor, *at least in her own home.* In the Forge house, everything was store-bought with flavors as shallow as an August pond, so she had to work twice as hard to create half the depth, but so be it. She doubted that kind of people could even tell the difference between a well-raised meat and supermarket cardboard. White folk were stupid like the sun was bright. Which was to say, shatteringly" (62; emphasis mine). In this novel, at least, there is room for an interiority, a momentary home for Black genius, served with a large helping of white stupidity, a quality of living that Maggie also surmises as she quits the track for the Thursday edition of the *Winchester Mail* and its "coarse savory dishes."[67]

But the knowledge that Maryleen discovers and the boy Henry divines eventually lets loose a hierarchy of relations that sends Maryleen packing. Henry is *forged* from the white power his father's lexicon possesses, the breaking of female horseflesh and a desire to ride her while broken, and the sexual knowledge of his mother's transgression. All three of these scenes carry information as power, and when Maryleen returns to the Forge kitchen, without knowing from her own community what has become of Filip, she enters into a domain that can now be claimed by him. And in a series of exchanges in that before-six-a.m. kitchen, including "the sight of his flesh made Maryleen rear back in distaste and alarm," it is Maryleen who becomes that broken filly who rears, noticing that Henry "looked like a buzzard off a gut pile" (62). As she goes about procuring the eggs that Filip usually brings to her, she moves away from Henry's sharp gaze, but he stalks her nonetheless and when she commands him to wake his father and ask how she's to get to the market without a driver, Henry pauses midstride in his acquiescence and calmly retorts, "You can't tell me what to do."

From then on, Maryleen's fear rises to panic and when she confronts Henry about his story of Filip and Lavinia, she explodes, "He touched your whore mother. . . . BECAUSE SHE WANTED IT!" Fully possessed now of his stature in relation to Maryleen and no longer a "boy," a furious Henry (who says, in telling the truth he gleans from Maryleen to his father and now to her, "All I want is to grow up,") orders her to leave ("Get out of my house") (66). Of this moment, Maryleen remembers: "Only later would she look back furiously and think of herself as some slave ordered about by a little boy who had just discovered he would be master someday, talking big at the kitchen girl, who obeyed him, not even stopping to snuff out the candle, just grabbing her jacket and a black goatskin purse she'd spent a week's wages on. The door spun a draft that gutted the candle and left Henry in the darkness behind her" (66).

Maryleen confronts the arrogance of her own biography and notices a "sneaky joy" as she hurries away from the Forge residence, asking: "What had she been thinking, turning down colleges and ending up in a white kitchen like that? What exactly had she been trying to prove? Or avoid?" (67). She packs a bag and, without leaving a note for her parents, she leaves for New York City to "find a job in a restaurant and then figure it out from there" (67–68). Maryleen, gifted cook, single Black female, wearing a skirt "under which no hint of a figure could be discovered" travels toward Cincinnati— Morrison's fictive cosmos, perhaps—on the way to New York City and a Clearing of sorts where only she can be the proper host and witness to and of her own flesh.

Maryleen walks out of the novel's frame with determination. We do not hear from her again until much later. Having evacuated the African-descended help—both Filip and now Maryleen—Henry Forge does indeed grow up, sexually and otherwise. After a sexual encounter with a cousin (Loretta) in the tack room of the barn—one in which the innuendo of racialized sexual difference—"I never said coloreds have big cocks"—looms large, Henry takes the opportunity to diminish Filip's horsemanship by noting that he trained and rode Tennessee Walkers—"heavy on their bones with their absurdly long underlines. And, too, they were the province of Filip, a man he could not think of without his stomach turning to a hard plum" (81). Henry's sexual life is now a boring psychoanalytic tale. In the interim before the cousin's arrival, Henry is provided with a tutor, Gerald Price from New Jersey, and at sixteen, he instructs Price to start with *On Horsemanship*, noting, "Do you know that evolution is a ladder to perfection. . . . You can chart the development of the horse right up the ladder" (73). His reading is obsessed with *parts* of the horse but not the whole, and his approach to the sport and to what will become the legacy he built will fall upon assessments that disarticulate flesh, human and otherwise. As Morgan notes: "And the boy paid keen attention to *the assemblage of a horse's body, particularly the shoulder blades, or arms, these if thick and muscular present a stronger and handsomer appearance, just as in the case of a human being*" (75; italics in original). The disarticulation of flesh and bone and now the disarticulation of a whole to its *parts* paves the way for Henry's dynasty of horseflesh.

In the haze of sexual knowledge and its currency, and the distributive outcome of racial hierarchies, Henry is free to utilize this knowledge in two ways: he causes a scene in front of his cousins at the dining table—a scene that travels from dining room to hallway to staircase, where Henry reminds his father, still the "tyrant" (91) of the first section of the novel that "You weren't even enough for your own wife!" (92). In the only moment of the novel where John Forge seems to have a *beating* heart, he says, "I made you to break my heart?" Father John dies in 1965, just a few paragraphs later, and Henry, like Faulkner's Thomas Sutpen before him, sets about to reshape Forge Run, reseeding with fescue and clover in the fall of the following year, and like all betters, swindlers, and track enthusiasts, he picks up a mark named "Hellbent . . . a spirited horse, fast, and almost perfectly formed" (92).

hum:animal

By the time we arrive at the novel's second chapter, "The Spirit of Lesser Animals," hum:animal is indistinguishable, as the mechanics of horse breeding required by the Jockey Club begin to bleed into what makes for good Forge family stock. Hellbent becomes dam to several horses, but Secretariat's line seems to continue on uninspired. Morgan writes:

> But your father [Henry] procured a mate that fateful day in Saratoga: a woman thin as a pin with a glassy blonde bob and lips painted burgundy, displaying near-perfect conformation with only minor defects: pigeon-toed with a hard voice; but also restlessness, the quality of perpetual dissatisfaction. . . . You call this woman Mother. She is one-half responsible for your

corporeal organization, your particular form of accumulated inheritance. Together with your father, she is a conduit of the great law, the Unity of Type. (98)

The "Unity of Type" argument, fostered by Étienne Geoffroy St.-Hilaire and Richard Owen, is in contrast to the "conditions of existence" theory supported by Georges Cuvier and Charles Bell, proving that all science is one degree of separation from racist pseudoscience. Darwin would later bring the two debates into conversation for developmental biology, but the currency of nature versus nurture and other racialized differences that dot the landscape of what is discoverable as science or by science does not escape popular imagination. And what passes for scientific inquiry when gendered embodied beings are present is the stuff of the kinds of feminist interrogations launched by Haraway and discussed several chapters ago in this book.

Ruminations about hum:animal are ample fodder for horse *and* human propagation. Later Henry observes that the first time he met Judith, Henrietta's mother, he was "easily impressed by her . . . conformation" (120). The difference between human and horse is captured in the aftermath of Judith's departure from Forge Run; for Henrietta, "every corner of the house is filled with the purpose of your father's life. Which is . . . you . . . or a horse" (119). This Mother leaves Henrietta and Henry for (as Henry says) "a German Jew," and so Henrietta's fate is sealed in the imbricated arc of her father's anger and her own abandonment. Hers manifests in a strange and brutal necessity. Having no Maryleen like her father to banish from the Forge residence, Henrietta imagines that her problem is the absence of

> a girl to stand behind her in the looking glass . . . to ease her grieving limbs into white cotton drawers and a long chemise; to snap her stockings into garters and cinch up a corset until it was too tight for her to draw breath, much less cry; to secure the caging crinoline; to tug over her head a dress of flat black . . . but she didn't have twenty yards of black Parisian cotton or a veil or a colored girl. . . . And because she didn't have that girl to rail against, to beat about the head and shoulders, because there was no one weaker, she flung her black bonnet against the walls of her mind and clattered about like a drunkard and wailed at the vaporous absent bitches hate sonofabitch-spoilevilrottenfuckfuckniggers, because there was no one else around smaller and weaker than she was. (121)

The scene is pivotal for this section of the novel because it brings about Henrietta's meltdown in school where she uses the word "nigger" and is sent home. She recalls that when her mother left "she would no longer tolerate humans" (122). Hum:animal difference and racialized taxonomies of being gather together for Henrietta. Where there is no slavocracy still intact, one will be invented.

It is at this point that Henry takes over his daughter's education by removing her from school. From here on, the knowledge being produced is all about how to create the perfect racehorse. These lessons include having Henrietta at thirteen watch a mare being bred—an event which occasions the disgust of the men in the brood mare barn and eventually the rumors in the town about the Forge family's unconventional interpersonal dynamic. This is followed by her reading of the worn black ledgers belonging to generations of Forge farm inhabitants and managers and discovering therein the corollary to the taxonomies her father outlines in his lesson and the psychic desire of Henrietta to have a "colored girl" she can abuse. The list is as expected: "One negro woman named Prissey, $500; One negro girl named Senna, $350; One negro woman named Phebe, $300" (140).

And like a thief in the night, after Henrietta's full history lessons have been on display, she returns to Forge Run from visiting her mother in Germany, and Henry, wildly bereft without her, chastises her for leaving and then kisses her full on the mouth, thus beginning his incestuous relationship with his daughter. Breeding in horse and human lines is always already a negotiation with acceptable forms of incest. As Morgan remarks, "The Forges, once a distinct subspecies, are quickly becoming a closed gene pool with a natural history all their own" (149). Two weeks after her return, Henrietta begins to sleep with various grooms on the property, and Hellbent's line becomes Hellcat's to continue. By Henrietta's nineteenth year, a filly named Seconds Flat matures and runs in the Kentucky Derby. And during this catastrophic race, where three horses are put down, and the jockeys are "starved and sweated down to weight," Morgan reminds us that the present violence of the sport of kings has its historical backdrop which is always already: "*the sun shines bright on my old kentucky [sic] home tis summer the darkies are gay*" (160).

There is simply no sport of kings without the continued and public telling of the place of the African-descended, while at the same time, the missing girl of Henrietta's imaginary is called forward in this hellscape of tradition and heredity at the scene of domestic life. Domesticity is fractured, however, by its incestuous nature; it is now Henry and Henrietta who maintain the order of the slavocracy—to increase their issue, no matter the cost. At the end of this chapter, it is certain that this "sport" will have its flesh. When

Henrietta meets Allmon Shaughnessy, his "footsteps approached on the cupped planks of the el porch," which should remind us of that very same el porch in Charles Burnett's short film *The Horse* where three white men sit in judgment of the (death) work of people of African descent. Shaughnessy's hiring at Forge Run closes the book's second chapter, and the third opens upon the city of Cincinnati and its abattoir, so close to where the African-descended, where animal life, live and work. Cincinnati—first home of Ford's assembly line, born in the gallows of animal flesh.

a river runs through it

The forging of Cincinnati from what the French named "La Belle Rivière"—the Ohio River—is recounted as the novel opens up to embrace Allmon's genealogy. This story begins not with human or horseflesh but with swine, as Morgan writes:

> The newcomers drive all their pigs into her. The swine befoul her and roam wild into the seven hills and beyond, where they breed: doubling, trebling, making a second city of swine. On the low banks of the river, blocks south of the new brick residences, the citizens build their first abattoir and in the years to come . . . [pigs] make fat rivers of flesh in the streets so wealthy women will refuse to leave their homes for all the shit. . . . Whacked steadily from behind by the drovers' staves, each wave of squealing hogs pushes the hogs ahead of them to the slaughter. . . . All hanging in a line, swaying side to side along the pulley as their bodies are opened, showing waved lines of rib and vertebrae like the keys of a warped piano, the heads sawn off. Now to the disassembly: a drop onto the table, then quick mechanical thudding, the fall of cleavers, the flinging of component parts—hock, shoulder, loin. In sixty seconds, the hog is gone and meat is made, the dumb passage of life. (187–88)

The true bottom of this new place made by the making of meat from flesh is Bucktown, which "smells like an open coffin" (188). And Morgan reminds us that the cage for animal life and the abattoir erected to murder "it" is no different than a neighborhood made for the African-descended makers and builders of this gleaming other "white" city on a hill: "He labors. He labors and the city grows. But whenever his own numbers swell, he's chased back into Bucktown, his clapboard home burned, some of his number left swinging from lampposts" (188).

Into this proscenium, Allmon's life unfolds, and it is a tragedy laced with all the ways in which Black life can be taken. Allmon is the seed of his father, a trucker named Mike Shaughnessy, "that fucking Irish fuck" and his mother, Marie, a preacher's daughter, "Marie the sweet, Marie the naïve, Marie, the first in the family to escape Over-the-Rhine with a high school diploma and an associate's degree and a dream of being a teacher" (190). From the beginning, it is clear that Marie and Allmon will never travel beyond Northside—will never go north, but always south, further into the despair created by the abattoir of hum:animal slavery. Where he lives is always already defined for Allmon by some travesty of history, as the Over-the-Rhine neighborhood in Cincinnati where he and his mother make their home is a Fugitive Slave Law (1850) incarnation. Forge Run is built with enslaved labor, and Blackburn Penitentiary where Allmon is incarcerated for a time rises out of the ashes of America's burning postemancipation question: what to do with a free Black person?

Neither Marie nor her preacher father—"the Reverend"—will survive this section. The one dies of untreated lupus and the other from a stroke/heart attack that takes him in his sleep.[68] When the ER physician who treats her discovers "lupoid lesions that had ravaged her neck and torso," he says, "Jesus Christ. Who let this happen to her?" (280). Thus, echoing Patsey's outcry in Northup's narrative, "What will become of me?" Before the end of this tale, Allmon is twice a felon, incarcerated as a juvenile and as an adult. The first offense is for a crime he did not commit, an irony because he is accused of setting his deceased grandfather's church aflame; the second offense is not a crime, if grief in and of itself is a crime. When Allmon is told of his mother's passing, he has nowhere for his grief to go, and in a desperate move to get back home in the wake of his mother's death he attempts to drive there. He doesn't even know how to drive yet and so is apprehended quickly. Allmon steps outside the vehicle while his interiority flashes: "Whatever. Nothing mattered" (288).

The echoes of earlier parts of this book's brief work on animal life and blackness and that nagging "whatever" and its meaning for Black life are reprised in this moment of Allmon's despair. His naming too, so reminiscent of that old text *Everyman*. All-mon is a twentieth-century Black reflection of that purposefulness in generality. Dying alone in a shotgun house perched at "the edge of the world" (253), Marie, praying to a God she fears never listens, craves hum/animal distinction, but notes that there is no such distinction without the difference that gender makes in its wake. She asks,

"Why did you curse me with this female body? . . . Make me an animal, so I won't know anything. Make me a man so I won't give a damn about anyone" (278). As Marie meets her death and her son travels south to Kentucky only to flee in less than twenty-four hours and be arrested for possession of crack cocaine and an unregistered firearm, it is clear that Morgan holds no brief for the bright spots of Black pleasure, can tell us nothing about an interiority that possesses only the fleeting memory of a buoyant childhood taken by the harsh realities of an unachievable adulthood.

In fact, the chief flaw of the novel is that it understands Black life as the sum of what all happens to a person, rather than a negotiation among elements of being, doing, and living etched in accident and love. What Morgan creates for her Black characters is a hellish landscape of hatred, despair, and revenge. This is because the author mistakes the righteous rage of Black people as a kind of hatred that simmers and gains purchase on a life incapable of transformation *in* relationship. What we have in the novel is a deep and unsettled ambiguity about blackness that does not mar the force of its hum:animal revelations, but nevertheless prevents several of Morgan's African-descended characters from having more complex relationships with their own trauma. This ambivalence is remarked upon in the novel itself, by one of its African-descended characters. As Allmon's grandfather, the Reverend, says to him: "Now most people, they choose fancy things and money, because you can see all them, you can hold all them in your hand. But all them things you can't see is what matters most. They live in the mind and the heart. The perfect things, like justice" (237). What people of African descent seek is justice, *not* revenge, necessarily. Justice is a practiced insurgence, a quality of being with that often escapes a more static imaginary and makes perfection a striving, rather than an attainment. But it is a lesson, at least in this novel, too little, too late for Allmon. So the story of Allmon Shaughnessy unfolds as a flinty knife of hatred and revenge outside of the possibility for justice, which can channel that rage, define it and bring it to fruition in connection with *an* other.[69]

During his last stint in prison, Allmon learns to groom horses. He comes to the horse earlier in the novel through an affinity with its suffering. In his youth, he attends a local carnival without his father, who lies in a drunken stupor on the couch in his mother's home. While there, Allmon notices a horse that "isn't impressive, just a nag snatched up by a carnie for forty bucks at the slaughterhouse in Peoria . . . a disheveled thing perched on tender, surbated hooves" (199). And yet in another moment a stranger is described as having "thin hair like a horse's neglected mane" (205). While Morgan's world of horseflesh melds Black and white, male and female, human and animal, it somehow seems to forget, or better yet, abandons the world that blackness created through hum:animal life and renders that world unattainable to Allmon. Allmon sees the animal's suffering but can only understand it through his own need *not* to suffer, rather than through a shared history that can sustain him. Even when that hum:animal relationship in blackness comes forward in the flesh in the fifth chapter, in the person of African-descended jockey "Reuben Bedford Walker III of provenance unknown and character indeterminate" (409), Allmon cannot understand Reuben's rapid-fire articulation of the messy stuff of being that brings him to his seat across the table from him. Reuben, in a retort to Allmon's words "You ain't nothing but a jock," dazzles our senses with "Nothing but a jock? I'm nothing you can even imagine, you fucking river rat! Not with your borrowed dreams! I am the Defender of Myself, wizard of the saddle, untutored genius, the first with the most! . . . Confabulate and fabricate! No one knows my name—or my history! Hallelujah and fuck you! I piss on family and order, I lie and I counterfeit! No mother made me, I bore my own damn self. I got a contraband brain and Napoleonic balls. Twenty-nine horses shot from under me, and still I ride on. Can I get a goddamn Amen!" (432–33). Reuben's denunciation of all that makes for good and normative living is impressive, and his candor and penchant for hyperbole don't sit well with Allmon. The queerest character in the novel, his repudiation of *everything* is instructive and, yes, insurgent. Reuben's wholesale embrace of his own genius *is* the legacy that is Allmon's too, but he can only see Reuben as an impossibility. Moreover, Reuben's assertion that "No mother made me" concretizes the hyperbolic masculinity that Reuben possess—he is the quintessential, queer trickster and wholly unavailable to Allmon, who is stricken by his over-the-top monologues.

The novel's fourth chapter, "The Survival Machine," opens with another interlude, this time the story of an enslaved ancestor of the Reverend, Marie, and Allmon named Scipio, who escapes from "the heart of Kentucky" and means to cross the Ohio River into Cincinnati (290). We learn that Scipio's Kentucky is on the outskirts of Paris (home to the Forge family), and it is most likely that the story he tells about his enslavement is frightfully close to the experience of the enslaved at Forge Run or farms nearby. Moreover, the incest narrative, which enlivens this fourth chapter, gets its Black counterpart in this moment if we think of enslaved people of African descent and their white masters in any territory or geography as less than two genera-tions away from practices that produced unclaimed or unnamed progeny. So when Henrietta eventually sleeps with Allmon and becomes pregnant, whether it's her father's or her lover's child hardly abates the suspicion that incest most surely haunts this birth and all others in the novel, including, yes, the horses.

But this story is no escape from slavery but an anvil that catches you up in your own emancipation, as on the way to his Ohio freedom, Scipio meets up with a very pregnant enslaved woman named Abby, with whom he (re-luctantly at first) travels on the four-day journey to the banks of the Ohio, only to inadvertently kill her in their desperate swim against the current to freedom. Scipio is a man whose "spirit [is] riven by fear. His brief dreams are like jars shattering. For twelve days, he has lived in terror" (301). Since the days and years are no doubt compounded for him, I doubt those twelve days are the sum of all his fears and the reference to twelve is both biblical and slightly recalls another portion of twelve in Northup's narrative. As Abby and Scipio cross the river, he loses sight of her. In his panicked at-tempt to locate her in the muddy, rapidly moving water, "without warning, she yanks him beneath the surface, and with blind horror, Scipio kicks downward. Quick as lightning, guided only by instinct, his foot finds her belly. Her hands release, and like a stone, Abby drops away" (304). As they headed into the icy water, Abby was not only with child but also in labor.

Partner to our Platt (née Northup), Scipio too must harm a Black woman to reach freedom and the future it promises. A Black woman carrying that "future"—if our queer vision of survivance *pace* Edelman can stand shoulder to shoulder with Spillers's attention to mothers and "issue"—must be *ar-rested* at all costs. At this point our narrator addresses us directly, like some-thing out of a Bronte sister saga: "But oh, reader, now Scipio has found some-thing worse than slavery, and will live fifteen more years trying to forget it" (305). If indeed that something worse is the taking of Black *female* life, then the answer to that question, posed at the beginning of this hum:animal study, is surely again, should you take the whip when the overseer hands it to you? Scipio is *not* literally handed the whip, but he inherits the psychic dilemma that the slavocracy necessitates: save the self and the potentiality of joining the hum/animal distinction, or choose to die rather than *perish* in a fraudulent category of being. How much of that survival is built upon the annihilation of the very *future* it is intended to complete? How much of the will to survive is pent up in, ruled by, the taxonomies of hum/animal?

"so it's the miscegenation, not the incest, which you cant bear"

> Have I exceeded the bounds of the form, committed a literary sin? I say there's no such thing—any striving is calcined ash before the heat of the ever-expanding world, its interminability and brightness, which is neither yours nor mine.
>
> **C. E. MORGAN**, *The Sport of Kings* (2016)

Like the human characters in this tale, even the foal of Seconds Flat is born into a deeply racialized world, with her "coat of miscegenated depth, neither black nor brown with a white marking between her eyes" (309). The veterinarian, Lou, is called to the brood mare barn to attend to the foaling and notices the "too-intimate touch" of father to daughter, but moves past this moment, eager to "get off Forge land" because, as her husband intoned as she left the house in the early hours of the morning, "Those Forges are motherfucking nuts" (310; 307).
An other
group of
motherfuckers.
On the outskirts of this world somewhere in the north, Maryleen as insurgent subject emerges in shadow and in judgment with pen poised: "Somewhere, Maryleen sharpened her pencil to a knife's point and began to write" (311). Writing perhaps to tell another story that, like Faulkner before her, Morgan feels unable to tell. The one of that insurgent female, who moves swiftly out of the scene's framing and beyond our collective vision, but soon walks through the front door of the Forge household to pass judgment once again. So we have the possibility of another story, another narrator waiting in the wings, destined to tell a similar tale but through gift and genius—a gift and a genius that Morgan can't seem to harness in this tome about hum:animal belonging, being and bereavement.

But Maryleen's storytelling is forestalled by Allmon's as we move back to Blackburn and Allmon's participation in the thoroughbred boot camp in the early 2000s, where among the incarcerated, on Valentine's Day, a white trainer tells the group of initiates, "As far as I'm concerned, the only ones who earn the right to say that [they love horses] are the grooms. You feed a horse, you brush a horse, you pet a horse, then you can say you love it. We have an old saying in this sport: Treat your horse as your friend, not as your slave. That's what I'm talking about. Now come on up here and meet your first horse" (316). Allmon learns to overcome his initial fear of the sheer power of horses and in a familiar, but distanced second-person voice, the narrator speaking through Allmon notes without irony "the future came and wrenched open your eyes when you were a kid, and once your broken eyes healed, the only thing you could see was: horse" (317).

Allmon's talent with horses lands him at Forge Run. His first encounter with Henry is four months into his stint at the farm and it is clear that the two men do not and will not get along, as Allmon's touch on the foal soon to be named Hellsmouth is special and Henry envies the groom but maintains his status by reminding Allmon "that horse you're looking at is two hundred and fifty years old . . . it broke the ground you're standing on, it built that house I live in, and it bred itself. It's entitled—do you understand me—*entitled* to exist in its own flesh, because of its history" (320). The only other character in the novel who "bred itself" is Reuben. While this moment seems to be surely the mother. fucker. moment of the novel, I want to argue that this slippage into what seems like a repudiation of the female—no mother made me—is where the novel takes a hum:animal turn, where Hellsmouth becomes the embodiment of a kind of femaleness, mothered in itself, and insurgent. Hellsmouth is "entitled to exist in its own flesh," and perhaps what Henry misunderstands here is that the horse is no "it" but a "she."

It is clear, for Henry at least, that the rudimentary elements of the slavocracy endure, and the hum/animal life he imagines brings rights-bearing logic to the trafficking in horseflesh—and it is marshaled to put Allmon in his place, indeed to put Hellsmouth above her human groom. What does it mean to be "entitled to exist" in one's own flesh, in conditions where such flesh has a corollary in a ledger entry: sire, dam, foal, dam, sire, colt, filly, and so on? In the wake of his pronouncement, Henry looks for "a cowed spirit" (320) but finds none. Instead, he sees Allmon's steely resolve when Allmon answers Henry's question "What do you want?" with "I want what you got."

In this space of Allmon's ambition and Henry's taxonomies of power and inheritance, Allmon's love affair with Henrietta blossoms. Their relationship unfolds as a series of quick and brutal exchanges, instigated by Henrietta's myopic education: about Allmon's racial identity—"If you don't look white, you're not white. At least in the real fucking world" (332); about the difference between northerners and southerners—"Southerners, on the other hand, know perfectly well they're ignorant; the problem is they're proud of it" (323); and of course, about Darwin—"Do you know who Darwin was?" . . . he found the key to the best idea anyone ever thought up. He found the key to life" (325). The miseducation of Henrietta Forge is so great that only in moments of their lovemaking—in feed and tack rooms, never in beds—can they see their way through the blind ambition of overcoming laced with ignorance and an internalized warped sense of personal and collective human/horse histories of belonging. In one moment when the two broken beings attempt to speak to one another, Henrietta asks, "What's the best thing you can think of?" Allmon answers: "The river . . . Because my momma . . . I know she's on the other side. It's like she's alive and just waiting for me to come home." Henrietta answers: "You're the best thing I can think of. I feel like the real me when I'm with you, and I've been waiting my whole life for that" (351). It is the most interiority we will get from either of them and it is not near enough to sustain their connection to one another, not in the face of Henry's tyrannical greed and jealousy and Allmon's consuming hatred and ambition.

Henrietta's South is a white South, the South of her father and her whole line. Hum:animal struggles to regain its equilibrium in this chapter. In some moments we can see their coming together: "She knew the velvet of a horse's muzzle was as tender as the flesh of a woman's inner thigh" (340), or while remarking upon Allmon's conformation: "His body was perfection. . . . He stood eight heads high" (341). In this chapter, hum:animal is torn apart by the intervention of breeding, family, and the making of horseflesh into "auctionable flesh" (338).

The lofty strivings of the human, perched above all others in mastery and, yes, awe are nothing but *slave* to the machinations of biology and sex, and so the house of Forge comes tumbling down once again before the miscegenated ghost of hauntings past as Mack, the soon-to-be-trainer of Hellsmouth, who hails from "Crapalachia" (418), "a stereotype of a stereotype, that was Holler" (354), lets loose his knowledge of the affair between Henrietta and Allmon in a casual conversation with Henry. The reprisal is swift and sets in motion the deal between Allmon and Henry: that Allmon will leave Forge Run and take Hellsmouth to Mack's barn to be trained to race, and that Allmon will stay away from Henrietta in exchange for futures on the completion of a successful third year of racing for the bold "black" ("miscegenated") filly.[70] It is stunning but predictable that another divulged affair sets the last stages of the plot in motion.

When Henrietta learns that she is pregnant, she "knew with absolute certainty that there was no animal on earth less free than herself. . . . Only women—not science—knew how the species reproduced: the next life nothing new at all but an undulation, a spillover from the abundance of the last"

(370). It is the bearing of children in a world that hates women that connects Henrietta's *gendered* observations with those of Allmon's mother, Marie: "There's a war on women in this world! They're killing us left and right, and when they don't do it with their own hands, they do it with ours" (223). While Henrietta's life with her father is always a contestation, her reproductive self shifts and alters her temporality, pulls her into sharper focus not as a self, but as *an* other "stretched taut between generations." For Henrietta before pregnancy "her pussy was like something she invented—sui generis. . . . But, pregnancy shattered that illusion like so much cheap mercury glass. What differentiates man from animal is deferral of appetite. . . . Woman was a tensile thing stretched taut between generations" (376).

When Henrietta awakens to Marie's "war," and her place in it, it is much too late for her. She confronts Allmon with her growing incubation, and he wonders if the baby is his. As he leaves the property, Henrietta, hurt and desperate, asks him, "What could you possibly have to win?" His reply is stinging: "It's a black thing, you wouldn't understand" (374). It is the presence of the child that sharpens the novel's work on race so that its threat as a temporal declension in history—a looking b(l)ackward—is measured by a future that cannot be known but is nevertheless solidified. The enfleshment of the child is a kind of living otherwise held away from white vision. In the wake of Allmon's departure, her next moment is with her "Father and Lover. He was always there. He had given birth to this house, given birth to history. He had given birth to her" (374). In this model, Henry Forge is the author of all that there is; his character takes on the capacities of architecture, history, and reproduction. It is an odd reversal of the language Henry uses to confront his rival, Allmon. It is no longer the horse but the human who gives rise to the house at Forge Run and the perfection, once prized by Allmon's grandfather as "justice" is only the centerpiece of a long-standing white supremacy uttered by Henry to his daughter: "I love you, Henrietta. . . . But I also love perfection" (362). Morgan's horse is not just metaphor but an embodied measure of the racialized tension in the novel. Their lives and those of other animals are the length and measure of the failure of our fledgling democracy, whose pitiable lungs still want for proper air.

Henrietta is pages away from her own death in childbirth months later when she says to her father: "You better pray it's not yours—don't you know old seed produces weak plants?" (375). Henrietta dies producing a child whose birth inspires the obstetrician to declare: "He's alive. He's perfect. He's perfect." And then Henry reacts: "At first he recoiled, his mind rearing like a frightened horse. Then, with shaking hands, Henry drew the tiny, perfectly formed brown baby to his chest and looked in astonishment at the only family he had left" (391). It seems that Henry's plan for perfection and Allmon's plan for revenge have come into full flower in the person of the baby boy who will eventually be named Samuel, like that Forge ancestor who separated from his white family with an enslaved other and set out to found a legacy in Kentucky soil.

$C_{19}H_{20}N_2O_2$

> America has many ills, but none greater than the refusal of so many to think long and hard, to think critically. We must learn to be choosers, not merely receivers; to be self-critical; to cast a superstitious eye on the powers that be, including one's own unearned power. We want easy answers, but we must refuse them. The only true answer is to think.
>
> **C. E. MORGAN**, *The Sport of Kings* (2016)

In the penultimate chapter, named for the horse Hellsmouth, who embodies the legacy of the great Secretariat, Henry falters, with his "grief beyond the capacity of his flesh" (397), bewildered by the new racial landscape he must navigate. In this space he moves about the house at Forge Run like a wounded ghost, immersing himself in "Henrietta's beingness" (403) and reading the journals she kept, filled with the conversation about Henry's lessons that they would not have, could not have. Henry now realizes that "death and perfection could not both exist" (404). When he sees Henry for the first time since his departure from Forge Run, Allmon learns about Henrietta's death, and when he asks about the baby, Henry lies because "the child—the wrong color but the right blood—was his" (423). It is a simultaneous blow, a twofold grief. Even in the arc of his mourning, Henry's breeding logic and enslaver's mind cannot get away from the ledgers and the debts and perfection. "Allmon, who now had nothing in the world but a horse that didn't belong to him," collapses into the hay in "grief and rage" (423).

After a blistering seven-lengths win in the Laurel Futurity in November of 2005, Hellsmouth comes up with a hairline fracture between cannon bone and fetlock and she is put on stall rest. Pages earlier, during the cooldown after Hellsmouth takes the October Champagne Stakes, Allmon begins to feel ill. "He'd been staring down at his own hands in mystification, lost in thought. He said the first words that came to mind: 'My hands feel broke'" (417). Hum:animal connection rears its head in the novel as bloodlines shrink and so does the narrow passage occupied by a mutual and imbricated fate of horse and human. Such passage is antitemporal, its recursivity a matter of flesh *rearticulated*. As they near the Derby, Allmon's sickness, diagnosed by Reuben—"Something tells me you've got the flushing disease—a precious gift from your mama, perhaps?"—intensifies. His reply to Reuben's quip is harsh, but he is troubled by "a knowing that was very deep like bones at the bottom of the river" (452). The same river that swallows up Abby's pregnant descending form rises up again to claim Allmon's ancestor Scipio in an interlude before the opening of the novel's last chapter, "The Interpretation of Horses." But this river has the bones of hum:animal comingled; it is the pigs of Cincinnati's slaughterhouses, the horseflesh of Kentucky's finest sport, and the bodies of humans sold for cash.

As Allmon struggles with his mama's disease, the focus is on the difference that gender makes, as Hellsmouth continues to stomp the competition, winning by twenty lengths in the Florida Derby with her speed and strength and no small amount of mare-ishness: "Now Stop the Music, poor fool, pulled up alongside [Hellsmouth] in his cooldown loop. Hell turned to him, her lips curled, her eyes like globes of a newly charted world. As the cameras rolled, she snaked out and bit the gelding savagely on the tender flesh of his ear. Both jocks cried out, wrestling for space, until Hell finally galloped away, a spring in her step and blood in her mouth" (462). That "newly charted world" opens up as potentiality for Henry and for Allmon as a messy terrain of hum:animal being and belonging that is haunted by the gifts from the dam's, not the sire's, line. As one of the novel's racing reporters, Jeff Burrow, writes:

> Hellsmouth has never been just another equine athlete. In a sport overrun with huge colts and powerhouse geldings, she's a filly, and a tremendous one at that, and that makes her unique. If despite this loss, she manages to conquer the Derby's mile and a quarter, it won't be just a win for Hellsmouth, but a testament to the power and potential of her sex in this sport. In a world that downplays the accomplishments of women at every possible turn, a great female athlete is representative, whether she likes it or not. They change their sport and public opinion . . . this big filly runs for all fillies, and the distinction still matters. (472)

And indeed, the "distinction still matters." As Henry's father John and his father before him tried to move the *human* line to perfection, they held no brief for the heart of the dam. And yet, the end of the line for horse and human is laid at the dam's feet—it was the heart of the dam, after all, which gave Secretariat what he needed to finish in 2:24 flat in the Belmont Stakes, garnering him the 1973 Triple Crown.[71] An unbeaten record to this day. It is the horse's genius that breaks through hum:animal for Henry. After a loss right before the Derby, Henry muses: "If Hellsmouth is not his perfect thing, then what exactly is she? What if she isn't his at all, or worse, not a thing at all? What if she—" (472). What if there is something about being that cannot be comprehended through the violent history of a farm ledger, or the lineaments refined through blood, or the necessary liquid at the end of a syringe? It is clear that Henry has nothing but a miseducation to fall back on, so he cannot fully comprehend what is beyond his own limited vision—he literally runs out of room in his own imagination. *The Sport of Kings* is relentless in its critique, and moments of realization like this one for the males in the novel do not hold. It is *female*ness—Lou, Maryleen, Henrietta, Hellsmouth, and Marie—that understands fully what hierarchies are in place and how to dream another world. Maleness in this novel is weakened by its own elevated sense of itself or haunted by a lesson of the same.

The section on Hellsmouth is about picking your poison, about hum:animal life and the lessons it must teach but which are often ignored. Into this scene, on the morning of the Derby, walks Maryleen, who gets her full name in this iteration, "Maryleen Jesse Deane" (476). In fact, the naming of Maryleen is clearly an allusion to the infamous Paula Deen, who paid her African-descended cook Dora Charles $10 an hour for decades, making her a "culinary sharecropper."[72] Under the pretense of an interview on the day of the Derby about the Forge farm and its winning filly Hellsmouth, Maryleen returns and walks through the front door. Henry does not recognize her and as their conversation unfolds like bleeding ink on fine paper, she lets him know "I plan to publish a book in June, just in time for the Belmont. I intend to tell the real story of your family, of this house, of Kentucky. I intend to tell the truth" (476). Henry's panic is immediate, and their conversation is interrupted by their neighbor Ginnie, who comes into the study with baby Samuel to inquire about the raised voices. At this point, Maryleen turns to see the brown baby, and when Ginnie reveals that he is Samuel's grandson, Maryleen erupts in laughter, which carries her out the front door again as Henry "the voice of pure rage" screams: "GET OUT OF MY HOME!" once again.

Maryleen's discovery of the ruination of Henry's racist vision for his family takes her to the track to find Allmon, but before their brief exchange, we are yanked back to a Forge Run nestled in the antebellum South. As Henry drives with Samuel to the Derby, he sees "the fullness of [Henrietta's] face fleshing his. Her blood coursing through him." This flesh and blood moment yields a realization for Henry: "Henry, you spread your daughter's legs the way you split a tree to build a house. Was it worth it?" (480). Time "flows backward, like the Ohio" and deposits us in the wake of a Forge ancestor and master, Edward Cooper Forge, in the aftermath of the loss of his son, Barnabas Monroe Forge. In his anger, he goes to the quarters of the enslaved and demands that a woman named Phebe "increase his stock" with an enslaved man named Benjohn then and there, saying, "Give me a buck" (483). After this brutal scene he goes in search of Prissey—who is in the original ledger that so fascinates Henrietta ("one negro woman, Prissey, $500")—and sexually assaults her. After he rapes her, "she reaches around his bulk and, with all the weary resignation, which seems the lone inheritance of woman, she comforts him" (484). It is a brutal telling and a terrible scene, one that binds the lot of women in the narrative together, stepping in time to the needs, wants, demands of hum:animal slaughter.

Hellsmouth wins the Derby by enough to secure what looks like a potential Triple Crown—if accomplished in this fictional world, it would be the first for a filly in the history of the grueling three-race series. In this moment, Henry's realizations come in never-ending waves and "so began the third and final movement of Henry Forge's life" (494). For Henry in the novel's last fifty pages, it is all too little too late.

In the interlude that precedes the last full chapter, we are allowed the space for that insurgent female subject. The narrative turns backward to Scipio on the banks of the Ohio, fifteen years after his own crossing with Abby, as he witnesses the near-drowning of his eight-year-old daughter, Laney. He saves her and when she is safe on the bank of the river, "Scipio began to beat her" (498). They are perched on the edge of a place, at least before the Fugitive Slave Law of 1850, where they are neither enslaved nor freed. In this liminal space, she looks at her father, stricken with grief and rage—a twinned emotion throughout Morgan's tome—and she sees what he sees and comes to a realization:

> Abruptly, confusedly, Laney turned to see what he was staring at. . . . It was not just the expanse of Kentucky with its fine gradations of summer green, the sloping rise of gorgeous hills that led to a graceful interior. This time she saw something inside of the prettiness, something that had captured her father's gaze, or perhaps captured him. She saw the shadows between the trees, the grave-black spaces that could harbor secrets. Or people. . . . Your father is still hiding there, a voice inside her said—not her own voice but

many voices, like the elders were speaking in the round of her heart. Your father never escaped, he couldn't. White folks won't give you nothing you don't demand, and you got to demand your soul long after the body reaches freedom. Then, like a good soldier, you got to fight for the souls of others, and if necessary you offer up your most precious thing—your life—to do so. (500)

The difference between poetry and rhetoric is being willing to kill yourself. At this moment, Laney runs out of the scene, "arms outstretched" and vows to "take up arms in God's great war" as an underground railroad lieutenant. *She* is the insurgent Black femaleness that is the counterpart to Maryleen, who keeps the story of the Forges . . . and when she reaches Allmon at the barn on Derby day says to him: "Do I have a story for you" (485). At this point in the novel, it is a story that we all know well, and so Morgan leaves it to our imaginative rehashing. Maryleen never gets to tell her story in the novel itself, it sits somewhere at the periphery, a dog's vision.

At the post-Derby celebration the afternoon after Maryleen's morning visit, Henry announces that he is "pulling Hellsmouth from racing" and "I will contribute no more horses to this sport" (502, 503). Moving through the stupefied press conference crowd, Henry brings Hell home despite the protestations of her trainer and feels "The sensation was deliciously unfamiliar. Was this finally joy?" (504). Regardless of what Henry knows and learns in these last moments, regardless of his invitation to Allmon to come to Forge Run—"Why don't you bring my car to the farm tomorrow. I'll do my best to explain" (507)—when Henry turns Hellsmouth out and sees her in the paddock, he muses, "The greatest dreams of humans were nothing but clumsy machinations next to the natural ambition of animals" (518). But Henry *is* that animal with ambition and he still cannot see past his own taxonomic logic. The world as he knows it must be ordered into its hum/animal parts; he fails to see that his very living has shattered the precise instrument of measure and sense-making that he utilizes on the daily. His tools are simply not up to the task; it is the same realization that Derrida comes to in his philosophical approach to the consideration of animal life in *The Animal That Therefore I Am*.

Allmon's story of incarceration is finally told in these last pages, as if it's some release we need before he does come not *to* Forge Run but *for* it—he shoots the two brood mares, Forge's Fortune and Seconds Flat, in an attempt to end Hell's line. Before he kills the dams, he looks around the opulence of the barn and notes, "It's sickening, a veritable temple of tack and flesh" (530).

After killing the horses, he says: "But where is Henrietta—no, Hellsmouth!" (531). Hum:animal burns brightly in Allmon's mind, the female insurgent in this moment is Hell, who escapes his attempt to murder her and takes off, "finding the concrete of the road, where she beats her drum out into the wider, waiting world" (532). Allmon sets the house ablaze and ties Henry to the old whipping post, that first abattoir and founding scene of the enslavement engendered and turned into the soil at Forge Run. Holding his son for the first time, Allmon is in deep despair and after laying Samuel on the ground, out of harm's way, he takes his own life. The last image of this scene is of Hellsmouth, who "bloomed suddenly out of the dark, she was gleaming with sweat and bright red with reflected fire. Samuel screamed in delight as the filly galloped toward them. . . . She was almost perfect. She was ready for more" (540). It is indeed the females in this novel who "do fine in this book, including fillies, but not mothers, daughters, and wives—women defined by their relationships to men—suffer silence, sickness, abuse, and early death."[73] I am not sure if *The Sport of Kings* will be a feminist classic, but I am sure that it is a remarkable achievement of a novel that even critics understand through its hum:animal vision.

The unsatisfying ending—Will Hell race again? Will Henry keep to his series of realizations?—is coupled with an epilogue where the ghostly but embodied Allmon hitches a ride with a trucker named John so that he can go to the river and join his mother, a light burning on the other side of the river where she calls him by his "given name" (545). Schulz's review perhaps says it best; the novel "hovers between fiction, history and myth, its characters sometimes like the ancient ones bound to their tales by fate, its horses distant kin to those who drew the chariot of time across the sky."[74] It is indeed, as Audre Lorde once said, "a biomythography." What is left to contemplate after this novel's star explodes and collapses many worlds is to contemplate the *sovereignty* of yet *an* other world. It is to this last task that my nose, still to the ground, takes me.

6   **sovereignty : a mercy**

Where else but in this disorganized world would such an encounter
be possible?

TONI MORRISON, *A Mercy* (2008)

The animal is a necessary reminder of the limits of the human; its
historical and ontological contingency; of the precariousness of the
human as a state of being, a condition of sovereignty, or an ideal of
self-regulation.

ELIZABETH GROSZ, *Becoming Undone* (2011)

But what were these lessons, and what exactly did [Michael] Vick
admit? Perhaps much like the dogs he raised, fought, and killed, he
learned to bare his teeth only when told.

MEGAN GLICK, "Animal Instincts" (2013)

nemesis

In the revised and expanded edition of *The Dreaded Comparison:
Human and Animal Slavery*, originally published in 1988 and about
which Alice Walker once said, "A powerful short book, which can
be read in an hour . . . will take a lifetime to forget," Marjorie Spiegel brings to bear a series of always awful and sometimes artful
proofs about the relationship between the suffering—think Ben-
tham (1789) and Levinas (1947; trans. 1987)—of nonhuman animals
and the situation of the enslaved.[1] At one point in her critique,
Spiegel turns to Sterling Brown's 1968 essay "Negro Character as
Seen by White Authors." While noting the postemancipation shift
in the attitude of whites toward their Black counterparts, Brown
uses the image of the "docile mastiff" turned rabid "mad dog" to
draw readers' attention to the stereotyping of blackness as bestial.
Spiegel then observes, "In seeing comparisons of Blacks to animals

that were so prevalent in the period literature of his study, Brown accepted and, through his response, subsequently strengthened the negative views about animals held by the racist authors. . . . Brown's indignation at these offensive books blinded him to the fellow victims of their propaganda."[2] Spiegel's assessment pulls in two directions. The first is more obvious—that stereotypes of animals are universally held. The second is more opaque— that blackness's normative gaze upon the animal therefore prohibits ethical relation. This second prohibition is a phenomenon that is repeated across accountings of *ethical* relation to animal life and the African-descended. In an encounter with the animal, enslaved experience can justify dropping the bottom out of the question of blackness's ethical commitment to the animal other. This is a fundamental problem.

In the course of her examination of animal and human suffering—and this is an important detail because no moment of comparison in this book opens the possibility of shared pleasure, only pain—Spiegel makes the obligatory liberal nod toward the condition and sentiment of the "Native American." Spiegel writes in a chapter on hunting, "Notably, traditional, culturally intact Native Americans and many other aboriginal peoples hunted out of real necessity, with respect for, and in harmony with, the balance of nature. Theirs was not a profane act, nor an unconscious attempt to symbolically conquer chaos. . . . Harmony and respect were central to an entire worldview, a view of the universe, with which the very lives of Native Americans were imbued, from birth until death, and, in their philosophy, from death until rebirth."[3] Now that's a mouthful.

This type of conceptualization of Indian life is not uncommon, and Philip Deloria painstakingly documents how we as an American culture arrived at such overwhelming and overarching collective sentiment about "Native Americans" in his important book *Playing Indian*. What I am interested in for the purposes of this larger project is not how or why we arrived at our conclusions about Blacks' and Indians' relationship to the animal, but rather how we might think through these historicized entanglements. I say "historicized" because views of Indian life and animals are sedimented in an archaic—to borrow from Deloria—historicization of an "Indian time' before settler colonialism—a kind of anti-temporality where subjects and their relations are locked in static rapport. By comparison, views of Black life and animals solidified across slavery's four-hundred-year history, as Spiegel's book relentlessly catalogues. The possibility for blackness to relate to animal being is constantly foreclosed by the threat of falling into becoming already the animal other and various forms of animality packaged for us through the deploying of "like" as blackness. As Megan Glick aptly notes, "To imagine a state of literally becoming-animal is to imagine a state of dehumanization so profound as to be too dehumanizing to talk about."[4] Zakiyyah Iman Jackson's *Becoming Human* cuts through swaths of philosophical thought to move beyond becoming-animal toward an understanding that the animality of the human and the human's dependence upon blackness for its outside are coterminous in an anti-Black world.

What is interesting about Spiegel's frontloading of negative Black relation to the animal via Brown's work is that she ends her observations with several quotes in support of her comparative argument—three of these are pulled from Frederick Douglass and the most famous African American vegetarian/fruitarian, Dick Gregory. Spiegel begins with the most oft-quoted line of Douglass's section on "Treatment of Animals" from "Address before the Tennessee Colored Agricultural and Mechanical Association" (September 1873). Douglass begins: "There is no denying that slavery had a direct and positive tendency to produce coarseness and brutality in the treatment of animals, especially those most useful to agricultural industry. Not only the slave, but the horse, the ox and the mule shared the general feeling of indifference to the right naturally engendered by the state of slavery. The master blamed the overseer; the overseer the slave, and the slave the horses, oxen and mules, and violence and brutality fell upon the animals as a consequence."[5] The place of the overseer and the enslaved and the ethical question that their relation brings forward have already been broached earlier in this book.

The line of descent that Douglass draws here perhaps has allowed Black studies to decenter the place of the animal in the question of Black being. When we get to Douglass's phrase "violence and brutality fell upon the animals," we are led to believe that the chief perpetrators of violence toward the animal are enslaved subjects. Violence from Black beings toward animal beings is naturalized under a totalizing system of descending degradation. But the important kernel here is in the following line: "Not only the slave, but the horse, the ox and the mule shared the general feeling of indifference to the right naturally engendered by the state of slavery." The capacity for same-feeling or shared feeling is opened up by Douglass's remarks, as is his investment, albeit ambivalent, in hum/animal distinction.

Nevertheless, Spiegel sees what she wants to see, as the rest of the paragraph clearly defines Douglass's conceptualization of hum:animal, as he notes: "One of the greatest pleasures connected with agricultural life may be found in the pleasant relations capable of subsisting between the farmer and his four-legged companions" and later he urges "and to do this, there is but one rule, and that is, uniform sympathy and kindness," noting that "a horse is in many respects like a man."[6] In fact, Douglass's animal-forward lesson in agrarian life represents the chief tension of the present animal studies quandary: what is the balance between sameness and difference, civilizing mission and gentle hegemony? In this balance the place of suffering and its recognition in the *other* is necessary for achieving *relation*. Yet, Douglass's interest here derives from pleasure, not pain. His interest is in some form of companionate life. In Spiegel's ordering, the matter of relation—hum:animal—is drawn in racialized terms. Such terms produce the relationship of the African descended to animal life in constricted space; blackness is shackled to a racialized ordering defined by the human and it cannot *respond*. So the question becomes, what if the animal responded in a kind of undifferentiated way; exercising a nineteenth-century promiscuity that might be frowned upon in public or a twentieth-century idea of life as a single referent that in turn produces a violent reaction from the state and the community? This is not to say or contest saying that hum:animal isn't made up of the matter of race; the distinction, as others like Zakiyyah Iman Jackson (*Becoming Human*) and Joshua Bennett (*Being Once Property Myself*) have pointed out, carries with it other *matter* as well—the terms of the "political" or the mark of sexual difference, for example.

Black relation to the animal is rendered as a blind spot, impossible outside of our becoming animal because of the machinations of slavery, while Indian relation to the animal is naturalized, as part of a cultural matrix, universalized to the point of becoming the great Indian chain of being. Years ago, I wrote an article about Afro-Native literature and the importance of thinking through the issues of sovereignty and emancipation together.[7] I now pick up the loose thread of that argument in order to think through the relationship of these stereotypical views of Black/Indian relation to the nonhuman animal world. In early critical literatures about the capacities of both populations, at least, it seems as if "freedom" and "self-determination" are a task that Indian and Black peoples are not up to accomplishing on their own. Moreover, I want to argue, this fitness for self-government is *not* dependent upon the relations among humans, but is mired in one's relationship to the nonhuman animal and even concerns the very nature of what it means to be "sovereign." This arrangement makes the present-day "question of the animal" absolutely beholden to the articulation of aspects of sovereignty and freedom constitutive of Indigenous and Black life, respectively. How we go about thinking through these articulations is part of my interest in what follows.

beast and sovereign

In the first volume (there are two) of a series of lectures given in Paris from the fall of 2001 to the spring of 2003—stretching from the 9/11 events to the rise in US militarism in Afghanistan and Iraq—Jacques Derrida set out to contemplate both beast and sovereign. Given the international events and the changes in geopolitical cultures that they signaled, I take this contemplation of beast and sovereign as startlingly necessary engagements with hum:animal infrastructures. At the beginning in December 2001, Derrida observes, "We had above all to explore the 'logics' organizing both the submission of the beast (and the living being) to political sovereignty, and an irresistible and overloaded analogy between a beast and a sovereign supposed to share a space of some exteriority with respect to 'law' and 'right' (outside the law: above the law: origin and foundation of the law)."[8] As with his work on the hum/animal distinction discussed in an earlier section of this book, Derrida returns to the *gendered* nature of the alignment of companionable forces existing in relative *distinction* to one another. Here, the beast (*la*) is feminine and the sovereign (*le*) is masculine, and he goes on in his beginnings, which are always already recursive, to say that it is "as if we were naming in it, ahead of time, a certain coupe, a certain coupling, a plot involving alliance or hostility, war or peace, marriage or divorce—not only between two types of living beings (animal and human) but between two sexes which, already in the title, and in a certain language—French . . . are going at each other, are making a scene" (1–2). Are behaving like/as animals? Such behavior could be the sexual embrace of lovers, or the violence between intimates: neighbors, friends, colleagues. The point is that this coupling, uncoupling of difference/indifference works in two directions, always. The pressure between like and as again rests in the very meaning of the distinction, which reveals and occludes.

As the sovereign philosopher winds his way through a myriad of texts (Hobbes, Schmitt, Lacan, Flaubert, to name a few), we discover that the beast and the sovereign stand not at opposite poles from one another but in complex and imbricated relation where consumption, abjection, inside and outside blur and bring forth a multitude of possibilities within the law and outside of it, where, given the interests of this project and the preceding chapter, insurgence surely lay—"identity and difference coexist" (14). Nestled inside this "difference," this trope of diversity as argued earlier in this project, is the extent to which living being and biosphere take hold, how marking/making difference is to confer unsettled discursive force to each, creating not a binary but *relation*. Taking the whole of sovereignty as his object, Derrida understands "it" (always living, not quite dead, in a state of potential rebirth as *an* other) as "political, social or individual" (14). A third of the way into his discursive adventure in his "Fifth Session," Derrida returns to this "couple," marking the relationship between beast and sovereign as a kind of sexual play, with queries that belie this unsettled sex in relation: "What if, at bottom, the distinction between *what* and *who* came to sink into indifference, into an abyss?" (137). This bottom, this abyss has been the concern of queer theorists from Leo Bersani to Kathryn Bond Stockton, and it serves to unsettle and expose *queer* relation as one of the lost nodes of sovereignty's constituency.[9] Native Hawaiian (Kānaka Maoli) theorist and scholar J. Kēhaulani Kauanui reminds us that same/sexual practices make up definitions of sovereignty that potentially burst the bubble of its *political* matter. I will take up Kauanui's concerns shortly. But the task of this chapter is not to posit queerness or becoming with the animal as necessary escape hatches for our work on sovereignty. This dialogue is ongoing in queer studies, and I do not wish to contribute to it by depositing a new line of thought, but to perhaps free us from it.[10] I am simply following the trace, tracking animal life and letting it be, foregoing sign, metaphor, or likeness. In this final chapter I want to think, after Kandice Chuh, *otherwise*.

The beast drags the sovereign, the sovereign drags the beast into its orbit, and the possibilities of sovereignty cohere in its sacred and theological origins in Western thought. For Derrida, to contemplate them in their origin is to see their "being-outside-the-law" as both maker of laws and mark of their constitutive possibility for destruction, being both without law and above the law, the condition of the beast is one and the same with the condition of the sovereign. As one and the same, beast and sovereign create an origin story of the coterminous nature of *power* itself. Definitions of sovereignty therefore depend upon *la bête*—a taming that is not outside or above, but within—and the desire to exist in a feral state, to be *unmanned*, is a property of sovereignty that produces self-determination as animal instinct; a kind of coupling, but I would contend here and as I have elsewhere in this book, an animal instinct (what if the animal responded?) laced though with *female insurgence*.

Moreover, Derrida reminds us through readings of Rousseau and Hobbes that the beast has its own doppelganger, the "brute" which involves a kind of "bestiality of the animal" (21), though later he will also ask "(what does 'brute' mean)?" (55). We need to be reminded that the first purveyor of definitions of sovereignty, Jean Bodin, was also a scholar of sorcery, naturalism, and, yes, demonology. What opens up is the capacity for animal life—its nonhuman parts—to be expressed in a particular and affective quality of the old theology. In Derrida's first session of thirteen, we see the concept of "mercy" aligned with "enslavement" in a heavily commented upon stretch of text from Plutarch's *Essays*. It is the quality of *mercy* and its relationship to sovereignty, to *life* that piques my interest in Toni Morrison's text by the same name and produces the reading that unfolds—soon—after this bit of philosophical meandering.[11] For now, we rest on our haunches.

Practices of captivity provide the occasion for the practice of "mercy," which then becomes the right and true expression of what it means to be *good*. Notice how I do not say what it means to be *ethical*. Sovereignty brings forward not just the drag of the right and proper animal, though there is that too, but most particularly, the problem the beast and its machinations propose for the management-making, time-bending operations of the Anthropocene and its structures of government. Sovereignty in Indigenous thought—a thought that expands through the Americas to that place called "the Continent" and even in/of the "Old World"—brings to bear the question of the beast as *relation*, as it contests that radical and impossible Western fabulation known as *the self* and provides instead the possibility of connection to the life of beings, both like and unlike (identity and difference).[12] The Western self is indeed a curiosity, a capacious separation from life itself, but in the name of such life it and it alone can carry. The coupling of the beast and the sovereign, represented in Derrida's second lecture, as a "hymen," by its feminine part, which will yield, must yield (?) to penetration, is a vestige of earlier work of Derrida that sought to produce invagination as the blurring of difference, as *différance*. As someone with a vagina that remained so during early biological processes of differentiation, I will ignore these particular bleatings among the order of men whose capacity for knowledge always falls short of the mark. I am falling back upon the biological more to prove a point about *having* and perhaps *naming* and the power that such adventures in a lexicon can and do afford. And after Derrida comes Agamben, and then Lacan (parenthetically) and then Deleuze . . . I perhaps *follow* the modeled mode of caustic critiques.[13] But I digress.

In Derrida's collection of lectures, a good substitution for the beast is "the slave, the woman, the child," as this arrangement of analogous beings is repeated more than once (33, 66). An adequate "correlate" of sovereignty is "fear" (39); "Sovereignty causes fear, and fear makes the sovereign" (40), at least after Hobbes. Gender creates the particular problem the beast and the sovereign pose for one another; to be treated "'like beasts' is to be non-men" (74). But to *be* a beast is to be sovereign, if not *the* sovereign. So, again, we turn ourselves to the importance of the word "like" and the exchange of "like" for "as" that is so necessary to break the conundrum that *hum/animal* proposes for *living*. The condition of sovereignty cannot be inhabited by the feminine, female. or woman; these entities are surrogates for beast (slave, woman, child). This same constellation comes up in Karen Barad's work where she notes that "the point of challenging traditional epistemologies is not merely to welcome females, slaves, children, animals and other dispossessed Others . . . into the fold of knowers but to better account for the ontology of knowing."[14] But some of the fundamental questions in animal studies are not only what or who the animal is, exactly, and how can we know, but also who has the right to name or know? It is hard to get away from a value-added approach to thinking animal.

Given all the fine talk about language, the work of gender in Derrida's lectures is fettered by analogies and almost always sloppy (purposefully), at least from the standard of feminist rigor. These somewhat bankrupt analogies seem to place slave, woman, and child in various states of being dominated, mastered, domesticated. And, because the center does not hold, or at least its opposition (beast/sovereign) does not cohere, the nature of the difference that makes for a *gendered* submission is up for serious debate. What happens to slave, and woman, and child as a consortium of oppositions betray obvious binaries? This entity (slave, woman, child?) is a possible collective that rises at the level of the condition of the beast, in a confidence that rather overshadows the ipseity—the oneness, the individuality of the differentiated *sovereign*. This *collective*, not one being, but being in the one as many, is the enmeshed voice of the three (enslaved) women who articulate themselves in Toni Morrison's *A Mercy*. They represent *altogether* an insurgence, *an* other that time and perhaps place (?) cannot account for.

While I shall get to Morrison's novel anon, the deferral is necessary because what is at stake in the muddled terrain of sovereign states and beings is not only the work of gender but also affective life itself. We must remember that the qualities of what is *good*, what constitutes a good life, harken back to what makes the *political* in the first place, at least philosophically. In her study of Kahnawà:ke political life, Audra Simpson asks at first, "What happens when we refuse what all (presumably) 'sensible' people perceive as good things? What does this refusal do to politics, to sense, to reason?"[15] For Simpson, "settler occupation" has an "ongoing life, which has required and still requires that they give up their lands and give up themselves."[16] So, while this book has called for the release of *living* from the engaged terms of the *political* that seem to strangle it, Simpson seems to remind us that the Kahnawà:ke "do all they can to *live* a political life robustly."[17]

The political life that Simpson brings to us entails a self, but one borne in relationship to others and in such relation, the terrain is messy, and, yes, *gendered* as Simpson's discussion, forged from the perspective of the discipline of anthropology, centers questions of belonging during a period of contested conversation about tribal membership; conversations which involved statements like "Who is your mother?" or "Why are we not going through the women?" (8, 9). A very different question from the one I have explicated earlier in a public television short documentary on MOVE where a person on the street asks the MOVE member, "Who is the father of these children?" As the stranger reminds this MOVE member, finding the right and proper father is the backbone of civil society and its social contract.[18] But where shall we go, what shall we do to find our mother? Derrida points toward how *gender* matters, while Simpson, like Spillers, approaches another question about enfleshment altogether—not just a woman, but a mother too. Living a political life is always already a gendered one, or one steeped in gender. Perhaps that civil society that is so embraced by the pessimism is indeed always the provenance of men, and the space of sovereignty, disrupted by the beast, by the feminine, is a place of potential insurgence. Aileen Moreton-Robinson recognizes that "Native epistemologies . . . provide the cultural criteria for who belongs, where you belong and how you belong in relation to humans, non-humans as well as nation and territory."[19] I want to note that Simpson and Moreton-Robinson's inquiries span continents and tribal locations, but each questions the grounding of epistemology and how "cultural criteria" are marked (Moreton-Robinson) and how they might be embodied (Simpson).

Later, Simpson calls to question the very nature of *nation*, asking "how to be a nation, when much of one's territory has been taken," thus bringing the vexed problem of *geography*—which is the political apportioning of land— to the question of sovereignty, which a Eurocentric philosophy of right can only think of in terms of a power always already endemic to the having of/ possession of the land itself, through inhabitation or natural right.[20] How to be an Indigenous nation is underscored by the legal determinations of a "foreign government," that denies the presence of "a governmental system" or "philosophical order," for Indigenous peoples. Later, Simpson observes that being "different" is "defined by others and will be accorded a protected space of legal recognition *if* your group evidences that 'difference' in terms that are sufficient to the settler's legal eye" (22). This last part is perhaps the racial stew in which historically underrepresented groups swim for their recognition.

In the end, Simpson reminds us that all of these qualifying factors do not "speak of sovereign political orders with authority over land and life" (10). What she offers is a "grounded refusal, not a precipice" (10), one better understood from the vantage point of the concept of "nested sovereignty" (11). To nestle or be nested is to be in a state of comfort *and* necessary and protected concealment. There is no doubt that the question of the animal at the heart of Western notions of beast and sovereign do not figure largely in the political imaginaries of sovereignty as it is understood after settler colonialism, but the question does produce the order of things in which such sovereignty nestles and is nested even. And so too does the tail end of consideration of sovereign right as a condition (but perhaps not a practice) of being unearth the precarity of its own narrowly focused contemplations through Western thought.

Stretching back to the Reformation's consequence—the exploration of the Atlantic and the coming of colonizing forces embodied in peoples of European descent—one of the chief interpretations of "others" at the point of contact was their relationship with land, and in particular the *use* of such land, understood through modes of husbandry. So, it is often our relationship with the animal, and "its" mastery that sets us apart as citizens, non-others—those who belong in and to the nation. "Yes, you *live* among animals, but can you put them to proper use?" To live requires the ability to designate, rather than to practice a kind of *letting be*. The standard is doubly bound. On the one hand, we are to work the land and her animals for our industry and pleasure. On the other hand, we will be told at any moment what is "proper" to animal life and what is *good* for the land in the performance of both tasks. This too is the work of sovereignty (though now understood as rather bankrupt in its *gender* from this foregoing discussion) from the vantage point of settler colonialism.

sovereignty matters

> The romance of sovereignty ... rests on the belief that the subject is the
> master and the controlling author of his or her own meaning.
> **ACHILLE MBEMBE**, "Necropolitics" (2003)

Scholarship on sovereignty and dispossession occur across a range of tribal homes—from Robert Warrior (Osage) to Philip Deloria (Standing Rock Sioux), from Jodi Byrd (Chickasaw) to J. Kēhaulani Kauanui (Kānaka Maoli), and Aileen Moreton-Robinson (Quandamooka First Nation) to Jean O'Brien (Ojibwe).[21] Each scholar invoked here adds another entry point for a complex discussion of sovereignty in US Indigenous intellectual traditions, and more to the point, one that moves away from the singularity of the individual's (historically the king, but also the sovereign who claims such right *for* everyone) claim to sovereign right, toward a collectivity that cannot be so easily managed or understood. As Simpson reminds us, through the words of the Kahnawà:ke Membership law (2008), "We *reject* all efforts to assimilate and extinguish our community under the guise of absolute individualism" (14). In fact, such "relatedness" "does refuse logics of the state" (15). It is "relatedness," both an articulation of belonging in terms of some forms of Native sovereignty *and* the sign of the inherent collapse of beast and sovereign in the very same models of state-making that require such *distinction*, that so concerns me in this project and that comes to a head in this final chapter. Simpson's focus in *Mohawk Interruptus* is to remind us that nation recognition *in* state formation produces an anterior logic wherein Native sovereignty is an *effect* of a set of forceful interactions with settler governments. In this logic, Native sovereignty is consequential to the presence of the settler governmentality, rather than a form of relation that "predate[s] the advent of the settler state" (19). What then to do with our *prior* relation? As sovereignty tries to detach itself form the *beast* (a self?) which it cannot govern, it reveals its consequential and ongoing relationship to its feral parts, feminine, ungovernable, and perhaps, indiscriminate. This is the *nestled* nature of sovereignty.

   In her introduction to *Sovereignty Matters*, Joanne Barker notes that one prevailing definition of sovereignty in Indian country "emanates from the unique identity and culture of peoples and is therefore an inherent and inalienable right of peoples to the qualities customarily associated with nations."[22] It is now a matter of standard critical practice to understand the series of decisions emanating from the Supreme Court's Chief Justice John

Marshall as contradictory and convoluted on the matter of Indigenous sovereignty and the US federal government.[23] What is noteworthy for our discussions here is that "Marshall's fictionalized accounting of the doctrine of discovery" or "aboriginal title" rather than full title produced the definition of sovereignty and Indigenous self-governing powers *for* domestic and international entities.[24] Sovereignty in its current iteration under biopower has a global reach, but it fails to engage matters of sovereignty among Indigenous peoples, thus relegating discourse about "native" sovereignty to more domestic matters or colonial histories and elevating theoretical and philosophical discussions of sovereignty to the sphere of the global.[25] In this configuration, it is *that* sovereignty that concerns us most when thinking about the biopolitical—and I hope I have argued here in this project that this kind of privileging doesn't quite hold as a center and is in fact, contested (as my brief read of Derrida's work demonstrates) *in* itself.

In truth, the making of Indigenous *legal* sovereignty is as much a matter of global concern in 1823 as it is today. From the perspective of Justice Marshall's plan for Indigenous self-determination, dispossession could be affected through civilizing efforts of husbandry and farming, key components in the very definition of what "land" means in the prevailing culture. In essence, one could argue that the philosophical tradition that tracks sovereignty back to a "king" is one characterized by a particular kind of blindness, like a horse moving fast along the inside lane, trained for likeness, who shies at sudden difference at every turn. Anywhere there is settlement, or a claim to land itself, the shadow of the animal appears and is *companionate* in this process of making-sovereign, and *insurgent* for its coming to fruition.

As practices of enslavement among tribal peoples demonstrate, laborers of African descent in captivity produced *wealth* and *cultural capital* for those participatory nations, thus producing a tension that has lasted for centuries in Indian/African-descended communities and intersectional work. Jodi A. Byrd's *The Transit of Empire* (2011) tracks the confluence of natural events and human endeavor to understand the *interpolation* of indigeneity in the making of a multiracial society. She manages to deftly articulate when and where Native-ness presents a challenge to and then necessarily is obfuscated by the emerging nation's desire to honor its melting pot (in name only). In this matrix, after Barker above, Byrd challenges the racialization or the multi-ethnicization of the United States as a rhetoric and practice that undermines and obfuscates Indigenous sovereignty; there is no instance where sovereignty can be seen, it is always already brought forward in direct contradistinction to the pull of the "racial." In particular,

Byrd observes: "This notion of becoming savage is what I call the transit of empire, a site through which the United States with ties to Enlightenment and Victorian colonialism propagates itself through a paradigmatic 'Indianness' tied now to the global ascendency of liberalism."[26] For Byrd, in this "paradigmatic Indianness" Indian peoples represent the "already known," the been-there-done-that of US empire so that they serve a "mythological function" which shores up the liberal project of multicultural inclusion that relies upon our continued obfuscation of what happened "back then." Temporally, this is the site of impossible reckoning, as *US* sovereignty is predicated on this constant absenting. After our walk through Derrida's concerted explication of sovereignty as a philosophical standard, I hope it is clear that the sovereignty in US governmentality is nestled in contradiction and occlusion.

In a collection of essays written over two decades, Aileen Moreton-Robinson (*The White Possessive*) attempts to direct Indigenous studies away from a model of articulating culture toward a model of understanding forms of ontological and epistemological differentiation. She is also one of the first scholars in the discipline to challenge the too-easy positing of queer theory's "subjectless critique" (in a discussion of Andrea Smith's work) as the more capacious category from which to consider indigeneity and its "ethnographic entrapment."[27] The move here is from seeing Indigenous peoples as "objects of study" to focus on certain ontologically derived truths, one of which is that the existence of "Indigenous peoples . . . threatens the self-realization of patriarchal white sovereignty's interior truth."[28] Given that these interior truths are forged not in human being but in the relatedness of *being* itself, then this direction for Indigenous studies work opens up sizable terrain for work on sovereignty, on beast and sovereign, on the relatedness of *animal* life. The horizon that the word cloud beast/sovereign beckons toward is rich and demands our engagement.

A better approach to thinking indigeneity from the vantage point of queer studies would be the work of J. Kēhaulani Kauanui in *Paradoxes of Hawaiian Sovereignty* (2018). Like Moreton-Robinson, Kauanui embraces "privileging Indigenous methodologies as a way of decolonizing knowledge production."[29] By bringing forward the interplay among gender, land, and "savage sexualities," Kauanui perceptively evades "queer" as an addendum to strategies of being/belonging, and instead, toggles back and forth thinking through "practice[s]" rather than "tradition[s]" in Kānaka Maoli living that produce and resist colonial structures like heteronormativity.[30] None of us are exempt from the sphere of influence such structures of control exert. The pressure to belong is both within and without and as Kauanui tracks efforts from missionaries and Hawaiian chiefs to curtail sexual practices deemed either "savage," or not in alignment with prevailing norms, she proposes that "any rigorous examination of sexuality in relation to colonial domination necessarily entails a focus on sovereignty and its sexual implications."[31] In essence, the trace or tracking that Kauanui performs echoes the gendered course of *le et la* that Derrida begins with in almost every lecture/session, but cannot hold on to, thus constantly sending up the problem of gender in our work on sovereignty's (colonial) trace.

The Indigenous studies work on sovereignty examined here comes from a period of intense reconceptualization of the relationship between indigeneity and Black studies from roughly 2010 to 2016. This relationship's long arc, however, begins in the 1920s and 1930s with writings of Carter G. Woodson and Kenneth W. Porter in the *Journal of Negro History*; was reimagined at the turn of the century at the 2000 Dartmouth conference organized by Tiya Miles, then a dissertation fellow; and perhaps got its most significant reinvigoration from the efforts of Black studies scholars like Frank B. Wilderson III (2010) to distinguish between the "antagonisms" that accrue to Black ("Slave") and Indigenous ("Savage") subjects.[32] Wilderson's distinction is grounded in a series of statements about what *constituencies* matter most. Wilderson states that though "the restoration of sovereignty—would surely obliterate the cartographic integrity of the United States, it is not a foregone conclusion that this demand would obliterate the subjective integrity of the Settler/Master. By dismantling the cartographic institutionality of the nation-state, a return to Native American paradigms of sovereignty need not destroy the spatial and temporal capacity . . . of *Human* existence."[33] The status of the human is a problem for blackness as the human is always already constituted in opposition and erasure of African-descended (Black) being. The mistake Wilderson makes is in viewing the human as the privileged node of being proper to Indigenous or, for that matter, Black *life* (MOVE is an example here). If this is not the case in some instances—and I believe it is not—then we run the risk of misunderstanding the constituents of Indigenous sovereignty, crafted and, yes, *nestled* in nation or tribe. The assumption here, at first, is that the relationship to *land*, in and of itself a living entity, is tangled up in the miasma of the human. Or that the human, as it is construed in and by certain philosophical inquiry, is the only entity that carries an ontological capacity that can be called "being." What I want to open up here is the possibility that "Human existence" might not be the only actant (Bennett) when the return of land is initiated.

Most recently, Tiffany Lethabo King has contemplated the intersection of Black and Native futures in her award-winning *The Black Shoals* (2019), where she also sees the efficacy of "Native and Black people to refuse the narrow and violent conception of the human. Black and Indigenous protests against conquistador ways of life have already been talking to one another in ways that exceed certain forms of humanist narrativity and intelligibility."[34] King's work "pushes through abstract theoretical impasses between Black and Native studies" and along with Stephanie K. Dunning's *Black to Nature* (2021), both see some value in Jared Sexton's call in "The Vel of Slavery: Tracking the Figure of the Unsovereign" (2014) to adhere to the most "radical elements of Black politics," ones that "refuse to (and cannot) make claims to anything."[35] I see this call in King as less rigid than Sexton's more definitive stance; hers is another opening for questioning how we got to the *human* as a determining node of agency for *life*. For Dunning, Sexton's focus on the loss of the African subject's indigeneity, coupled with the fact that "land ownership itself (as a system) *requires* the very oppression we want to see undone"[36] makes for an approach to *land* that is deeply rooted to total "abolition."[37] King notes that Sexton's call for a kind of landlessness in relation to a radical call for abolition doesn't always center what or who sovereignty is *for*. Moreover, the being of blackness stands as a non sequitur in the language of the metaphysics and if *land* is conceived as such a burden for thought as well, then the only *life* that is sustainable within such a paradigm is indeed the empty category of the *human* and its white constituencies.

My contemplations here about sovereignty are not meant to wade completely into an already robust debate, but instead to contemplate what is missing in sovereignty's intended script. I am simply opening the category of sovereignty itself to its own contradiction (beast and sovereign) and, yes, *lie*. But to return to Wilderson just for the moment, it is clear that the privileging of a distinctly "human" experience does not guide the entirety of Wilderson's inquiry, as he is quick to garner from scholars like Haunani-Kay Trask and Vine Deloria Jr. the "barrenness of Western metaphysics, as opposed to the plentitude of the Indigenous spirituality."[38] In fact, Wilderson acknowledges that the core animation of Indigenous thought and living is "among animate and inanimate"—thus, gesturing to a relation that is not contained in the constituencies that animate thought along the lines of the ontological, always already suspect because of its value-laden understanding of *being*.[39] It is clear that Wilderson wants to acknowledge the difference Native kinship might make, but he does not want to valorize it as such; this is a break in the theoretical scaffolding that persists as these modes of relation are not consequential in the paradigmatic work that follows. Wilderson's critical reading of a conversation between Audre Simpson and Taiaiake Alfred identifies a key opposition in the terms "nation" and "sovereignty," where for Simpson, the first term is connected to "being" and the second to "authority to exercise power."[40] While Wilderson's critical flows tend to provide more nuance and capaciousness, his conclusions revert to more paradigmatic locations for the sovereign subject's *impossibilities*, thus curtailing the more interesting and impactful utility of his theoretical intervention.

These conversations recognize the intense interplay between emerging state and established nation(s), a will-to-possession that is both geographical and performative, a shadow play of enormous consequence that confuses contact with conquest. Our popular understandings of sovereignty flatten the middle ground to the black and white thinking of *before* and *after*. Such rumination reminds me of Hortense Spillers's early reading of Harriet Jacobs's *Incidents*, where she notes that the Black female body can be stolen and inhabited at *any time*—a terrorizing atemporality—by her white mistress.[41] Such dispossession of land, culture, and body creates instabilities across a range of inhabitations and identities.

Taking one more glance at Spiegel, in the same chapter on "Hunting" where she gives praise—specious though it might be—to Native lifeways, she also states rather offhandedly, "Hunters may pay up to $50,000 to legally kill an endangered polar bear in Canada, purchasing a hunting license from a Native American tribe that peddles them for cash." So much for the peace, love, and coconuts argument about Native culture that ends the chapter. Here, the beautiful fiction of Indian essence falls away when it comes into direct contact with the implications of sovereignty—when it comes time to self-determine, the Indigenous body is a mere peddler, a Black-market capitalist. So too does Black life falter in the wake of emancipation, as Spiegel quotes Sterling Brown's opinion that "in freedom they are beasts."[42] The twin images of the sovereign and the beast are brought to bear here in a stunning kaleidoscopic interplay. I endeavor to participate in and interrupt a global conversation about sovereignty and biopower along with scholars like Charles Mills, Achille Mbembe, and Aileen Moreton-Robinson, while also exposing the conversation about the body and governmentality and intellectual work in Native American and Indigenous studies that should already inform it. As Byrd notes, this is a story about "land, labor, journey and displacement."[43]

I hope to understand this connection among Black, Indian, and nonhuman animal about "land, labor, journey and displacement" as it is drawn in

Toni Morrison's *A Mercy*—a peculiar, pithy, but dense homage to relations among peoples in the fledgling United States (circa 1690), the time that "race" forgot. Carrying with us the scaffolding made by the imbrication of sovereign and beast, I move next to this slippage among human, animal, blackness, and indigeneity that Morrison attempts to address in her ninth novel.

beasts of burden

After the 1871 congressional decision to suspend treaty-making practices with Indigenous groups, the United States entered into a colonial power relationship with Native peoples, argues Kevin Bruyneel in *The Third Space of Sovereignty*. In the period between 1871 and the political movements of the 1960s that brought forth moments like the American Indian Chicago Conference (AICC), this colonial relationship devolved. Thinking through Bruyneel's arguments (and by extension Jodi Byrd's and Philip Deloria's) about the necessary and mythic disappearance of the "Indian" into an archaic past or a mythologized multiracial future, I am intrigued by how this naturalizing of Indian being through issues of nonsovereign rule can be understood in tandem with self-determination and emancipation, nodes which find the Indian and Black other deteriorating into an(other) naturalized state—(in)to a beast, who cannot be governed by itself or others. In Jacques Derrida's *The Beast and the Sovereign*, he notes: "Here, whenever we speak of the beast and the sovereign, we shall have in view an analogy between two current representations (current and therefore problematical, suspect, to be interrogated) between this type of animality or living being that is called the 'beast' or that is represented as bestiality, on the one hand, and on the other a sovereignty that is most often represented as human or divine, in truth anthropo-theological."[44] Thus, the condition of sovereignty depends upon the nonhuman animal, or to echo Derrida, "a *type* of animality," making ideas of animal being intrinsically bound to the ability of the sovereign to self-determine not only his/her own fate but that of others. Derrida paints the landscape of interaction between beast and sovereign with the stuff of fairy tales—the big bad wolf, among others—demonstrating that the "archaic" or the "unheimlich" is in play during this scripted interaction. To be sovereign—the ability to govern (self-govern), to think oneself competent enough to self-govern—is to be civilized, a mission demonstrated in one's ability either to tame or to determine the conditions under which the animal matters, and if I were inclined to be thinking more necropolitically, the conditions under which the animal always already dies.[45]

To solidify what I mean by this archaic past that I also mentioned earlier, I turn to Bruyneel's apt description of the Catch-22 of what he terms—and this is perhaps another mouthful—"the modern American liberal democratic settler-state." In Bruyneel's assessment of the Mille Lacs Band of Ojibwe's response to Wisconsin Governor Jesse Ventura's challenge to Native sovereignty, he notes there are "two prevalent American sentiments" about Indigenous people's political status: "The first sentiment is that indigenous tribes and nations claim a form of sovereignty that is unclear because it is not easily located inside or outside of the United States. . . . The spatial logic is quite simple: if the tribe is 'part of the United States,' it is not sovereign, but if it is to be sovereign, it cannot be part of and thus make demands on the United States. The second sentiment is that the treaty-secured rights of indigenous tribes stem from an archaic political time that cannot assume a modern form. . . . [In sum] Chippewa sovereignty is not permitted to develop into a modern form and engage in practices commensurate with present-day American political life."[46] In many ways, the primary problem is geographic; the secondary problem is temporal. I am intrigued by the "political status" Bruyneel alludes to here, and especially his appeal to "American political life." The animal studies debate is steeped in discourse of the political, and in fact comes out of a historically grounded moment—the advent of post–World War II technologies like the prison camp or the CAFO—but it has little or nothing at all to say about how understandings of sovereignty and emancipation in its US context might change the landscape and focus of animal studies work. This is a serious frustration for me as a scholar who reads at the intersection of queer, feminist, and critical race studies. For animal studies scholars, politics *is* consumed with the distinction of hum/animal, yet it cannot see the ways in which this hum/animal relationship is etched upon discourses of freedom and sovereignty in relation to Black and Indigenous lives, here or elsewhere. From my vantage point, it appears that sovereignty—as a political effect—came to die in the Americas. That Euro-American struggle for independence keeps working itself over and through the effigy of *that king*; and yet, as these notions of freedom morphed (in a postdemocratic epoch) into *modes* of governmentality, the question of sovereignty and its afterlife in the Americas should be of particular concern to animal studies scholars and advocates.

Assessments of what Black "freedom" at the time of emancipation and beyond would look like travel along the lines of the racist to the truly celebratory. While the state of Black persons in the United States is neither colonial nor postcolonial, this neither/nor boundary, this inability for blackness to settle into its progress, is reflective of the same states of injury and redress outlined by postcolonial theorists. Once formal campaigns—to repatriate Blacks to Liberia, for example—ceased, the Black body, like its Indian counterpart circa 1871, was cast in a web of constant attempts at domestication—no longer what Bruyneel calls a "foreign concern," Indianness (and I would add blackness here as well) becomes a domestic problem to be solved through attempts at veritable eradication. What I want to offer here is that Indigenous and Black being come together as a "foreign concern" during the same period before such entities then become a domestic concern.[47] Black and Indian life circulate around one another, hover even, like the strands of DNA touching and arching out from one another in a patterned dance, skirting the dictates of what's foreign and what's domestic in lockstep with nonhuman animal life, a becoming that morphs into *animal* life. I want to turn now to Morrison's *A Mercy* to demonstrate ways in which this attempt to answer the question of Black freedom and Indian sovereignty is managed by Morrison. I also want to draw our attention to how the novel clears the way for such domesticating through the constant troubling of animal life.

the "quiet of animals sated at last"

We are a nation obsessed with origins. If one were to listen to the hue and cry from different quarters of this country's tea party revolutionaries, we would think that our origins certainly do not reflect the diversity of persons who pepper this small portion of the globe we call home. In *A Mercy*, the notion of "origin" is always already that: a notion—usually vague and unimpressive as a foundational idea of something. When we wish in our present tense for "how things were," we reset the clock on the past, populate it with those whom we imagine reflect our core values as a nation and then repackage that thing called history for more popular consumption. Even the fabulousness that is Lin-Manuel Miranda's *Hamilton* follows a scripted understanding of the political.[48] Anyone who wants to get back to that mythical happy nation that our founding fathers authored hasn't had the pleasure of reading the tedious diary entries of Cotton and Increase Mather, or delighted in the musings of one Michael Wigglesworth, or contemplated Thomas Jefferson's more self-reflexive chapter called "Manners" in *Notes on the State of Virginia* on the devastating psychic havoc that centuries of slavery can wreck upon kin, home, and, ultimately, nation, or ventured to read William Apess's (Pequot) stunning autobiography or had a look at David Walker's strident and purposeful *Appeal*. When we start to have conversations about who belongs where, when, and why, I am reminded that except for certain tender mercies like acts of friendship, salvation, and sustenance, many of us, in fact, do not "belong."

Diversity in this nation is not new. It is, in fact, plainly put, "a mercy," if a mercy can be understood to encompass all of the acts between (human) beings that comprise the nature of diversity itself—in these times, our very biodiversity is dependent upon "a mercy." Acts of acknowledgement, kindness, and bravery are thought to pull human being from the arc of cruelty and isolation into the bandwidth of compassion and consideration of the other. Those same acts in turn must also pull nonanimal human being from the brink of extinction. A mercy is a pause in the temporal order of things where the present outwits our attempts to grapple with a past/the past; it is a shift in relations across the board. A mercy, at least in Morrison's novel, might be a kind of queer temporality, a sort of sordid relationality that acknowledges the twin impact of settler and enslaved economies.

A mercy, according to the OED, can be a blessing or a relief. In many ways a mercy is an ethical commitment. In his brief essay on "The Name of the Dog, or Natural Rights," Emmanuel Levinas observes, "with the appearance of the human—and this is my entire philosophy—there is something more than my life, and that is the life of the other."[49] In the Cartesian tradition that Levinas follows, it is important that the animal is distinct from the human. For some philosophers, this difference is speech, for Levinas, it is the face. The "face" holds the possibility for recognition, for exchange, for mercy.[50] Animals are thought to be incapable of such reciprocal gazing. Female as animal is infused with such incapacity. As I have argued throughout this book, this distinction or nonrelation is the lie that nestles at the heart of hum/animal. Derrida is right to posit that *la* in relation to *le* unmakes the binary of beast and sovereign.

In her review of Morrison's novel, Elizabeth McHenry writes that the book is "a story about a world in which acts of mercy prove ambiguous, and the lines between cruelty and compassion are murky at best."[51] Indeed, somewhere between the ambiguous and the murky, "cruelty and compassion," the ethical commitment floats, awaiting our attention, our action. *A Mercy* tells the story of Florens, Lina, Sorrow, and Jacob and Rebekka Vaark. On a small but steadily growing farm in Virginia, Jacob, an orphaned immigrant hailing from Amsterdam, acquires Florens, Lina, and Sorrow, one surrendered, one left over, the other sold cheaply. I will examine at some length the scene in the novel that describes how Florens comes to be on the Vaark farm. The central action of the novel revolves around Florens's sexual obsession with and journey to find a blacksmith who has knowledge of healing herbs that might bring Jacob's wife Rebekka back from the brink of a smallpox death. The same death that ultimately claimed her husband.

The opening of the novel is decidedly *animal*. Florens is the first character we meet, and the second voice, though in third person unlike Florens's inhabited narrative, is the man who will become her owner, Jacob Vaark. In classic Morrison fashion, Florens comes to us out of the ether in the middle of recounting a difficult experience, enjoying our ability as readers to be shocked into the time of the novel. Morrison writes: "Don't be afraid. My telling can't hurt you in spite of what I have done and I promise to lie quietly in the dark. . . . I will never again unfold my limbs to rise up and bare teeth. I explain. You can think what I tell you a confession, if you like, but one full of curiosities familiar only in dreams and during those moments when a dog's profile plays in the steam of a kettle."[52] Hum:animal emerge early in this text and of course, there goes that dog again, like the picture in Louis Cartwright's hands in Edward P. Jones's *The Known World*, the image of the dog, the play of possibility beyond the frame, literal or literary. Florens's desire parallels Jones's Louis, who too wants to lick the pooled water from his lover's skin; Florens's quest for the unrequited love of the blacksmith rests in the shock of her own desire as Morrison tells us, "The shine of water runs down your spine and I have shock at myself for wanting to lick there" (44). And the madness of teeth bared, limbs *un*folding. In the classic definition of "bared," the process is not a revelation but an unconcealment—the removal of a covering from something. But this is no secret being exposed; this act is making known what is always already there. Think Heidegger here. Think Agamben. Think too, precarious life, and those ants under a rock. In this newer new world, precarity is most definitely at issue, especially as it pertains to hum/animal life.

Florens also brings with her the *beast*, a moment in the text that is located in a temporal past. Recalling the "boneless bears in the valley," Florens's memory is visceral, "Their smell belying their beauty, their eyes knowing us *from when we are beasts also*" (5; emphasis mine). The beast breaks into the narrative as a possibility in relation to a somewhat altered past perfect condition, *la* comes from a time called "from when." I am not the first or last critic thinking with Morrison's stunning ninth novel to focus on what gender *means* in the context of the story's unfolding. Marc C. Conner ob-serves that "Florens [unlike Jacob] moves into and through a landscape in which dominion does not exist, and the only language available to her is a female language that does not wish to dominate, but only to find the way."[53] Conner also notes that "Native American characters and culture are consistently valorized in Morrison's work . . . ; Lina speaks for the val-ues Morrison associates with native culture."[54] Jennifer Terry affirms this uncomfortable place in Morrison's work by noting that "tensions remain in the novel's activation of a Native American presence but Lina's prominence and particularity counter narrow stereotype."[55] I am not entirely sure that Lina's character counters narrow stereotypes of indigeneity, and I will speak to this issue in my assessment below.

Nevertheless, Conner is right to sense the proprietary nature of the female in this and other novels by Morrison. My argument expands that lens to the *beast* and its potential. The salience of the beast mistaken for some-thing else is contained in Jacob's first narration of the events that bring him to his journey in the novel. In his broken cosmos, Florens is an "ill-shod child," Sorrow is "the curly-haired goose girl," and "the acquisition of both could be seen as a rescue" and Lina "was a woman, not a child" (40). Later, we discover that at the sawyer's house where Jacob first encounters her, Sorrow was put to work "to mind the geese" (140). Remember Derrida's beast as "woman," "child," or "slave." The infantilization here is not so much about gender but about *animal* life in Jacob's world and its diminished being serves the stakes for new world sovereignty. That Lina is "a woman, not a child" in his eyes speaks to the elevation of her in Jacob's eyes. But this has nothing to do with her character but stems from the actual use of *capital* for Lina, as opposed to Sorrow and Florens who are "rescues." It is clear from Lina's only narrative that being rescued for her is no mercy, "[Jacob Vaark] mystified Lina. All Europes did. Once they terrified her, then they rescued her. Now they simply puzzled her" (51). In her own mind, being "rescued," like being "terrified" is in a litany of equivalent experiences that accrue meaning, thus slightly changing the terms of her own *purchase* and the sense that it was/is *mercy* that fuels has fueled her belonging.

This world that Morrison creates is forged out of the ashes of Bacon's re-bellion (1675–76)—a fact that one of the characters, Jacob Vaark, reminds us of in the first pages of the novel, "In this territory he could not be sure of friend or foe. Half a dozen years ago an army of blacks, natives, whites, mulattoes—freedmen, slaves and indentured—had waged war against local gentry led by members of that very class" (11). For Vaark, it's 1682 and

"Virginia was still a mess" (12). What is important about the novel's genesis, historically at least, is that internal contestations among settlers and tribes in the emerging and advancing colonies produced land loss for those Indian tribal nations involved and a proliferation of restrictive laws about slavery and the enslaved that became institutionalized as Virginia's slave codes in 1705.[56] It is my contention that beast and sovereign hover in Morrison's text as part of the somewhat unsettled soup of *being* she brings herself to investigate. Jacob Vaark wades into this mix as "a ratty orphan become landowner, making a place out of no place, a temperate living from raw life." The personification of *land* in this moment is important and the comparison of Jacob's patroonship and Henry Forge's Forge Run or Faulkner's Sutpen's Hundred cannot be overstated. The destiny of white men in settler slave encampments is to domesticate themselves and others. This "raw life" is given to Vaark as "one hundred and twenty acres of a dormant patroonship" (13). In short, the gift of *life* given to Vaark is an entitlement that doesn't even come from a direct line of welcome descent but is instead left to him from "an uncle he had never met from the side of his family that had abandoned him" (13). His land-ed-ness comes from the outrage of inconsequence, a gift of Indian land like a dangling participle in someone else's incomplete sentence. Later in the company of the "Papist" Maryland plantation owner D'Ortega, who owes Jacob a debt from a failed enterprise in human flesh, he insults D'Ortega's religion and feels the slight advantage over him that reminds him of being a "raw boy" (29). Sovereign tracks animal life always and every*where*.

In the opening pages we have a collection of females—Lina, Sorrow and Florens—poised in community; indeed, what Valerie Babb so astutely identifies as a tale that "enlists . . . marginalized voices to rewrite the origins narrative as a cautionary tale warning of the dangers of selfish individualism to any form of community."[57] The constant attachment to animal life, such that it becomes indistinguishable from what we would consider human, is reiterated and becomes central not only to the novel's metaphorical and representational landscape but also to its understanding of *being* itself.

The Indigenous character in the novel and the oldest of the three indentured "women" on the farm, Lina "had been purchased outright and deliberately" (40). In the only section dedicated to her story, Lina worries about the festive mood that overtakes the farm at the building of Jacob Vaark's "double-storied, fenced and gated [house] like the one he saw on his travels" (51). In true Thomas Sutpen form, Vaark sets to making his "design" come to fruition. Lina notes only: "Killing trees in that number without asking their permission, of course his efforts would stir up malfortune" (51). This is the first indication we get that Lina is different from Sorrow and Florens, the two orphan girls that Vaark rescues one at a time. I will return to Lina's relationship with the natural world in a bit, but I want to remark upon how Morrison positions Lina to literally read the threat that Black freedom poses to the territory and eventually the farm that they all inhabit. Upon meeting the unnamed blacksmith hired to work on the gates to Vaark's mansion, Lina recounts (53):

> Learning from Mistress that he was a free man doubled her anxiety. He had rights, then, and privileges, like Sir. He could marry, own things, travel, sell his own labor. She should have seen the danger immediately because his arrogance was clear. When Mistress returned, rubbing her hands on her apron, he removed his hat once more, then did something Lina had never seen an African do: he looked directly at Mistress, lowering his glance, for he was very tall, never blinking those eyes slanted and yellow as a ram's.

It is the animal who lets us know the condition of the human, and Lina disrupts the positionality of the blacksmith, through simile, calling his sovereign quest, perhaps, into question. Contemplating the blacksmith's relative freedom, Lina tells us "In the town [she] had been taken to, after the conflagration had wiped away her village, that kind of boldness from any African was legitimate cause for a whip" (53). The mention of the whip, I would argue, ties the African descended to the *fact* of slavery's hierarchies of flesh, as it also ties them to the collusion that makes such a system work. Lina's caution in regard to the blacksmith and her recall of the whip provides evidence of the presence of *both*. It is interesting that we find out about Lina's peoplelessness at the precise moment that she describes punishment for an exercise of free will, or because we are talking about a gaze here, punishment for what should be the face-to-face practice of ethical commitment to each other that (human) being entails, but instead produces at least in Lina's understanding a delegitimate dominance for someone who should be *less than*. This exchange is rehearsed again in the slice of apple offered the blacksmith by Jacob. Lina views such reciprocity as dangerous; in this space it is Lina who appears to keep to hierarchy. This troubling blackness "locked eyes" with Lina and also comes to them as a sexual threat in competition for female flesh, rather than in ethical relation (52).

Morrison has Lina not only repudiate this commitment in racialized terms but also states her relationship to such commitment through a discourse of homelessness. I would like to argue that this state of dispossession (if possession marks the "free," as in the paragraph above) unmakes Lina's relationship to sovereignty—she becomes a character for us in the midst of marking her own kinless and placeless state while referring to potential punishment for a simple act of practiced belonging—the face-to-face, eye-to-eye of the blacksmith and "Mistress," of Lina and the blacksmith, the former, an animal other, the latter, a contestation.

Unlike Florens and the blacksmith, Lina is also vexed by the animal, as just a few pages from the scene above, she tells us of the disease that took her "family and all the others." Morrison writes: "At first they fought off the crows, she and two young boys, but they were no match for the birds or the smell, and when the wolves arrived, all three scrambled as high into a beech tree as they could. They stayed there all night listening to gnawing, baying, growling, fighting and worst of all the quiet of animals sated at last" (54). But here we have a contradiction, as her kinless state and cultural solitude is cast in doubt by the presence of the "two young boys." Who are they to the girl who would become Lina? One could make the banal observation that her ideas of "family" might be bounded by female rather than male succession, but this move seems too easy, even "romantic," at best. Moreover, that this relationship to kin and nation is reduced to "family and all the others" in Morrison produces another kind of fiction in the novel— one in which Lina's relationship to a *prior* history, instead of the story of the Vaark farm in which, like Sutpen's Judith, Clytie, and Rosa, her narrative becomes part of the living of the other women, not girls, around her, is instead envisioned through the lens of "family" rather than tribe or nation. Morrison writes, "The shame of having survived the destruction of her *families* shrank with her vow never to betray or abandon anyone she cherished" (57). At the novel's close, it will be very difficult to assess just who Lina cherishes, if she does so at all. A woman in a newer new world who has just attached herself—and I'll get to this in a moment—to animal life around her and sees her relations as *family* . . . it feels like Lina's character is being hollowed out for a more fungible purpose in the novel. In many ways, Morrison attests to this with "she sorted and stored what she dared to recall and *eliminated the rest*, an activity which shaped her inside and out. By the time Mistress came, her self-invention was almost perfected" (59; emphasis mine). Indeed, it is hard to entirely comprehend what we are being encouraged to *see* here. Lina "nested with the chickens" for six years until Mistress arrived; the "self-invention" she manages could be nothing more than a mirror of the lives of the "Europes" around her, if it weren't for that *animal* life nestled with/"nested with." This remnant of sovereignty, the *la* of the beast, contemplates the inhabitants of the Vaark farm and realizes "that they were not a family—not even a like-minded group. They were orphans, each and all" (69).

In many ways, the novel is about the awful "quiet of animals sated at last." Remaking herself through bricolage from conquest in the Americas, Morrison writes that Lina was "relying on memory and her own resources, she cobbled together neglected rites, merged Europe medicine with native, scripture with lore, and recalled or invented the hidden meaning of things. Found, in other words, a way to be in the world. . . . She cawed with birds, chatted with plants, spoke to squirrels, sang to the cow and opened her mouth to rain" (57). A seventeenth-century Temple Grandin, she becomes the quintessential American by being dispossessed of the narrative of her past—in her state of relative cultural collapse, she turns to the animal and communicates.[58] Such communication does not signal meaning-making so much as it signals a becoming animal that serves as the rationale for the novel's treatment of Lina as a medium. This new world becomes thick with nonhuman animals, bringing the trace of the sovereign and the beast. Moreover, the unmooring of Lina and her subsequent new-world re-making prepares her for the following, at least according to Sorrow: "that Lina ruled and decided everything Sir and Mistress did not. Her eye was everywhere even when she was nowhere" (144). This eye reminds one of the ram's eye but is disembodied and becomes the lens of management, a panopticon Foucault would be proud of.

For Sorrow, Lina is the doer, the decider, as she has the power to take the first but not the second child of Sorrow: "Although Sorrow thought she saw her own newborn yawn, Lina wrapped it in a piece of sacking and set it a-sail in the widest part of the stream and far below the beavers' dam" (145). Lina's reach is literally biblical. But the animal beckons always, as even in Sorrow's short narration of the events that bring her to Vaark's farm, we are reminded that her imaginary "twin" is "nestling near" (139). Sorrow's journey to us is water-born, and so her animal life is centered upon mermaids (140) and whales (140, 150), a watery life that Black feminist scholar Alexis Pauline Gumbs describes in the following manner, "Marine mammals live in a volatile substance whose temperature is changing for reasons not of their own making. Their skin is always exposed, they are surrounded on all sides by depth. What could enable us to live more porously, more mindful of the infinite changeability of our context, more open to each other and to our own needs?"[59] While the usefulness of marine life is harnessed for the benefit of human being, there are instructive elements here that mirror this project's longing. In the above quote, taken from Gumbs's section on "vulnerability," she speaks to the necessity to open to one another, embracing a kind of vulnerability that is chosen rather than prescribed, one that moves away from the barrier to animal life in Black thought constituted in a broken ontology that instead counters with *relation*, even over ethics or *mercy*.

The possibility of becoming sovereign is couched in the most restrictive terms, where the beasts around the Vaark farm are tamed—where "Sir was a hurricane of activity laboring to bring nature under his control" (57); and where power over life and death is in full exercise. But this power is betrayed by the beast nestled/nesting within. This gentled moment is a call out to the *mother* who stands at the threshold, in the flesh (always a kind of *enfleshment*) a potentiality and a past. How Lina becomes sovereign in Sorrow's eye is perhaps the most intriguing story in the novel. Lina becomes a new-world subject, able to manage bare life. Her relationship to Sorrow and Florens is articulated in biopolitical terms, and my interest here is in how Lina seems to accomplish such power in the wake of having lost or relinquished her kin, her relationship to a founding indigeneity in the novel. Her power-not-power is perplexing. This is Lina's legacy in the novel, and one which she uses to rule over Sorrow and Florens by denying mother-right to Sorrow and becoming mother to Florens. Being sovereign entails power over life or death and its manageability as well as encompasses a certain kind of geographical reach, an inhabitation necessary to make the very idea of the capacity to rule possible. Lina might have some of the former in regard to the Black captives around her—and even this power is subverted in the text—but she does not have what I would call a geo-positive possessiveness integral to making sovereign practice work, at least not in its strictly euro-philosophical iteration. Moreover, this sovereign reach is constantly unsettled by the presence of animal life (human and otherwise), and Lina's positionality and her communication with animal life create several problems, including how to interpret the ethical life of the novel itself. In the next section I turn to a traditional philosophical ground in meanings of ethical relation/commitment to understand not only Jacob Vaark's turn toward having human chattel but how *mercy* works in the novel's meditation on sovereignty.

ethical lessons

I want to travel through the second brief section of the novel under the umbrella term "a mercy" and think through some of the novel's challenges to what I am thinking of as "the ethical commitment." I will start with Jacob's rescue of the raccoon. In many ways this scene is the first "human" act of the story, but it also involves an animal and demonstrates the ways in which saving the animal is always at the threshold of saving/rescuing human being (from itself). Morrison writes: "Jacob urged the mare to a faster pace. He dismounted twice, the second time to free the bloody hindleg of a young raccoon stuck in a tree break. Regina [the horse] munched trail-side grass while he tried to be as gentle as possible, avoiding the claws and teeth of the frightened animal. Once he succeeded, the raccoon limped off, perhaps to the mother forced to abandon it or more likely into other claws" (12). Between two animals—the mare and the raccoon—and two iterations of a "claw"—one belonging to the raccoon and another one to an unknown predator, Jacob commits his first act of mercy. It is 1682 and he is traveling via the Lenape Trail on his way to a plantation called Jublio (16) owned by a man in Maryland named D'Ortega. Jacob imagines a future for the animal that is suspended between "the mother" and "other claws," producing an act of mercy as a futility and also a hope.

The act of dislodging the injured raccoon is meant to tell us who Jacob is—the work with the animal is meant to steer us into future work with the human. In a scene from Douglass's *Narrative*, the act of freeing a nonhuman animal (the oxen) is meant to tell us what slavery is; it is crafted to speak to the very hierarchy that makes for slavery's infrastructure. We are called to know, as Douglass receives his beating from Mr. Covey, that nonhuman animal life is set above the lives of the enslaved. The practice of mercy in the slavocracy is foreclosed, but it is laced through with animal life. So too in this new world that Morrison envisions. The taking of the girl Florens in exchange for an unpaid debt appears to be "a mercy" of signature meaning. I would argue that a mercy toward nonhuman animals so informs what we would call human mercy, that we must consider them to be on par with one another—human acts scripted by a negotiation of hum/animal distinction. Yet, we find that all acts of kindness, as in the case of the raccoon that one could argue is freed for "death," are not always ethical acts. If the ethical commitment of the human is to the other—or as Levinas reminds us, "something more than my life," then what is Jacob's face-to-face commitment to Florens? We learn at the end of the novel that *A Mercy* is this solitary act—all of the others in the novel are just reverberations of the same, like a ripple on a pond.

Morrison provides some answer to the conundrum of this second act of mercy in Jacob Vaark's attitude toward trading in human cargo, noting "Flesh was not his commodity." But we are introduced to Jacob's distain for slave trading, not because of his absolute abhorrence of the thing itself—the trade in "flesh"—but because of the people with whom he associates such trade. He sees Maryland as a "palatinate [that] was Romish to the core. Priests strode openly in its towns; their temples menaced its squares; their sinister missions cropped up at the edge of native villages. Law, courts and trade were the exclusive domain and overdressed women in raised heels rode in carts driven by ten-year-old Negroes. He was offended by the lax, flashy cunning of the Papists."[60] Jacob is not repulsed by slavery, so much as he is unnerved by Catholicism: "There was something beyond Catholic in [D'Ortega], something sordid and overripe" (27). We have more descriptions of D'Ortega and his plantation's inhabitants—"a sloven man" (19); "their narrow grasp of the English language" (20); "the foolish, incomprehensible talk" (22); and the "curdled arrogant fop" (29). It is here that Morrison sets the tension in the novel in religious difference, rather than racial difference; a difference that reviewers have remarked upon as important in the text. But I would also add that along with racial and religious difference, there is sexual difference—or difference in sexual practice that appear in this first scene of contact. The sexual tension in this encounter with D'Ortega abounds and if anything D'Ortega's Catholicism indicates a nature declining toward the demise of the human, past its expiration point ("overripe"), and a concerted loss of a masculinity clearly needed for self-governance or at least the demonstrated capacity for sovereignty.

If the opening scene of Vaark's travel south holds open the possibility of his interspecies compassionate practice, the scene between (human) beings in the first section that arrests us is that between Jacob and Florens's mother—the woman we will eventually come to know through her own brief narrative at the novel's close. Morrison writes (30–31):

"Please Senhor. Not me. Take her. Take my daughter."

Jacob looked up at her, away from the child's feet, his mouth still open with laughter, and was struck by the terror in her eyes. His laugh creaking to a close, he shook his head, thinking, God help me if this is not the most wretched business.

"Why yes. Of course," said D'Ortega, shaking off his earlier embarrassment and trying to re-establish his dignity. "I'll send her to you. Immediately." His eyes widened as did his condescending smile, though he still seemed highly agitated.

"My answer is firm," said Jacob, thinking, I've got to get away from this substitute for a man. But thinking also, perhaps Rebekka would welcome a child around the place. This one here, swimming in horrible shoes, appeared to be about the same age as Patrician, and if she got kicked in the head by a mare, the loss would not rock Rebekka so.

"There is a priest here," D'Ortega went on. "He can bring her to you. I'll have them board a sloop to any port on the coast you desire . . ."

"No. I said, no."

Suddenly the woman smelling of cloves knelt and closed her eyes. They wrote new papers.

But what brings Vaark to this end? I would like to offer that the differences here could all be parsed through the article that moves us forward through acts of "mercy" throughout the text. Instead of "the" mercy—where "the" refers to something known to the listener, we have "a" mercy, an act more unknown and unspecified. What brings Jacob face to face with the mother about to give up her child is a turning point in the tension between Vaark and D'Ortega. "Jacob raised his eyes to D'Ortega's, noticing the cowardice of unarmed gentry confronted with a commoner. Out here in the wilderness dependent upon paid guards nowhere in sight this Sunday. He felt like laughing. . . . Where else could rank tremble before courage? Jacob turned away, letting his exposed unarmed back convey his scorn. It was a curious moment. Along with his contempt, he felt a wave of exhilaration. Potent. Steady" (29).

Immediately after this moment, Jacob passes the cookhouse, sees the woman in the doorway and is offered the child. Like Faulkner's Thomas Sutpen in *Absalom, Absalom!*, his visit to "the big house" produces an articulation of class difference so profound that it sets him to laughing—until he comes face to face with the woman. With the ethical commitment before him, Jacob can be persuaded to take the girl as an afterthought in a series of relations grounded in inequality: "[He] realized, not for the first time, that only things, not bloodlines or character separated them" (31). Class relations here, as evidenced by the myriad references to D'Ortega as effete, are laced with sex/gender.

A mercy here is a singular but mysterious act—known only to the interlocutors. In any event, this mercy's significance is not reciprocated by Jacob—he does not think of that moment literally in kind or in relationship to Florens's mother, but rather as evidence of his elevated stature in the world. This elevation causes him to have fantasies of building "a house that size on his own property" (31), again like Faulkner's Sutpen's Hundred and the "design" of its maker. Later in the same section, we learn that Jacob "did what was necessary: secured a wife, someone to help her, planted, fathered" (39). In Faulkner's text, Sutpen remarks, "I had a design. To accomplish it I should require money, a house, a plantation, slaves, a family—incidentally, of course, a wife."[61] While Morrison writes that "Jacob sneered at wealth dependent on a captured workforce that required more force to maintain" and that he would not be "trading his conscience for coin" (32), we have to return to the earlier scene of Florens's exchange to gain proper perspective upon this act of mercy.

Remember this: "This one here, swimming in horrible shoes, appeared to be about the same age as Patrician, and if she got kicked in the head by a mare, the loss would not rock Rebekka so" (31). Earlier, the death of their fifth child in this same manner has rocked his otherwise "capable" (23) wife, Rebekka, and so the substitute child—the enslaved—is valued, is exchanged because the "loss would not rock [her] so." Florens figured "death by mare"—two times, as the first mare (Regina, who has a name, though Florens's mother does not) carries Vaark to the D'Ortega plantation, bringing about her separation from her mother, and the second mare, having already killed the five-year-old Patrician is conjured here to produce a second value for Florens. The capriciousness of the animal is utilized by Morrison to mark Florens's situation in Jacob's eyes. The proximity to the animal makes her status as chattel even more cogent. The exchange of child for slave/child, the end of Vaark's bloodline, and the presence of the mare produce a culturally potent situation.

As the section closes, we see Jacob remember Regina, his leased mare, fondly by remarking upon the night sky a "canvas smooth and dark as Regina's hide" (40), as he washes away "the faint trace of coon's blood" (40). I cannot help but think about the double meaning of "coon" here. In the end, his walk in the "warm night air," his reflection upon the animal, brings him to the following conclusion: "Now he fondled the idea of an even more satisfying enterprise. And the plan was as sweet as the sugar on which it was based." Jacob settles upon his own plan for wealth procurement after a conversation with patrons at Pursey's tavern, but he also settles upon this plan in the wake of another scene with a horse, with the animal. On the way to his lodging, "he saw a man beating a horse to its knees. Before he could open his mouth to shout, rowdy sailors pulled the man away and let him feel his own knees in the mud. Few things angered Jacob more than the brutal handling of domesticated animals. He did not know what the sailors were objecting to, but his own fury was not only because of the pain it inflicted on the horse, but because of the mute, unprotesting surrender glazing its eyes" (33). Brutal handling of domesticated animals and attempts at domestication, at civilizing, at acculturation have more in common with what it means to achieve human being.

There are two gazes in this opening section: that of Florens's mother, who remarks at the end that she had "gathered you and your brother to stand in their eyes" "Because I saw the tall man see you as a human child, not pieces of eight [Spanish dollar]" (195), and that of the horse. In the end we realize that "a mercy" is not an act of God, but a deeply human endeavor: "It was a mercy. Offered by a human" (195). One could argue that the only human endeavor that matters is the ethical commitment to the other—who can be seen because of the commitment as "more than one's own life." It is clear that Florens's mother sees, recognizes, and inhabits this space called "a mercy"; it is also clear that Vaark's own vision is skewed by the way in which Florens is exchanged for so many things in the beginning of this novel; an exchange mediated by the persistent referencing to the animal. In the end, *A Mercy* rests on human, animal, gender, sex, class, and so much more.

The focus on the "human" in the novel is constantly interrupted by the gaze of the nonhuman other, which calls for sharper focus on the doers and the done too, demands a clearer perceptiveness about what freedom and sovereignty mean in the context of this new world order—whose logo-centrism necessarily and repeatedly puts (hu)man at odds with animal. In *Homo Sacer*, Giorgio Agamben sets forth the terrible possibilities of "supreme power" noting that "in the last analysis, [it is] nothing other than the capacity to constitute oneself and others as life that may be killed but not sacrificed."[62] The sovereign's political embodiment as sacred life extends both the right to power and its unaccountability, as sovereignty can be detected in the act of getting away with murder, over and over again. This actualization is remarked upon by Agamben and Derrida as dependent upon the condition of the hum/animal distinction, as the boundary between them is constantly called into crisis by "human" action, and into crisis by the very material conditions under which sovereignty obtains. What I am searching for here is a way for us to understand how much discourses of sovereignty, self-determination, and freedom are caught in the double temporal bind of a past that cannot be reconciled with a future and a kind of animal life that must be managed and reckoned with as a threshold moment for both Indigenous and Black peoples.

the open : ...

As I cease my writing of this book, the Supreme Court has just overturned *Roe v. Wade.* So much of the scaffolding of this work is *reproduction* and its grave consequence for hum:animal. Perhaps this relinquishment will open upon other questions that emerge simply because I have asked them and I wish for answers.

I began this journey with a question, "What happens when Black people *do* things with animals?" We have traveled to all of the places that *I* can think of to answer this question—and the answers have been devastating and cruel, loving and kind, cheeky and outrageous. *This* is what happens when you do things with animals, when you care not for the boundary that gives meaning to the word itself—*animal*—when you step outside of what you are supposed to do, and instead incline your head a little to what cannot be found on the page or in the landscape. The answers to my question reek of animal life, which is always already kind of awful/a kind of offal.

Together we have reimagined the stakes of enslavement for Black life, tracked the female (*the animal that I am therefore . . .*) at every turn, seen nonhuman animal life as consequential to world(s), birthed or yet to be born, chased the limit of the self, found the group and the collective. This book is no primer but a praxis, a Black feminist praxis. Its heroines do not always cohere in human being, but they are legion, and they are in these pages. Doing things with animals has been dangerous for some of us.

What *an other* brings to the table is its focus on the vulnerabilities and violence that craft insurgencies. What are the possibilities for ethical action, for an approach to *life* modeled by those people of African descent who threw their lot with animal life? How might we tell their stories? Will we even get the chance? As

I moved through this book's landscape laced with accident and love, I discovered something at the core of that civil rights mantra of nonviolence that I'd always thought was a bit weak in the face of the fire hoses. I was wrong. By thinking and living (*life*) hum:animal, I have come to understand that nonviolence is the only mode of living that doesn't center the self's survival as the only outcome of/for justice.

acknowledgments

When you work on a book across more than a decade (even publishing another one in the middle of such work) and move across four institutions in two states, looking to belong, you change your mind often and you have too many beings to thank to begin to do justice to the level of support you feel for who you are in the world.

While no significant funding organization supported this work, I am indebted to two research leaves granted by the University of North Carolina at Chapel Hill in the spring of 2019 and 2020 that allowed me valuable time to put these chapters together. If it weren't for the pandemic that pulled back the skin of human being, exposing its living for all of us to see, this project wouldn't have found its temporal location and I wouldn't have found valuable time away from the troubled and troublesome hallways of my place of work to write the first full draft of this book. Thank you to the archivists and librarians at UCLA and Temple University, you were all invaluable to this work and I see you and thank you.

I want to thank Ken Wissoker of Duke University Press for always believing in what I have to say and how I need to say it. I want to thank Liz Smith for shepherding this book to its rightful place on the shelf. Thank you to Cathy Davidson for always reading the work when it's messy and helping me to see dry sand through muddy water. Thank you to Cary Wolfe, fellow traveler in animal studies back in 1999 when we were colleagues at SUNY, who talked and walked animal with me and taught me that in forty degrees below zero wind chill, "cotton kills." To Alexander Weheliye, who was there at the beginning and whose fine mind still intrigues me. Thank you for the loving embrace of my Chicago dyke family, Lisa Freeman, Heather Schmucker, Jennifer Briar, Kat Hindman, and Jennifer D. Brody, intimate travelers for this journey in animal life. Thank you to my Duke colleagues: lover of dogs Cathy Rudy, horsewoman Kristine Stiles, and Ranjana Khanna, who were all at the table when we took part in a human/animal graduate/faculty seminar and taking a deep feminist dive into Derrida, I began to understand that to hail *an* other, *in theory*, was never going to be enough.

To my UNC colleagues, Elizabeth (Betsy) Olson, Pat Parker, David Garcia, Jennifer Washington, and Renée Alexander Craft, thanks for making the Chair-verse survivable, at least for a time. To my Critical Ethnic Studies colleagues, Emil Keme and Kumi Silva, words cannot express how your being in the world holds me down. To my rowdy ones, partners in justice and always ready to speak truth to power, Malinda Maynor-Lowery and Kia Caldwell, you are my sisters and my kin; I know we tried to do something important together and that bond endures. To my colleagues and students in American Studies, who inspire by their example. To Rachel Gelfand and Katelyn Campbell, who were research assistants for this book, and especially to Katelyn Campbell who helped to bring this project to production. To Kimber Thomas, Elijah Heyward, and Rae Garringer, who survived the wreckage of our Black worlds and my little queer world in the belly of a beast that just won't quit; I love you all for bringing who we are, for bringing your full selves, to the open. To Danielle Dulken, fellow rider and lover of equines, and Ben Apple, both family now.

To my family, Robert Warrior, Sylvia Villarreal, Tae Hart, Katie and Jack McCabe, and Luke and Laura McCabe, I love you to the moon and back; you are precious to me. To my North Carolina people, Meta Jones, Sunny, Tizzúnu, Roo, Aidan, Winnie, Webster, Jonathan, Willie, Kelly, Andrew, Starr, Molly, Glenn, Katy, Darian, Shayla, and Charlie, you are my heart and I know we love this place we call home together, despite its ruins. To my food studies family, Cynthia Greenlee and Kelly Alexander, you are my badass interlocutors, always. To the chefs and the barbacks and the front of house folks who always feed me, Gabe Barker, Heather Shores, and Bill Smith, thank you. To my trainer and friend Micky Purcell, thank you for seeing me each and every day and helping me always find my way back to Annie when I get lost in this world. To the squad, Annette, Danielle, and Antonia, we are still talking sh*t and writing books. To my coach, Emily O'Barr, without whom this book would not have reached beyond the threshold that is my doorstep, thank you. To Sweet Negritude, a living thing—I found a home at the end of the world in your lush interior and I am grateful. To Tiffany Lethabo King, thank you for embracing my two-spirited self, and for the gift of your gorgeous mind.

And to my fierce and fiery Annie, there is no part of you that I do not love: from the hoofprints still etched on my ass that you left when you needed to impart a portion of your biography to me, to the delicious feel of your muzzle at the day's end, to your *femaleness.* Being with you is the best part of any waking hour and I hope I have done some tiny bit of justice to the world we share and make together. Yours is a capacious nervous system connected to the vastness that is this earth's vibration. We beat as one heart.

abbreviations

GPJNFC   George P. Johnson Negro Film Collection (1916–1977), UCLA Library Special Collections

LACC   Los Angeles Community College

LAROH   L.A. Rebellion Oral History, UCLA Library

PEB   *Philadelphia Evening Bulletin*. Photographs included in PSIC records and also in the George D. McDowell Philadelphia Evening Bulletin Photographs. Temple University Library, Digital Collections.

PSIC   Philadelphia Special Investigation Committee, MOVE records, Temple University, Charles Library

abbreviations

notes

how to read this book

1 Chu, *Females*, 2. I want to thank my research assistant, Katelyn Campbell, for bringing this text to my attention.
2 hooks, *Appalachian Elegy*, 4. I want to thank Danielle Dulken, scholar extraordinaire, for bringing this text and its love for *animal* life and living to my attention.
3 Jodi A. Byrd speaks to *relation* when examining the work of Daniel Heath Justice. She notes, "It is the relations between them that matter the most . . . there are moments when the boundaries break down altogether to allow crossings, transformations, and stealings away." Lisa Lowe and Jennifer Nash, have both spoken to thinking through *relation* or relationality. Since their work doesn't necessarily focus exclusively on a non-species-centered approach to relation, I don't engage them more fully in this project. See Byrd, "What's Normative Got to Do with It?," 119; Nash, *Black Feminism Reimagined*; and Lowe, *The Intimacies of Four Continents*.

primer : what the animal said

1 I am grateful for remarks made by friend and colleague David Mitchell, whose response to this portion of my keynote for a conference at the University of Maryland was, in a word, brilliant.

1. vocabularies : possibility

1 Jean-Luc Nancy has described "world" in the following manner: "The becoming-world of the world means that 'world' is no longer an object, nor an idea, but the place existence is given to and exposed." Cadava, Connor, and Nancy, *Who Comes After the Subject?*, 1.
2 See Pickens, *Black Madness :: Mad Blackness*. She explains her use of the double colon in the introduction.

3   A recent keyword search for "blackness, human, animal" in the Duke library catalogue yielded zero results. African Americanists and African American intellectuals have been interested for quite some time in the relationship between blackness and the category of the human (W. E. B. Du Bois, Franz Fanon, Harold Cruse, Patricia Williams, and Hortense Spillers). Most recently, scholars have been investigating blackness in the context of posthumanism in a mode of critique called Afrofuturism. See "Afrofuturism," *Social Text* 20, no. 2, special issue 71 (Summer 2002).

4   I am reminded of Sylvia Wynter's argument in "1492: A New World View," where she asks scholars, "Can we therefore, while taking as our point of departure both the ecosystemic and global sociosystemic 'interrelatedness' of our contemporary situation, put forward a new world view of 1492 from the perspective of the species, and with reference to the interests of its well-being, rather than from the partial perspectives, and with reference to the necessarily partial interests, of both celebrants and dissidents?" (8). Black feminist scholars have returned to Wynter's work with some frequency, though there is room for debate about whether Wynter's thought holds a brief for the discipline. During my time as her colleague at Stanford (1993–1999), our paths did not cross.

5   "Human" refers to characteristics of the race, whereas "human being" refers to an individual. While I deal with/flirt with (human) being to some extent in this book, my intention is to float between the two signifieds/signifiers "hum/animal" as much as possible.

6   See Simpson, *Touching the Void*.

7   For information on the murder of Trayvon Martin in Sanford, Florida, see Lizette Alverez and Cara Buckley, "Zimmerman Is Acquitted in Trayvon Martin Killing," *New York Times*, July 13, 2013. For an outline of the facts in the case against officer Darren Wilson who shot and killed Michael Brown in Ferguson, Missouri, see Larry Buchanan, Ford Fessenden, K. K. Rebecca Lai, Haeyoun Park, Alicia Parlapiano, Archie Tse, Tim Wallace, Derek Watkins, and Karen Yourish, "What Happened in Ferguson?," *New York Times*, November 25, 2014. For a discussion of the chokehold death of Eric Garner in Staten Island, New York, see J. David Goodman and Al Baker, "Wave of Protests after Grand Jury Doesn't Indict Officer in Eric Garner Chokehold Case," *New York Times*, December 3, 2014. For a discussion of the shooting death of Walter Scott by Officer Michael Slager, see Jamelle Bouie, "Broken Taillight Policing," *Slate*, April 8, 2015. For a discussion of the lynching death of Lennon Lacy in Bladenboro, North Carolina, see Todd C. Frankel, "FBI Investigates Suspicious Death of North Carolina Teen Lennon Lacy," *Washington Post*, December 19, 2014.

8   See Bell, *Race, Racism and American Law*. See also Berlant, "Slow Death (Sovereignty, Obesity, Lateral Agency)," 760. Berlant's discussion of "event," "episode," and "environment" is particularly relevant.

9   Morrison, *Beloved*, 225.

10 Weheliye, *Habeas Viscus*, 1.

11 Weheliye, *Habeas Viscus*, 85.

12 Berlant, "Slow Death," 761.

13 Berlant's footnote to this particular phase of her argument—one that unpacks Giorgio Agamben's "overterritorialization" in *State of Exception* of what Berlant believes is "fundamentally a temporal" state in the rhetoric of indistinction—indicates that she is more interested here in interpreting the movement of the rock as a trope for the "activity of displacement." Anything other than "human" gets harnessed for the potentiality of human beings' ability to master.

14 Mills, *Racial Contract*, 10.

15 Stewart, *Ordinary Affects*, 1.

16 Stein, *Three Lives*.

17 See McKittrick, "Dear April"; Purifoy, "The Parable of Black Places"; and King, "Off Littorality."

18 Deleuze and Guattari, *A Thousand Plateaus*, 249.

19 Deleuze and Guattari, *A Thousand Plateaus*, 250.

20 See Freeman, *Time Binds*; and Muñoz, *Cruising Utopia*.

21 Bennett, *Vibrant Matter*, 24. Hereafter cited parenthetically in the text.

22 Kaba, *We Do This 'Til We Free Us*, 4. I want to thank Sunny Osment for bringing this book to my attention as the COVID-19 pandemic swirled around us.

23 Kaba, *We Do This 'Til We Free Us*, 20 (emphasis mine).

24 Moreton-Robinson, "The White Possessive," 20. I want to thank Robert Warrior for reaching out to Aileen Moreton-Robinson, who generously agreed to share a few essays before their publication.

25 Derrida, *The Animal That Therefore I Am*, 96; and Mbembe, "Necropolitics," 14–15.

26 Haraway, *When Species Meet*, 163. It is no small irony that this observation comes in an autobiographically driven chapter ("Able Bodies and Companion Species") that begins with a letter to her sportswriter father. Here, sports writing serves as a practice that often sutures relation between human and animal, as Haraway notes, "This chapter is a note of a sportswriter's daughter. It is writing that I must do, because it's about a legacy, an inheritance in the flesh. To come to accept the body's unmaking, I need to re-member its becoming" (162). Interestingly enough, it's the sportswriters who turned our attention to African-descended riders. See Hotaling, *The Great Black Jockeys*, on the place of Black jockeys in

histories of America's first sport. Also see Drape, *Black Maestro*. For a scholarly overview of the world of the enslaved, horses, and America's first sport, see Mooney, *Race Horse Men*.

27 Haraway, *When Species Meet*, 70.

28 Jackson, *Becoming Human*, 15. While my investigation certainly moves in the direction of the latter part of this statement, my inclination would be to steer away from giving over all manner of animal living to the realm of ontology altogether.

29 I want to thank audiences at the University of Maryland (October 2014) and George Washington University (February 2015) for their generous comments and responses to presentations on this next project. In particular, I want to thank colleague and friend David Mitchell (GWU), who was the first to reflect back that my work focused not on the idea of animal being as negative space but rather on the idea of the animal as a being in its own right, an entity capable of sharing in the luxury of human endeavor.

30 Heidegger, *Being and Time*, 11. Hereafter cited parenthetically in the text.

31 Derrida, *The Animal That Therefore I Am*, 96.

32 I have loved Merleau-Ponty's work for over thirty years, and I believe as Jane Bennett does that "[a] vital materialism attempts a more radical displacement of the human subject than phenomenology has done, though Merleau-Ponty himself seemed to be moving in this direction in his unfinished *Visible and Unvisible* [sic]." Bennett, *Vibrant Matter*, 30.

33 Bennett, *Being Property Once Myself*, 12 (emphasis in original).

34 The tension in the film and in the narrative that revolves around the ethical questions that are slavery's trace are paralleled in Yusoff's *A Billion Black Anthropocenes or None*. She speaks to "an actual mass slave suicide" upon which Dionne Brand's book *At the Full and Change of the Moon* is based. She also notes that filmmaker Steve McQueen's films *Caribs' Leap/Western Deep* look at parallel instances of suicide across two temporal and geographic locations. This adds to my argument that McQueen is focused on ethical questions that are particular to an African-descended being in his thinking about histories of enslavement.

35 Northup (*Twelve Years a Slave*, 78) describes Tibeats as "a small, crabbed, quick-tempered, spiteful man. He had no fixed residence that I ever heard of, but passed from one plantation to another, whenever he could find employment. He was without standing in the community, not esteemed by white men, nor even respected by slaves."

36 The only eyes that look onto the scene without flinching or looking away are the eyes of the plantation mistress. My concern in this scene is with the African-descended characters and their vision and not necessarily with phenotypically white subjects.

37 Weil, "A Report on the Animal Turn," 10.

38 Weil, "A Report," 13 (emphasis mine).

39 Calarco, *Zoographies*, 25.

40 Agamben, *Homo Sacer*, 8.

41 Northup, *Twelve Years a Slave*, 81.

42 Northup, *Twelve Years a Slave*, 85.

43 Steve McQueen, dir., *12 Years a Slave* (2013), 1:42:52.

44 Povinelli, *Economies of Abandonment*, 109.

45 Northup, *Twelve Years a Slave*, 198.

46 Spillers, "Mama's Baby, Papa's Maybe," 80. Hereafter cited parenthetically in the text.

47 Morrison, *Beloved*, 81.

48 McKittrick, *Demonic Grounds*, xvi–xvii.

49 I refer to the work of "flesh" in Afro-pessimism, a category that describes work on antiblackness in Black Studies. I capitalize the word "slave" because I am referring to this work, where it is often capitalized. See Sexton, Wilderson, Hartman, and Jackson, all discussed here. Also see Warren, *Ontological Terror*. As with my other work on Black thought, it is clear from this limited group that each author thinks differently about the paradigm, and I am waiting for the Black critic who will give us the full diversity of opinion about the pessimism in a review of this stunning body of work.

50 Merleau-Ponty, *The Visible and the Invisible*, 139. While I have thought about this moment in Merleau-Ponty since my time as an undergraduate, I want to acknowledge that Marquis Bey quotes the exact same passage in their stunning assessment of Black thought in *Black Trans Feminism*, 82. I came across it when I was asked to review their dossier and I'm glad I found a fellow traveler, though this is the only reference to Merleau-Ponty's work in the text, and the footnote to the quotation takes issue with the phenomenologist's grounding in the ocular and the boundedness of perception. Such an argument seems strange, given that Merleau-Ponty's project is to contest the extent to which the ocular and perception itself are limited—this is why the *elemental* qualities of flesh are much more appealing than their more material manifestations, at least for Merleau-Ponty.

51 Povinelli, *Economies of Abandonment*, 6. The purpose of this particular project is for Povinelli to let loose the term "late liberalism"—which she defines as a particular outgrowth of the failure of liberalism's relationship with capital in the face of "new social movements" and challenges to the state that have brought about its eventual and perhaps future perfect collapse (26–29).

52 Povinelli, *Economies of Abandonment*, 197, 203.

53 Jackson, *Becoming Human*, 194.

54 McKittrick, *Demonic Grounds*, ix.

55 My reading of the whip departs from Saidiya Hartman's conceptualization of the whip in *Scenes of Subjection*. Hartman's assessment sees the internalization of the whip as a form of potential disciplinary power and what it might engender in the self. I take my cue from Spillers in thinking through the positionalities at the two ends of slavery's most common instrument of torture. Our differences need not be at odds with one another, since Hartman is thinking through the whip as a felt trope in performance and I am thinking about its hum:animal connections.

56 In Sexton's *Amalgamation Schemes*, gender most often occurs in relationship to other intersectional realities, and when we do get gender on its own, it is inhabited by white females: "Beyond the expanded set of victims vulnerable to the putative menace of lascivious Blacks, what makes multiracialism an augmentation of the negrophobia typically accredited to white supremacy is the variation it seeks in the functions of female gender" (62).

57 See Sexton, *Amalgamation Schemes*, 217.

58 Wilderson, *Red, White & Black*, 18.

59 See Wilderson, *Red, White & Black*, 38.

60 See the discussion of Levinas and Blanchot in Cools, "Revisiting the *Il y a.*"

61 See Calvin Warren's conclusion in particular to *Ontological Terror: Blackness, Nihilism, and Emancipation.*

62 Wilderson, *Red, White & Black*, 141.

63 In an earlier discussion of white feminist thought, Wilderson (*Red, White & Black*, 132) remarks: "The foundation of all White feminist thought maintains its coherence not primarily thorough a conscious understanding of how the White female body is exploited, but through the unconscious libidinal understanding that, no matter how bad exploitation becomes, the White body can never fall prey to accumulation and fungibility."

64 Wilderson, *Red, White & Black*, 122. In a previous generation of pessimistic thought on "the Negro," a scholar like Nahum Dimitri Chandler relegates Wynter and Hartman to footnotes, though he does take on the difference that gender might unmake in his work on Spillers.

65 Wilderson, *Red, White & Black*, 57.

66 Wilderson, *Red, White & Black*, 38.

67 Povinelli, *Economies of Abandonment*, 4.

68 Povinelli cites Linda Simon, "William James's Lost Souls in Ursula Le Guin's Utopia," 4n7.

69 Povinelli, *Economies of Abandonment*, 124.

70 In his assessment of pragmatist William James and mathematician Alfred Whitehead (Deleuze focuses on his work in *The Fold*), Didier Debaise puts forth another new materialist intervention in the prob-

lem of metaphysics and its static (a word Whitehead also uses in regard to human beings' approach to the world) ontology. Debaise (*Nature as Event*, 13) writes: "The ontology of the moderns comprises the manner in which they have attempted to express the permanently repeated gesture of dividing bodies and their qualities while continually masking this very operation. In short, this ontology presupposes the gestures, techniques and operations of division." What is always astonishing to me is how these predominantly white and male scholars find the bending of time, the disruption of place, and the thought that produces a necessary question mark of the binary as illuminating surprises. Debaise's book signals that the movement toward another way to view *matter*—the how and the why—is nothing more than the work of new-world subjects (white men) to join what has already been said and come before.

71   Bogost, *Alien Phenomenology*, 7. The book is in Cary Wolfe's "posthumanities" series, which has published more than sixty books in the field.

72   In the same year, Kalpana Rahita Seshadri published *HumAnimal: Race, Law, Language*; much of her focus is on language and silence as an efficacy for rendering the distinction ineffective and, perhaps, obsolete.

73   Ahmed, *Cultural Politics of Emotion*, 145.

74   Wilderson, *Red, White & Black*, 313.

75   Wilderson, *Red, White & Black*, 315.

76   Wilderson, *Red, White & Black*, 315. In this excerpt, Wilderson quotes from Orlando Patterson's most influential *Slavery and Social Death*.

77   Wilderson, *Red, White & Black*, 2.

78   Wilderson, *Red, Black & White*, 2.

79   Wilderson begins his argument with two figures who stand outside institutional walls, occupying that space of insanity held open as a possibility of descent for the Black and Indigenous students who encounter these figures, but whose presence produces the beautiful phrase about ethics and violence I quote here.

80   Wilderson, *Red, Black & White*, 2.

81   Wilderson, *Red, Black & White*, 2.

82   See Chuh, *Imagine Otherwise*; and King, Navarro, and Smith, *Otherwise Worlds*. The latter volume was published about a year before a *New York Times* piece about Andrea Smith and the long and very public debate about her claims to Cherokee identity. Sarah Viren, "The Native Scholar Who Wasn't," *New York Times*, May 25, 2021, https://www.nytimes.com /2021/05/25/magazine/cherokee-native-american-andrea-smith.html.

83   Katie Calautti, "'What'll Become of Me?': Finding the Real Patsey of *12 Years a Slave*," *Vanity Fair*, March 2, 2014, https://www.vanityfair.com /hollywood/2014/03/patsey-12-years-a-slave.

84   Calautti, "'What'll Become of Me?'"

85   I allude to the work of Hammonds, "Black (W)holes and the Geometry of Black Female Sexuality."

86   Northup, *Twelve Years a Slave*, 129.

87   I note here that the Northup text published in 1853 is the transcription of his account as told to New York lawyer and legislator David Wilson. Sojourner Truth, "Ar'nt I a Woman?" Speech delivered to the May 29, 1851, Women's Rights Convention in Akron, Ohio. Historian Nell Painter points out that there are different versions of the speech, so it is impossible to know *exactly* what Truth said, but the words are now iconic. See Painter, *Sojourner Truth*.

88   Northup, *Twelve Years a Slave*, 152.

89   Northup, *Twelve Years a Slave*, 204.

90   Northup, *Twelve Years a Slave*, 204.

91   This allusion to the voice of the cyborg played by Arnold Schwarzenegger in *The Terminator*, trying to save the mother who will birth the insurgent white male subject in this back-to-the-future scape, is also instructive here. The lengths the machine will go to in order to have the mother of his new postapocalyptic nation survive are incredible and spawned a series of movies where Sarah Connor (played by Linda Hamilton) struggles at the end of her rope as well.

92   See Kyla Wazana Tompkins's critique of the new materialisms in "On the Limits of Promise of New Materialist Philosophy," https://csalateral.org/issue/5-1/forum-alt-humanities-new-materialist-philosophy-tompkins/.

93   See Raoul Peck's film *I Am Not Your Negro* (2016) for James Baldwin's account of that Black female child (Dorothy "Dot" Counts-Scoggins) who desegregated Harry Harding High School in Charlotte, North Carolina, alone. See also Redmond's essay on refusal, "'As Though It Were Our Own.'"

2. companionate : species

1   This conundrum is in evidence in Kathy Rudy's *Loving Animals*, where she articulates the liberation, welfarist, and rightist positions and comes at them through the lens of a feminist ethic of care tradition. Her goals are several—one is to consider "emotion . . . in the theory and practice of animal advocacy," while another is to question "the power structures that landed us in a world where abuse is accepted" (xvii–xviii). Another contradiction reveals itself, as to advocate is always already to produce structures of coercion and, yes, abuse.

2   See Firestone, *The Dialectic of Sex*; Haraway, *Simians, Cyborgs, and Women*; and Fausto-Sterling, *Sexing the Body*.

3   I want to make a distinction here between the rise of animal studies as a field of inquiry and the rise of animal liberation as a movement. In *For the Prevention of Cruelty*, historian Diane L. Beers observes that our citing of animal advocacy as a late modern phenomenon is simply incorrect and notes that "animal rights" go as far back as 1641 when the General Court of Massachusetts directly addressed the treatment of nonhuman animals in a document known as "The Body of Liberties." She offers that "When it comes to the animal advocacy movement, a historical amnesia effectively erases the significant legacies today's animal activists and society as a whole have inherited from their mostly forgotten predecessors. As we stumble uncertainly into the twenty-first century, this intriguing social justice cause marks nearly 140 years of persistent and diverse activism" (26). Nevertheless, she goes on to note that "Liberation ideology emerged mostly after 1975 and thus falls beyond the scope of this study, but it simply presents the most radical, uncompromising articulation of animal rights by demanding an immediate end to the speciesism (a concept similar to racism and sexism but applied to animals) perpetuated by humans" (14–15). But even in her work on the contemporary movement, she doesn't focus on MOVE's animal liberation or platform for "Life."

4   Peter Singer, "Animal Liberation," *New York Review of Books*, April 5, 1973. https://www.nybooks.com/articles/1973/04/05/animal-liberation/.

5   Élisabeth de Fontenay delivers a critique of Singer's utilitarian efforts in *Without Offending Humans*, her short book on animal rights. She notes that "Peter Singer's utilitarianism consists in determining the just or unjust character of actions based on the good or bad character of their effects: a perspective according to which the axiological must precede the deontological" (53). The critique continues, and it is rather eviscerating, but spot on, as the argument is more utilitarian than efficacious. It makes claims in order to get students of animal life to *see* the qualitative relationship between human and animal suffering, but its methods produce taxonomies of value that remain uncomfortable and wholly damaging to the argument about animal liberation in the first place. Later she concludes, "For them [Peter Singer and Paola Cavalieri], the vocabulary of rights is merely a convenient way of presenting certain demands but is in no way adequate to speaking about the interests of animals" (63–64).

6   Scholarly accounts vary widely in the dates of production for these two films. I have chosen to use the dates selected by the UCLA Film and Television Archive.

7   See Boisseron, *Afro-Dog*, specifically, her discussion of PETA.

8   Every rule has an exception, and so I would be remiss if I were to forget Paul Patton's "Language, Power, and the Training of Horses" in Wolfe, *Zoontologies*.

9 I am following Lisa Lowe's (*The Intimacies of Four Continents*) astute call for us to read across the archive in order to make connections among peoples and their relationships to discourses of "freedom" under liberalism.

10 Lowe, *Intimacies*, 3.

11 For one of the most detailed and persuasive accounts of the shortcomings of animal rights theory, see Donaldson and Kymlicka, *Zoopolis*. The authors call for a more robust animal rights approach using political theories of citizenship and hence "a more relational theory of justice" (23).

12 I want to note here that the word *species* has its place in Black pessimism stretching from Fanon to Hartman to Sexton, and Frank Wilderson spends time with this discussion in Black thought. I am more concerned with how species plays itself out in animal studies work; species there is about beings other than humans, whereas species in Black studies work is a work of distinction within the human. I opt for science *over* philosophy in this instance.

13 Haraway, *Companion Species Manifesto*, 53.

14 Agamben, *The Open*, 91.

15 Haraway, *Companion Species Manifesto*, 5.

16 To read across Haraway's work is to encounter a terrain of possibility that is ever shifting. In yet another work on hum:animal "becoming-with," *Staying with the Trouble*, she notes, "In human-animal worlds, companion species are ordinary beings-in-encounter in the house, lab, field, zoo, park, truck, office, prison, ranch, arena, village, human hospital, forest, slaughterhouse, estuary, vet clinic, lake, stadium, barn, wildlife preserve, farm, ocean canyon, city streets, factory, and more" (13).

17 This was the West Philadelphia home of Louise James. See Wagner-Pacifici, *Discourse and Destruction*, 32.

18 If one were to follow the religious trajectory and claims of the group, they grew out of Rev. Marshall L. Shepard's Mount Olivet Tabernacle Baptist Church, as many of the original members worshipped there. See Washington, "MOVE: A Double Standard of Justice," 73. The PSIC produced a written history of MOVE and indicates that "there was no MOVE until Leaphart met Glassey in Powelton Village in the spring of 1971. . . . When Leaphart did some repair work on Glassey's second floor apartment at 3312 Race St." This meeting is corroborated in the transcript of John Africa's (Vincent Leaphart's) trial; Glassey testifies that he met John Africa "in the spring of 1971." PSIC, Box 64, Folder 30. The "MOVE History" document also notes that Glassey was a part-time teacher at a Philadelphia community college and chronicles the public myths about who was actually the founder of MOVE, Glassey or Leaphart? The first seventeen pages document MOVE's early history, noting that both Delbert Africa and Sharon Cox have minimized Glassey's input into the

document that became known as the group's "Guidelines." PSIC, "MOVE History," Box 8, Folder 5, pp. 2 and 4–6.

19 Feldman, "MOVE Crisis," 8.

20 See Washington, "MOVE." See also Wagner-Pacifici, *Discourse and Destruction*, 31. See also Murray Dubin, "MOVE Credo: Revolution Ain't Verbalized," *Philadelphia Inquirer*, August 9, 1980, 14-A.

21 In their book *Burning Down the House*, John Anderson and Hilary Hevenor, residents of Philadelphia, almost completely omit MOVE's animal liberation work, noting that "in those days, especially, there was always something to demonstrate against: scientists, universities, visiting circuses" (10–11). Many MOVE members to this day are weary of giving interviews. Based upon the way in which their words are extracted in the Anderson and Hevenor text, I can see why. I want to thank Tiffany King for letting me know about this particular account of MOVE in the city.

22 Wagner-Pacifici, *Discourse and Destruction*, 14.

23 Across documents in the Temple University PSIC MOVE records, it is clear that despite being visited by and advocated for by Dick Gregory in 1978, MOVE members were not convinced by Gregory or moved by his attempts to help them.

24 Wagner-Pacifici, *Discourse and Destruction*, ix–x.

25 Haraway, *Companion Species Manifesto*, 36.

26 In Derrida's *The Animal That Therefore I Am*, he opens with a contemplation of nakedness, noting that he works "in order not to give the appearance of training [*dressage*], already, of a habit or a convention that would in the long term program the very act of thanking" (1).

27 Rose, "Human Sciences in a Biological Age." Quoted in Frost, *Biocultural Creatures*, 14 (emphasis mine).

28 In their examination of the MOVE conflict, Assefa and Wahrhaftig (*Extremist Groups*, 7) observe the importance of thinking about and working with their philosophy: "Whether one agrees with them or not to understand the premises underlying MOVE's world view in order to understand their behavior and the dynamics of the conflict."

29 Frost, *Biocultural Creatures*, 12.

30 Frost, *Biocultural Creatures*, 9.

31 The MOVE records consist of photographs, taken mostly by *Philadelphia Evening Bulletin* photographers, Philadelphia Special Investigation Committee (PSIC) interviews, transcripts, and historical documents. The PSIC was established by executive order 5–85 by Mayor W. Wilson Goode on June 19, 1985.

32 See Feldman thesis and the interview with both Winterbourne siblings regarding Powelton Village activism. Delbert Africa called the east Powelton group "a bunch of white, middle class academics who are acquiring

land through absentee ownership and driving poor black people out of their homes" ("Powelton Groups Clash Over Houses," *Philadelphia Daily News*, January 29, 1974). In addition, as early as April 25, 1975, Powelton Village neighbors had been showing up in the courts in particular distress about the animals and "garbage" on MOVE property. Community members had shown up to block a petition by MOVE members before the zoning board to place a kennel on their property. John T. Gillespie, "MOVE Appeals to Zoning Board over 20 Stray Dogs," *Philadelphia Evening Bulletin*, April 25, 1975. See also Gillespie, "Neighbors Complain about Threats from MOVE Members," *Philadelphia Evening Bulletin*, April 29, 1975. PSIC, Box 39, folder marked "MOVE, Radical Group, 1975."

33   PSIC, MOVE Records, September 4, 1985, Box 8, Folder 2, p. 2.

34   In Dorothy Roberts's groundbreaking study of reproduction and race, *Killing the Black Body*, she notes, "As I have charted the proliferation of rhetoric and policies that degrade Black women's procreative decisions, I have also noticed that America is obsessed with creating and preserving genetic ties between white parents and their children" (246).

35   Wilderson, *Red, White & Black*, 126.

36   Haraway, *Companion Species Manifesto*, 2–3.

37   See Schwartz, *Birthing a Slave*, 14. Thanks to Danielle Dulken for bringing this book to my attention.

38   Leslie Bennetts, "She Says Natural Childbirth and REALLY Means It," *Philadelphia Evening Bulletin*, August 10, 1975. PSIC, Box 39, folder marked "MOVE, Radical Group, 1975."

39   Assefa and Wahrhaftig, *MOVE Crisis in Philadelphia*, 4.

40   Washington, "MOVE," 67. Washington's sense of MOVE's beginnings is confirmed by a PSIC memo from William B. Lytton to Dan Dunne. On July 8, 1985, he requests "clippings going back as far as 1972 concerning MOVE." PSIC, MOVE Records, Box 7, Folder 3. Linn Washington's presence as a reporter in Powelton Village during the events that led to MOVE's first confrontation with Philadelphia police is confirmed in a PSIC interview with Mercel E. Randolph on August 22, 1985, where he recalls events surrounding the police barricade and members of the community and press who tried to intervene. PSIC, Interview with Mercel E. Randolph, Box 8, Folder 1, p. 2.

41   Ramona Africa, "Letter to Commission in support of her motion to dismiss the complaint of Andino Ward (father) and Birdie Africa for harm inflicted on the minor," PSIC, Box 7, Folder 3, p. 3 of 9. Another PSIC document adds the Bronx Zoo and the American Veterinary Medical Association to the list of institutions protested by MOVE. About veterinary medicine, a MOVE picket sign read, "Veterinary medicine is a science of imbalance, that is a direct imposition on animals causing diseases

and sickness." PSIC, "Move History," Box 8, Folder 5, pp. 10–11. In a *Philadelphia Evening Bulletin* opinion piece from October 25, 1975, Charles Lewis notes that "MOVE is intensely iconoclastic. It has demonstrated against human rights activist Dick Gregory, civil rights leader Dr. Ralph Abernathy, as well as the Philadelphia Zoo, Barnum and Bailey Circus, and a host of other American institutions." PSIC, Box 39, folder marked "MOVE, Radical Group, 1974 + prior."

42   "SPCA Raps Dog Bill," *York Dispatch*, February 17, 1972. Several documents across the PSIC MOVE papers note the presence of MOVE's animal liberation platform. In a June 10, 1985, memo detailing PSIC chief of staff Bill Lytton and staff member Dan Dunn's interview with former police commissioner Joseph O'Neill, O'Neill notes that "Although MOVE had made its first public appearance at the Philadelphia Zoo some time previously, and the police had collected 'a good deal of intelligence prior to that time,' Mr. O'Neill stated that May 20, 1977 [when the barricade was placed on the MOVE block], marked a 'turning point.'" PSIC, Box 7, Folder 3, p. 1 of 6. He also notes in this same interview that the purpose of tearing down the MOVE house shortly after the surrender of its occupants after a four-hour siege (4:00 a.m. to 8:15 a.m.) was to "prevent it from becoming a 'cult symbol'" (p. 5). This fear of MOVE as a cult can be traced back to documents gathered during the commission's work. One such document is a June 1985 issue of *The Cult Observer* put out by the American Family Foundation. On MOVE, it states: "The Christian Movement for Life, which later became MOVE, was founded in 1972 by Glassey, a white former student activist with a master's degree in social work, and Leaphart, a black handyman and philosopher who later changed his name to John Africa," labeling MOVE "a violent back-to-nature group." This nomenclature makes its way into various testimony and media observations of the group. PSIC, Box 7, Folder 1, *The Cult Observer* 2, no. 6: 12. In an interim briefing memorandum from Tino Calabia (civil rights analyst) to Edward Rutledge (the mid-Atlantic regional director), Calabia refers to them as "the cult known as MOVE." PSIC, Box 7, Folder 3, June 3, 1985.

43   Quoted in Washington, "MOVE," 69.

44   MOVE, *20 Years on the MOVE* (MOVE, 1986, date unclear, author's personal library), 2.

45   For early print news media coverage of PETA, see Milford Prewitt, "Research Monkeys Seized," *Baltimore Sun*, September 12, 1981. In this piece, a George Washington University student identified as Alex Pacheco is named as the "founder and director" of PETA. See also Associated Press, "Laboratory Accused of Abusing Monkeys," *Evening Sun* (Hanover, PA), September 12, 1981. The AP story was picked up by a number of local

newspapers across the country, thus ushering in PETA's presence in animal welfare and liberation.

46   Wagner-Pacifici spends an entire chapter on "domesticity" and its relationship to public and institutional perceptions of the MOVE organization before the bombing and during the nine months of hearings after it. MOVE's practices were an affront to neighbors and they "were accused by neighbors and citizens in the area [Osage Avenue] where they lived of not living in the common manner that the normal citizen lived." PSIC, Interview with Lucien Blackwell, September 4, 1985, Box 8, Folder 2, p. 1.

47   John T. Gillespie, "MOVE Rejects 'Modern Life-Style,'" *Philadelphia Evening Bulletin*, April 4, 1975. PSIC, Box 39, folder marked "MOVE, Radical Group, 1975."

48   PSIC, Box 39, folder marked "MOVE, Radical Group, 1975." April 21, 1975.

49   Interview with Gerald Africa, September 11–13, 1985. PSIC, Box 8, Folder 1, p. 14.

50   Ellen Karasik, "Inspection of MOVE Planned," *Philadelphia Inquirer*, July 31, 1976. PSIC, Box 39, folder marked "MOVE, Radical Group, 1976."

51   Interview with Gerald Africa, Box 8, Folder 1, pp. 14–15. In another interview with Stanley Vaughan, Investigator Scott asked about "any foul odors" at the MOVE house on Osage Avenue. Although Vaughn replies in the negative, it is clear that Scott's questions lean toward public perceptions of hum:animal relations rather than actual observations from MOVE neighbors. The interview transcript also reveals: "He [Stanley Vaughan] said he also recalled that Ramona Africa had informed him that they took in stray dogs off the street and cared for them. However, Mr. Vaughan did not observe any dogs." PSIC, Stanley Vaughan Interview August 27, 1985; Box 8, Folder 1, p. 3.

52   MOVE, *20 Years on the MOVE*, 12.

53   See Laura Murray, "MOVE: Deputies Caused Baby Death," November 11, 1976. PSIC, Box 39, folder marked "MOVE, Radical Group, 1976" and "Includes MOVE Children."

54   One of the PEB photographers (Don Camp) captured a picture of the bulldozed headquarters on August 8, 1978. It is a scene of Black residents in the background looking on and Black children in the foreground playing as if the scene behind them were a commonplace occurrence.

55   Ramona Africa's handwritten letter to the PSIC, "Facts Regarding May 13th," Box 7, Folder 5. See also the account of William Africa: "The second sister was about six months pregnant too. She was arrested, taken to Eighth and Race. Four cops held her down, spread-eagled, and a Black matron named Robinson kicked her in the vagina until she lost her child," in K. Moore and I. Lacey, "Million $ MOVEment?," *Hera: A Philadelphia Women's Publication* 4, no. 1 (Summer Solstice, 1978); PSIC, Box 7,

Folder 3. This same account is repeated almost verbatim in *20 Years on the Move* (12). LaVerne Sims Africa's testimony before the PSIC commission is also quoted at length in Feldman's senior thesis ("Move Crisis," 1987).

56   Wilderson, *Red, White & Black*, 124.

57   Wilderson notes that "the significance of this is that the blood on the floor of her cell is hers and probably that of the baby aborted during the beating." Wilderson, *Red, White & Black*, 125–26.

58   Field, "Rebellious Unlearning," in *L.A. Rebellion*, 99.

59   Wilderson writes without benefit of the astute feminist critiques of the L.A. Rebellion school, but this scene in Gerima's film is addressed in Jan-Christopher Horak's "Tough Enough: Blaxploitation and the L.A. Rebellion," in Field, Horak, and Stewart, *L.A. Rebellion*, 139–41. Here, they note that Gerima believed that "the oppression of African American women is also a function of the emasculation of African American men" (140).

60   Morgan Woolsey, "Re/soundings: Music and the Political Goals of the L.A. Rebellion," in Field, Horak, and Stewart, *L.A. Rebellion*, 190.

61   I feel that Delany's argument for public sex, for the old Times Square before its turn toward family and corporate sponsorship, should be understood as part of that movement to think through Black geographies of being, incorporealization, and meaning. For Delany, the cleaning up of Times Square all but obliterated our chance for "contact" across differences in race and class.

62   Wilderson, *Red, White & Black*, 131.

63   Wilderson, *Red, White & Black*, 132.

64   See A. W. Geiselman Jr., "MOVE Figures Upset," and "'Stop It! Enough!' MOVE Cultist Yells," *Philadelphia Evening Bulletin*, July 9, 1981. PSIC, Box 39, folder marked "MOVE, Radical Group, Raids 1981."

65   A. W. Geiselman Jr., "MOVE Founder Asks Acquittal, Sobs: You Got Our Babies!," *Philadelphia Evening Bulletin*, July 17, 1981. PSIC, Box 39, folder marked "MOVE, Radical Group, Trials, 1981." It is also noted in the same collection of *PEB* articles that MOVE members went on another hunger strike.

66   See A. W. Geiselman Jr., "U.S. Jury Acquits MOVE's Founder," *Philadelphia Evening Bulletin*, July 23, 1981. PSIC, Box 39, folder marked "MOVE, Radical Group, Trials, 1981."

67   Adrian Lee, "But the Children Knew Love," *Philadelphia Evening Bulletin*, February 11, 1979. See also Dianne C. Gordon, "MOVE Kids Given Clothing and Toys," *Philadelphia Evening Bulletin*, August 9, 1978; Jill Porter and Frank Dougherty, "11 MOVE Kids Get 1st Taste of Play," *Philadelphia Daily News*, April 9, 1978; and Adrian Lee, "Fate of the MOVE Kids," *Philadelphia Evening Bulletin*, January 10, 1980; PSIC, Box 39, folder marked "MOVE, Radical Group, Children." In addition,

Heidi Feldman's March 15, 1987, interview with Sue Africa describes how MOVE members had to consistently fight misconceptions of them as a group (Feldman, "MOVE Crisis," 91). Feldman herself notes that "A certain image of MOVE was perceived and maintained by those reporters who covered MOVE, and there was no change in that image throughout the years, even during periods when MOVE's members had changed or MOVE's relationship with its neighbors had changed" (120).

68   Wagner-Pacifici, *Discourse and Destruction*, 56.

69   Wagner-Pacifici, *Discourse and Destruction*, 57. For a discussion of domestication, animal life, and slavery, see David Lambert's discussion of "domestication," which relies heavily on Jacoby's "Slaves by Nature?" Lambert, "Runaways and Strays: Rethinking (Non)human Agency in Caribbean Slave Societies," in Wilcox and Rutherford, *Historical Animal Geographies*, 185–98.

70   Wagner-Pacifici, *Discourse and Destruction*, 148.

71   Heidi Feldman writes that "on the same day as the Osage Avenue incident, Chester police attempted to enter the MOVE house in Chester in order to inspect for violations. When denied entry, they shot tear gas into the home, forcing Mary Africa and her five children out of the house. The children were placed in foster care by Children and Youth Services, later to be returned to their mother after a legal battle. As part of the settlement, Mary was ordered not to return to Chester." Feldman, "MOVE Crisis," 2. See also reporting about the MOVE group at the Flint Street residence in Rochester, New York, and the arrest of nine members, including John and Sue Africa, by federal agents. The account also documents the continuation of their raw food diet and their affection for stray dogs and cats in the neighborhood. Ashley Halsey III, "Tracing the Movements of MOVE Group," *Philadelphia Inquirer*, May 17, 1981. For reporting on their Richmond location, see Julia Lawlor, "Va. MOVErs Held on Child Neglect Charges," *Philadelphia Evening Bulletin*, January 16, 1980. PSIC, Box 39, folder marked "MOVE Radical Group: Raid/ Trials, January 1980."

72   PSIC, September 4, 1985, Box 8, Folder 2, p. 1. Blackwell had also written a letter to the city on July 28, 1978, vouching for MOVE members—"I know these people and their children to be very healthy, strong and mentally aware"—and in support of their application to receive funding for a parcel of rural land. PSIC, Box 8, Folder 4.

73   See Assefa and Wahrhaftig, *The MOVE Crisis in Philadelphia*, 11. See also Ramona Africa, "MOVE wouldn't accept the farm because it was a trick the government was tryin' to use to get MOVE isolated by ourselves so they could kill us without any witnesses." PSIC, Box 7, Folder 5. Quoted also in Feldman, "The MOVE Crisis," 88.

74 Feldman, "The MOVE Crisis," 9.

75 Feldman, "The MOVE Crisis," 12.

76 Feldman, "The MOVE Crisis," 13–16.

77 Feldman, "The MOVE Crisis," 22.

78 Several sources report the fact that Frank Rizzo was up for re-election and that setting white and Black Philadelphians against one another was one of the pivot points of his particular political platform. Susan Whitehorne, a resident in Powelton, noted that "working class Black people" and those that owned their houses were the most annoyed with MOVE (Feldman, 25).

79 Feldman, "The MOVE Crisis," 11.

80 *Hera: A Philadelphia Women's Publication*, PSIC, MOVE records, Box 7, Folder 3. The incident which sparked the confrontation with police is described in Marc Schogol and Robert K. Terry, "Commune Members Clash with Police, Six Arrested," *Philadelphia Inquirer* article, March 26, 1976. PSIC, Box 39, folder marked "MOVE, Radical Group, 1976, Includes Children."

81 *Hera: A Philadelphia Women's Publication*, PSIC, MOVE records, Box 7, Folder 3.

82 While a PSIC-sponsored early history of MOVE indicates that their animal activism waned as early as 1974, it is clear from later statements of MOVE members and even recent coverage that MOVE's commitment to animal liberation, as a *practice*, rather than a politic, was ongoing. PSIC, "MOVE History," Box 8, Folder 5, p. 14. The PSIC document notes that "while MOVE still occasionally mounted protests against animal related groups and politically progressive groups and individuals, MOVE's activities became increasingly focused on such government related targets." PSIC, Box 8, Folder 5, p. 13. Simultaneous with this move toward government institutions is the injunction granted the city of Philadelphia "sharply curtailing and constraining MOVE's activities on municipal property." Janine Philips Africa, when interviewed about her release, noted that she "raised therapy dogs in her cell and raised vegetables in the prison yard." Ed Pilkington, "Chuck Sims Africa Freed: Final Jailed MOVE 9 Member Released from Prison," *Guardian*, February 7, 2020. https://www.theguardian.com/us-news/2020/feb/07/chuck-sims-africa -move-9-freed-philadelphia. Thanks to my colleague Annette Rodriguez for letting me know about the therapy dog mention.

83 Temple University Urban Archive. Series 1, Subseries 1–2, WPVI News Footage—Public Affairs Presentation of WPVI-TV, "Visions of a New Day. MOVE," written, produced, and directed by Ademola Ekulona, recorded May 15, 1976, airdate June 13, 1976. In the roughly twenty-minute segment, we learn that the documentary was prompted by the group's claims that the infant, Life Africa, was killed by police. As the voiceover

narrator comments at the segment's end, "The death of the baby, Life Africa, and the resulting investigation may be headline news, but what's more important is the uncompromising confrontation of MOVE and society. This is a new American revolution." On April 29, 1976, the Philadelphia City Council called for an investigation of the death of the infant (Janine Africa's baby). An investigation was found to be unwarranted because the MOVE babies in general had no birth certificates, so how could an investigation proceed without a record of birth? We also learn from Phil Africa that "it is a policy that the mothers always keep their children with them"—perhaps a beginning for attachment parenting before William and Martha Sears could "found" the movement in 1985.

84   WPVI News footage. The segment's commentator notes that "MOVE receives a number of visitors. Groups of Quakers and foreign students who came to hear about the MOVE way of living."

85   The Black Artist's Group (BAG) historian Benjamin Looker observes that Rutlin came out of a more politically activist community than did other BAG members, as he was a "longtime member and former chairman of the local CORE (Congress of Racial Equity) chapter." Looker, *"Point from Which Creation Begins,"* 47. Rutlin traveled to Chicago to be part of Gwendolyn Brooks's writing workshops at her home and to collaborate with another group, AACM (Association for the Advancement of Creative Musicians). There are always six degrees of separation between radical thought and revolutionarily minded people—Luisah Teish, who had come to St. Louis to dance with Katherine Dunham, came out of the BAG. As a graduate student working on a dissertation that focused on African retentions, I participated in ceremonies and rites led by Teish in Ann Arbor in the 1990s. Teish "injected a strong feminist consciousness into BAG's dance wing" (see Looker discussion of Teish, 134). Moreover, if we think across genres of revolutionary expression, we can see connections between BAG's creative writing classes (which Rutlin organized) and the literary influence on early L.A. Rebellion filmmakers like Charles Burnett, who enrolled in literature classes at Los Angeles Community College *before* he began making films in the mid-1970s.

86   Ajulé-of-the-Shadows, liner notes. Solidarity Unit, Inc., *Red, Black and Green* (1972). Eremite reissue, 2008 (emphasis mine). From the author's private collection.

87   *20 Years on the MOVE*, 20.

88   *20 Years on the MOVE*, 26.

89   Haraway, *Companion Species Manifesto*, 12.

90   Wagner-Pacifici, *Discourse and Destruction*, 56–77 (emphasis mine).

91   Jason Osder, dir., *Let the Fire Burn* (2013), 25:25.

92   One PSIC document that attempts to approach the early history of MOVE in the city details the observations of the wife of Vincent Leaphart (aka John Africa), who moved to a raw diet because of her involvement with the Kingdom of Yahweh ministries in 1965, whose "recommendations [were] to eat a diet of raw vegetables, fruits, and juices." PSIC, "MOVE History," Box 8, Folder 5, p. 4. This is perhaps why early documents point toward the religious overtones of MOVE's ideology. See also Evans, *MOVE: An American Religion*.

93   NPR, May 13, 2015.

94   See Fiscella, "Removing MOVE," who calls for an intersectional analysis of the MOVE organization.

95   Wagner-Pacifici, *Discourse and Destruction*, 26.

96   Interviews with Powelton Village community activists by student researcher Heidi Feldman while she was an undergraduate at Swarthmore College, quoted in Wagner-Pacifici, *Discourse and Destruction*, 153. LaVerne Sims denies these efforts on behalf of the Quakers in a November 9, 1985, letter to PSIC Commissioner William Brown: "And altho there have been talk about the Quakers offering us land this is not true." PSIC, Box 7, Folder #7-2.

97   Quoted in Wagner-Pacifici, *Discourse and Destruction*, 33.

98   Audre Lorde, *Zami*, 89.

99   Washington, "MOVE," 75.

100   Wagner-Pacifici, *Discourse and Destruction*, 40.

101   Washington, "MOVE," 68.

102   Osder, *Let the Fire Burn*, 1:09:30.

103   Osder, *Let the Fire Burn*, 1:27:09.

104   Quoted in Wagner-Pacifici, *Discourse and Destruction*, 41; also shown in Osder, *Let the Fire Burn*.

105   Wagner-Pacifici, *Discourse and Destruction*, 42.

106   Redmond, "Politics of Identification," 38.

107   This ending is even more poignant in the wake of the 2021 story of the remains of MOVE family members being held by the Penn Museum without MOVE family member's permission or knowledge. See Craig R. McCoy, "New Controversy Arises over MOVE Remains," *Philadelphia Daily News*, April 22, 2021.

3. diversity : a scarcity

1   In philosophical terms, *being* is not necessarily the same as existence, so I do want to mark that Grosz and Lippit are speaking in somewhat different registers here.

2   This particular point could be greatly enriched by readings in Marxist thought. See Hennessy, *Profit and Pleasure*; and Kevin Floyd, *Reification of Desire*.

3   I am thinking here about Charles Mills's *The Racial Contract* and his introductory remarks about white supremacy in particular. Mills writes: "White supremacy is the unnamed political system that has made the modern world what it is today. A standard undergraduate philosophy course will start off with Plato and Aristotle, perhaps say something about Augustine, Aquinas, and Machiavelli, move on to Hobbes, Locke, Mill, and Marx, and then wind up with Rawls and Nozick. It will introduce you to notions of aristocracy, democracy, absolutism, liberalism, representative government, socialism, welfare capitalism, and libertarianism. But though it covers more than two thousand years of Western political thought and runs the gamut of political systems, there will be no mention of the basic political system that has shaped the world for the past several hundred years" (1). See also Zambrana's analysis of diversity culture and URMs (Underrepresented Minorities) and her discussion of what CRT brings to the table of ideas and why it is feared. She writes, "For example, it has been empirically documented, but institutionally denied, that URM research agendas that tackle and uplift deep-rooted racial, ethnic, and gender inequality in research publications are not given the same weight, legitimacy, and acclaim. Closely related to this conundrum is the traditional objection to the use of nonmainstream theoretical frameworks such as CRT and intersectional theory that instigate analyses by examining power relations, historic antecedents, and repeated patterns of inequity throughout the life course." Zambrana, *Toxic Ivory Towers*, 213–14.

4   In step with thought on the decentering of the Enlightenment self, Sarah Jane Cervenak remarks in the first chapter of *Wandering: Philosophical Performances of Racial and Sexual Freedom*, "The fraudulence of an inherent association between Enlightenment subjectivity, whiteness, male gender identity, able-bodiedness, and a putatively unaffected and self-directed *straight* comportment will be exposed and will lead to an interrogation of its contemporary, unchecked, illusory reenactments." Cervenak, *Wandering*, 26.

5   Wolfe observes, "The question squarely before us, of course, is whether [Lyotard's] reconceptualization of the subject enables us to fundamentally rethink the relations of language, ethics, and the question of the animal." The question remains, what subjects are at play here? Wolfe, *Zoontologies*, 13.

6   Ahmed, *On Being Included*, 141. Ahmed gives credit to two other critics for their look at diversity work on campus: Chandra Talpade Mohanty

in *Feminism without Borders* (2003) and M. Jacqui Alexander in *Pedagogies of Crossing* (2005).

7   For a comprehensive treatment of the term "dominion" and its impact and meaning for animal life, see Scully, *Dominion*. See also Wise, *An American Trilogy*.

8   Zambrana, *Toxic Ivory Towers*, 84.

9   DeSouza, *How Art Can Be Thought*, 9.

10   Ahmed, *On Being Included*, 147.

11   See Christopher Newfield's body of work on higher education: *Ivy and Industry*; *Unmaking the Public University*; and *The Great Mistake*.

12   In her astute assessment of the meaning of diversity in K-12 schools, my colleague Antonia Randolph observes that "a particular logic of diversity . . . elevates the status of multiracial schools and of certain minorities, but leaves the low status of Black schools and Black students intact. [This book] is about the meaning of race and ethnicity, when we are instructed to appreciate diversity, but not talk about race. . . . In short, it is about the trade-offs that come with moving from social justice to diversity as the dominant frame for thinking about minority status." Randolph, *The Wrong Kind of Different*, 1.

13   For a sustained discussion of how "diversity" works at the public University, see Newfield, *Unmaking the Public University*, especially the chapter entitled "Diversity in the Age of Pseudointegration" (107–22). Newfield argues that the civil rights gains of the late twentieth century worked to establish less cohesion in the middle class, marking the interests of those who gained from civil rights over and against a population that in many ways also benefited from civil rights legislation. This practice of divide and conquer made diversity on college campuses an effective and persuasive rhetoric to engender disunity in the middle class.

14   In his very cogent readings of philosophy's take on "the question of the animal," Matthew Calarco notes that the same charge of trafficking in identity politics can and has been leveled at animal rights activists. "I do believe much of contemporary animal rights discourse and politics is in fact another form of identity politics or has had precisely the effect of further fragmenting the left, both for good and for bad. Many animal rights theorists and activists see themselves as uncovering some sort of fundamental identity (for example, sentience or subjectivity) shared by all animals (or, rather, the animals they believe worthy of ethical and political standing) in order to represent that identity in the political and legal arena." Calarco, *Zoographies*, 7.

15   Quoted in Ahmed, *On Being Included*, 170.

16   Jones, *The Known World*, 3.

17   Jones, *The Known World*, 9.

18   Bassard, "Imagining Other Worlds," 413.

19   The toll slavery takes on young lives is later spelled out in Jones's novel when in the next to last chapter, he tells the story of Morris and Beau Calhenny, who "when they . . . had been boys, they were almost as close as brothers." "When the two reached the age of fourteen, there was the inevitable parting and they never came back together in the same way." Jones, *The Known World*, 341.

20   See Morrison, "Unspeakiable Things Unspoken."

21   Jones, *The Known World*, 356–57.

22   Jones, *The Known World*, 188.

23   Jones, *The Known World*, 189.

24   Bassard also points out this moment in *The Known World* where Calvin sees the photograph and notes, "There was a whole world off to the right that the photograph had not captured." Jones, *The Known World*, 189.

25   Jones, *The Known World*, 385.

26   Jones, *The Known World*, 386.

27   Derrida, *The Animal That Therefore I Am*, 55.

28   Calarco, *Zoographies*, 23 (emphasis in original).

29   Derrida takes on a famous moment—the dog Bobby in the concentration camp—in Levinas's work on ethical relation. Derrida, *The Animal That Therefore I Am*, 117–18). He writes: "The animal remains for Levinas what it will have been for the whole Cartesian-type tradition: a machine that doesn't speak, that doesn't have access to sense." Calarco, reading the same passage in Levinas, remarks that "Levinas's efforts to draw a sharp break between human beings and animals on this issue is not just bad biology—it is also bad philosophy, inasmuch as it uncritically reinforces the metaphysical anthropocentrism of the Western philosophical tradition." Calarco, *Zoographies*, 62. Calarco later spends a chapter on Agamben's *The Open*, where he reiterates that philosopher's phrase "lethal and bloody." Calarco, "Jamming the Anthropological Machine: Agamben," in *Zoographies*, 79–102.

30   Derrida, *The Animal That Therefore I Am*, 21.

31   Derrida, *The Animal That Therefore I Am*, 14.

32   Communication from Calvin Warren during a visit to and discussion with my Critical Ethnic Studies class, September 7, 2020. While writing this book, I came across a number of misunderstandings, corrections, and, yes, arguments about the accuracies of interpretation. I also witnessed several missed readings, a problem that this book is poised to address. One of my favorite moments in these readings occurs in Calarco's footnotes—always the place where authors try to say what they really mean, and even sometimes there, they fail. Calarco notes that "Derrida's writings on animality have been badly misread in most cases and are still in

need of careful exposition." Calarco, *Zoographies*, 137. And the footnote to this statement is "I have no desire to attack any particular authors for egregious misreadings, although several examples could be given." He then refers to Cary Wolfe's work for "more reliable and interesting readings." Calarco, *Zoographies*, 161n44.

33   In her first tome about animal nature, *Primate Visions*, Donna Haraway reminds us of the power of naming: "The paucity of African names in paleoanthropological and primate literature speaks volumes about the limitations of Adam's claims to species fatherhood" (281).

34   Lippit notes, "As Adorno and Horkheimer insist, the idea of human superiority has been restated so frequently that it has become an unqualified truth." Lippit, *Electric Animal*, 10.

35   Agamben, *The Open*, 79.

36   Scholars like Charles Mills in *The Racial Contract* have begun, through the terrain of analytic philosophy, to ask questions about contract theory and who or what it attempts to write. Like Simone de Beauvoir before him, who saw marriage as a contract between men for whom women are the language, Mills reimagines the social contract as between two white signatories, whose relationship solidifies the thing called "white supremacy" and subsequently creates an unethical commitment to govern and establish laws that is the very underpinning (and one made in bad faith) of modernity. It would be interesting to see this branch of philosophy take on the claims made in continental philosophy about the difference between human/animal being (see Lyotard in particular). Most recently, in 2020, two scholars broached the question of the animal in relation to blackness: Joshua Bennett, *Being Property Once Myself: Blackness and the End of Man*, and Zakiyyah Iman Jackson, *Becoming Human: Matter and Meaning in an Antiblack World*. Both authors brilliantly speak to some of the same moments in Black thought and utilize Spillers's work with flesh, animality, blackness, and the work of Black cultural production to bring consequence to human/animal distinction *and* relation.

37   For more work on this problem of the autobiographical, see Lindon Barrett's posthumously published book, *Racial Blackness and the Discontinuity of Western Modernity*. In his chapter on Olaudah Equiano/ Gustavus Vassa, Barrett notes, "The pivotal scene of manumission both coalesces and disfigures the presiding autobiographical identity by consolidating the autobiographer within the political structures of modernity but, at the same time, reiterating the emphatic self-difference signaled in the caesura between 'Olaudah Equiano' and 'Gustavus Vassa.'" Barrett, *Racial Blackness*, 55. In the same year (2014), Rebecka Rutledge Fisher published a reading of Equiano's narrative utilizing the work of Du Bois and his thought on being and becoming (*Habitations of the Veil*).

38   Agamben, *The Open*, 80. The tension between "the animality and the humanity of man" is brilliantly tackled in Zakiyyah Iman Jackson's *Becoming Animal*.

39   Fred Moten comments on the American academy's obsession with a certain interpretation of Agamben's "bare life" in the following manner: "There is a certain American reception of Agamben that fetishizes the bareness of it all without recognizing the severity of the critique he levels at movements of power/knowledge that would separate life from the form of life. . . . The constant repetition of bare life bears the annoying, grating tone that one imagines must have been the most prominent feature of the voice of that kid who said the emperor has no clothes. It's not that one wants to devalue in any way the efficacy of such truth telling, such revelation; on the other hand, one must always be careful that a certain being positive, not positivism, doesn't liquidate the possibility of political fantasy in its regulation of political delusion." Moten, "The Case of Blackness," 218n6.

40   Butler, *Precarious Life*, 6.

41   For a detailed discussion of William James's pragmatism and its influence on generations of American writers, artists, and musicians, see Ananat, "The Music of William James."

42   I purposefully use the word "things" here to remind us of the problem of the human, and to signal that once the human split itself as species into a thousand tiny fractures of categorizable differences, the whole economy of structured being collapsed with it.

43   Derrida, *The Animal That Therefore I Am*, 62.

44   In the beginnings of his second chapter, "But as for me, who am I (following)?" Derrida speaks to gender, but in an old paradigm of heteronormative encounter that produces some of the effect of his following/followed play; see Derrida, *The Animal That Therefore I Am*, 58–61. Calarco also points to the place of gender in Derrida's philosophical cosmos, while writing about Derrida's contribution to the philosophical question of the animal. Calarco notes, "Derrida argues that the meaning of subjectivity is constituted through a network of exclusionary relations that goes well beyond a generic human-animal distinction. He has coined the term 'carnophallogocentrism' to refer to this network of relations and in order to highlight the *sacrificial* (carno), *masculine* (phallo), and *speaking* (logo) dimensions of classical conceptions of subjectivity." Calarco, *Zoographies*, 131.

45   If I were to engage Derrida on this issue of force, I would have to agree with him that a system of laws that requires force is inherently unjust. For some of the best feminist takes on Derrida's essay, "The Force of Law: The 'Mystical Foundation of Authority,'" see Drucilla Cornell and Nancy Fraser in Holland, *Feminist Interpretations of Jacques Derrida*.

46   Dorothy Korber, "Truth Can Hurt: Exotic Pets Are Still Wild at Heart," *Sacramento Bee*, March 8, 2005. LaDonna and St. James Davis owned the chimp, Moe, who was not involved in the attack itself, though he was taken from their home in 1999 after biting off part of a woman's finger.

47   Associated Press, "Rampaging Chimps Killed," *Windsor Star*, March 5, 2005.

48   Amy Argetsinger, "A Tale of Moe: California Couple's Love for Wild Animals Turns Tragic," *Longview [Washington] Daily News*, May 31, 2005.

49   Associated Press, "Chimp Attack Victim Stepped in to Save Wife," *The Californian*, March 7, 2005.

50   Associated Press, "Husband Stepped in to Save Wife in Brutal Chimp Attack," *The Signal*, March 7, 2005.

51   David Pierson and Mitchell Landsberg, "A Primate Party Gone Horribly Awry," *Los Angeles Times*, March 5, 2005.

52   Amy Argetsinger, "The Animal Within," *Washington Post*, May 24, 2005.

53   Woods, *Bonobo Handshake*, 32.

54   Hare and Yamamoto, "Moving Bonobos Off the Scientifically Endangered List," 248.

55   Woods, *Bonobo Handshake*, 111.

56   I am indebted to friend and fellow lover of great apes Karen McCall, who pointed this out to me and handed me a copy of Sarah Blaffer Hrdy's *The Woman That Never Evolved*. Haraway spends some time critiquing the "sexual politics" of Hrdy's vision for primate study in her chapter on Hrdy, "Sarah Blaffer Hrdy: Investment Strategies for the Evolving Portfolio of Primate Females," in *Primate Visions* (1989).

57   See my discussion of modes of refusal in Black thought in chapter 1. See also King, "Humans Involved"; and Simpson, *Mohawk Interruptus*.

58   Haraway, *Primate Visions*, 6.

59   Woods, *Bonobo Handshake*, 171.

60   MacKinnon, "Of Mice and Men," 264.

61   Haraway, *Primate Visions*, 1.

62   Haraway, *Primate Visions*, 2.

63   Zakiyyah Iman Jackson argues for the simultaneity of definitions of blackness and animality in *Becoming Human*.

64   For popular press reviews of Haraway's *Primate Visions*, see physical anthropologist Susan Sperling, "A Jungle of Our Imagination," *Los Angeles Times Book Review*, September 17, 1989; University of Pittsburgh professor of film and English Dana Polan, "'Primate Visions' Challenges Traditional View of Apes," *Pittsburgh Press*, June 9, 1990; and professor of physics at Stonehill College Chet Raymo, "Gorillas in the Myth," *Boston Globe*, July 20, 1992.

65 Haraway's text came well before Stoller's leap into Foucault's work, on the cusp of Judith Butler's *Gender Trouble* and certainly after the French feminists had their way with him. Perhaps because hers is feminist science, rather than feminist critical theory, we have ignored its contribution? Nevertheless, it is an important and deliberately messy work.

66 Haraway, *Primate Visions*, 289.

67 Haraway goes on to recount the fascinating story of how the work done by primatologists at Berkeley and Stanford, which was especially front and center in the famous *National Geographic* story on Jane Goodall's gorillas, became more widely known. But, she argues, the work that several international students of primatology executed at Gombe in the mid-1970s would come to be the hallmark of what she calls a particular pedagogy that would become the standard in ethology. See chapter 7, "Apes in Eden, Apes in Space: Mothering as a Scientist for *National Geographic*," in *Primate Visions*.

68 I am alluding here to my second monograph, *The Erotic Life of Racism*, where I produce the acronym HER to think through some of the problems posed by competing genealogies of critical queer work. Jackson's *Becoming Human* also tracks sex/gender and reproduction. See her chapter "Organs of War," 159–98.

69 Haraway, *Primate Visions*, 152n16, 402.

70 We see this centering of the African mother in P. D. James's dystopian novel *The Children of Men* (1991), ironically enough, set in 2021, the year in which this book was finished. Eerie that.

71 Haraway, *Primate Visions*, 284.

72 Grosz, "Feminism, Materialism, and Freedom," 154.

73 Rosi Braidotti, "The Politics of 'Life Itself' and New Ways of Dying," in Coole and Frost, *New Materialisms*, 204. Braidotti borrows her thinking from the work of Rose in *The Politics of Life Itself*.

74 Barad, *Meeting the Universe Halfway*, 409n11.

75 Barad, *Meeting the Universe Halfway*, 58.

76 Quoted in Bennett, *Vibrant Matter*, 85.

77 Bennett, *Vibrant Matter*, 84.

78 Bennett, *Vibrant Matter*, 86.

79 See cultural historian Joanna Bourke, *What It Means to Be Human*, where she speaks to Kant's proposal against animal cruelty—a proposal much thought about in animal studies work.

80 See Leonard Nelson, "Duties to Animals," in Godlovitch, Godlovitch, and Harris, *Animals, Men and Morals*, 149–55.

81 My project attempts to create some distance between the ethical and the political, or at least to return to the trace of *gender* in the making of the political, while simultaneously thinking through the distinction

(hum/animal) as the rather silent backdrop to our considerations of agency, life and being.

82 Barad, *Meeting the Universe Halfway*, 225.

83 Barad, *Meeting the Universe Halfway*, 225 (emphasis mine).

84 Brian Luke, "Justice, Caring and Animal Liberation," in Donovan and Adams, *Feminist Care Tradition*, 125.

85 See Erica Fudge's discussion of human culture and animals in her book *Animal*. In her short section "Puppy Love," she asks a simple but important question: "Is a pet an animal?"

86 Levinas, *Difficult Freedom*, 153.

87 Levinas, *Difficult Freedom*, 153.

88 Levinas, *Difficult Freedom*, 153.

89 Theodore Ruch penned the term "primatology" in his 1941 comprehensive bibliography on primates "beginning with ancient texts and concluding in 1940" (Haraway, *Primate Visions*, 24). Zakiyyah Iman Jackson's discussion of philosophical discourse about apes occurs throughout her project. Earlier, in a discussion of Derrida on Heidegger, she notes, "The entanglement of literary form and genre with an imperialist and racially sexuating mode of grasping, I suggest, draws black mater into the orbit of *the* animal and animality into the domain of *the* black" (*Becoming Human*, 101).

90 Levinas, *Difficult Freedom*, 153.

91 See Sarah Ellis, "Spring Valley High School Incident: Black Lives Matter, Others Rally in Response to Incident," *The State*, November 1, 2015. The best reading of the Charleston massacre at Mother Emanuel church and the life of convicted murderer Dylann Roof is Rachel Kaadzi Ghansah's "A Most American Terrorist: The Making of Dylann Roof," *GQ*, August 21, 2017.

92 Bennett, *Vibrant Matter*, xi.

93 In "Berlin: A Spectacularly Gendered Cinematic Landscape of Dystopian Devastation," Susan Ingram argues for a gendered reading of the film.

94 Reviewers and fans alike have noted the film's borrowing from *Fahrenheit 451*, *Brave New World*, and *1984*. The film was panned by critics, although it has garnered a cult fandom over the years. Wimmer is credited with creating a martial art form for the digital age called "gun-kata"—a form that has its most stunning debut in the film during its closing scenes. This same filmwork is replicated in the *Matrix* series by the Wachowskis (Lana and Lilly).

95 In the second film in *The Terminator* series, *Terminator 2: Judgment Day* (1991), scientist Miles Dyson (played by Joe Morton), sits on the floor riddled with bullets and holds an incendiary device in his hands while

the child, John Connor (Edward Furlong), leader of the (future) resistance, and the mother (Linda Hamilton) escape toward the future for humanity. Interestingly enough, Christian Bale also gets a chance to play John Connor in the series in *Terminator Salvation* (2009).

4. love : livestock

1   This is being challenged with the publication of the wildly acclaimed novel *The Prophets* by Robert Jones Jr. (2021).
2   Bennett, *Being Property*, 3. Joshua Bennett's beautiful and evocative readings of African American fiction from Wright to Morrison to Hurston and its animal figures thinks through the impossible predicament of seeing oneself through the animal. In particular, see his discussion of love in chapter 2, "Cock," 86–87. See also Dunning, *Black to Nature*.
3   Bennett, *Being Property*, 87.
4   One particular article of note is Gates, "'What's Love Got to Do with It?'" The debate about Black love continues in Kathleen M. Puhr's assessment of Gloria Naylor's work, "Healers in Gloria Naylor's Fiction." Michelle Cliff also joins the conversation with a meditation on Black women writers through the work of Ntozake Shange, "'I Found God in Myself and I Loved Her/I Loved Her Fiercely.'"
5   hooks and West, *Breaking Bread*, 117.
6   Spillers, "Mama's Baby," 80.
7   hooks and West, *Breaking Bread*, 117.
8   hooks and West, *Breaking Bread*, 144.
9   Povinelli, *Empire of Love*, 177.
10 hooks and West, *Breaking Bread*, 146.
11 About aesthetic value and natural qualities, David Theo Goldberg attests: "Those critics committed to the moral irrelevance of race tend to assume that racists inevitably combine these two strains, aesthetic values and natural qualities, into a spurious casual principle." Goldberg, *Racist Culture*, 31.
12 Povinelli, *Empire of Love*, 2.
13 Derrida, *The Animal That Therefore I Am*, 96.
14 Wise, *An American Trilogy*, 32. See also the discussion of "scrub" cattle in Rosenberg, "No Scrubs." Rosenberg reminds us that the largest federal agency that emerged at the turn of the century was the USDA and that the management of the reproductive life of livestock was intimately connected to that of human being.
15 Derrida, *The Animal That Therefore I Am*, 62.
16 Quoted in Field, Horak, and Stewart, *L.A. Rebellion*, 8 (emphasis mine).

17 Charles Burnett, oral history by Jacqueline Stewart and Allyson Field, June 15, 2010, transcript, LAROH.

18 See Streeby, *Imagining the Future of Climate Change,* for her discussion of Octavia Butler's work and her time in the public library. For an engagement of Purvis Young's work that makes reference to his time in the public library, see Sharon P. Holland, "'Put Honey in the Sky Where It Could Drip and Make the World Sweet': Looking for Purvis Young and Thomas Samuel Doyle, but Seeing Something Else: Meditations on the *Matter* of Black Freedom," in Herman, *Unfinished Business of Unsettled Things.*

19 Interestingly enough, for the purposes of this study's focus on MOVE and their love affair with the word "motherfuckers," this ad hoc group of faculty and students at UCLA was also known as the "Mother Muccers." Naremore, *Charles Burnett,* 13.

20 Jacqueline Stewart and several other film historians and critics set about to conduct oral histories with all of the students who took classes at UCLA from 1968 to 1998. Many of these oral histories are housed in UCLA's Film and Television Library's online database.

21 Charles Burnett, oral history.

22 See Jim Jarmusch, *Ghost Dog: The Way of the Samurai* (1999). Ghost Dog (Forest Whitaker) lives on the rooftop of an abandoned building somewhere in New Jersey, next to his beloved pigeon roost—pigeons he uses to convey messages between himself and his mob employer. In fact, it is revealed later in the film by a mobster named Old Consigliere (Gene Ruffini) that the pigeon Ghost Dog uses to send messages is actually a passenger pigeon—a breed that became extinct in 1914, thus lending to Ghost Dog's somewhat paradoxical and archaic existence.

23 George P. Johnson Negro Film Collection 1916–1977 (hereafter GPJNFC). UCLA Library Special Collections, Box 59—Clippings, Miscellaneous. "Book for Kids Depicts Life of Negro Cowboys," *Los Angeles Sentinel,* May 19, 1966. I want to thank film scholar Jacqueline Stewart for taking the time to speak with me (May 9, 2018) and pointing me toward this rich collection of clippings, postcards, journal entries, and ephemera that create the world of Blacks and horses in the mid-1960s and 1970s.

24 GPJNFC, Box 33, "Negros as Cowboys." Clipping from unknown news source, "Black Cowboys Is Subject on WTTW." Johnson's clipping has a query below in his own handwriting: "Negroes on TV?" See also Stewart, *Migrating to the Movies,* 197.

25 GPJNFC, Box 56, Folder 8. Clipping, news source unknown. "The Black West," Robert Lewis Shayon, November 14, 1970.

26 GPJNFC, Box 56, Folder 8. Clipping, news source unknown. "The Black West," Robert Lewis Shayon (emphasis mine).

27 GPJNFC, Box 59, Folder 1–5. Though Genesis III released its collection of films and was reviewed in 1970, two newspapers note 1972 showings. See Kent Donovan, "Short Flics Exhibit Merits of Avant Garde Films," *Manhattan [Kansas] Mercury*, February 6, 1972; and Sharon Cohen, "Short Films Say Much," *Tampa Tribune*, January 29, 1972.

28 GPJNFC, Box 53, Folder 25, miscellaneous.

29 Charles Burnett, oral history.

30 The cameraman on the film is Ian Conner.

31 Wilderson, *Red, White & Black*, 118.

32 Walker, "Am I Blue?," 7.

33 Derrida, *The Animal That Therefore I Am*, 96.

34 Naremore observes that Burnett disclosed that the smile elicited from Stan during the movie's last scenes was due to something that happened off camera Stan was reacting to, rather than the true emotion he wanted to depict at that time. Naremore, *Charles Burnett*, 45–46.

35 Naremore, *Charles Burnett*, 23.

36 Larry Clark, *Cutting Horse* (2002), UCLA Film, Video and Media Laboratory Archives.

37 See Chris Norton, "Black Independent Cinema and the Influence of Neo-Realism," *Images Journal*, http://www.imagesjournal.com/issue05/features/black.htm. Norton notes, "Contemporaneity is an important aspect in realist films only because of the social consciousness that these pieces strive to alert and awaken. A need to see reality dealt with as it truly exists." Cited also in Povinelli, *Economies of Abandonment*, 103.

38 My contention here is in direct contradistinction to the work of Nathan Grant, who believes that "it is not his job at the slaughterhouse that is responsible for his state of ennui." Quoted in Massood, "An Aesthetic Appropriate to Conditions," 35.

39 Povinelli, *Economies of Abandonment*, 30.

40 Povinelli, *Economies of Abandonment*, 31, 32.

41 Povinelli, *Economies of Abandonment*, 103 (emphasis mine).

42 Povinelli, *Economies of Abandonment*, 130.

43 Kari Weil, "Report on the Animal Turn," 13.

44 Raengo, "Encountering the Rebellion," in Field, Horak, and Stewart, *L.A. Rebellion*, 304. Raengo references my earlier piece on Black love and Burnett's work: Holland, "(Black) (Queer) Love."

45 Povinelli, *Economies of Abandonment*, 110.

46 Povinelli, *Economies of Abandonment*, 112.

47 Povinelli, *Economies of Abandonment*, 102.

48 See Brantz, "Recollecting the Slaughterhouse," 121. Brantz observes, "The most important of these inventions was the two-story disassembly line. Invented in Cincinnati but perfected in Chicago, the disassem-

bly line gave Henry Ford his ideas for a prototype for car production. It consisted of an overhead rail system by which animals were hoisted and moved through compartmentalized workstations, where one man would slit the animal's throat, another would tear off its hide, a third split the carcass, and on and on until the dressed carcass was hoisted into a rail car and sent on its way to consumers."

49 Massood, "An Aesthetic Appropriate to Conditions," 37.

50 Hozic, "The House I Live In," 471.

51 Hozic, "The House I Live In," 473. Burnett might be referring to a two-part article run by the *Los Angeles Times* in 1992, one of which (September 8) was written by Robert A. Rosenblatt and was titled "Home Loan Gap: Banks Are Behind in S&L Lending to Minorities."

52 Massood, "An Aesthetic Appropriate to Conditions," 38.

5. horse : flesh

1 From the fall of 2015 to the spring of 2018, I edited *south: a scholarly journal*.

2 Thompson, *Better Off without 'Em*, 108.

3 Gordon, *Lord of Misrule*, 181. Of the "backstretch," C. E. Morgan's Black jockey Reuben in *The Sport of Kings* muses: "The backstretch, that theater of quarrel and striving and hangover work, of labor white and brown and poor all over, of motormouth agents and trainers chewing out assistants, of milkshaking vets hauling gear bags" (409).

4 hooks, "27," *Appalachian Elegy*, 37.

5 In 2022, Geraldine Brooks published *Horse*, which brings to life the story of an enslaved groom/trainer named Jarret. At several moments in a narrative that weaves in and out of the nineteenth and twenty-first centuries, Jarret cautions the granddaughter (Marry Barr) of his enslaver (Dr. Warfield) to stay away from the barn. There are several studies across genres that attend to Black presence in the sport. See Hotaling, *Great Black Jockeys*; Saunders and Saunders, *Black Winning Jockeys in the Kentucky Derby*; Drape, *Black Maestro*; Scanlan, *The Horse God Built*; McDaniels, *The Prince of Jockeys*; and Mooney, *Race Horse Men*.

6 Associated Press, "Klan Leader Grants Interview," *Asheville Citizen-Times*, March 8, 1990.

7 In fact, the sense that women abound in the sport, except at the racetrack, is addressed by Jane Smiley on two occasions: "But more than one horseman, at the racetrack and elsewhere, has noted that women have a special talent with horses and a special attraction to them. Perhaps this special talent is simply a talent for relating" and "A natural audience for a

horsey activity, girls and women, who have not been appealed to, tend to feel out of place at the racetrack." Smiley, *A Year at the Races*, 62, 166.

8 I am also reminded of Midas Dekkers in *Dearest Pet*, where he speaks to men, horses, and statues, "In order to understand the love of a man for his horse all one need do is look around a historic city. Everywhere one sees statues of men on their horses, seldom if ever of men with their wives. With such an intimate bond between horse and rider, it is understandable that men should sometimes wish to mount their steed." Dekkers, *Dearest Pet*, 18. It is true that another arc of this book would suggest inclining ourselves to sex with animals, but my inquiry does not flow in that direction, as I am more concerned with liberation, a letting go more in step with modes of consent, than with modes of libertine desire, although there is that too.

9 Gordon, *Circumspections*, 36.

10 Gordon, *Circumspections*, 23.

11 Schwartz, *Birthing a Slave*, 5. I want to thank Danielle Dulken for bringing this book to my attention.

12 Schwartz, *Birthing a Slave*, 28.

13 Schwartz, *Birthing a Slave*, 69.

14 Gordon, *Circumspections*, 19, 52.

15 Gordon, *Circumspections*, 1, 56.

16 I am aware that the use of the word calls forward both Derrida and Fred Moten's use of his work around the term "invagination" in *In the Break: The Aesthetics of the Black Radical Tradition*. I want to note the relationship here between Spillers's comment about the male being "handled" by the African American female and the extent to which invagination in Moten's usage calls forth a possibility of an *enfleshment* that produces a break for ontology's ruling anti-ethic.

17 Gordon, *Circumspections*, 21–22 (emphasis in original).

18 See Ronald S. Coddington, "The Capture of Ambrose Burnside's Valet," *New York Times*, "Opinionator," July 21, 2011. https://opinionator.blogs .nytimes.com/2011/07/21/the-capture-of-ambrose-burnsides-valet/.

19 Gordon, *Circumspections*, 58, 59.

20 Gordon, *Circumspections*, 59.

21 Wu, *Chang and Eng Reconnected*, 5.

22 Wu, *Chang and Eng Reconnected*, 120.

23 Wu, *Chang and Eng Reconnected*, 81, 120.

24 Gordon, *Circumspections*, 2.

25 See Edward Troye, "Richard Singleton," https://www.youtube.com /watch?v=zCbID7wKdEI. A telling virtual snapshot of the extent to which subject and objects are still managed in the world of equestrian sport and the art world that manages its aesthetic life.

26 Mackay-Smith, *Race Horses of America*, 55.

27 Mackay-Smith, *Race Horses of America*, 56.

28 Mackay-Smith, *Race Horses of America*, 156. J. Winston Coleman Jr. mentions the daughter of William A. Dawson and this very painting in *Three Kentucky Artists*, 61.

29 Jane Smiley, "Jaimy Gordon's *Lord of Misrule*," *Washington Post*, November 16, 2010. See also John Madera, "Jaimy Gordon, *Lord of Misrule*," *Review of Contemporary Fiction* 31, no. 2 (2011): 188–89; and Michael Sragow, "Jaimy Gordon: a Literary Winner from the Outside Track," *Baltimore Sun*, April 6, 2011, https://www.baltimoresun.com /entertainment/bs-xpm-2011-04-08-bs-ae-jaimy-gordon-20110408-story .html.

30 Smiley, *A Year at the Races*, 229.

31 On the brutality of the sport, Smiley notes: "A horse's life is rather like twenty years in foster care, over and over and discovering that, not only do the other students already have their social groups, but also what you learned at the old school hasn't much application at the new one. We do not require as much of any other species, including humans." Smiley, *A Year at the Races*, 139.

32 A notable exception is the mercurial literary blog by John Latta, *Isola di Rifiuti*, http://isola-di-rifiuti.blogspot.com/2011/01/blog-post.html.

33 Gordon, *Lord of Misrule*, 17, 31.

34 Gordon, *Lord of Misrule*, 147.

35 See Saunders and Saunders, *Black Winning Jockeys in the Kentucky Derby*, 87–96. For more on Kentucky Derby jockeys, see also Drape, *Black Maestro*; and McDaniels, *Prince of Jockeys*.

36 One of the most well-known writers about racing in the United States and in Ireland is Bill Barich. See *A Fine Place to Daydream*.

37 Gordon, *Lord of Misrule*, 25. Hereafter cited parenthetically in the text.

38 Sheila Hamanaka and Tracy Basile, "Racism and the Animal Rights Movement," quoted in A. Breeze Harper, "Vegans of Color, Racialized Embodiment and the Problematics of the 'Exotic,'" in Alkon and Agyeman, *Cultivating Food Justice*, 222.

39 Julie Guthman, "'If They Only Knew,'" in Alkon and Agyeman, *Cultivating Food Justice*, 264.

40 Alkon and Agyeman, *Cultivating Food Justice*, 15.

41 Probyn, *Carnal Appetites*, 57.

42 Probyn, *Carnal Appetites*, 55.

43 Amirah Mercer's discussion of the rich tradition of veganism is a primer for study of African-descended contributions to the practice. See "A Homecoming," *Eater*, January 14, 2021, https://www.eater.com /22229322/black-veganism-history-black-panthers-dick-gregory-nation

-of-islam-alvenia-fulton. I want to thank my colleague Kelly Alexander for pointing me in the direction of this piece.

44 On May 9, 2017, the *New York Times* published a piece by Kim Severson, "A Powerful, and Provocative, Voice for Southern Food," about John T. Edge and his hold on the discipline and practice of southern foodways. Many of the interviews in the piece pointed toward the issues of gender, race, and power that go unacknowledged in the field. Severson followed up that piece with another on June 29, 2020, as calls increased for Edge to resign from his directorship of the Southern Foodways Alliance ("A White Gatekeeper of Southern Food Faces Calls to Resign"). My own colleague (Marcie Ferris) in food studies at UNC stepped cautiously in responding to the critiques of Edge, preferring to keep her comments to noting "the demons of his white Southern past." The second article on the crumbling Southern Foodways Alliance mentions Cynthia Greenlee, historian, James Beard award-winning food writer, and deputy editor of its journal, *Gravy*. In the summer of 2020, Greenlee published a special issue (no. 75) focused on writers, chefs, and practitioners of color. See also Harris, *High on the Hog*.

45 Agamben, *The Open*, 26.

46 See Jacques Derrida on the question of responding versus reacting in the debate about the human/animal distinction. Derrida, "And Say the Animal Responded?," in *The Animal That Therefore I Am*, 81–82.

47 I would like to thank Heather Mallory at Duke University in Romance Languages for forwarding the reference to Madame de Sévigné's letters.

48 Tompkins, *Racial Indigestion*, 11.

49 Fanon, *Black Skin*, 89. An earlier translation (1991) of the same words is: "I came into the world imbued with the will to find a meaning in things, my spirit filled with the desire to attain to the source of the world, and then I found that *I was an object in the midst of other objects.*"

50 Oliver, *Animal Lessons*, 108.

51 Kathryn Schulz, "Track Changes: Race and Racing in C. E. Morgan's *The Sport of Kings*," *New Yorker*, May 2, 2016.

52 Morgan, *Sport of Kings*, 11. Hereafter cited parenthetically in the text.

53 See Wolff, "William Faulkner and the Ledgers of History." Morgan's novel is definitely a homage to Faulkner's genius, and I can't help but see that her Judith and Henry are mirrors of the same named characters in Faulkner's *Absalom, Absalom!*

54 Though John uses the word "women" here, he yokes them to a body whose chief expression is its reproductive force, one that disqualifies them from the sphere of men, thus emphasizing femaleness over and above anything else.

55 Egerton, *Southern Food*, 23.

56 Quoted in Nancy Carter Crump, "Foodways of the Albemarle Region," 5.

57 Wiegand, *Outer Banks*, 4.

58 See Halberstam's *Queer Art of Failure* for its explication of the Parker and Lord film.

59 Wiegand, *Outer Banks*, 7.

60 Crow, Escott, Hatley Wadelington, *History of African Americans*, 72.

61 Wiegand, *Outer Banks*, 12.

62 Egerton, *Southern Food*, 24.

63 Egerton, *Southern Food*, 25.

64 Morgan, *Sport of Kings*, 5 (italics in original). Hereafter cited parenthetically in the text.

65 See Roundtree and McCabe, *Mighty Justice*.

66 Quashie, *Sovereignty of Quiet*, 6, 9.

67 Gordon, *Lord of Misrule*, 157.

68 The white doctor who treats Marie midway through this second section, in response to Marie's request for treatment, intones, "Lupus doesn't get much research. Mostly, colored women get it. There's really nothing else to do but take steroids. We're all still following a script that was written fifty years ago" (257).

69 I am thinking here of the 2011 film version of Kathryn Stockett's 2009 novel *The Help* and its depiction of one of the Black characters (Minny, played by Octavia Spencer) baking a chocolate pie filled with excrement as a form of revenge on her racist employer (Hilly, played by Bryce Dallas Howard). These are fantasies of a white author who understands that a freed Black person will automatically rise to cut down its white counterpart when given the chance. This vision of Black freedom is a rather limited one.

70 A "black" horse is technically not a color of horse, but a variation of bay that can be either dark bay or "liver chestnut."

71 Lawrence Scanlan's biography of Secretariat focuses on horse and human and the role that groom Eddie Sweat played in Secretariat's success. See Scanlan, *The Horse God Built*. It is a unique study of the backside of the racetrack and he notes that "the track's best and most devoted grooms, for all of the nineteenth century and most of the twentieth, were black" (108). He also tells the story of Eddie "Shorty" Sweat, self-identified as a South Carolinian from the Gullah culture. Before the pandemic, I had hoped to tell this story of Sweat's relationship to African-based tradition and horse love, but was unable to do this round of archival research for this project, given the frequent closures of archives.

72 Kim Severson, "Dora Charles Moves on from Paula Deen, and Makes It All About the Seasoning," *New York Times*, April 31, 2005, https://www

.nytimes.com/2015/09/02/dining/paula-deen-chef-dora-charles.html.
See also Tipton-Martin, *Jemima Code.*

73 Schulz, "Track Changes."
74 Schulz, "Track Changes."

6. sovereignty : a mercy

1   Alice Walker, foreword to Spiegel, *Dreaded Comparison*, 13.
2   Spiegel, *Dreaded Comparison*, 34–35.
3   Spiegel, *Dreaded Comparison*, 64.
4   Glick, "Animal Instincts," 642.
5   Brotz, *African-American Social and Political Thought*, 292.
6   Brotz, *African-American Social and Political Thought*, 292.
7   See Holland, "'If You Know I Have a History.'"
8   Derrida, *Beast and the Sovereign*, xiii. Hereafter cited parenthetically in the text.
9   See Bersani, "Is the Rectum a Grave?," *October* 43 (Winter 1987): 197–222; and Stockton, *Beautiful Bottom.*
10 Indigenous studies scholars Mark Rifkin, Lisa Tatonetti, Jodi Byrd, and J. Kēhaulani Kauanui have all investigated and/or posited queer/ness as a fruitful node of inquiry and attention in Indigenous studies. By thinking through what queer does for indigeneity, they complicate the possibilities for gender in history, culture and community praxis. See Rifkin, *When Did Indians Become Straight?*; Tatonetti, *Written by the Body*; and Kauanui, *Paradoxes of Hawaiian Sovereignty.*
11 As a mirror to my frustration here, Derrida remarks upon the condition of philosophy in relation to the political in his second of the thirteen lectures: "What is always remarkable with the great philosophers of politics, with all philosophers when they deal with politics, is that, more than ever, their philosophemes are also, in a very marked way, those of citizens and politicians of their own time, implicated and exposed in the national political field of their time." *The Beast and the Sovereign*, 51.
12 I want to thank Robert Warrior for reaching out to Aileen Moreton-Robinson, who shared a few unpublished essays on the matter of sovereignty. In particular, Moreton-Robinson limns the place of identity as a construct within Western thought that produces the erasure of Black and Indigenous peoples, evacuates their being for the becoming always of white forms of identity. See Moreton-Robinson, "The White Possessive."
13 Derrida refers to this moment of argument with Lacan's "aggressive seminar" from years ago in what he calls a "chatty parenthesis." *The Beast and the Sovereign*, 143.

14 Barad, *Meeting the Universe Halfway*, 378.

15 Simpson, *Mohawk Interruptus*, 1.

16 Simpson, *Mohawk Interruptus*, 2.

17 Simpson, *Mohawk Interruptus*, 3 (emphasis mine).

18 Derrida, *Beast and the Sovereign*, 29.

19 Moreton-Robinson, "The White Possessive," 10–11.

20 Simpson, *Mohawk Interruptus*, 11. Hereafter cited parenthetically in the text.

21 See Warrior, *Tribal Secrets*; Deloria, *Playing Indian*; O'Brien, *Dispossession by Degrees*; Byrd, *Transit of Empire*; and Kauanui, *Paradoxes of Hawaiian Sovereignty*. The global discussion of sovereignty in Western thought begins after the Reformation with the collapse of the relationship between king and church, as humans began to contemplate and exercise emerging schemas of power. The discussion of sovereignty has been ongoing, and its strongest contemplation has appeared across a range of scholarly work, both legal and otherwise, in Indigenous studies with the earliest contemporary contribution coming from none other than Vine Deloria Jr. (*Custer Died for Your Sins*, 1969). In the wake of previous generations of scholars, Robert Warrior published his first book, *Tribal Secrets*, which offers a cogent starting point for understanding the key moments in a thoroughgoing intellectual history. Jean M. O'Brien's path-breaking book *Dispossession by Degrees* works through a plethora of public records and "scattered evidence" (126) to arrive at a new methodology for understanding how, when, and why Indian peoples became dispossessed of their land. This work certainly laid the methodological ground for Tiya Miles's *Ties that Bind*. In the story of Doll, Miles demonstrates the complex merging of whiteness, blackness, emancipation, sovereignty, and freedom, demonstrating that no story of emancipation can be entirely told without the presence of Indigenous peoples, without a sense of sovereignty's power over life and land.

22 Barker, *Sovereignty Matters*, 3.

23 See Richotte, *Federal Indian Law and Policy*.

24 Barker, *Sovereignty Matters*, 6, 8.

25 In a footnote to the introduction, Barker notes "the fact is that indigenous peoples have made an important difference in what sovereignty means." Barker, *Sovereignty Matters*, 29n67.

26 Byrd, *Transit of Empire*, 10.

27 Moreton-Robinson, *The White Possessive*, xvi. Moreton-Robinson's critique is of Andrea Smith's GLQ piece, "Queer Theory and Native Studies," 195n10. Smith's work follows upon the late Patrick Wolfe's important essay, "Land, Labor, and Difference." While Smith's work is both generative and important, it is difficult to produce *this* work about

ethical life building upon the work of someone who makes their living through the devaluation of what it means to be Cherokee in this world. A detailed investigation of the controversy over Smith's Cherokee belonging can be found in Sarah Viren, "The Native Scholar Who Wasn't," *New York Times*, May 25, 2021, https://www.nytimes.com/2021/05/25/magazine/cherokee-native-american-andrea-smith.html.

28 Moreton-Robinson, *The White Possessive*, 189.

29 Kauanui, *Paradoxes*, 33.

30 Kauanui, *Paradoxes*, 35.

31 Kauanui, *Paradoxes*, 156.

32 Wilderson, *Red, Black & White*, 150. See also Miles and Holland, *Crossing Waters, Crossing Worlds*. The book is the result of that contentious conference, "Eating Out of the Same Pot," which we address in the introduction, along with some historical contextualization of the rise of the study of the African diaspora in Indigenous histories, cultures, and intellectual traditions.

33 Wilderson, *Red, White & Black*, 150 (emphasis mine).

34 King, *Black Shoals*, 73. See also Barnor Hesse's illumination of "white sovereignty" through the work of Charles Mills and Achille Mbembe to name (Mills) and concretize (Mbembe) white supremacy as both a stabilizing factor in Western philosophy and a kind of operationalized violence. Hesse, "White Sovereignty."

35 King, *Shoals*, 147, 148; Sexton, "The Vel of Slavery."

36 Dunning, *Black to Nature*, 97.

37 Dunning, *Black to Nature*, 121.

38 Wilderson, *Red, White & Black*, 175.

39 The phrase "animate and inanimate" repeats itself three times across Wilderson's chapter on "The Ethics of Sovereignty." *Red, White & Black*, 165, 169, 177.

40 Alfred, *Peace, Power and Righteousness*, quoted in Wilderson, *Red, White & Black*, 184.

41 Where mainstream queer temporality always already sees this space as playful, in my work and in the wider work of Black/Indigenous studies, dominant modes of thinking about the temporal (and I include queer studies in that) forget about the terror, while Jacobs and Hartman, Byrd and Deloria along with a host of other scholars have been reminding us of the terror of time stretched beyond recognition.

42 Brown, quoted in Spiegel, *Dreaded Comparison*, 36.

43 Byrd, *Transit of Empire*, 33.

44 Derrida, *Beast and the Sovereign*, 14.

45 See Mbembe, "Necropolitics."

46 Bruyneel, *Third Space*, xiii.

47 Bruyneel, *Third Space*, 148.

48 It is my sense that *Hamilton* fulfilled two liberal racial national desires: the nation's need for a more accurate script for African-descended inclusion in its founding, and the collective need to embrace and make more palatable an American art form (hip-hop) that already had a global reach.

49 Levinas, in Calarco and Atterton, *Animal Philosophy*, 50.

50 This is a quick and dirty assessment of Levinas and his use of the trope of the face. I am aware of the ongoing debates about different interpretations of what Levinas meant at any given time about the "face," both in his initial conceptualization in *Totality and Infinity* (1961) and in later works. This assessment from Dermot Moran in his *Introduction to Phenomenology* sums up the impossibilities inherent in coming to any conclusion about how to deploy Levinas's concept of the face: "*Totality and Infinity* is a difficult book, with no clear structure, highly repetitive in style replete with turgid prose, idiosyncratic use of philosophical terms, and contradictory assertions—more an impressionistic collage of ideas than a philosophical treatise. . . . The book is best known for its conception of ethics and of the face-to-face relation." Moran, *Introduction to Phenomenology*, 342. Regardless of its theoretical or philosophical machinations and import, it has had a profound effect in phenomenologies of the popular, even serving as the basis for an ethics in veganism, where proponents have claimed that they will not eat any food with a face. For an extended discussion of the face in Levinas, see Perpich, "Figurative Language and the 'Face' in Levinas's Philosophy."

51 McHenry, "Into Other Claws," 16.

52 Morrison, *A Mercy*, 3. Hereafter cited parenthetically in the text.

53 Conner, "'What Lay Beneath the Names,'" 123.

54 Conner, "'What Lay Beneath the Names,'" 123.

55 Terry, "'Breathing the Air of a World So New,'" 135.

56 For a discussion of Bacon's rebellion and Indigenous tribes, see Rice, "Bacon's Rebellion in Indian Country," 730, 732. It is clear from Rice's work that the motivating force for this conflict and several others, like the Anglo-Dutch Wars of 1672–74, have to do with land, territory, and religion.

57 Babb, "'E Pluribus Unum?,'" 148.

58 Grandin and Johnson, *Animals in Translation*. See the chapters entitled "My Story" and "How Animals Perceive the World" for an explanation of Grandin's use of autism to understand animal behavior.

59 Gumbs, *Undrowned*, 61.

60 Morrison, *A Mercy*, 15. Hereafter cited parenthetically in the text. In their historical revision of the colonies before the American Revolution, Peter

Linebaugh and Marcus Rediker quote Kerby A. Miller, "On numerous occasions in the late seventeenth and early eighteenth century, colonial officials in Newfoundland, Nova Scotia, New York, and the West Indies feared that Irish 'papists' were plotting insurrection with negro slaves or foreign enemies." Miller, *Emigrants and Exiles*, 146–47. Linebaugh and Rediker, *Many-Headed Hydra*, 197. The footnote to this quotation draws from a range of sources that vary in date (1743 to 1982) and genre (archival to critical).

61 Faulkner, *Absalom, Absalom!*, 218.
62 Agamben, *Homo Sacer*, 101.

bibliography

"Afrofuturism." *Social Text* 20, no. 2, special issue 71 (Summer 2002).

Agamben, Giorgio. *Homo Sacer: Sovereign Power and Bare Life.* Translated by Daniel Heller-Roazen. Stanford, CA: Stanford University Press, 1998.

Agamben, Giorgio. *The Open: Man and Animal.* Translated by Kevin Attell. Stanford, CA: Stanford University Press, 2004.

Ahmed, Sara. *The Cultural Politics of Emotion.* New York: Routledge, 2004.

Ahmed, Sara. *On Being Included: Racism and Diversity in Institutional Life.* Durham, NC: Duke University Press, 2012.

Alfred, Taiaiake. *Peace, Power and Righteousness: An Indigenous Manifesto.* Ontario: Oxford University Press, 2019.

Alkon, Alison Hope, and Julian Agyeman. *Cultivating Food Justice: Race, Class and Sustainability.* Cambridge, MA: MIT Press, 2011.

Ananat, Ryan Snyder. "The Music of William James: Pragmatism as Improvisational Lyricism." PhD diss., University of Michigan, Ann Arbor, 2009.

Anderson, John, and Hilary Hevenor. *Burning Down the House: MOVE and the Tragedy of Philadelphia.* New York: Norton, 1987.

Assefa, Hizkias, and Paul Wahrhaftig. *The MOVE Crisis in Philadelphia: Extremist Groups and Conflict Resolution.* New York: Praeger, 1988.

Babb, Valerie. "'E Pluribus Unum?' The American Origins Narrative in Toni Morrison's *A Mercy.*" *MELUS* 36, no. 2 (Summer 2011): 147–64.

Barad, Karen. *Meeting the Universe Halfway: Quantum Physics and the Entanglement of Matter and Meaning.* Durham, NC: Duke University Press, 2007.

Barich, Bill. *A Fine Place to Daydream: Racehorses, Romance, and the Irish.* New York: Vintage, 2006.

Barker, Joanne, ed. *Sovereignty Matters: Locations of Contestation and Possibility in Indigenous Struggles for Self-Determination.* Lincoln: University of Nebraska Press, 2005.

Barrett, Lindon, Justin A. Joyce, Dwight A. McBride, and John Carlos Rowe, eds. *Racial Blackness and the Discontinuity of Western Modernity.* Urbana: University of Illinois Press, 2014.

Bassard, Katherine Clay. "Imagining Other Worlds: Race, Gender, and the 'Power Line.'" In "Edward P. Jones's *The Known World*," special issue, *African American Review* 42, no. 3–4 (Fall-Winter, 2008): 407–19.

Beers, Diane L. *For the Prevention of Cruelty: The History and Legacy of Animal Rights Activism in the United States*. Athens: Ohio University Press, 2006.

Bell, Derrick A. *Race, Racism and American Law*. 6th ed. Boston: Aspen, 2008.

Bennett, Jane. *Vibrant Matter: A Political Ecology of Things*. Durham, NC: Duke University Press, 2010.

Bennett, Joshua. *Being Property Once Myself: Blackness and the End of Man*. Cambridge, MA: Harvard University Press, 2020.

Berlant, Lauren. "Slow Death (Sovereignty, Obesity, Lateral Agency)." *Critical Inquiry* 33 (Summer 2007): 754–80.

Bersani, Leo. "Is the Rectum a Grave?" *October* 43 (Winter 1987): 197–222.

Bey, Marquis. *Black Trans Feminism*. Durham, NC: Duke University Press, 2022.

Bogost, Ian. *Alien Phenomenology or What It's Like to Be a Thing*. Minneapolis: University of Minnesota Press, 2012.

Boisseron, Bénédicte. *Afro-Dog: Blackness and the Animal Question*. New York: Columbia University Press, 2018.

Bourke, Joanna. *What It Means to Be Human: Historical Reflections from the 1800s to the Present*. Berkeley, CA: Counterpoint, 2011.

Brand, Dionne. *At the Full and Change of the Moon*. New York: Grove, 1999.

Brantz, Dorothee. "Recollecting the Slaughterhouse." *Cabinet 4* (Autumn 2001): 118–23.

Briggs, Laura. *How All Politics Became Reproductive Politics: From Welfare Reform to Foreclosure to Trump*. Berkeley: University of California Press, 2017.

Brotz, Howard, ed. *African-American Social and Political Thought 1850–1920*. New Brunswick, NJ: Transaction (Rutgers), 1992.

Bruyneel, Kevin. *The Third Space of Sovereignty: The Post-Colonial Politics of U.S.-Indigenous Relations*. Minneapolis: University of Minnesota Press, 2007.

Butler, Judith. *Precarious Life: The Powers of Mourning and Violence*. New York: Verso, 2004.

Byrd, Jodi A. *The Transit of Empire: Indigenous Critiques of Colonialism*. Minneapolis: University of Minnesota Press, 2011.

Byrd, Jodi A. "What's Normative Got to Do with It? Toward Indigenous Queer Relationality." *Social Text* 38, no. 4, special issue 145 (December 2020): 105–23.

Cadava, Eduardo, Peter Connor, Jean-Luc Nancy, eds. *Who Comes After the Subject?* New York: Routledge, 1991.

Calarco, Matthew. *Zoographies: The Question of the Animal from Heidegger to Derrida.* New York: Columbia University Press, 2008.

Calarco, Matthew, and Peter Atterton, eds. *Animal Philosophy: Essential Readings in Continental Thought.* London: Continuum, 2004.

Cervenak, Sarah Jane. *Wandering: Philosophical Performances of Racial and Sexual Freedom.* Durham, NC: Duke University Press, 2014.

Chu, Andrea Long. *Females.* London: Verso, 2019.

Chuh, Kandice. *Imagine Otherwise: On Asian Americanist Critique.* Durham, NC: Duke University Press, 2003.

Cliff, Michelle. "'I Found God in Myself and I Loved Her/I Loved Her Fiercely': More Thoughts on the Work of Black Women Artists." *Journal of Feminist Studies in Religion* 2, no. 1 (Spring 1986): 7–39.

Coetzee, J. M. *The Lives of Animals.* Princeton, NJ: Princeton University Press, 1999.

Coleman, J. Winston, Jr. *Three Kentucky Artists: Troye, Hart, Price.* Lexington: University of Kentucky Press, 2009.

Conner, Marc C. "'What Lay Beneath the Names': The Language and Landscapes of *A Mercy*." In *Toni Morrison: Paradise, Love, A Mercy*, edited by Lucille P. Fultz. New York: Bloomsbury, 2012.

Coole, Diana, and Samantha Frost. *New Materialisms: Ontology, Agency, and Politics.* Durham, NC: Duke University Press, 2010.

Cools, Arthur. "Revisiting the *Il y a*: Maurice Blanchot and Emmanuel Levinas on the Question of Subjectivity." *Paragraph* 28, no. 3 (November 2005): 54–71.

Crow, Jeffrey J., Paul D. Escott, and Flora J. Hatley Wadelington. *History of African Americans in North Carolina.* Raleigh: Division of Archives and History, North Carolina Department of Cultural Resources, 1992.

Crump, Nancy Carter. "Foodways of the Albemarle Region: 'Indulgent Nature Makes Up for Every Want.'" *Journal of Early Southern Decorative Arts* 19, no. 1 (May 1993): 1–36.

Debaise, Didier. *Nature as Event: The Lure of the Possible.* Translated by Michael Halewood. Durham, NC: Duke University Press, 2017.

de Fontenay, Élisabeth. *Without Offending Humans: A Critique of Animal Rights.* Translated by Will Bishop. Minneapolis: University of Minnesota Press, 2012.

Dekkers, Midas. *Dearest Pet: On Bestiality.* Translated by Paul Vincent. London: Verso, 1994.

Delany, Samuel R. *Times Square Red, Times Square Blue.* New York: New York University Press, 1999.

Deleuze, Gilles, and Félix Guattari. *A Thousand Plateaus: Capitalism and Schizophrenia.* Translated by Brian Massumi. Minneapolis: University of Minnesota Press, 1987.

Deloria, Philip J. *Playing Indian.* New Haven, CT: Yale University Press, 1999.

Derrida, Jacques. *The Animal That Therefore I Am.* Translated by David Wills. New York: Fordham University Press, 2008.

Derrida, Jacques. *The Beast and the Sovereign, Volume I.* Edited by Michel Lisse, Marie-Louise Mallet, and Ginette Michaud. Translated by Geoffrey Bennington. Chicago: University of Chicago Press, 2009.

deSousa, Allan. *How Art Can Be Thought: A Handbook for Change.* Durham, NC: Duke University Press, 2018.

Donaldson, Sue, and Will Kymlicka. *Zoopolis: A Political Theory of Animal Rights.* Oxford: Oxford University Press, 2011.

Donovan, Josephine, and Carol J. Adams, eds. *The Feminist Care Tradition in Animal Ethics.* New York: Columbia University Press, 2007.

Drape, Joe. *Black Maestro: The Epic Life of an American Legend.* New York: Harper, 2006.

Du Bois, W. E. B. *The Souls of Black Folk.* New York: Norton, 1999.

Dunning, Stefanie K. *Black to Nature: Pastoral Return and African American Culture.* Jackson: University of Mississippi Press, 2021.

Egerton, John. *Southern Food: At Home, on the Road, in History.* New York: Knopf, 1987.

Evans, Richard Kent. *MOVE: An American Religion.* Oxford: Oxford University Press, 2020.

Fanon, Frantz. *Black Skin, White Masks.* Translated by Richard Philcox. New York: Grove, 2008 [1952].

Faulkner, William. *Absalom, Absalom!* New York: Library of America, 1990.

Fausto-Sterling, Anne. *Sexing the Body: Gender Politics and the Construction of Sexuality.* New York: Basic Books, 2000.

Feldman, Heidi. "The MOVE Crisis: A Case Study in Community Conflict." Senior thesis, Swarthmore College, 1987.

Field, Allyson Nadia, Jan-Christopher Horak, and Jacqueline Najuma Stewart, eds. *L.A. Rebellion: Creating a New Black Cinema.* Oakland: University of California Press, 2015.

Firestone, Shulamith. *The Dialectic of Sex: The Case for Feminist Revolution.* New York: Bantam Books, 1971.

Fiscella, Anthony T. "Removing MOVE: A Case Study of Intersectional Invisibility within Religious and Legal Studies." *International Journal for the Study of New Religions* 7, no. 1 (2016).

Fisher, Rebecka Rutledge. *Habitations of the Veil: Metaphor and the Poetics of Black Being in African American Literature.* Albany: State University of New York Press, 2014.

Floyd, Kevin. *The Reification of Desire: Toward a Queer Marxism.* Minneapolis: University of Minnesota Press, 2009.

Francis, Vievee. *Horse in the Dark: Poems.* Evanston, IL: Northwestern University Press, 2012.

Freeman, Elizabeth. *Time Binds: Queer Temporalities, Queer Histories.* Durham, NC: Duke University Press, 2010.

Frost, Samantha. *Biocultural Creatures: Toward a New Theory of the Human.* Durham, NC: Duke University Press, 2016.

Fudge, Erica. *Animal.* London: Reaktion Books, 2002.

Gates, Henry Louis, Jr. "'What's Love Got to Do with It?': Critical Theory, Integrity, and the Black Idiom." *New Literary History* 18, no. 2 (Winter 1987): 345–62.

Glick, Megan. "Animal Instincts: Race, Criminality, and the Reversal of the 'Human.'" In special issue, "Species/Race/Sex," *American Quarterly* 65, no. 3 (September 2013).

Godlovitch, Stanley, Roslind Godlovitch, and John Harris. *Animals, Men and Morals: An Inquiry into the Maltreatment of Non-humans.* New York: Taplinger, 1971.

Goldberg, David Theo. *Racist Culture.* London: Wiley-Blackwell, 1993.

Gordon, Jaimy. *Circumspections from an Equestrian Statue.* Providence, RI: Burning Deck, 1979.

Gordon, Jaimy. *Lord of Misrule.* Kingston, NY: McPherson, 2010.

Grandin, Temple, and Catherine Johnson. *Animals in Translation: Using the Mysteries of Autism to Decode Animal Behavior.* New York: Simon and Schuster, 2005.

Grosz, Elizabeth. "Feminism, Materialism, and Freedom." In *New Materialisms: Ontology, Agency, and Politics,* edited by Diana Coole and Samantha Frost. Durham, NC: Duke University Press, 2010.

Grosz, Elizabeth. *The Nick of Time: Politics, Evolution, and the Untimely.* Durham, NC: Duke University Press, 2004.

Gumbs, Alexis Pauline. *Undrowned: Black Feminist Lessons from Marine Mammals.* Chico, CA: AK Press, 2020.

Halberstam, Jack. *The Queer Art of Failure.* Durham, NC: Duke University Press, 2011.

Hammonds, Evelyn. "Black (W)holes and the Geometry of Black Female Sexuality." *differences* 6, no. 2–3 (Summer-Fall 1994): 126–45.

Haraway, Donna. *The Companion Species Manifesto: Dogs, People, and Significant Otherness.* Chicago: Prickly Paradigm, 2003.

Haraway, Donna. *Primate Visions: Gender, Race, and Nature in the World of Modern Science*. New York: Routledge, 1989.

Haraway, Donna. *Simians, Cyborgs, and Women: The Reinvention of Nature*. New York: Routledge, 1991.

Haraway, Donna. *Staying with the Trouble: Making Kin in the Chthulucene*. Durham, NC: Duke University Press, 2016.

Haraway, Donna. *When Species Meet*. Minneapolis: University of Minnesota Press, 2008.

Hare, Brian, and Shinya Yamamoto. "Moving Bonobos Off the Scientifically Endangered List." In "Bonobo Cognition and Behavior," special issue, *Behaviour* 152, no. 3–4 (2015): 247–58.

Harris, Jessica B. *High on the Hog: A Culinary Journey from Africa to America*. New York: Bloomsbury, 2011.

Harris, Sylvia. *Long Shot: My Bipolar Life and the Horses Who Saved Me*. London: HarperTrue, 2011.

Hartman, Saidiya. *Scenes of Subjection: Terror, Slavery, and Self-Making in Nineteenth-Century America*. Oxford: Oxford University Press, 1997.

Hearne, Vicki. *Adam's Task: Calling Animals by Name*. New York: Skyhorse, 2007.

Heidegger, Martin. *Being and Time*. Translated by Joan Stambaugh. Albany: State University of New York Press, 2010.

Hennessy, Rosemary. *Profit and Pleasure: Sexual Identities in Late Capitalism*. New York: Routledge, 2000.

Herman, Bernard L., ed. *The Unfinished Business of Unsettled Things: Art from an African American South*. Chapel Hill: University of North Carolina Press, 2022.

Hesse, Barnor. "White Sovereignty (. . .), Black Life Politics: 'The N****r They Couldn't Kill,'" *South Atlantic Quarterly* 116, no. 3 (July 2017): 591–93.

Holland, Nancy. *Feminist Interpretations of Jacques Derrida*. University Park: Pennsylvania State University Press, 1997.

Holland, Sharon P. "(Black) (Queer) Love." *Callaloo* 36, no. 3 (Summer 2013): 658–68.

Holland, Sharon P. "'If You Know I Have a History, You Will Respect Me': A Perspective on Afro-Native Literature." *Callaloo* 17, no. 1 (1994): 334–50.

hooks, bell. *Appalachian Elegy: Poetry and Place*. Lexington: University Press of Kentucky, 2012.

hooks, bell, and Cornel West. *Breaking Bread: Insurgent Black Intellectual Life*. Boston: South End, 1991.

Hotaling, Edward. *The Great Black Jockeys*. Rocklin, CA: Prima Publishing, 1999.

Hozic, Aida A. "The House I Live In: An Interview with Charles Burnett." *Callaloo* 17, no. 2 (Spring 1994): 471–87.

Hrdy, Sarah Blaffer. *The Woman That Never Evolved.* Cambridge, MA: Harvard University Press, 1981.

Ingold, Tim. *The Perception of the Environment: Essays on Livelihood, Dwelling and Skill.* London: Routledge, 2000.

Ingram, Susan. "Berlin: A Spectacularly Gendered Cinematic Landscape of Dystopian Devastation." *Space and Culture* 17, no. 4 (2014): 366–78.

Jackson, Zakiyyah Iman. *Becoming Human: Matter and Meaning in an Antiblack World.* New York: New York University Press, 2020.

Jacoby, Karl. "Slaves by Nature? Domestic Animals and Human Slaves." *Slavery & Abolition: A Journal of Slave and Post-Slave Studies* 15, no. 1 (April 1994): 89–99.

Jones, Edward. *The Known World.* New York: HarperCollins, 2003.

Kaba, Mariame. *We Do This 'Til We Free Us: Abolitionist Organizing and Transforming Justice.* Chicago: Haymarket, 2021.

Kalof, Linda, and Amy Fitzgerald. *The Animals Reader: The Essential Classic and Contemporary Writings.* Oxford: Berg, 2007.

Kauanui, J. Kēhaulani. *Paradoxes of Hawaiian Sovereignty: Land, Sex, and the Colonial Politics of State Nationalism.* Durham, NC: Duke University Press, 2018.

King, Tiffany Lethabo. *The Black Shoals: Offshore Formations of Black and Native Studies.* Durham, NC: Duke University Press, 2019.

King, Tiffany Lethabo. "Humans Involved: Lurking in the Lines of Posthumanist Flight." *Critical Ethnic Studies* 3, no. 1 (Spring 2017): 162–85.

King, Tiffany Lethabo. "Off Littorality (Shoal 1.0): Black Study Off the Shores of 'the Black Body,'" *Propter Nos* 3 (2019): 40–50.

King, Tiffany Lethabo, Jenell Navarro, and Andrea Smith. *Otherwise Worlds: Against Settler Colonialism and Anti-Blackness.* Durham, NC: Duke University Press, 2020.

Levinas, Emmanuel. *Difficult Freedom: Essays on Judaism.* Translated by Seán Hand. Baltimore, MD: Johns Hopkins University Press, 1990.

Linebaugh, Peter, and Marcus Rediker. *The Many-Headed Hydra: Sailors, Slaves, Commoners, and the Hidden History of the Revolutionary Atlantic.* Boston: Beacon Press, 2000.

Lippit, Akira Mizuta. *Electric Animal: Toward a Rhetoric of Wildlife.* Minneapolis: University of Minnesota Press, 2000.

Looker, Benjamin. *"Point from Which Creation Begins": The Black Artists' Group of St. Louis.* St. Louis: Missouri Historical Society Press, 2004.

Lorde, Audre. *Zami: A New Spelling of My Name*. Freedom, CA: Crossing, 1982.

Lowe, Lisa. *The Intimacies of Four Continents*. Durham, NC: Duke University Press, 2015.

Mackay-Smith, Alexander. *The Race Horses of America, 1832–1872: Portraits and Other Paintings by Edward Troye*. Saratoga Springs, NY: National Museum of Racing, 1981.

MacKinnon, Catherine. "Of Mice and Men: A Feminist Fragment on Animal Rights." In *Animal Rights: Current Debates and New Directions*, edited by Cass R. Sunstein and Martha C. Nussbaum. New York: Oxford University Press, 2004.

Massood, Paula J. "An Aesthetic Appropriate to Conditions: Killer of Sheep, (Neo)Realism, and the Documentary Impulse." *Wide Angle* 21, no. 4 (October 1999): 20–41.

Massumi, Brian. *What Animals Teach Us about Politics*. Durham, NC: Duke University Press, 2014.

Mbembe, Achille. "Necropolitics." *Public Culture* 15, no. 1 (2003): 11–40.

McDaniels, Pellom. *The Prince of Jockeys: The Life of Isaac Burns Murphy*. Lexington: University Press of Kentucky, 2013.

McHenry, Elizabeth. "Into Other Claws: *A Mercy*, by Toni Morrison." *Women's Review of Books* 26, no. 4 (July/August 2009): 16–17.

McKittrick, Katherine. "Dear April: The Aesthetics of Black Miscellanea." *Antipode* 54, no. 1 (January 2022): 3–18.

McKittrick, Katherine. *Demonic Grounds: Black Women and the Cartographies of Struggle*. Minneapolis: University of Minnesota Press, 2006.

Merleau-Ponty, Maurice. *The Visible and the Invisible*. Translated by Alphonso Lingis. Evanston, IL: Northwestern University Press, 1968 [1964].

Miles, Tiya. *Ties that Bind: The Story of an Afro-Cherokee Family in Slavery and Freedom*. Berkeley: University of California Press, 2005.

Miles, Tiya, and Sharon P. Holland. *Crossing Waters, Crossing Worlds: The African Diaspora in Indian Country*. Durham, NC: Duke University Press, 2006.

Miller, Kerby A. *Emigrants and Exiles: Ireland and the Irish Exodus to North America*. New York: Oxford University Press, 1988.

Mills, Charles. *The Racial Contract*. Ithaca, NY: Cornell University Press, 1997.

Mooney, Katherine C. *Race Horse Men: How Slavery and Freedom Were Made at the Racetrack*. Cambridge, MA: Harvard University Press, 2014.

Moran, Dermot. *Introduction to Phenomenology*. London: Routledge, 2000.

Moreton-Robinson, Aileen. "The White Possessive: Identity Matters in Becoming Native, Black and Aboriginal." *Borderlands Journal* 20, no. 2 (2021): 2–26.

Moreton-Robinson, Aileen. *The White Possessive: Property, Power, Indigenous Sovereignty*. Minneapolis: University of Minnesota Press, 2015.

Morgan, C. E. *The Sport of Kings*. New York: Picador, 2016.

Morrison, Toni. *Beloved*. New York: Knopf, 1987.

Morrison, Toni. *A Mercy*. New York: Vintage, 2008.

Morrison, Toni. "Unspeakable Things Unspoken: The Afro-American Presence in American Literature." *Michigan Quarterly Review* 18, no. 1 (1989): 1–34.

Moten, Fred. "The Case of Blackness." *Criticism* 50, no. 2 (Spring 2008): 177–218.

Muñoz, José Esteban. *Cruising Utopia: The Then and There of Queer Futurity*. New York: New York University Press, 2009.

Naremore, James. *Charles Burnett: A Cinema of Symbolic Knowledge*. Oakland: University of California Press, 2017.

Nash, Jennifer. *Black Feminism Reimagined: After Intersectionality*. Durham, NC: Duke University Press, 2019.

Newfield, Christopher. *The Great Mistake: How We Wrecked Public Universities and How We Can Fix Them*. Baltimore, MD: Johns Hopkins University Press, 2016.

Newfield, Christopher. *Ivy and Industry: Business and the Making of the American University, 1880–1980*. Durham, NC: Duke University Press, 2004.

Newfield, Christopher. *Unmaking the Public University: The Forty-Year Assault on the Middle Class*. Cambridge, MA: Harvard University, 2011.

Northup, Solomon. *Twelve Years a Slave: Narrative of Solomon Northup, a Citizen of New York, Kidnapped in Washington City in 1841, and Rescued in 1853*. Edited by David Wilson. Chapel Hill: University of North Carolina Press, 2011.

O'Brien, Jean M. *Dispossession by Degrees: Indian Land and Identity in Natick, Massachusetts, 1650–1790*. Lincoln: University of Nebraska Press, 1997.

Oliver, Kelly. *Animal Lessons: How They Teach Us to Be Human*. New York: Columbia University Press, 2009.

Painter, Nell. *Sojourner Truth: A Life, a Symbol*. New York: Norton, 1997.

Perpich, Diane. "Figurative Language and the 'Face' in Levinas's Philosophy." *Philosophy and Rhetoric* 38, no. 2 (2005): 103–21.

Pickens, Therí Alyce. *Black Madness :: Mad Blackness*. Durham, NC: Duke University Press, 2019.

Povinelli, Elizabeth A. *Economies of Abandonment: Social Belonging and Endurance in Late Liberalism.* Durham, NC: Duke University Press, 2011.

Povinelli, Elizabeth A. *The Empire of Love: Toward a Theory of Intimacy, Genealogy, and Carnality.* Durham, NC: Duke University Press, 2006.

Probyn, Elspeth. *Carnal Appetites: Food, Sex, Identities.* London: Routledge, 2000.

Puhr, Kathleen M. "Healers in Gloria Naylor's Fiction." *Twentieth Century Literature* 40, no. 4 (Winter 1994): 518–27.

Purifoy, Danielle. "The Parable of Black Places." *Transactions of the Institute for British Geographers* 46, no. 4 (December 2021): 829–33.

Quashie, Kevin. *The Sovereignty of Quiet: Beyond Resistance in Black Culture.* New Brunswick, NJ: Rutgers University Press, 2012.

Randolph, Antonia. *The Wrong Kind of Different: Challenging the Meaning of Diversity in American Classrooms.* New York: Teachers College Press, 2013.

Redmond, Shana L. "'As Though It Were Our Own': Against a Politics of Identification." In *Critical Ethnic Studies: A Reader,* edited by Nada Elia, David Hernández, Jodi Kim, Shana Redmond, Dylan Rodríguez, and Sarita Echavez See. Durham, NC: Duke University Press, 2016.

Rice, James D. "Bacon's Rebellion in Indian Country." *Journal of American History* 101, no. 3 (December 2014): 726–50.

Richotte, Keith, Jr. *Federal Indian Law and Policy: An Introduction.* New York: West Academic Publishing, 2020.

Rifkin, Mark. *When Did Indians Become Straight? Kinship, the History of Sexuality and Native Sovereignty.* Oxford: Oxford University Press, 2011.

Roberts, Dorothy. *Killing the Black Body: Race, Reproduction, and the Meaning of Liberty.* New York: Vintage Books, 1997.

Rose, Nikolas. "The Human Sciences in a Biological Age." *Theory, Culture, and Society* 30, no. 1 (2013): 3–34.

Rose, Nikolas. *The Politics of Life Itself: Biomedicine, Power, and Subjectivity in the Twenty-First Century.* Princeton, NJ: Princeton University Press, 2006.

Rosenberg, Gabriel N. "No Scrubs: Livestock Breeding, Eugenics, and the State in the Early Twentieth-Century United States." *Journal of American History* 107, no. 2 (September 2020): 362–87.

Roundtree, Dovey Johnson, and Kathleen J. McCabe. *Mighty Justice: My Life in Civil Rights.* Chapel Hill, NC: Algonquin Books, 2019.

Rudy, Kathy. *Loving Animals: Toward a New Animal Advocacy.* Minneapolis: University of Minnesota Press, 2011.

Saunders, James Robert, and Monica Renae Saunders. *Black Winning Jockeys in the Kentucky Derby*. Jefferson, NC: McFarland, 2003.

Scanlan, Lawrence. *The Horse God Built: The Untold Story of Secretariat, the World's Greatest Racehorse*. New York: St. Martin's, 2007.

Schwartz, Marie Jenkins. *Birthing a Slave: Motherhood and Medicine in the Antebellum South*. Cambridge, MA: Harvard University Press, 2006.

Scully, Matthew. *Dominion: The Power of Man, the Suffering of Animals, and the Call to Mercy*. New York: St. Martin's Press, 2002.

Seshadri, Kalpana Rahita. *HumAnimal: Race, Law, Language*. Minneapolis: University of Minnesota Press, 2012.

Sexton, Jared. *Amalgamation Schemes: Antiblackness and the Critique of Multiracialism*. Minneapolis: University of Minnesota Press, 2008.

Sexton, Jared. "The Vel of Slavery: Tracking the Figure of the Unsovereign." *Critical Sociology* 42, no. 4–5 (December 2014): 583–97.

Simon, Linda. "William James's Lost Souls in Ursula Le Guin's Utopia." *Philosophy and Literature* 28, no. 1 (2006): 89–102.

Simpson, Audra. *Mohawk Interruptus*. Durham, NC: Duke University Press, 2014.

Simpson, Joe. *Touching the Void*. New York: Perennial, 1988.

Smiley, Jane. *A Year at the Races: Reflections on Horses, Humans, Love, Money, and Luck*. New York: Anchor Books, 2004.

Smith, Andrea. "Queer Theory and Native Studies: The Heteronormativity of Settler Colonialism." *GLQ* 16, no. 1–2 (2010): 41–68.

Spiegel, Marjorie. *The Dreaded Comparison: Human and Animal Slavery*. New York: Mirror Books, 1996.

Spillers, Hortense J. "Mama's Baby, Papa's Maybe: An American Grammar Book." *Diacritics* 17, no. 2 (Summer 1987): 64–81.

Stein, Gertrude. *Three Lives*. New York: Grafton, 1909.

Stewart, Jacqueline Najuma. *Migrating to the Movies: Cinema and Black Urban Modernity*. Berkeley: University of California Press, 2005.

Stewart, Kathleen. *Ordinary Affects*. Durham, NC: Duke University, 2007.

Stockton, Kathryn Bond. *Beautiful Bottom, Beautiful Shame: Where "Black" Meets "Queer."* Durham, NC: Duke University Press, 2006.

Streeby, Shelley. *Imagining the Future of Climate Change: World-Making through Science Fiction and Activism*. Berkeley: University of California Press, 2018.

Sunstein, Cass R., and Martha C. Nussbaum. *Animal Rights: Current Debates and New Directions*. New York: Oxford University Press, 2004.

Tatonetti, Lisa. *Written by the Body: Gender Expansiveness and Indigenous Non-cis Masculinities*. Minneapolis: Minnesota University Press, 2021.

Terry, Jennifer. "'Breathing the Air of a World So New': Rewriting the Landscape of America in Toni Morrison's *A Mercy*." *Journal of American Studies* 48, no. 1 (February 2014): 127–45.

Thompson, Chuck. *Better Off without 'Em: A Northern Manifesto for Southern Secession*. New York: Simon and Schuster, 2012.

Tipton-Martin, Toni. *The Jemima Code: Two Centuries of African American Cookbooks* (Austin: University of Texas Press, 2015.

Tompkins, Kyla Wazana. "On the Limits of Promise of New Materialist Philosophy." *Lateral: Journal of the Cultural Studies Association* 5, no. 1 (Spring 2016).

Tompkins, Kyla Wazana. *Racial Indigestion: Eating Bodies in the 19th Century*. New York: New York University Press, 2012.

Wagner-Pacifici, Robin. *Discourse and Destruction: The City of Philadelphia versus MOVE*. Chicago: University of Chicago Press, 1994.

Walker, Alice. "Am I Blue?" In *Living by the Word: Selected Writings 1973–1987*. New York: Mariner Books, 1989.

Warren, Calvin L. *Ontological Terror: Blackness, Nihilism, and Emancipation*. Durham, NC: Duke University Press, 2018.

Warrior, Robert Allen. *Tribal Secrets: Recovering American Indian Intellectual Traditions*. Minneapolis: University of Minnesota Press, 1995.

Washington, Linn. "MOVE: A Double Standard of Justice?" *Yale Journal of Law and Liberation* 1, no. 1 (1989): 67–82.

Weheliye, Alexander G. *Habeas Viscus: Racializing Assemblages, Biopolitics, and Black Feminist Theories of the Human*. Durham, NC: Duke University Press, 2014.

Weil, Kari. "A Report on the Animal Turn." *differences* 21, no. 2 (2010): 1–23.

Wiegand, Elizabeth. *Outer Banks Cookbook: Recipes and Traditions from North Carolina's Barrier Islands*. Guilford, CT: Globe Pequot, 2008.

Wilcox, Sharon, and Stephanie Rutherford, eds. *Historical Animal Geographies*. London: Routledge, 2018.

Wilderson, Frank B., III. *Red, White & Black: Cinema and the Structure of U.S. Antagonisms*. Durham, NC: Duke University Press, 2010.

Wise, Steven M. *An American Trilogy: Death, Slavery and Dominion on the Banks of the Cape Fear River*. Philadelphia: Da Capo, 2009.

Wolfe, Cary. *What Is Posthumanism?* Minneapolis: University of Minnesota Press, 2010.

Wolfe, Cary, ed. *Zoontologies: The Question of the Animal*. Minneapolis: University of Minnesota Press, 2003.

Wolfe, Patrick. "Land, Labor, and Difference: Elementary Structures of Race." *American Historical Review* 106, no. 3 (June 2001): 866–905.

Wolff, Sally. "William Faulkner and the Ledgers of History." *Southern Literary Journal* 42, no. 1 (Fall 2009): 1–16.

Woods, Vanessa. *Bonobo Handshake: A Memoir of Love and Adventure in the Congo*. New York: Penguin, 2010.

Wu, Cynthia. *Chang and Eng Reconnected: The Original Siamese Twins in American Culture*. Philadelphia: Temple University Press, 2012.

Wynter, Sylvia. "1492: A New World View." In *Race, Discourse, and the Origin of the Americas: A New World View*, edited by Vera Lawrence Hyatt and Rex M. Nettleford, 5–57. Washington, DC: Smithsonian Institution Press, 1996.

Yusoff, Kathryn. *A Billion Black Anthropocenes or None*. Minneapolis: University of Minnesota Press, 2018.

Zambrana, Ruth Enid. *Toxic Ivory Towers: The Consequences of Work Stress on Underrepresented Minority Faculty*. New Brunswick, NJ: Rutgers University Press, 2018.

index

insurgence, 43, 135, 201, 209–10, 213, 229, 233, 254. *See also* Black female insurgency

Intimacies of Four Continents, The (Lowe), 272n9

Jackson, Zakiyyah Iman, 12, 27–28, 125, 128, 224–25, 285n36, 289n89

Jacob, Harriet, 237

James, William, 32, 286n41

Jones, Edward P., 98–104, 242

Jones, Everett L., 146

Jones, Meta, 10

justice, 24, 126–30, 134–36, 150, 209

Kaba, Mariame, 9–10

Kahnawà:ke (peoples), 232

Kant, Immanuel, 288n79

Kauanui, J. Kēhaulani, 227, 234–35, 298n10

Killer of Sheep (Burnett), 20, 26, 53, 68, 146–48, 153–56, 159–64

King, Tiffany Lethabo, 236

Known World, The (Jones), 98–104, 242

Ku Klux Klan, 169

labor. *See* work

Lacan, Jacques, 228

land, 234–37, 244

L.A. Rebellion, 145–46, 151, 154, 277n59, 280n85

Latour, Bruno, 33, 122. *See also* actor-network theory; new materialism

Leaphart, Vincent, 57. *See also* MOVE organization

Le Guin, Ursula, 32

Let the Fire Burn (Osder), 77

Levinas, Emmanuel, 30–32, 105–6, 115, 127–28, 189, 222, 241, 249, 284n29, 301n50

life: affective, 152, 229; animal, xi–xiii, 3–24, 50–54, 77–78, 93–94, 102–7, 158–61, 183–208, 223–54, 266n28; bare, 21–24, 248, 286n39; Black, 16–22, 35–44, 50–59, 81–87, 149–64, 208–9, 223–26; as existence, 33, 37–38, 45, 97, 107, 121–23, 136; female, 39, 44; human, 33–34, 45, 61, 79, 102, 107, 112, 236, 248; hum/animal, 229, 242; hum:animal,

54–66, 88–89, 119–30, 145–61, 173, 179–83, 210, 218, 255; insurgent, 39, 43–44, 81, 125, 230, 254; nonhuman, 16–18, 23–24, 93–94, 225, 228, 240, 249, 254; sanctity of, 46–47, 65, 79–80, 94, 228, 244, 253. *See also* being; sentience

Lippit, Akira Mizuta, 90–96, 281n1

livestock, 11, 154, 190

Lord, Peter, 195

Lorde, Audre, 10, 19, 32, 41, 44, 54, 85, 155, 221

Lord of Misrule (Gordan), 169, 178–79, 183

love, 13, 139–45, 164

Loving Animals (Rudy), 270n1

Lowe, Lisa, 54, 263n3, 272n9

Luke, Brian, 126

Lyotard, Jean-François, 92–94

Mackay-Smith, Alexander, 175

MacKinnon, Catherine, 116

"Mama's Baby, Papa's Maybe" (Spillers), xii, 18, 22–24, 27, 30, 119

Martin, Trayvon, 264n7

masculinity, 146–48, 155–57, 173, 198, 210, 218, 250

Massood, Paula J., 161–64

materiality, 45, 48

matter, 44–45, 129, 163, 269n70

Mbembe, Achille, 11, 55

McCall, Karen, 287n56

McHenry, Elizabeth, 241

McKittrick, Katherine, 25

McQueen, Steve, 16–22, 41–42, 49, 69, 173, 266n34

meat, 20, 24, 29, 33, 102, 123, 128, 133

Meeting the Universe Halfway (Barad), 122

mercy, 228, 241, 248–53

Mercy, A (Morrison), 196, 201, 229, 238–44, 248–53

Merleau-Ponty, Maurice, 15, 26, 30, 59, 97, 100, 105, 142, 266n32, 267n50

Miles, Tiya, 235, 299n21

Mills, Charles, 5–6, 19–20, 33, 96, 109, 282n3, 285n36. *See also* contract theory

Miranda, Lin-Manuel, 240

modernity, 91–96

Printed and bound by CPI Group (UK) Ltd, Croydon, CR0 4YY

09/06/2025

14685753-0002